D0875188

STRINDBERG AS DRAMATIST

AUGUST STRINDBERG

EVERT SPRINCHORN

STRINDBERG AS DRAMATIST

NEW HAVEN AND LONDON
YALE UNIVERSITY PRESS

Designed by James J. Johnson and set in Melior Roman type. Printed in the United States of America by Vail-Ballou Press, Binghamton, New York.

Portions of this book were published earlier as "Introduction," from A Madman's Defense by August Strindberg, translated by Evert Sprinchorn, copyright © 1967 by Evert Sprinchorn, and reprinted with the permission of Doubleday & Company, Inc.; "Strindberg and the Greater Naturalism," in The Drama Review (Winter 1968), copyright 1968, and reprinted with the permission of The Drama Review; "Julie's End," in Essays on Strindberg, ed. Carl Reinhold Smedmark, copyright 1966, and reprinted with the permission of Carl Reinhold Smedmark; "The Logic of A Dream Play," in Modern Drama 5, no. 3 (1962), copyright 1962 by the University of Toronto and "The Zola of the Occult: Strindberg's Experimental Method," in Modern Drama 17, no. 3 (1974), copyright 1974 by the University of Toronto, and reprinted with the permission of Modern Drama; "Strindberg and the Wit to Go Mad," in Scandinavian Studies 48, no. 3, copyright 1976 and "Hell and Purgatory in Strindberg," in Scandinavian Studies 50, no. 4, copyright 1978, and reprinted with the permission of Scandinavian Studies; "Introduction," from The Chamber Plays by August Strindberg, copyright © 1962 by Evert Sprinchorn and Seabury Quinn, Jr., and reprinted with the permission of the publisher, E. P. Dutton.

Library of Congress Cataloging in Publication Data

Sprinchorn, Evert.
    Strindberg as dramatist.

    Includes bibliographical references and index.
    1. Strindberg, August, 1849–1912—Criticism and interpretation.   I. Title.
PT9816.S64   839.7'26   81-23992
ISBN 0–300–02731–1   AACR2

10 9 8 7 6 5 4 3 2 1

"You get nowhere if you assume that the vital basis of man is nothing but a very personal and therefore very private *affaire scandaleuse*. This is utterly hopeless, and true only to the extent that a Strindberg drama is true. But pierce the veil of that sickly illusion, and you step out of your narrow, stuffy personal corner into the wide realm of the collective psyche, into the healthy and natural matrix of the human mind, into the very soul of humanity."
—Jung, "Some Aspects of Modern Psychotherapy"

"There is no occupation so coarse, so lacking in sensitiveness as the writer's. If you only knew what sort of life this is, in which one must, as a writer must, strip oneself naked in public, how he must like a vampire suck blood from his friends, from his nearest and dearest, from himself! And if he doesn't, he isn't a writer."
—Strindberg, Letter to von Heidenstam

"Creative writers are valuable allies and their evidence is to be prized highly for they are apt to know a whole host of things between heaven and earth of which our philosophy has not yet let us dream. In their knowledge of the mind they are far in advance of us everyday people, for they draw upon sources which we have not yet opened up for science."
—Freud, "Delusion and Dream in Jensen's *Gradiva*"

"The creative writer should have no grave; his ashes should be scattered in the wind and he should exist only in his works, if they have the power of life in them. People should accustom themselves to viewing him as something other than an ordinary human being and not judge him, but consider his personality as something beyond their comprehension."
—Strindberg, *En blå bok I*

CONTENTS

Illustrations follow pages 50 and 152.

PREFACE

To judge from what has been written about him, Strindberg is surely one of the more bewildering figures in modern literature, fascinating in fleeting moments to most readers but difficult to comprehend. The bewilderment arises because his path through life and art appears to be so erratic and capricious. He made his way by leaps and bounds, kangarooing from wife to wife, from misogyny to mother worship, from poetry to prose, from novel to drama, from historical research to fairy tale and legend, from Nietzscheanism to socialism, from atheism and materialism to mysticism and spiritualism, from naturalism to expressionism, from writing to painting to alchemy, from Stockholm to Berlin to Paris to Graz and on to a hundred other places. I doubt that any other writer was so constantly on the move as Strindberg, so reluctant to settle down. In Stockholm alone he resided in twenty-two different places during his life,[1] and his foreign residences could easily add another one hundred to the list of his postal addresses.

This extraordinary restlessness, inherent in his personality, became a crucial element in his method as an artist. In midcareer he wrote of himself that he might rightly be called a seeker who "experiments with points of view. A complex of individualities, stemming from many crossbreedings affecting blood and brains, of many stages passed through, for which the author simply makes himself a medium or 'automatic writer.'"[2] Experimenting with points of view, with philosophies and postures, he saw himself as a kind of scientist, at a time when science and the experimental method seemed to hold all the answers to man's problems; and in exploring the different aspects of the personality he was doing what an actor does when he plays different roles. Strindberg developed a creative method that allowed him to be both actor and scientist. Though he wandered through all the fields of literature, he always returned to the drama. As a youth he wanted to go on the stage and did not only because he had a poor voice. His first effort as a writer took the form of a play. Near the end of his life he finally got his own theatre, realizing a lifelong dream, and when he died he was at work on a play. The stories, poems, and essays were in a sense preliminary studies and experiments necessary for the writing of the plays, which constitute approximately 30 percent of his oeuvre.

The present volume focuses on the dramas and takes up Strindberg's other writings only in order to show the continuity of his progress as an artist. And since a study of all his plays, of which there are about sixty, would tend to obscure what is significant in Strindberg's production, I have narrowed the focus even further and confined myself mainly to four groups of plays: the sex tetralogy of the 1880s, the dream tetralogy of 1898–1901, the Vasa trilogy of history plays of 1872 and 1899, and the Chamber Plays of 1907. These plays represent the different phases of Strindberg's development, and in them lies the essential Strindberg.

ACKNOWLEDGMENTS

Most of the material in the chapter "A Life on Stage" appeared as the introduction to Strindberg's *A Madman's Defense*, published by Doubleday Anchor Books, New York, in 1967. The chapter on the Chamber Plays served as the introduction to a translation of these plays published by E. P. Dutton, New York, in 1962. "The Greater Naturalism" was first printed in the Winter 1968 issue of *The Drama Review*. "Tragic Ends and Means" was a contribution to *Essays on Strindberg*, published by the Strindberg Society, Stockholm, in 1966. "Beyond Naturalism," originally entitled "The Zola of the Occult" and read at the international symposium arranged by the Strindberg Society in Stockholm in 1973, was printed in *Strindberg and the Modern Theatre*, published by the society in 1975, and also in *Modern Drama*, September 1974. "The Guinea Pig" was a paper delivered at the annual meeting of the Society for the Advancement of Scandinavian Studies in May 1975 and was printed under the title "Strindberg and the Wit to Go Mad" in the Summer 1976 issue of *Scandinavian Studies*. Some of the matter in "The Chastising Spirits" and "Paradise" was first presented at the annual meeting of the Society for the Advancement of Scandinavian Studies in May 1977 and later printed under the title "Hell and Purgatory in Strindberg" in the Autumn 1978 issue of *Scandinavian Studies*. "The World of Dreams" was printed in *Modern Drama*, December 1962, with the title "The Logic of *A Dream Play*." "Making Music" began as a talk delivered on the Third Programme of BBC Radio in August 1978.

These articles have been revised and expanded for the present volume. The rest of the material has not been printed before.

Translations, unless otherwise indicated, are my own.

Of the major European writers August Strindberg has had the worst press and has been the least understood. One reason is that he wrote in a minor language, and his forceful prose, free-flowing, seemingly spontaneous, eminently readable, a prose that revitalized the Swedish language, is difficult to translate into another language, even Danish or Norwegian. Another reason is that he was enormously productive, publishing as much in his sixty-three years

CHAPTER ONE

A LIFE ON STAGE

on earth as Bernard Shaw in his ninety-four. Although Strindberg's life was not too short for him to write so much, nearly everyone finds life too short to read so much. *Ars longa, vita brevis.* Nor can it be said that one spoonful of Strindberg is like the next and that to know *The Father* is to know the Strindberg oeuvre. His prose style evolved over the years, becoming more lambent and allusive, more improvisatory, and more directly responsive to his subconscious. His ideas changed, too, and to those who had not followed him closely the changes could appear to be disconcerting volte-faces. The Danish literary critic Georg Brandes was greatly amused when he learned that between January and March 1866 Strindberg had become an atheist,[1] and he found it difficult to take seriously a man who could change his religion with the season.

Actually, Strindberg's path towards atheism was a fairly long one that can be clearly traced in his writings. Ten years later, however, in 1896, an extraordinary reversal did occur when the convert to atheism went through a psychological and intellectual crisis, and emerged from it a Swedenborgian mystic. Everyone was astonished, Strindberg's friends as well as his enemies—even Strindberg himself. The man he had been was now a stranger to him. While he chose to regard the experience as a stage on life's way, most critics, including that arch-rationalist Brandes, chose to see it as a mental collapse,[2] not as a step forward to greater knowledge and insight but as a falling back into superstition and primitive mysticism.

Once Strindberg had been certified by the critics as having earned a place with the great madmen of literature, it was no longer necessary to study him as thinker and artist, however interesting he might be as a psychiatric case. Why trouble to explain what could not be explained ra-

1

tionally? And Strindberg did nothing to make himself appear less mad. In fact, he called attention to his odd behavior, advertised his irrationality, even falsified evidence to prove he was mad at times; for if ever madness was part of a man's method, it was so in Strindberg's case. His purpose was to explore the dark continent of the mind, the largely uncharted realm to which rational thought had only limited access; and to prove that he had been there he had to come back hollow-eyed, physically wasted, and spiritually ravaged. Venturing into that savage world involved a great risk on Strindberg's part, not only a risk to his faculties but a risk to his reputation as an artist. But it was the sort of risk that every soaring spirit has had to take. "Where danger is, salvation blooms also," said Hölderlin in his poem "Patmos."

One consequence of Strindberg's great adventure was that it made an appreciation of his art all the more difficult. A life already rich in political controversy and sexual scandal now assumed the proportions of a spiritual pilgrimage—or an ironic tragedy, depending on how one looked at it. But no matter what the point of view, the art he produced became merely the lens through which one viewed the man. This was regrettable but understandable since Strindberg, even more than Wilde, made his life into a work of art. Even the great crisis of 1896, with its unexpected aftermath, seems to have been planned by a master dramatist. It gave his whole life a dramatic contour, introducing a peripety precisely when it was needed.

But from then on, the life of the man was confused with the work of the artist. The critics took his writings to be a transcription of his life, an outpouring of personal experiences, the trivial mingling indiscriminately with the significant, a chaos of events with little esthetic order and less philosophical sense. Not since Rymer dismissed *Othello* as the tragedy of a handkerchief and Voltaire and Hume pronounced Shakespeare a barbarian, a disproportioned and misshapen genius totally ignorant of theatrical art, have men of reason so erred in their judgment. Blinded by the received notions of what art should be, they were unable to appreciate what theatre art could be in the hands of a genius and failed to recognize that the barbarian element—that is, the element alien to their view of art—was the source of Shakespeare's vitality. In Strindberg's case the men of reason did not take the trouble to look for the esthetic principles behind his more difficult works because they saw in them only the cracked image of a disturbed mind. The possibility that their own spectacles might be cracked and their own view of the world distorted did not occur to them until about the time of the First World War. Then they made the mistake of thinking that Strindberg's madness was part of the madness of the world and that once the world had recovered its sanity Strindberg would lose his relevance.

2

Wanting very much to be a man of his times and, if possible, ahead of them, the young Strindberg accepted the ideas about art that were considered advanced in mid-nineteenth-century Scandinavia. From the French and English writers he learned that art should reflect reality and that it should be based on the direct observation of life itself. Any artistic convention that interfered with the faithful reproduction of reality was to be questioned. On the other hand, one traditional principle of art remained unquestioned: art must be a distillation of life, a concentrated image of nature imbued with meaning. With his keen eye, facile pen, and omnivorous interest in all things great and small, the young Strindberg recreated in words all the bustle of Stockholm, the look of its buildings, the sound of its traffic, the emotions of its people. He also had a mind quick enough to see the contradictions between the life of its leading citizens and the ideals they held, and nerve enough to describe what he saw.

In his early writings he was only bringing Sweden abreast of literary developments in England and France. He did not create his own distinctive kind of literature until he took up the leading social questions of the time: feminism and the rise of the lower classes. On the former he took a stand to the right; on the latter, a stand far to the left. A politician canvassing for votes or a writer seeking fame and fortune would not have divided the ranks of his supporters in this way, but Strindberg was driven by a need to examine these questions as deeply as possible. As a child he had learned to be skeptical of anything that passes as an eternal verity, and as a journalist he had observed that what goes on in the corridors of power is a travesty of justice. He knew that what masquerades as truth in political and social matters is only the opinion of those in power and that law, science, art, and morality are, as he said in his inflammatory "Little Catechism for the Lower Classes," the means by which the upper classes keep the rest of society in an inferior position.* The woman question, which was debated even more intensely in Scan-

* August Strindberg, *Samlade skrifter*, ed. John Landquist, 55 vols. Stockholm, 1912–20, 16:176. References to this edition will be cited hereafter in the text as SS, followed by the volume and page number.

dinavia in the 1880s than in America in the 1960s and 1970s, resolved itself in Strindberg's mind into a class question, since all the feminists were from the upper classes—intellectual women, well educated, with plenty of time on their hands to read Ibsen, write articles, and entertain politicians either in the salon or the bedroom. They constituted at most 10 percent of the population, yet their views were taken as representing those of women in general. Strindberg never denied the right of the feminists to have their say, but he wanted the opposition to have its say, too. What infuriated him was that the feminists, in league with the moralists and monarchists, tried to silence him. In the controversy surrounding the publication in 1884 of his stories about sex and marriage, they nearly succeeded.

Knowing that truth was relative to time and circumstances, Strindberg believed that the artist could, at best, only give versions of the truth, the value of the different versions depending on the honesty, passion, insight, and technical skill of the artist. To get at the truth of a situation the artist must necessarily distort reality, which is what Aristotle meant when he said that poetry is more philosophic than history. The artist must focus on a certain aspect of his subject, must choose and select what to emphasize from the infinite number of possibilities, must constantly refine the matter and pare away what seems extraneous until he has exhausted the subject—or himself. Some artists can work in a detached manner, coolly and determinedly giving shape to their visions. Strindberg preferred not to work that way. Writing about a subject without passionate involvement was to him a form of artistic expropriation.

When he took to investigating the social class system in Sweden, he kindled his creative fires by identifying with his mother, who had been a servant, rather than with his father. "I'm a born democrat," he told his publisher, "even though (by means of an aristocratic-bourgeois father) fate hurled me into the upper class where I have never felt at home. I love the bums in the street and I want to write for them. . . . And here I am writing books for the lower classes so expensive that they can never buy them. And using a 'cultured' language they can't understand. I must—as my democratic friends put it—lower myself. I'm not writing for immortality or for the Swedish Academy." [3]

When he wrote about his childhood, he emphasized the misery and poverty of his home, which in reality was a conventional middle-class home without any unusual tragedies occurring in it; he painted a picture much darker in tone than the one his sisters would provide years later when they tried to set the record straight.[4] It was not simply a desire to evoke sympathy for the working classes or for himself that led Strindberg to write this way. Nor was it entirely the artistic need to give a unity of tone and a center of attention to the picture. It went beyond propaganda and art. It was the actor's desire to enter into a role as completely as possible, to make himself over, stripping away attributes that did not fit the part and adding traits that filled out the role. The actor's way to the truth was Strindberg's way. Cast as Othello, he would have become the part by remembering the times he had been deceived by a trusted friend and the times he had suspected his wife of unfaithfulness. If there had been no such times, either he would not have undertaken the role or he would have created in life the situation in the play, casting friends and wife in roles that they did not know they were enacting.

His type of actor was the one who seeks inner truth, not external verisimilitude. This approach to the truth may seem utterly subjective and unreliable. But Strindberg saw that in the study of human beings it was perhaps more valid than the conventional literary approach, in which the author's imagination was seldom tested against actual human behavior but always against the accepted artistic conventions of human behavior, conventions which, for all one knew, might be positively Ptolemaic, or at least Rymerian. It was Rymer who censured Shakespeare's characterization of Iago as against common sense and nature on the ground that the character of a trusted soldier had "for some thousands of years in the world" been that of an "open-hearted, frank, plain-dealing" man.[5] No matter that the world around him abounded in rascally and treacherous soldiers; the blinkered Rymer plodded on into absurdity. In the nineteenth century, writers of the realistic and naturalistic schools questioned these conventions and endeavored to give literature a solid foundation in fact by relying on personal interviews, medical reports, transcriptions of criminal testimony, and the like. "Human documents alone make good books," said the Goncourt brothers in 1879.[6] Strindberg approved, but he saw that a foundation made of documents of this sort was also a bit shaky, and he preferred studying people in the flesh to studying their records and catching them in the act to hearing their rationalizations. Hence he gave the title *Vivisections* to the series of essays in psychology that he wrote in the 1880s. (A second series of such essays occupied him in the early 1890s.) But these studies were at best only tentative probings that barely scratched the surface of the psyche. To go any deeper he had to use the scalpel on himself.

3

In Strindberg's view, what the experimental method was to science, role-playing was to literature. The scientist formulates a theory and puts it to the test in the laboratory. The artist who investigates human behavior and social relationships must do the same. He must experiment with points of view, his laboratory must be life itself, and eventually he must be his own guinea pig.

Strindberg was preeminently the actor aspiring to be a scientist. Stanislavsky's actors visited the flophouses of Moscow to observe the miserable existence of the human derelicts there in order to represent them on stage in *The Lower Depths*. For Strindberg the observation would have been only the first step in a long process that would have involved actually living as one of the tramps, a process that would not have been very productive unless one was to the manner born. Such a lengthy procedure, with its enormous cost in time and energy and its wear and tear on the psyche, prevents most artists from carrying out experiments of this sort; they prefer to rely on their observations of others and to draw on the few adventures of their lives. Strindberg's life was extraordinarily rich in experiences of all kinds. His histrionic personality constantly created dramatic scenes in his daily life. Everything he touched turned into theatrical gold. But this Midas touch was both the blessing and the curse of his existence. It gave him all the material an artist needs, but it also destroyed his relationships with others, often converting humanity into theatricality as it made life into drama. One of Strindberg's collaborators in the 1880s could never forget the look on his face when Strindberg was confidentially informed that the writer Victoria Benedictsson had decided to end her life and was at that moment in a nearby room passing into unconsciousness after ingesting a large amount of morphine. "[Strindberg] listened to me," said the writer, "with an expression that is branded in my memory, the look of a grim and unpitying cannibal without the slightest trace of human compassion."[7] Yet Benedictsson's death (on this occasion her attempt at suicide failed, but later she succeeded in killing herself with a razor) gave Strindberg ideas about the fate of Miss Julie.

What Victoria Benedictsson provided one night with a pathetic gesture, Strindberg's first wife, Siri, provided lavishly, day after day. His married life with her became a vast quarry which he worked a dozen years without fully exhausting. Siri became convinced that Strindberg could not be happy unless he was making a scene and that he deliberately provoked them.[8] Although he praised the domestic woman who would raise her husband's children, cook his dinner, and fetch his slippers, he married career women: two actresses and a journalist. Dr. Carl Ludwig Schleich, a close friend, said that Strindberg's marriages failed because he "used women for the sake of sensations, which he could provoke only by the most intimate observation, precisely like a fanatic Protestant who must always surround himself with Jesuit pamphlets. He did not live with his wives; he kept them under constant observation. They were the objects not of his caresses but of his surgical knife."[9]

His first attempt at creative writing took the form of a play on the adolescent theme of the reconciliation of father and son. It took full shape in his head and then poured onto paper in four days of feverish writing. His first significant work, written in 1872 when he was twenty-three, was also a play, *Master Olof*—so far in advance of what other Swedish playwrights were turning out that it was rejected by critics and producers before being recognized as the finest play written in Sweden up to that time. Time and again he was astonished to find that life arranged itself into scenes meant to be put on stage with himself as protagonist. The stage became the reason for his existence and the cause of his trials and tribulations. "It is strange," he said when he was in his fifties, "how the deeds (?) I reproach myself with have depended on, or been necessary for, my development, often appearing simply as reflex actions against outside provocations."[10] One of his alter egos says in a novel, "In order to write my *oeuvre* I have had to offer up my biography, my personality. Indeed, it struck me, quite early on, that my life was being put on stage for me in order that I might see it from all sides. That reconciled me to my misfortunes and taught me to think of myself as an object" (SS, 41:196). Not only did the conversion of life into theatre reconcile him to his misfortunes; it became life itself to him. "People and events took form, wove themselves together, and this kind of work gave me such great pleasure that existence became pure bliss while I was writing, and does so still. It is only then that I live" (SS, 54:467). To his diary on 25 January 1901 he confided, "Is it possible that all the horrible experiences of my life were staged for me in order to make me a dramatist who would depict all sorts of situations and all conditions of the soul? I was a dramatist by the time I was twenty. If my life had passed quietly and peacefully, I would have had nothing to depict." Even in his last play, *The Great Highway*, he was still the artist-actor, compulsively entering the drama. "If only I could remain a spectator, sitting with the audience; but I must mount the stage, perform, take part, and as soon as I find my role, I lose myself and forget who I am" (SS, 51:12).

In spite of the fact that Strindberg expressed himself in nearly every form of writing, the drama was the alembic of his thought and the generator of his art. The other major dramatists have confined themselves to the theatre or at best have let their genius disport itself in one other field: the sonnet in the case of Shakespeare, the short story in the case of Chekhov, and the expository essay in the case of Shaw. Schiller may be an exception, and his historical writings bear much the same relationship to *Don Carlos* and *Wallenstein* as Strindberg's nondramatic writings bear to *The Father* and *To Damascus*. When arranged in the order in which they were written, Strindberg's stories and novels, his poems and essays, however excellent in their own way, resemble an artist's sketches and drafts or an investigator's preliminary reports. He confessed, "The secret of all my stories, novels, tales is that they are dramas. You see, when the theatres closed their doors on me for long periods of time, I hit upon the idea of writing my dramas in epic form—for future use." [11]

The French critic Jolivet, after remarking that Strindberg's creative energies converge on the drama and find their ultimate expression there, arranged the works in three concentric circles: the articles and satires on the outermost circle, the autobiographical novels on the second circle, and the novels on the innermost circle.[12] Another arrangement might include Strindberg's letters, which he wanted incorporated in his autobiographical writings. The plays appear as the final distillation of his experiences, life boiled down to its essence, the letters representing what the artist starts with, the first impressions. After his thoughts had been condensed into a series of plays, Strindberg's interest in theatre would ebb, and his creative energies would flow into other areas, often remote from literature. During this time he would be gathering more experiences, deliberately placing himself in situations that would stimulate his mind. Sooner or later he would decide, or circumstances would decide for him, that a certain area needed to be investigated thoroughly. Then he would draw a line that seemed to penetrate the area and march off into the unknown. As a scientist and experimenter, he would think of himself as formulating a theory and putting it to the test. As an actor, he would think of the process as creating a role and acting it out.

Described topographically, the life work of Strindberg resembles a huge continent crossed by three mountain ranges. The first range, containing peaks like *The Father* and *Miss Julie*, occupies the mid-1880s. The second range divides the continent in two and includes plays like *To*

Damascus, A Dream Play, The Dance of Death, Gustav Vasa and *Erik XIV*, all written between 1898 and 1902. The third range, smaller than the other two, includes the Chamber Plays, written for the most part in 1907. Of these three ranges the second is the most majestic and the most forbidding, the Himalayas not only of Strindberg's life work but of the modern drama, and the product of two great upheavals that occurred simultaneously, one in Strindberg's life and the other in European culture.

4

The series of autobiographical novels that constitute the approach to *The Father* and *Miss Julie* reveal how the artist and scientist collaborate in Strindberg, and the fifth novel in particular, *A Madman's Defense*, shows how the scientist turns actor in order to carry out an experiment in psychology. In his introduction to the novel Strindberg says that he had determined to examine his life "carefully, discreetly, scientifically, with the aid of all the resources of modern psychology." In the context in which they appear these words sound like the talk of a deluded man; oddly enough, they are remarkably accurate, once it is understood that when Strindberg refers to his life he means the life that the actor-scientist has set up as a working model. He was not trying to write a book that would produce one of the conventional artistic effects, such as those associated with tragedy, melodrama, comedy, sentimental stories, horror tales, and so on. A novel by Zola, for instance, calls for a different attitude from the reader than a story by Poe, and what Strindberg gives us is, in a sense, Zola and Poe simultaneously. Consequently, the reader does not know whether he should identify with Strindberg's hero and be gripped by his mental collapse or stand comparatively aloof from the action, observing it with the detached curiosity of a scientist or a reporter. Not that Strindberg was trying to mix styles, but he was deliberately violating certain artistic conventions. He wanted to create a kind of novel more realistic than Flaubert's and more scientific or "experimental" than Zola's. Having learned from them in the past, Strindberg now wanted to improve on them. The French realists and naturalists constructed their novels by consulting newspaper reports, police files, medical journals, and seed catalogues; and the most crucial moments in their stories— those of suicide, murder, and rape, for example—were based on nothing more than educated guesses or simply were made out of whole cloth by a powerful imagination. The Swedish author wanted to bring literature

and life into closer correspondence. If literature were to have any util-
itarian value, there should be less guesswork in it. Therefore, one should
write about the life that one knows most about, one's own. This line of
reasoning led Strindberg to begin writing his autobiography in 1886,
when he was still in his thirties (figure 1).

By July 27 he had finished three volumes, which carried the story of
his life from the circumstances of his birth in 1849 to that "fateful stroke
of fortune" that sent him in 1875 to 12 Northgate Street in Stockholm,
where he met the woman who was to become his wife. While still at
work on the third volume, Strindberg wrote to his publisher, Bonnier, to
discuss plans for the next volume:

What volume 4 should contain is not quite settled. The proper thing would be to
march right ahead and include this unusual and highly dramatic story [of his
marriage] as part of my evolutionary history, but, unfortunately, one does not
possess exclusive proprietary rights over one's experiences, and the peace and
happiness of many people would be at stake if I followed that course. However,
there are other important considerations, and the question is whether the personal interests of a few individuals should prevent a whole life story, truthfully
told, from seeing the light of day for once. I have sacrificed all my peace and pri-
vacy and given myself completely to my flock; why shouldn't others also give a
little of themselves for a good and worthy cause? As you can see, my autobiography is no *Ehrenrettung* or whitewash; it is an analysis of the soul, psychological
anatomy.

My wife and I have often thought that for our own sakes and that of our children we should publish, anonymously and without mentioning any names, our
correspondence during the crucial year 1876 under the title *He and She*. Reading
over these remarkable documents that fill a whole volume, I found them so interesting in themselves, so well written, in part so beautiful, and reflecting so much
credit on all those concerned, that they could very well be read by the public not
as an attempt at a whitewash but as a novel with human interest, and not fic-
tionalized or prearranged but actually lived and experienced. If I were to go back
to constructing a novel now, it would be colored by new points of view and
would be untruthful.[13]

When he sent the *He and She* letters to his publisher, Strindberg argued that they would make a better work than a novel, since "a novel
would always look like a self-defence and would provide the occasion
for denials and misinterpretations, and would not be in style with the
great and unique work I have so far carried out" in the first three volumes
of the autobiography. He then went on to add:

It disgusts me to be nothing but an artist. My intelligence has evolved from
daydreaming to thinking. The deliberate summoning up of hallucinations at the

writing desk seems like masturbation to me. The novel and the theatre are about right for the ladies; let them take charge of these entertainments.

It is this battle against my calling that is undermining my health. I have seen through the shams of fiction writing, and I have no illusions about it. That's why I cannot work in that vein any more.[14]

The proposed volume was to tell the story of Strindberg's affair with Siri Wrangel (née von Essen) and would consist of the letters that had passed between them. Because Siri wrote these letters while she was still married to Baron Wrangel, who was himself romantically involved with another woman, the correspondence contained highly inflammable material that could not be rendered safe simply by replacing the names with asterisks, as Strindberg suggested. Having been prosecuted, albeit unsuccessfully, two years previously for transmitting to the reading public a blasphemous remark in one of Strindberg's stories, the publisher Bonnier immediately rejected Strindberg's proposal. Strindberg then wrote The Author, which dealt with the intellectual background of his works during the period 1877–87. This replaced He and She as the fourth volume in "The Story of the Evolution of a Human Being." Bonnier also rejected this manuscript, on the ground that Strindberg had exercised no restraint in attacking the younger generation of writers.

Well over a year after Bonnier refused to print He and She, Strindberg's attitude towards the novel as a genre remained the same. The novel is "false," he said.[15]

We really know only fragments of the lives of others, and the only novels we can write are those about our own lives. That is why The Son of a Servant represented the literature of the future; it pictured a certain human being and a certain epoch. . . . I have to write for those who understand me and according to my own thoughts, even at the risk of going unpublished. Since the ephemeral political and social questions, so-called, no longer hold any attraction for me, I'm hoping to get going on an artistic-psychological series of works, which should be capable of interesting both me and my public.

This letter was written on December 22, 1887, when he had finished perhaps a third or more of A Madman's Defense, although he refers primarily to other works that were in the planning stage. The autobiographical novel was finished three months later, in March 1888. Knowing that this slightly disguised story of his marriage had no chance of being published in Sweden as long as the chief participants were still alive; aware that by pursuing his own aims in literature he was alienating himself from the Swedish public; and probably deliberately challenging comparison with the psychological novels of Zola, Bourget, and the Goncourt brothers, Strindberg had written it in French and called it first "Histoire de mon mariage" and later *Le plaidoyer d'un fou.*

This fifth volume in his autobiography differs from the earlier ones in three seemingly superficial but quite significant respects. Not only is it written in French instead of in Swedish, but Strindberg's alter ego has changed his name from John to Axel: a different persona has been adopted. Furthermore, the book is devoted to a single subject, sexual jealousy, whereas the previous volumes pictured the hero as passing through several stages of life and as the focal point of a number of environmental and hereditary forces. These superficial differences suggest a major change of intention and method from those of *The Son of a Servant.* The tone of the latter is dry and unemotional, the prose is flat and economical. The tone of the *Defense* is supercharged with emotion of one kind or another, and its prose is over-rich. The words are not pondered but spewed forth. In *The Son of a Servant* the reader is asked to respond to a rather sober presentation of events and facts. In *A Madman's Defense* the reader is compelled to respond to an emotional hurricane of growing intensity, in which facts are uprooted and dispassion overwhelmed.

What brought about the change? and how could Strindberg justify to himself the fact that he had (apparently) abandoned his former position on the truthfulness of the novel and had reworked the material pertaining to his marriage into that despised form? There are two answers. The first concerns Strindberg's economic situation and the other the way in which a writer like Strindberg makes his life into a work of art.

I am not saying that Strindberg wrote the *Defense* to make money. From his letters it is clear that, by the time he had finished writing, he did not even want the work to be published. But his steadily worsening financial condition and his failure to sell his works put him in the proper frame of mind for writing this bitter novel. Very little money had come Strindberg's way after he stood trial in 1884 for the "blasphemous" remarks in *Married,* a volume of short stories. Although he was acquitted, publishers were disinclined to print what he wrote, and, in turn, his work became more immoderate in tone as he felt increasingly persecuted by women (who instigated the trial), by publishers (who were parasites living off authors), by other writers (who were deluded feminists and Ibsenites), and by the public (who were sheep without minds of their own). Like Rousseau, whom he resembles in many respects, Strindberg had a persecution complex. Perhaps he had more cause: he saw enemies all around him because they were all around him. "That you as an author," wrote his publisher Bonnier in July 1887 "are suffering an unfortunate unpopularity, an unpopularity without parallel, is a fact that cannot be unfamiliar to you, although, living far from home [Strindberg had left Sweden in 1883 and had been living in France and Switzerland], you cannot possibly imagine how terrible the situation really is" (letter of July 25, 1887).[16]

And the situation was indeed terrible. In March 1887 John Personne, a doctor of divinity, had published a pamphlet, *The Strindberg Literature and Immorality Among Our School Children*, which attacked Strindberg for trying to "provide for himself and his family by publicly smearing his wife" and accused Strindberg's publisher Bonnier of being no better than "a brothelkeeper and a fence." On top of that, in April had come the stormy meeting of the Swedish Association of Publishers at which the chairman, Albert Bonnier, was harshly criticized for issuing Strindberg's works. A great number of the members had walked out of the meeting in protest against Bonnier and had formed their own association.

In the meantime, Strindberg's marriage to Siri was breaking up, a process that had begun about the time of his trial for blasphemy in 1884. (See figure 2.) Although in the spring of 1887 he could describe his life as idyllic, on August 5 he began a long letter to a close friend by saying, "So the comedy of my marriage is over after ten years of delights and annoyances."[17] The rest of the letter sets the stage for *A Madman's Defense*. The suspicion that Siri is hiding something from him, the certainty that others know what the husband is always the last to know, the willingness to put the worst construction on trivial incidents, such as his wife's going to Dr. Forssberg for a massage, and the insistence on knowing that his wife has been unfaithful in order that he may have peace of mind—all is there. The whole letter is like a chapter from the novel.*

A week later Strindberg sent an application for divorce to Stockholm, but nothing came of this since the parties were not residing in

---

* Staaff's replies to Strindberg's persistent inquiries make it clear that there had been gossip about Siri's unfaithfulness in 1882 and 1883. At that time Staaff and Strindberg had been very close friends, sharing the same nihilistic view of society and belonging to a bohemian drinking club in Stockholm, organized by Strindberg, in which he and Siri jointly held the office of secretary. Strindberg wrote skits for the club and acted in them, while Siri regularly outdrank him. In 1892, after Strindberg's divorce from Siri became final, Strindberg asked Staaff to burn the letters of 1887, a request that the latter ignored. See Hans Lindstrom, "Strindberg, Per Staaff och En dåres försvarstal," *Ord och Bild* (1949), pp. 13–18.

Sweden. (In the back of his mind did not Strindberg know what answer he would get? Almost certainly.) About a month later Strindberg began to write *A Madman's Defense*.

5

If we consider Strindberg only as a husband, it seems clear that he wrote the book because his marriage was on the rocks and he saw no way to save it. If we consider Strindberg the creative artist, who deplored mere fiction-making and admired the scientist's laboratory methods in which the scientist must sometimes serve as his own guinea pig, then we must ask ourselves a disturbing and fascinating question: Was Strindberg's marriage going on the rocks because the artist-scientist was conducting an experiment with himself as guinea pig to be inoculated with the germs of sexual jealousy and the virus of insanity? Was Strindberg deliberately letting the ship be dashed to pieces because he wanted to discover—to quote from his own introduction—"some elements in the physiology of love, some clues to the pathology of the soul, and, into the bargain, a curious fragment from the philosophy of crime"?

A mad genius, paranoid and oedipal, is driven by some compulsion to set down the experiences he believes he has had—such is the usual view of the *Defense*. It seems an extraordinarily naive view that ignores the evidence offered by Strindberg's letters and takes no account of his avowed principles as an artist. A far more sensible view is that Strindberg created his experiences in order to write about them. Interested in exploring the frontier where jealousy encroaches on madness, he set up a model of the terrain in his own home. That is the scientific method. It is also a method not unfamiliar to actors. But Strindberg could not step out of his role without being called a fraud. He had to play the game for real, even if it meant injuring himself and others. When he compared himself to Hercules who lights his own funeral pyre, he was not joking.

To some, the suggestion I have offered here may seem absurd. To those who know Strindberg the question is not, Is it true? but, How true is it? Certain it is that Strindberg wrote best when he identified himself with a role. We know that when at work he took fiction for reality, just as an actor takes the stage for a real room. We also know that in the summer of 1887 he was looking for a good serious subject to write about and that he had never entirely abandoned the story of his marriage as a subject. We know, too, that in 1887 his plays were not being staged, his books were not being printed, and that he had "seven unpublished manuscripts lying around."[18] And as a noted Strindberg authority has convincingly argued, Strindberg's marital happiness stood in direct relation to his economic situation.*

As far as his career was concerned, the only encouraging signs came from Copenhagen, where there had been a growing interest in his work since 1879. The Danish capital began to look more and more like the only place where Strindberg might redeem his fortunes. If he succeeded there, he could return in triumph to Sweden, from which he had felt ostracized during the last three or four years. A Danish actor named Hans Riber Hunderup, who had recently acquired the management of a theatre customarily devoted to farces and musicals, decided to raise its artistic level by producing Strindberg's *The Father*—with a comic afterpiece lest the regular customers be offended. Hunderup was, of course, counting on the considerable notoriety that surrounded the play and its author.

Within a short time, Strindberg's fame was such that he was represented in the local wax museum. The published version of the play received mixed reviews that called attention to its controversial nature. The author was described as being on the brink of insanity; he was known to be seeking a divorce; and the play itself was presumed to be a direct transcription of the author's married life. Moreover, the radical element in Copenhagen, led by Georg and Edvard Brandes, were using the play to assail their opponents by pointing out that the stage of the Royal Theatre was denied to controversial writers like Strindberg. Georg Brandes himself directed the play, and its premier was, as a deliberate provocation, set for November 14, the birthday of Denmark's great romantic poet Oehlenschläger.

The effect of all this on Strindberg was twofold. On the one hand he saw that *The Father* might presage a happier phase in his career and bring about an improvement in his finances, which were now so desperate that when he and his family arrived in Copenhagen from Bavaria in the first week of November, he had to go first to a pawnbroker to raise money to claim his baggage. On the other hand, *The Father* revived in him the mood that had produced that masterpiece, giving rise simultaneously to anguish in the husband and creative excitement in the art-

* Harry Jacobsen, *Strindberg och hans första hustru* (Stockholm, 1946), p. 160. This is an indispensable study of the relationship between *A Madman's Defense* and the ascertainable facts about Strindberg's marriage. Both Lorentz Dietrichson, who knew Strindberg before the 1890s, and Johan Mortensen, who knew him later, agreed that lack of money, especially money as recognition for his literary accomplishments, was the primary reason for his irritableness and his rage. Johan Mortensen, *Strindberg som jag minnes honom* (Stockholm, 1931), pp. 70, 74.

ist. As we have seen, Strindberg had started to put the story of his marriage on paper in September. In August, when we may presume that the
novel was being planned, he had sent strange letters to faithful friends,
inquiring about the unfaithfulness of his wife. In October a new factor
entered the picture. At that time Axel Lundegård, who had been hired
to translate *The Father* into Danish, first wrote to him about the play.
On October 17 Strindberg replied with a letter that might have been
written by Bernard Shaw. He counseled that the role of the Captain be entrusted to

an actor of a rather lively disposition who with the superior, self-mocking,
slightly cynical air of a man of the world, fully conscious of his own merits, goes
in tolerably good spirits to meet his fate. . . .

A deceived husband is a comic figure in the eyes of the world, and even
more so in the eyes of a theatre audience. He must show that he knows this, and
that he too would laugh if only someone else were the cuckold.[19]

Yet on the very next day, October 18, Strindberg wrote an extraordinary five-page letter to a judge in Sweden in which he accused Siri of
being a whore and a lesbian and of attempting to have him locked up in a
lunatic asylum. It is this last idea, that of his wife trying to destroy him
by driving him insane, that is now added for the first time to the story of
his marriage as it takes shape in his mind; and, clearly, he got it from *The
Father*. In that play he had produced a masterpiece; why not try the same
theme again?

And now the actor in him takes charge. To write this story he must
become the husband being driven mad. He doesn't consult books, visit
the local sanatorium, or talk to his doctor. He immerses himself in the
role, just as he did when he wrote *The Father*. That play was supposed to
have been completely true to life—his life—when he wrote it; but now,
in the letter to the Swedish judge, Strindberg can say that he wrote *The
Father* only to "find out something" about his wife Siri; he can even venture the opinion that Siri got the idea of driving him mad with lies from
reading *The Father*!

By November 12, the day before the dress rehearsal of the play,
Strindberg has invested himself so completely with the mood and
qualities of the role that he is contemplating suicide and writes to Lundegård a letter in the form of a testament. He concludes it with the oft-
quoted lines:

It seems as if I am walking in my sleep, as if fiction and reality were mixed
together. I don't know if *The Father* is a fiction or if my life has been a fiction; but

I have the feeling that in a moment not far off I shall find out which is which, and then I'll crumble into dust either through insanity and a sick conscience or through suicide.[20]

The "sick conscience" betrays Strindberg's technique. For if it were true that Siri was driving him mad of her own volition, then *she* should have the sick conscience, not he. But if he is deliberately destroying his marriage and the happiness of his wife in order to experience sexual jealousy and insanity and to create a work of art, then and only then would *he* suffer from a sick conscience. And once he has had his experience and once fiction and reality have separated from one another and drawn back to their distinct spheres, what could he with his tender conscience do but kill himself or go mad—unless some part of the fiction turned out to be true. What irony! The more he can prove that he has been deceived, cuckolded, and driven mad, the more will his conscience be assuaged. But these considerations could not be allowed to interfere with his writing. In his preface Strindberg could say that he bitterly regretted having written the book. But the preface is dated 1887, while the book was not completed until March 1888. Nothing better demonstrates Strindberg's complete awareness of what he was doing while he was doing it.

Madness and the battle of the brains were among Strindberg's constant preoccupations. In the spring of 1887, a few months after writing *The Father*, he had returned to the subject of madness and delusions in an essay, "Soul Murder." Now, after another respite of a few months, during which he wrote the comic novel *The People of Hemsö*, he once again took up the theme of sexual jealousy and the madness it can inspire. *Othello* was the classic treatment of the theme. Shakespeare had improved on the countless Renaissance plays that dealt with the subject by building his plot on a fabrication, a lie invented by Iago. In *Othello* there was no adultery, no love triangle; there was only a mind being poisoned by a villain. In *The Father* and *A Madman's Defense* Strindberg further refined this plot idea by making the villain (villainess) into a mere flickering shadow projected by the fire in the hero's mind. Strindberg poisons his own mind, and the question of whether his wife Siri is or is not guilty of the crimes he charges her with is irrelevant.

The artfulness of *A Madman's Defense* must be apparent to everyone who reads it carefully. Strindberg, like Dante, writes in the first person but gives us two points of view: that of the omniscient author and that of the hero experiencing hell for the first time. The hero Axel is continually astonished and horrified at what is happening to him, while the

author Strindberg is carefully arranging matters to suggest Axel's growing madness and eventual mental collapse.[21]

Since he was not permitted to use the documentary approach—letting the correspondence speak for itself—or the fairly objective approach
of the first autobiographical volumes, Strindberg seems to have determined to write up the affair in the manner of a sensational French novel:
frank, scabrous, naturalistic. His immediate objective seems to be to de-
fame Siri, and she is given no chance to defend herself as she would have
had in the letters. But in order not to appear a complete cad, Strindberg
must convince the reader that he is Siri's victim. By building the novel to
show his mounting suspicions and his growing madness, he creates a
strange ambiguity. He cannot be trusted to tell the truth because he is
going mad; but if he is going mad, then there may well be some truth in
his accusation that his wife is deliberately driving him mad. He must
hate her for what she is doing to him, but only a great love can lie behind
that hate if his jealousy and his suspicions of her can drive him to the
brink of insanity.

This ambiguity produces a unique kind of love story, feverish but
cool, intense yet ironic, passionate but unsentimental, and above all ter-
ribly true in a way that art seldom is. Strindberg could honestly say that
the book was "true" and "corresponded to actual conditions,"[22] while his
wife could with equal honesty exclaim, "There is scarcely an incident in
it that doesn't have some foundation in fact—only everything is so horri-
bly twisted and distorted."[23] For the entire method of the novel is to
make use of distortion in precisely the same way that any great work of
art does, only here the method is applied where it has a double relevance—as art and as insanity.

Let me give just two instances that may serve to illustrate Strindberg's general method. In the novel there is a description of a rather wild
party that turns into an orgy of sorts and fills Axel with disgust, especially for his wife's lesbian girlfriend. Now there actually was at least one
such party in November 1885, when Strindberg was living in Grez,
France, and not long after it was over Strindberg wrote an altogether different description of it to his friend Verner von Heidenstam.

> Life is very sociable here. Old friends from Paris come out on Saturdays, and
> last Saturday we had ourselves a fair orgy that went on for two days, with sing-
> ing, guitar, tambourine, flute, and wild *joie de vivre*; a variety show (my own),
> dancing, billiards, midnight snack, pickled herring and breakfast at the Danish
> girls' [Sofie Holten and Marie David, the lesbians of the novel], dinner with our
> own *café chantant*, and dancing at the Chevillons' pension. Almost Decamer-

onesque (without the screwing, at least in public. This is regarded as a private matter) and everyone who had any talent had contributed some verses (I wrote a French chansonnette) or whatever. Nordström is a merry old soul(!) who sings, and sculptor Vallgren (with his wife) is a great ballad singer. We had everything you and I had written about (except naked women!). Fun and games and *joie de vivre*. And all because my very existence has never been so imperiled as now. One dances with the noose around one's neck and thinks: better make the most of it; tomorrow nothing but herring and potatoes. It's really a terrible crisis (evolution) that's going on, and the crash will soon come. And when I think of all the dinners and supper parties I've got to make up for from my pious theist period! [24]

One can see that in the novel, written some two years later, Strindberg has not invented a new episode; he has merely chosen to view the event through a dark and distorting lens that would make the weekend party harmonize with the mood his book required.

The second illustration is even more enlightening. At one point in the novel, Axel takes the long trip from Switzerland to Copenhagen to check on his wife's fidelity. He questioned everyone who might know the truth about her, but he was told nothing. Discussing his wife's possible unfaithfulness was "like trying to storm the walls of a fortress. People listened to me, they smiled at me, they stared at me as if I were some strange animal. And so, without obtaining the slightest bit of information from them, forsaken by all, most of whom were envious men desiring my failure as the only way to their success, I return to my prison where Maria [his wife] is waiting for me" (SS, 26:365).

Strindberg's letters tell a different story. Desperately in need of money, he went to Copenhagen to sell some articles to a newspaper and to break the boycott of his books by Swedish publishers. His efforts ended in failure. He found that the younger writers who envied his talents were, as readers for Bonnier's publishing house, rejecting his manuscripts. "In Copenhagen I faced a wall of prejudice," he wrote to his brother. "My publisher, with whom I have a five-year contract, didn't want to contract for anything more of mine. All I got was No! . . . And [since] I couldn't send for my family, I returned to them." [25] In the novel Strindberg's literary rivals appear as his sexual rivals, and the plight of a man who cannot raise any money is transformed into the frustration of a jealous husband who cannot find any evidence incriminating his wife.

What Strindberg, the perfect histrionic personality, is doing here every actor has learned to do at some point in his training. Stanislavsky made the technique an element in his system, calling it emotion memory, by which he meant the ability to feel and express an emotion in a particular scene by bringing to mind a personal experience that involved the same emotion under different circumstances. Without giving a name to it the twenty-two-year-old Strindberg in 1871 instructed a professional actor in the use of the technique, advising him to give conviction to the expression of sorrow on stage by conjuring up the memory of a deeply painful experience.[26]

In the final pages of the novel, Strindberg's guilty conscience over the writing of the book combines with his histrionic method of entering into the minds of his characters to produce one of the most sublimely ironic passages in literature. Says the hero of his wife: "The instinct for self-preservation had forced her to build up a melodramatic story that bore some resemblance to the facts and behind which she could shield herself from the attacks of her tormented conscience" (SS, 26:353). With that the artistry of the author and the madness of his protagonist, which have been cross-fertilizing each other throughout the novel, produce their crowning glory, and the process that shapes the plot is complete. In confounding art and life not even Pirandello affords so exquisite a moment.

Passages such as this remind us, moreover, that there is a crucial difference between an actor and an author. Strindberg is not simply enacting somebody else's scenes; he is creating his own. In this process he allows his present mood to play a major part. Consequently, since Strindberg was a man of many moods, he usually had more than one iron in the fire so that he could switch from one to the other to accommodate his moods. This is part of the secret of his amazing productivity. While he was completing his comic novel about the fisher folk of the Stockholm skerries, the idea for *A Madman's Defense* was already festering in his brain; and while writing *A Madman's Defense* he was simultaneously reworking his comedy *Comrades* and writing a volume of essays. Shortly after he had finished the *Defense*, he set to work on a series of stories about the people in the Stockholm skerries, darker in mood this time. After that came "Tschandala," another battle-of-brains story based on his experience with the overseer of a dilapidated Danish country estate on which Strindberg was living with his family. Once that was out of the way he wrote *Miss Julie*, the perfectly balanced summing-up of the love affair between Siri and Strindberg, the baroness and the son of a servant. He finished that on August 10, 1887 and then turned to write *Creditors*, the tragicomic treatment of what occurs in the first part of *A Madman's Defense*.

One of the most interesting features of the series of works inspired by his marriage is the order in which they were written. In *The Father*, the first of the series, the husband is driven mad and dies. In *A Madman's Defense* the battle between the husband and wife is not resolved; it ends where the last act of *The Father* begins. *Miss Julie*, the next work in the series, is nothing but a long seduction scene, the distillation of the first part of *A Madman's Defense*, only now it is the woman who is neurotic and who is driven to destruction. Finally comes *Creditors*, in which Strindberg ties up the beginning and end of the series by introducing the first husband of the woman and by having him come back to destroy the happy couple. As a demonstration of the skill with which a genius manipulates his material there is nothing more dazzling in dramatic literature than this series of works (unless it be the works Strindberg wrote a decade later). And few authors have let us examine so closely the creative process itself—the process by which "real experiences" are subjected to the pattern-making genius of the artist to produce different versions of the truth.

Although Strindberg began writing plays when he was twenty years old, he established himself as a writer with the publication of a novel, *The Red Room*, in 1879, when he was thirty. Until then he had supported himself by a variety of trades: editing an insurance journal, operating a telegraph office, working as a reporter for various newspapers, writing art and theatre reviews, and cataloguing the Chinese books and manuscripts in the Royal Library. *The Red Room*,

CHAPTER TWO

THE GREATER NATURALISM

which drew on Strindberg's encounters with aspiring poets, failed painters, actors in love, and businessmen in collusion, was a gathering of impressions forming a panorama of Stockholm life from dawn to dusk and from the corridors of power to the back streets of defeat. Nothing like it had appeared in Sweden. No one else had captured in words so precisely the rhythm of the city, the accent and character of its people. As soon as it was published, *The Red Room* was heralded—even by those who disliked being brought into contact with the seamier and more disreputable sides of life—as marking an epoch in Swedish literature. Long overdue, years after its appearance in France, England, and Russia, realism had finally penetrated the Scandinavian peninsula.

It was, however, realism with a difference. Strindberg was never a realist in the way Flaubert was: aloof, objective, and scrupulously indifferent to the fates of his characters. *The Red Room* is less a novel in which a person's life is allowed to unfold and develop than a series of sketches in the vein of the early Dickens. Although the people in these "scenes from the lives of artists and writers"—the subtitle of the book—were all easily recognizable as Stockholm types, and in several cases identifiable as individuals, Strindberg was unable to keep himself within the bounds of strict realism. He was more a painter than a photographer, and his love of the picturesque was always running away with him. The bold stroke, the bright splash of color, the dramatic contrast were as irresistible to him as to Dickens. The instinct for what was larger than life in scale and more compact in meaning drove him first to the novel and then, inevitably, to the stage. Even when he wrote realistic and naturalistic plays, he used theatre as a means of transcending the world of things. For the authors of well-made realistic plays, drama was the art of carefully motivating what was going to happen next in order to make it seem credible and therefore real. For Strindberg, drama was the art of intensifying the light cast on reality to the point at which an underlying truth and the deeper connection between events became visible. That was why, in each phase of his career, he turned to the theatre when he gave his ideas their final form.

He always regarded theatre as a kind of poetry, as the most heightened form of artistic expression, in which much more happens in each moment than in the sluggish and dilatory prose of the novel. In an age when verse was rapidly disappearing from the drama, he had to bring a different kind of poetry into the theatre. The main line of Strindberg's development, the line that leaps over all the apparent contradictions in his philosophical and religious development, is the line that traces his constant efforts to enhance the expressiveness of theatre. It is this ceaseless experimentation with theatrical art that has bewildered critics as much as it has stimulated dramatists.

Even such comparatively simple and straightforward plays as *The Father* and *Miss Julie* can easily be misunderstood and deprecated if regarded only as realistic or naturalistic works. In certain crucial respects they are much less realistic than *The Wild Duck* or *The Three Sisters*. Zola, the chief apostle of naturalism, was quick to find fault with *The Father* as a naturalistic play. Even *Miss Julie*, the drama that most fully answers the requirements of Zola's naturalism, is less naturalistic than Strindberg, in his preface, claims it to be. He labeled *The Father* simply "a tragedy," but he gave *Miss Julie* the subtitle "a naturalistic tragedy." This subtitle and the greater attention to physical detail in the play were probably due to Zola's criticism of *The Father*. In contrast to many readers and spectators who have been misled into thinking that that play was written in white heat by an inspired madman, Zola found the design of the play and the characters in it too obviously the product of careful calculation. The persons were too abstract, too manifestly the figures in a mathematical formula contrived to produce the desired result. Furthermore, the action was so radically truncated that the illusion of reality was bound to be shattered.

Having taken the pains to prepare his own French translation, which he mailed off to Zola with a covering letter asserting that the play had been "composed according to the experimental formula,"[1] Strindberg was undoubtedly upset by the Frenchman's criticisms. He might well have replied that in a tragedy the characters should appear larger than life and possess a somewhat abstract quality and that too much attention to realistic detail would detract from the grandeur of the design. *The Father*, after all, was meant to be a nineteenth-century version of Greek tragedy, and of Agamemnon in particular. But the rebellious Swede knew that unless he could find an audience outside his own country, stolid, philistine Sweden would silence him or force him to write only for the ladies' magazines. Having alienated the Swedish conservatives with his socialism and the liberals with his anti-feminism, he felt that his whole career as an original writer depended on attracting a following outside Sweden. No wonder then that he took Zola's criticisms to heart when he wrote his next play, *Miss Julie*. And having written it and made one or two fair copies, he perhaps feared that the play still would not seem naturalistic enough. Hence the preface, which has come to be recognized as the most concise and comprehensive statement of naturalistic theatre.

The two people Strindberg most wanted to please with his play were Zola and Antoine, the theoretician and the practitioner of the new movement. *The Father* was written before Antoine opened the doors of his Théâtre-Libre to the non-Boulevard drama, but *Julie* was written over a year later, by which time Antoine had become the most talked-about producer in Paris. The *Julie* preface shows very clearly how alert Strindberg was to what was happening in the French capital. There is scarcely a thought in this manifesto of naturalism that is original with him.

Zola's experimental formula[2] meant a concentration on the inner drama, an avoidance of theatrical tricks, a simplification of sets, and an adherence to the unity of time—in other words, a return to the principles of Racinian neoclassic drama. Echoing Zola, Strindberg averred that the theatre had reached a crisis, that the conventional intrigue drama was dead, and that only psychological drama could hold the interest of modern audiences. From Zola, too, comes the Darwinistic remark about humanity sloughing off its feelings as it evolves into a higher species that will not allow emotions to inhibit its thinking. From the Goncourt brothers come the idea of literature as case history, in which the writer is little more than a doctor's recording secretary or a court stenographer, and the conviction that the theatre is a declining art form fit only for women and children. From the French psychologists Théodule Ribot and Jean-Martin Charcot comes the theory that the ego consists of contradictory impulses, many of which may be buried beneath the level of conscious thought. From Hippolyte Bernheim comes the notion that hypnotic suggestion is a powerful force in life and much more common than generally supposed. From his familiarity with the European stage, as reflected in the Parisian papers and journals, derives Strindberg's call for solid

-rather than painted scenery (already in use in theatres that could afford it); for asymmetrical sets[3] (frequently used in French melodrama, sometimes in opera, and also in some productions of the Meiningen players); for real props (a fetish of the duke of Saxe-Meiningen); for the abolition of footlights to make facial expressions more true to life (the aim of theatre designers ever since the stage moved indoors in the seventeenth century); and for acting that would permit the performer occasionally to turn his back to the audience (already practiced by Porel as actor in the 1870s and as director in the 1880s at the Odeon theatre—Strindberg had seen him in 1876). Even the pantomimed action that Strindberg wants to substitute for an intermission is probably due to the growing interest in pantomime plays in Paris[4] in the 1880s. In making these points he seems to be addressing himself mainly to the provincial theatres, urging them to catch up with the latest trends. Ten years after Strindberg wrote his preface, Stanislavsky at the Moscow Art Theatre was still trying to get rid of canvas doors that billowed when they should have been slammed.

It is in Strindberg's plea for an intimate theatre that Antoine's influence is most apparent. Antoine's recent and unprecedented success was partly the result of having staged his plays in a small rented hall. Since his untrained actors did not know how to project in the manner of the skilled performers at the Boulevard theatres, they spoke in a natural conversational tone and acted pretty much as people do in real life. Thus, by a fluke, Antoine hit on the right acting method for the naturalistic drama.[5] The acting and the theatre were in almost perfect harmony. For Strindberg the great virtue of the intimate theatre was that it could be supported by a small intellectual coterie so that the dramatist would not be forced to write down to his audience. Secondarily, it offered the opportunity for subtle effects, the play of expression on the faces of the actors, the small gesture, the intimate tone of voice—all of which could not be "read" in the typical large theatre.

The writing of the *Julie* preface, like the opening of Antoine's theatre, occurred at a time when the naturalist movement was actually quite far advanced. Taine, Zola, the Goncourts had scored major victories all along the cultural front, and the theatre, that almost impregnable fortress of tradition and conservatism, had been the last area to be invaded. It was, however, at a critical juncture. The movement had won a major breakthrough in 1887 because of Antoine's young and enterprising spirit, but a group of young novelists, including some former Zolaites, had estranged themselves from the movement because of the sordidness of Zola's *La Terre*. At the same time, the Decadents, some of whom had begun as naturalists, were gathering their forces and in the next decade, under the banner of Symbolism, would outflank the naturalists. Consequently, when Strindberg leaped into the naturalistic saddle, he rode off in all directions.

2

Underneath this literary opportunism Strindberg had drawn up his own naturalist platform. Up to the mid-1880s his principal concern had been with social questions. These he had resolved, at least temporarily, in *The Author*, the fourth volume of his autobiography, written in 1886. He thereupon turned inward for his material, a course that would lead eventually to *A Dream Play*. This change reflected the interest in abnormal psychology that developed parallel with the rise of naturalism. During August 1886 he steeped himself in the "literature of insanity,"[6] and a few months later he wrote *The Father*. He felt, undoubtedly, that he was on the right track because of recent tendencies in the work of Zola and Ibsen.

The bedrock of his philosophy lay in the conviction that life was to be viewed less as a struggle against heredity and environment, as the naturalists insisted, than as the struggle of minds, each seeking to impose its will on other minds. Powerful minds were like charged particles attracting weaker particles, thus building up magnetic fields of influence. He found scientific support for his theory in the writings of Bernheim. Following up the latter's idea that "all who may be hypnotized are susceptible to suggestions," he wrote "The Battle of Brains" (1887), an essay in experimental psychology in which the Darwinian idea of the struggle for existence and the Spencerian idea of the survival of the fittest were applied to the life of the mind. Physical battle was obsolete; brawn had been conquered by brain and now it was a question of mind against mind and the power of suggestion. "Suggestion is only the stronger brain's struggle with and victory over the weaker," wrote Strindberg, "and this process is at work unconsciously in everyday life" (SS, 22:123), in political, religious, and artistic controversies, as well as in domestic squabbles. This essay, which anticipates the age of propaganda, of Madison Avenue and public opinion polls, provides the key to Strindberg's view of theatre and helps to define his position in the naturalist movement.

At first he had aligned himself with the naturalists because he saw them as exposers of the sham and "humbug" of modern civilization. If they did not precisely long for a return to nature, as the Rousseauistic

Strindberg did, at least they were opposed to the social establishment. At the same time he characterized realism (not naturalism) as the tendency in art to create illusion by the careful rendering of significant details. This was in 1882, before he had written his naturalist tragedies. A few years later, however, having written Miss Julie and having acquainted himself with the plays of the Théâtre-Libre, he felt it was necessary to dissociate himself from at least one branch of the naturalist movement and to distinguish between the "greater" and the "lesser" naturalism—which he proceeded to do in his essay "The Modern Drama and The Modern Theatre" (SS, 17:289), written in 1889. Here he says that the greater or higher naturalism is the naturalism

which seeks out those points where the great battles take place, which loves to see what one doesn't see everyday, which revels in the conflict of natural forces, whether they are called love and hate or the spirit of rebellion and the instinct for association, and which cares not whether a thing is beautiful or ugly as long as it is magnificent. [SS, 17:289]

The lesser naturalism allows no scope for the personality of the artist; it is merely a faithful imitation of nature, a kind of photography so inanely accurate that even "the speck of dust on the lens was included as part of the picture" (SS, 17:289). The lesser artist presents ordinary events and cannot see the forest for the trees, while the greater artist singles out the significant motif, which usually has something to do with life as struggle.

The greater naturalist follows the path blazed by the Zola who wrote Germinal and La Terre, not the Zola who in allowing L'Assommoir to be adapted for the theatre emphasized the environment of the action by having an extraordinarily realistic tavern and laundry erected on the stage. The lesser naturalist follows in the footsteps of Becque, whose Vultures, a realistic rendering of middle-class life, lacks temperament. This represents the objective approach loved by those "who lack personality, the soulless ones, as they should be called" (SS, 17:289). To Strindberg the great drama, the drama of Shakespeare, Racine, and Molière, was essentially psychological drama, a conflict of wills, in which the stage apparatus was reduced to a minimum. Shakespeare required scarcely any sets at all, and Molière's "marvelous vivisection" of Tartuffe "takes place on a stage with two taborets" (SS, 17:285). For the battle of brains no naturalistic set is needed. The Father and Miss Julie can be performed with a table and two chairs and a few props, such as a birdcage, a lamp, and a straitjacket.

Nevertheless, to judge from the preface to Miss Julie, Strindberg, in accord with naturalist thinking, wanted the set to be an active force in the drama. Environment and heredity were to be the jaws of the vise that would crush Miss Julie. The preface was written, however, to sell the play rather than to explain it. If we look at the play itself, we see what Strindberg actually had in mind for this set. He describes a manor-house kitchen of which the audience sees only the corner containing the large glass doors leading to the yard. (See figure 11.) This vaulted entry is a little stage-left of center. The other walls and the ceiling of the kitchen are masked by the teasers and tormentors, which means that in making some of their exits and entrances the actors would not use any doors. They would, in a sense, just fade in and out of the picture. Furthermore, the long deal kitchen table is cut off by the drapes or curtains serving as tormentors, for the audience is supposed to see only one end of it. "As far as the set is concerned" wrote Strindberg,

I have borrowed from the impressionists the idea of an asymmetric, truncated picture, and believe I have thereby enhanced the illusion, since, by not seeing the whole room and all its furnishings, the spectator will be induced to exercise his imagination to complete the room. [SS, 23:111–12]

This is a rather remarkable set that Strindberg prescribes, especially for this particular play, in which the heroine is to be trapped in the kitchen and forced to enter the valet's bedroom. One would have surmised that both the action of the play and the naturalist concern with milieu would have led the dramatist to specify a closed-in box set (SS, 50:285).[7] Yet Strindberg manifestly sought to avoid both this and the old-fashioned wing-and-drop set and endeavored to create instead the kind of effect the impressionist painters were achieving on canvas, presenting a corner of a room rather than the whole space. The incompleteness of the impressionist composition drew the artist and the viewer into closer personal contact, placing the viewer in the scene and compelling him to identify with the artist at a particular moment. From being "the representation of nature through imagination,"[8] as Humboldt had defined it at the beginning of the Romantic era, art had become, in Zola's definition, "a corner of creation seen through a temperament."[9]

In this, as in his replacement of the customary intermissions with a pantomime and a ballet and his reduction of the playing time to ninety minutes, Strindberg's ulterior purpose was to ensnare and hold an audience. If life to him was a battle of brains, the theatre was a submission of minds, achieved by the spectator's willing suspension of disbelief and the dramatist's hypnotic skills. If the subject matter was morally unpleasant or logically impossible, a conflict of minds would arise and the author-hypnotist would have to enhance the spell. Conventional naturalism created the illusion of reality by the accumulation of details (though its primary theoretical purpose was to establish the force of environment), whereas Strindberg assumed that the spectators could best be spellbound if they could be lured into the spirit of the game and made to supply what was missing. The dramatist's task was to supply what was significant.

One way of doing this was to give the selected objects a symbolic meaning. This is, of course, a basic artistic method, but Ibsen the realist and Zola the naturalist employed it with more than usual thoroughness, and Strindberg always appreciated the latter more as a symbolist than as a naturalist. Symbols now were not to be linked to the realms of the ideal and the supernatural; they were meant to adumbrate an inner, psychological action, to provide a focus for the mass of realistic detail, and to enlarge the scope of the work. In Zola's *La Bête humaine* the locomotive becomes a recurring symbol of the bestial drives of the engineer, just as in *La Curée* the entwining flowers (their names taken from seed catalogues) in the hothouse suggest the irresistible force of the sex drive. Ibsen's method is most apparent in *The Wild Duck*, but even in *A Doll's House* the denuded Christmas tree in the last act speaks vividly of the change in the Helmer household. In *Miss Julie* the boots waiting to be polished and the gaping speaking tube convey the haunting presence of Julie's father, the count. The songbird in the cage, the bird that Julie insists is her only friend and that Jean so brutally kills, underscores almost too heavily the situation in which the aristocratic girl finds herself. The set itself, the kitchen—naturalistic in that it takes us away from the parlors and drawing rooms of conventional realistic plays and speeds us on the way down to Wesker's kitchen and LeRoi Jones's toilet—is symbolic of the servants' world into which Julie has lowered herself. In contrast to most naturalistic plays, *Miss Julie* shows us a character out of her milieu.

Strindberg sought to preserve the integrity of the symbolic prop or set against a growing tendency to obscure it by amassing random details. He sought this more assiduously than Zola did, possibly more than Ibsen did, and certainly more than their successors did. He knew that he was swimming across, if not exactly against, the main current of the 1880s. The realistic spirit of the century had made stage successes of American melodramas like *Under the Gaslight* (1867) in which a train (two-dimensional) roared across the stage; of English dramas like Robertson's cup-and-saucer comedies, remarkable for the absence of a painted moon and the presence of real handles on the doors in the canvas flats; and of sensuous French comedies like *L'Ami Fritz*, which featured both a cherry tree that shed its blossoms and a genuine gourmet's dinner whose aromas were wafted out to the audience. The fact that the latter play was staged at the Comédie-Française in 1876 signaled the capitulation of the bastion of the classic drama to the newest trends. Inevitably, directors had to outdo one another in their search for novelty. In a letter of 1884, Strindberg joshingly told a Swedish producer that he was planning a modern comedy with "a locomotive (real, all fired up), a parsonage, an apple tree (real) in blossom, a tunnel, a train station, a room in a Swedish manor house, a mill, a coffin, a corpse, a bedroom with a double bed, a commode, and so on."[10] His own ideas emerge from a letter written in 1889 advising his wife on how to stage his one-act play *The Stronger*:

Set up on stage a corner, a crib or stall . . . of rehearsal props. Hang a few travel posters and theatre placards on the walls so that it looks like a café without the counter being seen. Set out an umbrella stand, a coatrack, etc.[11]

This is the *Julie* method again, the method of selective realism, and it is the method Strindberg was to develop later in such plays as *To Damascus* and *Charles XII*, where each set is built up out of a few suggestive elements. In the winter of 1896–97 Strindberg impressed Yeats[12] with these ideas for simplified and symbolic sets, and a decade or so later this approach to stage decoration, known as "synthesis," began to manifest itself in European theatres. One might be tempted to make some large claims for Strindberg as a scenic innovator were it not that this synthetic method is at least as old as the Elizabethan theatre, and probably as old as the Greek. It is, nevertheless, fair to regard Strindberg as its renewer.

3

As far as acting was concerned, Strindberg's views were, during the 1880s, more in line with the main drift of naturalism. The dominant style in serious plays was pompous and rhetorical, with the tragic actor relying on sweeping gestures and a voice that ranged from the elegiac to the stentorian. While this exaggerated style might have been appropriate in plays with exotic settings and superhuman heroes, it rang false in plays with everyday settings and middle- or lower-class people. The mode of drawing-room comedy was much more realistic. The best comic actors were masters of the light touch, the quick give-and-take of witty dialogue, the small but expressive gesture. Compared to tragic actors, they were cool and detached. It was this comic style that Strindberg opted in the 1880s for in his naturalist tragedies. Similarly, Chekhov wanted his plays performed by comedians and not by tragedians, and perhaps that is why he called his plays comedies: the tragic posture was alien to them.

When asked for advice on staging *The Father*, Strindberg replied that

the play can easily be ruined and made ridiculous. I would suggest, although I seldom interfere, that the part of the Captain be given to an actor of a rather lively disposition who with the superior, self-mocking, slightly cynical air of a man of the world, fully conscious of his own merits, goes in tolerably good spirits to meet his fate, wrapping himself as he dies in the spider webs that he cannot, because of certain laws of nature, rip asunder.

A deceived husband is a comic figure in the eyes of the world, and even more so in the eyes of a theatre audience. He must show that he knows this, and that he too would laugh if only someone else were the cuckold.

This is what's modern in my tragedy, and woe betide me and the mountebank if he goes out and acts *The Robbers* in this year 1887. No shrieking, no preaching. Urbanely, calmly, resignedly—as befits a basically strong soul who accepts fate in the modern form of erotic passion.

Remember that a cavalry officer is inevitably a rich man's son of good breeding who lives up to his own high standards in social behavior and is also well-behaved towards his soldiers.

In a word, not the coarse boor of stage tradition and army engineer propaganda. Moreover, he has risen above his profession, has exposed it, and is a scientist. For me he represents here especially a masculinity that some have sought to debase, cheat us of, and ascribe to the third sex. It is only with his woman that he is unmanly, for the good reason that she wants him that way, and the law of accommodation requires us to play the role our mistress demands. Yes, sometimes we have to pretend to be chaste, naive, ignorant, simply to get her to copulate.[13]

This was written in October 1887, a month before the Copenhagen production opened at the Casino Theatre. Having learned from that experience, Strindberg counseled the director of the Swedish production to play *The Father* in the manner of *The Wild Duck* as staged in Stockholm,

that is, not as tragedy, not as comedy, but as something in-between. Don't use a too fast tempo, as we did here at the Casino at first. Much better to let it move forward slowly, quietly, evenly, until it picks up momentum by itself in the last act. Exception: the Captain's speeches when his obsessions break out. These should be spoken hurriedly, abruptly; should be spat out with constant sudden transitions.[14]

Strindberg's advice can be misleading to modern actors and directors who do not set it against the background of nineteenth-century tragic acting. His later admonitions indicate that he would find American "method" acting quite unsuitable—too small, too easy, too mean, and too ugly. Twenty years after writing his principal naturalist dramas, Strindberg established his own intimate theatre, where he produced both The Father and Miss Julie. In 1908, when naturalism was everywhere triumphant, Strindberg abjured it in both stage decor and acting, declaring that realism and naturalism were past stages in the development of the theatre. He had read Gordon Craig's The Art of the Theatre immediately after it was published in 1905 and had met the author in 1906. Although he was unimpressed by Craig's ideas, he admired Craig's theatre designs.[15] Like Craig, Strindberg wanted simplified, abstract sets, and he was constantly experimenting with stage sets enclosed by drapes. Played on such a "drapery stage," said Strindberg, The Father would be "lifted from the heavy mundane world to the level of tragedy in high style. The characters [would] be sublimated, ennobled, and appear as if from another world."[16] During rehearsals he instructed his director to stage The Father as grand tragedy with magnificent voices and heightened passions. The actress who took the part of the maleficent wife was told to be "a lioness on stage, not to be tame, not to act as in drawing-room drama, not to fear the great outbursts, the ungovernable passions, the profound hate and overbearing arrogance of this demon woman."[17] We seem to catch here the first whiffs of expressionistic acting. But this, too, may be a false scent. The actors at Strindberg's theatre were young and inexperienced like those at Antoine's theatre twenty years before, and Strindberg may simply have been trying to get them to project. Bearing this out is the advice he gives Falck in the role of the captain. In contrast to what he told the actress playing Laura, Strindberg advised Falck,[18] the most experienced member of the troupe, to tone down his playing, to confine himself to the low register of his voice, to avoid sudden leaps from loud to soft, and to let the words come out naturally.

Clear, forceful speech that would capture the rhythms of his dialogue was the cornerstone of Strindberg's conception of good acting. Professional actors were in danger of slipping into the false accents of declamation. Strindberg's young actors, on the other hand, had not learned stage speech and were inclined to rattle off much of the dialogue, to breathe improperly and break up the rhythms, to swallow key words, and to emphasize the wrong words. Running through all his advice to young actors is an insistence on good stage speech. He did not want declamation, but he did not want natural speech either. The audience had paid to see and to hear; it was up to the actor to speak with the utmost clarity and to bring out all the nuances in the dialogue.

The salient fact emerging from all these contradictions, both real and apparent, is that the mantle of naturalism did not sit comfortably on Strindberg's shoulders. When he wrote *Miss Julie*, naturalism had already arrived at a crossroads. Some of its adherents attempted to make the novel and the stage painstakingly accurate copies of life. Arno Holz, for example, set forth in the 1890s his theory of a "consistent naturalism," which he summed up in the formula: Art = Nature − X, X representing such factors as the artistic means employed and the artist's personality.[19] Strindberg would have no truck with this trifling naturalism. "All my literary endeavors," he said toward the end of his life, "have been in reaction against *Kleinkunst* and petty realism" (SS, 53:100). The formula for an artistic realism and a heightened naturalism would read: Art = Nature + X. The kind of acting he wanted in his plays would unite realism with grandeur, but, as in Talma's definition of great acting, it would be a union of grandeur without pomp and nature without triviality.

Although I have seen at least seven productions of *Miss Julie*, some in English and some in Swedish, with the heroine played by such luminaries as Inga Tidblad, Karin Kavli, Viveca Lindfors, and Elizabeth Bergner, and by Meryl Streep in a performance that may fairly be said to have launched her as an actress (figure 12), I have never seen the end of the play carried off in a convincing manner. On the other hand, I have never seen Strindberg's stage directions followed faithfully. He knew the effect he wanted at the moment Julie exits to kill herself and worked hard to achieve it, but directors and designers have let him down.

CHAPTER THREE

TRAGIC ENDS AND MEANS

Strindberg is partly at fault because in explaining his play he had much more to say about psychology than about theatre and gave the impression that *Miss Julie* is a thoroughly naturalistic presentation of a woman driven to suicide, a casebook study fully documented. He has given so many reasons for Julie's suicide that one feels her death is overdetermined in a way that Hedda Gabler's, for instance, is not. There is Julie's lack of a will to live and her desire to put an end to the family of which she is the last and weakest member. There is her aristocratic shame at having sullied herself through intercourse with a lower species of life. Further, there are the more immediate and precipitating causes: suggestions prompted by the sight of the songbird's blood, the presence of the straightedge razor, the fear of discovery of the theft, and the final command given by Jean, the servant with a thirst for life. Although Strindberg was justifiably proud of this multiplicity of motives,[1] I doubt that the spectator can be aware of all of them when Julie walks off stage to end her life. And if he were, the play, however successful it might be as a nineteenth-century case history, would fail as a tragedy.

Nowadays the Julies of this world do not commit suicide. They cohabit with their butlers, servants, stable grooms, and chauffeurs and manage to live as happily with them as their sisters do with the proper young men they meet at their coming-out parties. The same was true in Strindberg's time, though to a lesser extent. Strindberg said that one of his models for Miss Julie was a certain Emma Rudbeck,[2] the wellborn daughter of a general. She seduced a stable boy, moved to Stockholm, and became a waitress. She did not kill herself. Whatever may be the principal cause of Julie's suicide, it cannot lie simply in class conflict. In the course of the last half-century, the class barriers that loomed so large to Strindberg and his audiences have been partially washed away by the currents of democracy and have left the true foundations of the play all the more clearly exposed. The rise of one class and the fall of another that are augured in *Miss Julie* have come to pass. Moreover, the drama itself has developed along the lines laid down by Strindberg so that his technique is no longer so bewildering. The result is that we are now in a position to see *Miss Julie* less as a social problem play than as a type of modern tragedy.

From the dramaturgical point of view, the first thing that strikes one is the degree to which the story material has been concentrated. Earlier one-act plays almost always concerned themselves with relatively trivial incidents and avoided any deep exploration of character. A joke, a *quiproquo*, a contretemps sufficed for a one-act comedy; a *méprise* or an unfortunate coincidence, for a one-act tragedy. In most cases, one felt the material was being stretched to cover thirty or forty minutes. With *Miss Julie*, one feels just the opposite. Although the play runs for an hour and a half, it is so crammed with story and motivation that the performers and the director must single out the important strands of the action or risk losing their audience.

The density of texture in Ibsen's plays has often been remarked, but Ibsen's kind of concentration differs from Strindberg's in that the Norwegian is intent upon withholding information until the most effective moment while the Swede is eager to tell all he knows at once. Ibsen constructs his plays like mystery stories that come to an end when the last and most vital piece of information is revealed. Strindberg, as he himself said, tends to spill everything immediately in his realistic plays,[3] and only after his Inferno crisis does he learn to hold back and mystify his audiences. Ibsen is more concerned to explore the past while Strindberg, even in a naturalistic work like *Miss Julie* in which those forces of the past, heredity and upbringing, have such a large part to play, seeks to depict the present. Ibsen's plays are constructed on the Scribean model and contain an exposition, a development leading to a climax, and then a denouement or catastrophe. The technical novelty in Ibsen's method was not, as Shaw says it was, the introduction of the discussion scene, but it was, rather, the penetration of the exposition into the rest of the play. The climax in an Ibsen play either consists in or is triggered by some crucial revelation of the past. Hence Ibsen's characters often seem to be patients on Freud's couch or ghosts clutching at cobwebs in some dingy Victorian mansion.

Miss Julie is different. Even though the past haunts Julie's mind and permeates nearly every moment of the play, the emphasis is on the present. Whereas Ibsen's plays are all exposition, *Miss Julie* is all climax and catastrophe. Bearing in mind the three-part structure of a conventional play, we may say that Ibsen stresses the first part, Strindberg the last. Ibsen's method is certainly more typical of the post-Renaissance drama and probably more sensible, for in drama, as in sex, the climax cannot be prolonged indefinitely; and when Strindberg finally came to write *Miss Julie* he had to reduce the playing time from the two or three hours of a standard play to ninety minutes—and of course he had to eliminate the act divisions, for an interrupted climax is no climax at all. I say when he finally came to write *Miss Julie*, for it is apparent that Strindberg could not have achieved this extraordinary degree of concentration, by which the nine years of his love life with Siri are distilled into ninety minutes of pure drama, without first having written his short stories about marriage, the plays *Sir Bengt's Wife* and *Comrades*, and the autobiographical novel *A Madman's Defense*. In a sense these took the place of the extensive notes and drafts that Ibsen made.

It is also clear, as Carl Reinhold Smedmark has pointed out, that Strindberg did not embrace the one-act form[4] as soon as he sat down to write about Julie. Indeed, Strindberg originally may have had a three-act play in mind, the first act ending with the dance of the peasants that forces Julie to retreat into Jean's room, the second act ending when Julie exits to pack her things and elope with Jean. But that scene is not nearly strong enough to serve as a second-act curtain, and Strindberg had to keep the action rolling on beyond this point without a break, even though it meant telescoping Midsummer Night so violently that it would have given pause to any realistic dramatist. When Strindberg set out, either consciously or unconsciously, to create one long stretch of rising action, intermissions had to be discarded and replaced with a dance and with pantomimes, landings that would permit the spectator to rest and relax on the way to the climax but not to escape from the influence of the author-hypnotist. Strindberg was experimenting with a form that improved on Zola's *nouvelle formule*—make it true to life, make it grand, and keep it simple—by making the spectator's agony brief and by letting the action rush to its conclusion without interruption. Commenting on the concentrated form of *Miss Julie*, Strindberg said,

In every play there is one real scene. That's the one I want. Why should I bother with what's leftover and give six or eight actors the trouble of taking care of it.

In France I always ordered five mutton chops, much to the astonishment of the autochthons. A mutton chop has half a pound of bone and two inches of fat. Within is the ball of lean meat—*la noix*. That I ate. Give me the nut is what I tell playwrights.[5]

In its final shape, *Miss Julie* bears only slight traces of its embryonic three-part form. It more resembles a two-act play formed by lopping off the exposition, with a consequent shift in the position of what used to be known as the peripety or plot reversal. Ordinarily, this would come at the end of the second act in a three-act play, the function of the third act being either to spell out the consequences of this reversal in the case of a tragedy or to restore the fortunes of the protagonist in the case of a comedy. In *Miss Julie*, however, about 40 percent of the play is rising action and 60 percent, catastrophe.

Apart from its position in the structure of the play, the peripety is a true peripety, bringing a change of fortune for both Jean and Julie. Once they seduce each other, their lives are changed irrevocably, and the world in which they move and think is turned upside down. The two-part structure of the play accords perfectly with the social and sexual reversal. (Dickens's *Little Dorrit*, which Strindberg, as a devotee of its author, may well have read, has the same structure, the second half of the story reversing the social relationships of the chief characters in the first half.) The first part of the play pictures Jean as slave and Julie as mistress; the second part shows Julie as slave and Jean as master. In the first part, Julie despises Jean for being vulgar, boorish, and animal-like; in the second part, Jean despises Julie for being dirty, impure, and unable to control herself. The noble lady lowers herself beyond the possibility of redemption while the slave rises above her. The aristocrat in the social sphere becomes the slave of the valet; the valet becomes the aristocrat in the sexual sphere. Much of the richness of this play, as of Strindberg's other writings in the 1880s, derives from his ability to fuse social and psychological motives. In his own marriage, the antagonism between him and his wife was, as he admitted, "the clash between the upper class and the lower class."[6] But the sexual, psychological, and inner conflicts are fundamental to the play; the social conflict is there to enhance the sexual conflict.

To focus more sharply on the basic conflicts, Strindberg makes use of small symbolic actions and parallels, devices that were to become the hallmarks of his dramatic technique in later years. The fact that Julie's pet dog Diana (!) has become pregnant by a mongrel foreshadows the peripety of the play, just as Jean's brutal beheading of Julie's pet songbird Serena (!) anticipates the final scene. The two dreams that Julie and Jean relate in the play complement each other so perfectly that one feels the ordering hand of the playwright more strongly here than elsewhere. In her recurrent dream, Julie finds herself on top of a high pillar from which she wants to climb down but cannot. Jean, in contrast, dreams of climbing up the thick, slippery trunk of a tree to rob a nest of its golden eggs. The transparent sexual imagery scarcely calls for comment, nor does the way in which these two dreams prefigure the action of the drama. Julie dreams of debasing herself—and will do so; Jean dreams of rising to the top—and will do so, at least for a moment. And in realizing their dreams, both will be disillusioned.

2

Concentrating on Julie we tend to forget that Jean experiences a minor tragedy. Once he mounts above Julie and robs her nest of its golden eggs, he is deprived of an object of worship. His is the slave's mentality, and without anything or anyone to look up to his life loses its meaning. Fortunately, there are always other masters to whom he can attach himself. Julie's father, the Count, is still there to inspire him with respect, as Strindberg says, even after Jean has possessed the daughter and seen how empty that pretty shell is. It is because there are always masters around and because Jean is a slave first, last, and always that he can retire from the battlefield unharmed, or at least not fatally wounded. Jean's life is defined by those above him, and, consequently, it has an aim and a purpose and a meaning. Without the aristocracy, God would not exist for Jean.

In contrast, Miss Julie's life lacks definition because there is nothing she can lastingly respect and revere. What one part of her being desires, the other part finds repulsive. She wants her fiancé to kowtow to her; she makes him jump over her riding crops as if he were a trained dog; but she has only contempt for him because he obeys her. When he refuses to jump, she hates him for that too. She enjoys seeing Jean kiss her shoe; she wants him to seduce her; she teases him until he does; but once he has blackened his lips on her shoe and ejaculated his seed into her, she hates him and herself for what they have done. Yet half an hour later she wants to repeat the whole business. Life for her is a balancing act in which she teeters between being slave and being master. As long as she plays her role in society, she can maintain her balance, but the moment she abandons that role and fully commits herself, she plunges from the pillar that haunts her dreams. Julie is destroyed because the game she has been playing becomes real.

To appreciate how this comes about, we have to consider another parallel that Strindberg employs, a parallel that is as essential to *Miss Julie* as exposition is in a conventional three-part play. Before the seduction, Jean tells Julie that as a small boy he stole apples from the Count's orchard, which is pictured as a Garden of Eden with its tree of life and, by implication, its tree of knowledge of good and evil. On another occasion he came into the grounds to work in the vegetable gardens. Driven by curiosity, he stole into the outhouse, a beautiful Turkish pavilion hung with honeysuckle. (Opulent bathrooms and air fresheners were not invented by Americans.) While he was in there, he heard people approaching. He was trapped. "There was only one way out for the upper-class people. But for me there was one more. And I had no choice: I had to take it" (SS, 23:138). Covered with muck and excrement, he ran through the strawberry patches and the raspberry and rose bushes until he caught sight of little Miss Julie. In her pink dress and white stockings, she appeared like an angel to him, a symbol of the hopelessness of ever rising above the class into which he was born. This was a crucial experience to Jean, and his whole view of life was shaped by this childhood expulsion from the Garden of Eden. The rest of his story about trying to commit suicide because he realized the impossibility of entering again the Eden out of which he had been cast is romantic exaggeration, reflecting his own daydreams, no doubt, but primarily intended, as he later admits, to impress Miss Julie.

Jean's parable serves as a background against which the rest of the play must be seen. When Julie is in the kitchen with Jean, and the farmhands and servants are heard approaching, Julie is in the same position as the boy Jean was. Now she is out of her milieu, enjoying the unsophisticated pleasures of the lower class. From the kitchen, which is in the servants' quarters and unconnected with the house, there is one proper way out for Jean and his class; but for Miss Julie there is yet another way—Jean's room—and she has no choice but to take it. And when she leaves Jean's room, covered with shame, she faces the black-liveried valet, a symbol of the hopelessness of ever changing her way of life.

This sense of physical entrapment is essential to a proper working of the play on stage. Without it, all the motives for Julie's end that Strindberg adduces seem only intellectual rationalizations. With it, they gather together to create a force of irresistible dramatic power. Before the seduction, Julie is a wild animal, hunted and pursued by her own desires. After the seduction, she is a trapped and caged creature hurling herself against the bars that imprison her. Jean's offer to elope with her is not an invitation to freedom but a temptation to enter a smaller, darker, narrower cage. Her suicide should have the same effect on us as the deliberate death of a wild animal that prefers to die rather than live in captivity.

Julie, however, is not only a wild creature; she is also a sophisticated human being. What distinguishes the human being from the animal is masochism, and what makes Julie the fascinating modern woman she is, is the extent to which she is half-man, half-woman, both hunter and hunted, both on top of the pillar and at the bottom of it, both master and slave. It is her unconscious desire to be trapped, her inner compulsion to defile herself that makes her modern—not, as Strindberg points out, because her type has not always existed but because it is now coming forward and attracting attention. Or, he might have said, because it is now being understood.

Julie kills herself not because she is an aristocrat but because she is Julie. Jean is ultimately no more than a part of her own being, a willing and convenient actor who can be assigned a major role in the drama she is constantly rehearsing and never finishing. But this time the drama is carried out to its logical end. By committing suicide Julie escapes from the net of conflicting desires. As with Hedda Gabler, her last moments are her noblest moments. Ibsen may have written *Hedda Gabler* (printed 1890) as a counterstatement to *Miss Julie* (printed 1888 and first performed 1889) or to Strindberg's short story "Upon Payment" ("Mot betalning," published in the collection entitled *Married II*, 1885), in which the sexually ambiguous woman who finds motherhood repulsive first appears. That Ibsen meant Hedda to be a sister under the skin to Helen, the woman in Strindberg's story, is obvious. He took the opening lines of the story and built on them. "Her father was a general, and she was quite young when her mother died. After that the visitors to the house were mostly men. And her father took charge of bringing her up" (*SS*, 14:302). In writing *Hedda Gabler*, Ibsen was invading Strindberg's territory and challenging him on his own ground. But Hedda's suicide is like Julie's in one important respect: there is a note of triumph sounded in it. If Hedda and Julie had chosen to live on as the vassals of Brack and Jean, we could speak of a defeat; but not now. Hedda's fear of scandal, her contempt for the philistine Judge Brack, her awareness that she has failed to realize her ideals—either immediately in her own life or vicariously in Lövborg's—constitute the negative aspect of her suicide. But she also kills herself because she wants to bring back into the world some of the glamour and grandness it lost when the middle class took power; she wants to show Brack that there are more things in heaven and earth than are dreamt of in his philistinism ("People don't do such things!"); she wants to prove to herself that Lövborg's ideals and hers can be realized, if only fleetingly; and she wants for once in her life to do something exciting instead of just hearing about it from Lövborg's lips. Much of this complex motivation must inevitably escape the attentive spectator and even the careful reader because Ibsen, working within the formal limits of the pièce bien faite, had to rush his ending. Hence Hedda's decision to kill herself appears impulsive, irrational, and capricious, rather than arrived at step by step. Strindberg, on the other hand, by minimizing the exposition and prolonging the catastrophe, painstakingly carves out each of the steps that carry Julie to her end.

3

More instructive than Ibsen's play is a group of long one-acts written in France since 1940. The superficial similarity of Genet's Deathwatch and The Maids and Sartre's No Exit to Miss Julie and Creditors is immediately apparent and testifies to the vitality of a form that Strindberg may be said to have reinvented: the ninety-minute one-act spellbinder, long enough to allow the full development of a rich subject, short enough to demand and receive the audience's complete concentration. No Exit is a three-character drama in which all three are trapped in situations that represent their lives. But since they are all dead there can be no change or resolution as there can be for Miss Julie. The Maids, Genet's most revealing play, strikes me as being modeled both in form and content on Strindberg's Miss Julie. Here is the essence of Genet's thought. Everything he wrote before it was in preparation for it; everything he has written since is an elaboration on it.

Genet presents a sado-masochistic ritual in which two maids play the roles of mistress and maid; that is, maid A plays the mistress, and maid B plays maid A. In taking the part of the tyrannical mistress and in reviling B, A is simultaneously achieving the position she herself both hates and envies, heaping abuse on the position she in fact occupies, and providing B with the pleasure of being spat on. After a bit of this the roles can be switched, so that every nuance of sadism and masochism can be enjoyed. Nothing could be more perfect, except to have it go on forever. This it cannot do, for reality in the person of Madame always threatens to arrive on the scene and interrupt their pretense. Hence an alarm clock must be set to warn them of their mistress's expected arrival. Regrettably, the maids trap themselves by unsuccessfully trying to betray Madame's lover to the police. When Madame finds out what they have done, their game will have to end once and for all. They must either destroy their mistress or themselves. They therefore decide to play the game in earnest and act out the ritual to its ultimate conclusion. They will poison their mistress, and they will act out the poisoning. As the real mistress approaches, the weaker of the two maids takes the part of the mistress and proves herself the stronger by commanding the other maid, who is of course playing the weaker maid, to give the mistress-maid the poisoned tea. In this manner, the weaker maid manages to combine in herself both the sadist and the masochist, both the slave and the master. In her last moments she ecstatically achieves the synthesis that in life could only be hers in pretense. She dies both by her own hand and by that of another.

The end of *Miss Julie* is remarkably similar. Julie's problem is twofold. She herself is the mistress and therefore cannot "play" that role, and she has found no one who can play the game with her and keep it at the desired pitch of excitement. But as her father the Count approaches, she does find a partner who will play the game to the end. She orders Jean to order her to kill herself. She, the weaker of the two, who has not strength enough to kill herself, seems stronger at the end when she tells Jean what to do. Jean seems weaker because he is incapable of acting until the Count rings the bell. Like Genet's Madame, the Count is the primum mobile in this universe of slaves and masters rotating around each other, and Strindberg was wiser than Genet in keeping this force offstage. As in Strindberg, class distinctions are used in *The Maids* to earmark the master and the slave, the sadist and the masochist. Other distinctions can serve the same purpose. In *Deathwatch*, for instance, which is set in a prison cell, degrees of criminality separate the envied from the envious, the glorified ones from the self-haters; and in *The Blacks* Genet expresses the distinction in terms of the white and black races. In nineteenth-century Europe, the sado-masochistic relationship could best be suggested by using the social class structure. In twentieth-century America, it is most forcefully brought out by using black skins and white skins to distinguish the players in the game. It would be quite in keeping with the inner spirit of Strindberg's play to adapt it for present-day American audiences by making Jean a black man and Julie a white Southern belle, as has often been suggested. On the other hand, Tennessee Williams's *A Streetcar Named Desire*, which struck many Swedes as a Southern version of *Miss Julie*, differs fundamentally from Strindberg in that the heroine's behavior is motivated by her feelings of guilt. She knows she is responsible for destroying her husband who killed himself when confronted by her revulsion at his homosexuality. Guilt, which plays such a large part in Ibsen's works and accounts for his use of the retrospective technique, is not an important factor in Strindberg's naturalistic works, nor in the ritualistic works of Genet. "The naturalist has wiped out guilt along with God," said Strindberg in his preface to *Miss Julie*—and so has the existentialist. The roots of the sado-masochistic relationship may quite possibly lie in the sex act, so that the male-female conflict that Strindberg emphasizes in his works may be the psychological and physical basis of the social conflict of classes. Nevertheless, as Genet's homosexual plays make clear, male and female should be understood as representing attitudes rather than organs.

Just as *Miss Julie* is an attempt by Strindberg to reduce or distill the action of the conventional well-made play to nothing but climax and catastrophe, so Genet in *The Maids* has in effect extended and prolonged the last moments of *Miss Julie*. The whole of Genet's play spells out what happens on the last pages of Strindberg's play. At that point, Jean and Julie are no longer the comparatively free creatures they were at the beginning. The possibility of keeping Julie as his mistress on the estate does not appeal to Jean when he is reminded of the consequences, the pregnancy and scandal that will come inevitably if their affair continues. On the other hand, the possibility of eloping with Julie is cut off by the cook Christine. Julie is confronted by the alternative prospects of a life with Jean or a life with father. Either way, she is faced with humiliation, degradation, scandal, her own unhappiness, and that of others. The situation is stalemated with both Jean and Julie knowing that the only real end must be Julie's suicide. But neither of them is able to bring about this resolution: Julie because she is weak, Jean because he is afraid. Only something that can give her strength and him courage can make them move. The only thing that can give her strength is something outside her, and the only thing that can give him courage is some greater fear. Not until the Count rings the bell are Jean and Julie able to act.

4

To bring off the end, which obviously gave Strindberg some difficulty, he had to steal a sunrise from Ibsen and some hypnosis from the French school of psychology. These two devices were necessary to lift the play from the level of realism to the ritualistic level on which Genet's play is enacted. The spirit of the end is violated by realistic acting and realistic sets. To escape realistic acting, Strindberg calls for Julie to be hypnotized, and her last long speech is spoken in an ecstasy. To rid himself of the realistic set for which he had argued so eloquently in his preface but which at this moment would betray the spirit of Julie's speech, Strindberg calls for the long slanting rays of the early morning sun to fall on Jean alone. But I have never seen a production in which this direction is followed. The spectator should be aware of nothing but a black, undefined object in the sun and the voice of the transported Julie. To realize Strindberg's intentions the audience must be as hypnotized as Julie.

Under hypnotic suggestion, largely self-induced, Julie has jumped from one orbit to another, where Jean cannot follow her. If the audience were aware now of the psychological motives for her death, they would be left behind with Jean. The ending will not work unless the world of reality momentarily fades away. The gaping mouth of the speaking tube is ominously present throughout the play and functions dramaturgically in much the same way as the gods do in Greek tragedy. When it speaks, Jean and Julie are forced to act. But Julie can act only by entering her play-world where to act in one sense means to act in another. When she is hypnotized and transported, the stage world of audience and actor coincides with the play-world of Julie. In the rest of the play, the setting and the performers are imitations of the world the audience knows. In this last scene, the audience is at one with Julie, no longer watching but participating, and the real world has ceased to exist for both. When the bell rings again for the last time, this mood is shattered, and Julie is shoved over the edge of the abyss to her death, for by this time the real world stands for death. Although Strindberg at first planned to have Julie die on stage, it is not necessary for us to see her die. We experience the effect of the razor slash when the bell rings. Here Strindberg succeeds better than Ibsen did in *Rosmersholm*. Rosmer and Rebecca talk each other into a double suicide, and they too must be in some exalted state that belies the heavy Victorian set in which they stand. Ibsen follows their last exit with a speech by the housekeeper, in which she describes their deaths, and it results in a fatal collapse of the action to the realistic level.

Miss Julie demonstrates both the effectiveness and the limitations of stage realism. It enables the spectator to identify to a certain extent with the protagonist and with the situation on stage, but it inhibits the expansion of the spirit. When considered in relation to the end of the play, the long uninterrupted stretch of action and its realistic basis serve as a runway for a flight into another realm. The audience should take off with Julie, experiencing with her the growing terror of entrapment, the ecstasy of escape, and then, for one brief instant, the blow that brings oblivion. In that lies the essence of romantic theatre. The spectator begins as a witness to a realistic event and ends as a participator in a ritual.

Genet's technique consists in beginning the ritual in medias res. On anyone not in a frame of mind to accept his peculiar ritual, his play will have the same effect as the Catholic liturgy on a nonbeliever, who may find the ceremony curious, instructive, and beautiful but who will not share in it directly. Genet's world is a world of fantasy with piquant touches of reality. His characters are not real, nor are they meant to be. Genet capitalizes on the fact that theatre is an illusion by presenting his world of illusions as theatre. His evil is not evil in any practical sense since it exists only in the form of fantasy; as soon as his ritual of sadism and masochism becomes real, it comes to a halt.

In contrast to Genet, Strindberg gradually entices the spectator into the ritual. For him, the ritual in the play reflects a ritual in real life. When Genet's maid dies, only a marionette dies; when Julie dies, a woman dies and a world with her.

5

A proper understanding of the ending of Miss Julie goes a long way to answering the objections raised against the play as tragedy. In the view of most critics, neither this play nor The Father is tragic because the naturalistic philosophy implicit in them allows for no spiritual meaning in the universe. The Darwinian scheme imposes no moral order on existence, and without that there can be no tragedy, tragedy being irreconcilable with chaos. As part of a spiritual universe, the tragic hero enjoys a measure of free will allowing him, for a moment at least, to become godlike, as Oedipus does when he plucks out his eyes and astonishes even the gods by going beyond the fate they had ordained for him. In the naturalistic view, mortal man lacks free will and is simply the victim of heredity and physical circumstances. Because of the way in which they were raised, Miss Julie is neurotic and the Captain paranoid.

Strindberg met these objections head on, and in writing *Miss Julie* and *The Father* he deliberately set out to emulate ancient tragedy. Whereas Ibsen sought to avert odious comparisons by giving *Ghosts* the modest and ironic subtitle "a domestic drama," Strindberg pointedly called *Miss Julie* "a naturalistic tragedy" and gave it the length and structure of ancient Greek tragedy. And with *The Father*, which is always thought of as purely personal, altogether subjective drama, he transplanted Aeschylus's *Agamemnon* into the nineteenth century. In it he continued his study of the feminist movement of the 1880s by introducing into the French problem play, which was the highbrow drama of the time, Darwinist ideas about the struggle for survival and Marxist ideas about social evolution. A number of French plays and novels* written from 1860 to 1886 were more blatantly misogynistic than anything

---

*Among novels: *L'Affaire Clemenceau* (1866) by Dumas *fils* and *Charles Demailly* (1860) and *Manette Salomon* (1867), both by the Goncourt brothers. These three novels treat of the destruction of a decent man by an evil woman. In *Charles Demailly* the husband is dishonored and driven to madness and death by the jealousy his wife arouses in him. Among plays: *L'Homme-femme* (1872) and *La Femme de Claude* (1873), both virulently misogynistic works by Dumas *fils*. Closer to Strindberg's play in time is Guy de Maupassant's story "Monsieur Parent" (1885), in which a man is tortured by doubts as to the parentage of the child who has given him the only real joy he has known in life. Jolivet, *Le Théâtre de Strindberg* (Paris, 1931), pp. 157–59, notes the similarities between this story and *The Father*, which are very superficial. A more remote source has been suggested by Margaret Clark, who makes an interesting case for Samuel de Constant's 1783 novel *Le Mari sentimental*, in which a wife brings about the madness and suicide of her husband, an army captain, by isolating him from his friends and spreading harmful rumors about him. "Strindberg and Samuel de Constant, the Source of *The Father* and of Strindbergian Sociology (1883–1887)," *Revue de littérature comparée*, 42 (1968):583–96.

Being well read in French literature, Strindberg certainly knew some of these works. Still, there is a world of difference between Strindberg's play and these French fictions, and they only serve to show that plots involving destructive wives, troubled husbands, and doubtful children were recurrent in French literature. For the French writers, the wife's lover was, more often than not, the operative force. In Strindberg, the unconscious thoughts determine the course of events.

Strindberg himself says, and there is little reason to disbelieve him, that he was spurred to write *The Father* because a play by Jules de Glouvet on the subject of paternity had stirred up a minor tempest among the Parisian literati. *Vivisektioner* (1894), ed. Torsten Eklund (Stockholm, 1958), pp. 36–37. *Le Père*, a work by Glouvet, was indeed published in the early months of 1886, but far from provoking much discussion, it seems to have plummeted to the depths of Parisian intellectual life without producing a ripple on the surface.

Strindberg had written, and he felt that his views on the woman question, if expressed in the fashionable mode of a play about a demonic woman, would be given a more sympathetic hearing in France than they had received in Sweden. The subject of paternity—*pater semper incertus*—may or may not have come to him while he was reading about Gustav III,[7] as he said it did, but it certainly did not come out of his own marriage. He chose to make use of it because he had read a Marxist interpretation of the *Oresteia*, an article by Paul Lafargue called "Le Matriarcat,"[8] published in 1886. Lafargue argued that Aeschylus's trilogy reflected the development of ancient society from an organization in which the mother was central, because parentage could only be indubitably determined by her, to a social organization in which the father was central. This interpretation was not new, having been advanced by J. J. Bachofen some years before; Lafargue gave it added cogency by combining it with the theory of the origin of the family that Friedrich Engels had recently enunciated.

Before he began to write *The Father*, Strindberg familiarized himself with all these new and stimulating ideas about man's prehistory (SS, 14:239–40; 54:269ff.),[9] and, having himself experienced the onslaught of the feminist hordes, he now speculated on the possibility that history was completing a cycle and that Europe was entering a second matriarchal era. In *The Father* man makes his last stand. Strindberg surrounds his beleaguered captain with women who take on all the female roles: mother, wife, mistress, and child, with the unseen mother-in-law representing the old matriarchal order. But the beleaguered soldier is not defeated by numbers. The women are triumphant because in the struggle for survival physical strength is no longer a necessity. The battle of the sexes, which was won by the brute caveman in the distant past, has now become a battle of brains, of cunning, and in that conflict the more highly developed moral sense of man would prove to be his undoing.

Once he had the subject firmly in mind, he was able to raise it above Darwinian and Marxist concerns by placing the heart of the conflict within the hero. Combining sociology with psychology, Strindberg could suggest that the predisposing cause of the decline of modern patriarchal society lay in man's adulation of mother (SS, 14:237–39; 54:273–74).[10] The Captain is defeated because he has a mother fixation. In the climactic scene at the end of Act II he discloses that when he made love to his wife he was embracing his mother. While all the women in the house have been superstitiously worshipping a phantom called God, the Captain has been adoring an idol called Mother. In the last act he comes to her. The Captain is lured into the straitjacket (which corresponds to the net in *Agamemnon*)[11] only because he becomes a child again in the hands of his old nurse, the only truly motherly woman in his life.

The Father was intended to be part of a trilogy,[12] the rest of which never materialized. Instead, *The Father* should be regarded as part of a sex tetralogy, the first play in it being *Comrades* (1886–87), a spoof of Ibsenism, feminism, and unisexism. The confusion of the sexes is the main subject. *A Doll's House* is turned upside down, with the husband coming on as the doll, dressing up (almost) as a Spanish dancer for a costume ball (Nora's tarantella), and slamming the door on his wife, while Nora's "most wonderful thing of all" turns out to be a man who can dominate a woman. Out of this sexual ambiguity and reversal of roles arises the tragedy of *The Father* (1887), in which the sexual crisis of modern Europe is seen as having its source in the historic development of the family. In the third play, *Miss Julie* (1888), the sex struggle is combined with the class struggle. Finally, in the tragicomedy *Creditors* (1888), the struggle is pictured as purely one of brains, and the tetralogy returns to its starting point with husband and wife playing at brother and sister and treating each other as comrades.

To make tragedies out of *The Father* and *Miss Julie*, Strindberg had to find a modern equivalent for the Greek sense of fate. In *The Father* fate, he said, takes the form of erotic passion,[13] by which he meant the incestuous aspect of the lovemaking of the Captain and his wife. In *Miss Julie* the heroine's faulty upbringing, her weak constitution, and her social position all add up, as Strindberg remarks in his preface, to an equivalent of fate or the universal law of the Greeks. Then, having deprived his protagonists of free will by seeing them as creatures in a Darwinian world, he gave it back to them when he made them the final arbiters of their fates. Miss Julie makes the decision to kill herself and stages her own death. The Captain has all along been acting out his destiny, his wife only playing the part he has assigned her. He is an Othello who creates his own Iago. Though they are the slaves and victims of their passions, Julie and the Captain end up being more free than any Greek hero because they are their own oracles. The god is within them. Hearing its voice, Julie tells Jean what he must do, and the Captain lets the nurse play mother to him and slip the straitjacket over him. As surely as the heroes of Greek tragedy, Julie and the Captain embrace their fates, Julie taking in her hand the razor that represents the masculine element in her and the Captain submitting to the straitjacket that represents the oedipal longings that have determined the course of his life.

These are rationalistic answers to those who feel that *The Father* and *Miss Julie* do not belong in the august company of the great tragedies of the past. But there is more to the argument. Strindberg knew that tragedy was essentially irrational and that the paradox of tragedy was that it produces a sublime effect while dealing with the most horrible acts and disclosing the most awful truths. The tragic catharsis results from seeing what lies beyond reason and reasoning beyond what is seen. The strict naturalist could not view life tragically because he limited himself to things he could explain, never venturing into the heart of darkness. He was satisfied to reason about what happened in the world by studying the facts. The tragedian wanted to explain the facts, which meant going beyond them. That was why Strindberg sought a higher naturalism. He was not content to reproduce reality as accurately as possible. He needed to create a second reality, an exaltation of life.

Writing in 1887 on the intrigues and machinations of men and women in the battle of the sexes, Strindberg said, "All these ideas and schemes that I have ascribed to human beings, and especially to women, I have purely and simply transferred from the unconscious, the obscure realm of the instincts, to the conscious realm" (SS, 54:304).

He said this before he wrote the plays. It was easy enough for the polemicist to discourse in an essay on man's unconscious thought; it was quite another matter to bring the unconscious on stage with such immediacy that the spectator would feel that he has actually entered the world where fantasies are the only real facts and where the inner life becomes the outer life. This was the challenge the dramatist faced, the challenge that he answered in the strongest scenes of *The Father* and *Miss Julie*. He wanted to raise the viewer to the sphere in which Julie exists at the moment when she decides to end her life and to let him fall with the Captain into the pit of madness. With a fine actress and a director who has faith in Strindberg, Julie's moment of Dionysian ecstasy and Apollonian beauty can become the spectator's too. And with an actor like Lars Hanson, the Captain's collapse can become divinely tragic. For those who saw his portrayal of the Captain in 1953 (figure 13), when he was old enough to possess the wisdom and experience to understand the role and still young enough to have the strength and endurance to play it, all the things they had heard about tragedy and read about catharsis became vivid and real. When the old nurse, the surrogate mother, put the strait-jacket on the Captain and brought him back to his childhood, to the fate he had been trying to master all his life, as Oedipus had tried to master his fate, the drama achieved a power beyond the power of words to explain. The Captain's cry of despair and recognition when he woke from his trance and struggled against his bonds was as piercing, trenchant, and true as the cry of the blinded Oedipus. If *The Father* is not a genuine tragedy, neither are the Greek tragedies.

1. Strindberg in 1886—37 years old and hard at work on his autobiographical novel *The Son of a Servant*.

2. Siri von Essen, Strindberg's first wife. Photographed c. 1881–85.

3. Strindberg. Oil painting by Christian Krohg, 1893. Another version of this painting was purchased by Henrik Ibsen and hung in his study. "I can't write a line," said Ibsen, "unless that crazy man is there to stare at me with his mad eyes." Strindberg is wearing the cape that the Stranger has on at the beginning of act 4 of *To Damascus*. Courtesy of Norwegian Folkmuseum, Oslo.

4. Strindberg in the midst of his Inferno.
Photographed in Ystad, Sweden in the
summer of 1896.

5. Strindberg, c. 1910.
Drawing by E. Nerman.

6. The young rebel at the age of 21
—shortly before he began to write *Master Olof*.

7. Strindberg in 1886 in Gersau, Switzerland. Courtesy of Nordiska Museet.

8. Strindberg in 1907.

9. Strindberg, his last walk, in snow flurries, 9 April 1912.
(Photo by Magnus Wester.)

10. Strindberg's funeral procession through the streets of Stockholm, 19 May 1912. Courtesy of Stockholms Stadsmuseum.

Strindberg's exploration of sex and marriage culminated in *The Father* and *Miss Julie*, written in 1887 and 1888. During the next few years he traversed the same ground in a number of plays, but they seem to be afterthoughts, exercises in technique rather than deeper probings into human nature. *The Stronger*, for instance, one of Strindberg's best known plays because it is often used in acting classes, is technically noteworthy because one of its two charac-

ters never says a word. *Creditors*, a ninety-minute one-act play like *Miss Julie*, is another tour de force. Strindberg thought it even "better than *Miss Julie*, with three people, one table, two chairs, and no sunrise."[1] It also differs from *Miss Julie* in offering cynicism and sarcasm in place of grandeur and passion, surprise in the place of catharsis, and an epileptic fit in the place of an ecstatic death. He called it a tragicomedy, and it is the kind of play Nietzsche would have made out of Coward's *Private Lives*. Having reduced his naturalist tragedies to scenes "from the cynical life" (*SS*, 19:148), Strindberg could find nothing more to say on the subject of marriage. The first major phase in his career had come to an end. When his divorce from Siri became final in 1891, he fired off a few more short plays as parting shots aimed at her, and then he gave up playwriting—for the time being.

When he turned to the drama again in 1898, he was a different man. What happened to him during the intervening years constitutes one of the most fascinating chapters in the history of European literature, not merely because of the change in outlook of this one man but because the crisis in Strindberg's life[2] coincided with the crisis in European culture that occurred in the 1890s. No other writer brought the issues of the age into such sharp focus. His life became the burning glass of an epoch.

That is what he wanted it to be, but only in retrospect is it possible to see how well he succeeded. Putting his finger on the pulse of the times was never enough for him; he wanted to be part of the throbbing spirit itself. In the 1880s, he had made himself a center of controversy on the two most warmly debated issues in Scandinavia, feminism and socialism, by taking the part of "The Son of a Servant." That was the title of his autobiography, and in the role of a mother-fixated revolutionary he had been able to see more deeply into the issues than anybody else, except Ibsen. Now he had to start over again. It was a case of the actor looking for a new role, the artist looking for a new subject worthy of his genius, the scientist looking for a new formula. It was the age of science; Strindberg wanted to be a scientist more than anything else, and to science he turned for the stimulus his creative energies needed.

2

At first, all he had to go on was the conviction that matter and spirit are one. What eluded him was what he as artist and scientist needed most: a sense of design or purpose that would transform chaos into cosmos, at least tentatively. In 1891, when his marriage had been dissolved and his children taken from him, "existence and the universe itself" appeared to him, as he said, "a colossal humbug,"[3] and all attempts to explain the universe and to find a meaning in existence were bound to be fruitless. Three years later, when he was a homeless wanderer in Europe, his attitude changed. Now he hoped that he might discern a meaning to existence. Instead of dismissing all explanations with a skeptical shrug, he opened his mind to all ideas and waited for the word to come. Drifting from town to town, he put himself at the disposal of his unconscious, often obeying impulses that resulted in strange behavior. (See figure 3.)

In a letter to a friend, he compared himself to the prophet Ezekiel, who found himself lifted up between the earth and the heaven. "I don't know what fate holds in store for me, but I feel the 'hand of the Lord' upon me. There's going to be a change. Whether upwards or straight down to the center of the earth, who can tell?"[4] Strindberg saw a bit of himself in Ezekiel because of the prophet's strange behavior. Obeying his Lord, Ezekiel ate a book, slept only on his left side for long periods, and baked bread with dung in it. To his neighbors, these strange acts were irrational; to Ezekiel, they were full of symbolic meaning.

More than anything else Strindberg wanted the inner voice to speak to him, and he tried various means of letting that voice be heard. The difficulty was that there were so many voices speaking to him, voices of social custom and practical morality, of received ideas and school-taught logic, that it was impossible to distinguish the authentic inner voice. To hear it, he had to retune his mind and his whole sensory apparatus.

The drift of his thought is clear enough. Nihilism could not satisfy him nor could a purely naturalistic or materialistic view of life. Like

Samuel Butler and Bernard Shaw, he was convinced that the Darwinists "were pitchforking mind out of the universe,"[5] and he was hoping to bring something like mind or spirit back into his life. In 1895 he told the woman who had become his second wife that he was trying desperately "to poeticize his existence—without succeeding."[6] He had to give a meaning to life if he was to live at all. "Cast out into the desert like the son of the servant [bondwoman], I am born for the desert where I shall perish alone. Or else I shall have to create a god for myself who will protect me against the evil spirits."[7]

A year later, in 1896, Strindberg plumbed the depths of his being and out of the experience emerged a different man, who created a new kind of drama. The new Strindberg saw himself as a "Zola of the occult."[8] The phrase, which was dropped in his mind by a theosophist correspondent, is particularly apt since it suggests both how long and how short the journey was from naturalism to mysticism.

The main tenet of Zola's naturalist creed was the validity of scientific experimentation as the source of knowledge. Abjuring metaphysics as idle speculation, Zola placed his faith in the experimental methods of the laboratory scientist, and, as a disciple of Zola, Strindberg embraced the doctrines of materialism, determinism, and experimentalism. But in regard to the last of these, he found his master's devotion somewhat lax. Zola was not a dedicated experimenter; too often he let the conventions of fiction substitute for the facts of life. How do we know, asked Strindberg about one of Zola's scenes, what a dying man says or thinks when there is no witness to his suicide (SS, 18:458)? With greater rigor than Zola, Strindberg maintained that in the realm of psychology, which after all was the concern of most creative writers, the best subject is oneself and that experiments in subjective motivation must be performed largely on oneself if they are to have any validity.

3

In the 1880s his studies in human behavior had brought him to the point where life was seen almost exclusively as a psychological struggle. It was a view that combined evolutionary and psychological theory by reducing the struggle for existence to a battle of minds. It was, of course, a limited view, and Strindberg was not satisfied with it even as he formulated it. It isolated man from the rest of the universe. Having probed man's mind as deeply as he could, he now endeavored to place man in a larger scheme. He reverted to a plan that he had drawn up as early as 1883, a survey that was meant to encompass the whole phenomenal world. He outlined the scope of the work in a letter written in 1895.

I begin in the volcanoes where I seek out the earth's elements and their transmutations into one another. I descend into the depths of the sea with the deep-sea diver to observe the beginning of life out of water. I rise with the balloonist into the air to draw from their observations my conclusions about the atmosphere, the early form of the earth, and its relation to the heavens and other worlds.

Return to the earth. Begin with the stones, and the first forms of life. Linger over animal-plants (insectivorous plants?) and pause especially at the frontier between plants and animals.

Pass on to the plants, which are for me living beings, with nerves, possibly sense perceptions, conceivably consciousness.

To animal life.

Then raise myself toward the firmament, which I find, with corroboration from my observations and with proof based on the accepted laws of science, is not what others believe it to be.

Thence to man, who is not simply an animal—who perhaps like the earth itself has had a pre-existence.

Whether I shall finally come upon God . . . remains to be seen.[9]

Strindberg refers to this plan in his novel *By the Open Sea* (*I havsbandet*), written in 1889 and 1890, when he has the scientist hero Inspector Borg survey the various kingdoms of nature in order to deduce from his observations either "the great cohering principle, if there was such a thing, or the universal chaos, which was more probably the case" (SS, 24:57). Resuming his nature studies in 1891, Strindberg devoted himself to chemistry and botany. In his search for the great cohering principle, he sought to combine the realms of inorganic and organic matter in one grand synthesis in which the universe would reveal a kind of order without having any teleological end. Accepting the principle of evolution, he applied it rigorously to all aspects of the physical world. If all life had evolved from simple cells, it followed that all matter could have evolved from some basic particles. Transmutation of the elements was a necessary continual process in the universe, as was the transformation of inanimate matter into living spirit.

The scientist whose concept of the universe harmonized most fully with Strindberg's was Ernst Haeckel, a German biologist and naturalist who out-Darwined Darwin as an expounder of evolution, eliminating from the Englishman's theories all religious loopholes. His *History of Creation* (*Natürliche Schöpfungsgeschichte*), which went through many editions in the nineteenth century, traced the development of the earth and its inhabitants and pointedly dismissed any supernatural god from having had any part in this development. Haeckel's god was simply nature itself, and "the firm foundation for this religion of Nature," said Haeckel, "is formed by the monistic conviction of the unity of all natural phenomena, the unity of mind and body, of force and matter, of God and Universe." His philosophy of monism was, he affirmed, the basis of truth, which had lost its way during the Middle Ages, "when Christianity asserted its sovereignty over the whole world" and when "the most offensive barbarity and the deepest immorality prevailed everywhere."[10]

In 1893 Strindberg wrote *Antibarbarus* to refute the beliefs of the offensive barbarians and put forward a "new view of chemical processes in accordance with the dominant monist theory concerning the unity of all nature as it has been employed in the other sciences by Darwin and Haeckel" (SS, 27:115). Strindberg sent a copy to Haeckel, who thanked him for it and said he saw nothing "crazy" in it.[11]

It is understandable that the extreme reductionism of Haeckel's monism would have appealed to Strindberg in his efforts to bring coherence to the apparent chaos of nature. In the light of Strindberg's later religiosity, however, it is surprising that he could have adopted a philosophy that was as utterly materialistic as Haeckel's.

Strindberg's world in 1894 was one in which there was no personal god, no eternal life of the individual soul, no purpose beyond that of improving the race. For Strindberg, the key to this Lucretian scheme of things lay in the transmutation of elements, and his chemical experiments were directed at proving that the so-called elements were not irreducible. His experiments did not convince anyone besides himself, and his scientific essays did not win him the support for which he had hoped.

Strindberg came to attribute his failure in the laboratory to the monistic theory. When he wrote *A Dream Play*, Strindberg alluded symbolically to this failure in the scenes having to do with the riddle of the universe (*världsgåtans lösning*). Two years previously Haeckel had summed up his life's work in a book called *The Riddles of the Universe* (*Die Welträthsel*), which sold thousands of copies. Here he reaffirmed his monistic philosophy, denied freedom of the will, the existence of a personal god, and declared that the soul was "purely a product of the poetic imagination." The study of cells has made possible, he said, "an explanation of those physical, chemical, and even the psychological processes of life—those mysterious phenomena for whose explanation it has been customary to postulate a supernatural 'vital force' or 'immortal soul.'"[12]

Anticipating the reductive materialism of Jacques Monod, he emphasized that all problems of consciousness, of spirit and soul, could be reduced to physiological problems, and from these to physical and chemical problems, so that all organic phenomena, everything that is called
life in the usual sense of the word, is the result ultimately of the peculiar
chemico-physical properties of carbon. Carbon "is the remarkable substance that effects the endless variety of organic syntheses and thus may
be considered 'the chemical basis of life.'"[13] Organic chemistry is essentially the chemistry of carbon.

Haeckel admitted that science and philosophy were not in agreement and held that the philosopher's ignorance of science was the cause
of this disharmony. In a passage that may have provided the idea for the
quarrel of the learned faculties in A Dream Play, Strindberg derogates
the politicians, the educators, the ministers of justice, and the divines of
the church for not having kept up with advanced knowledge. Indra's
Daughter interrupts the squabbling deans to summon them to the opening of the door behind which lies the answer to the riddle of the universe. To open the door she asks the Glazier to come with his diamond. It
is odd, even in a dream, that a glazier rather than a locksmith should be
summoned, but it is logical here because the Glazier's instrument holds
the key to the riddle of the universe. A glasscutter contains a diamond,
and diamond is the hardest form of carbon, which is the basis of all life
and the secret of creation.

Of course when Haeckel's carbon opens the door, it reveals absolutely nothing. The biologist who had averred that the soul was the invention of the poet's imagination now sees the emptiness of a soulless
universe. He throws his glasscutter into the fire along with the other delusions of mankind, while Indra's Daughter explains to the Poet that the
real secret of the universe concerns the perennial tension existing between the male and female principles.

The Glazier is pictured in A Dream Play as an old man, and already
in 1896 Strindberg had begun to suspect that Haeckel was senile. "The
man is old," * he wrote in a letter. Haeckel himself wrote in his preface to

*Strindberg to F. U. Wrangel, 13 July 1896, Brev, 11:265. It has been suggested by
Maurice Valency (The Flower and the Castle [New York, 1963] pp. 332, 424) that Strindberg had in mind the French astronomer Leverrier when he had a glazier open the door to
the secret of the universe. Having discovered the planet Neptune in 1846 by predicting
mathematically where it should be, Leverrier was hailed by all nations as a genius who
held the key to the heavens. One might object that Leverrier would make a better glazier if
his name were Levitrier. On the other hand, there is the curious circumstance that Leverrier
has an indirect connection with dreams and could easily have been drawn into Strindberg's

Die Welträthsel that he was now in his sixty-sixth year and that this work marked "the close of my studies in the monistic conception of the universe." He also expressed regret that this "System of Monistic Philosophy" would never be carried to completion. "My strength is no longer equal to the task, and many warnings of approaching age urge me to desist. Indeed, I am wholly a child of the nineteenth century, and with its close I draw the line under my life's work."[14]

A few years later, Strindberg, insisting upon the necessity of a Creator, scoffed at Haeckel's "automobile universe—self-propelled but without a motor" (*SS*, 47:462).

4

Strindberg's great project, a work in the tradition of Spencer, Haeckel, Humboldt, Bacon, and Aristotle—names that Strindberg himself invoked—was to begin with the heavens, proceed to an investigation of the earth and its various forms of life, and conclude with a study of *homo spiritualis*, the highest form of earthly being. But this was not to be a mere compendium of received knowledge nor a Spencerian synthesis worked out in the library. Strindberg saw himself as a scientist who would conduct experiments in all fields, observe with his own eyes, and from his assembled observations (the equivalent of Bacon's *Sylva Sylvarum*) draw some conclusions about the government of the universe. This project was of such consuming interest to him that, like an obsessed scientist, he rejected opportunities for financial gain, abandoned his family, and sacrificed his health—all in order that he might penetrate more deeply into the secret heart of things.

His impatience to get to the later stages of the project was such that as early as May 1895 he hoped to finish his study of the material world and prepare himself for the religious phase.[15] In the previous year he had added to his fund of knowledge about psychology by conducting certain experiments in the derangement of the senses. Knut Hamsun, who was investigating what he called "the subjective knowledge of the blood," praised Strindberg in 1894[16] for his earlier attempts to formulate a mod-

---

Dream Play. Strindberg owned a copy of Camille Flammarion's study of extrasensory phenomena, *The Unknown*, which was published in France and translated into Danish and into Swedish in 1900, only a year before *A Dream Play* was written. The curious fact is that in the chapter on dreams, Flammarion, who was an astronomer, mentions that Leverrier appeared to him several times in his dreams. See Flammarion, *Det Ukendte. Iagtagelser og Studier fra det mystiske Sjælelivs Omraade*, trans. Ingeborg Borgen and Kj. Müllen (Copenhagen, 1900), pp. 407, 413, 419.

ern psychology and predicted that Strindberg's greatest accomplishments in this field were still to come. By going without sleep and dissipating himself, Strindberg in 1894 honed his nerves and sharpened his senses in order to raise his soul to a higher level[17] of evolutionary development. Sickliness, nervous disturbances, and an overwrought condition could be signs of an extreme sensitivity and an increased vitality. A person who suffered from them, like Inspector Borg in By the Open Sea, might be the beginning of a new race, or at least a new variety of human being, who consequently would appear to older generations as sick or unsound (SS, 24:56; 27:540).

From another point of view, however, this heightened sensitivity could be regarded not as evolutionary progress but as a regression to a former stage of life. By exploring his subconscious, Strindberg was effecting a recapitulation backwards. There was an apparent contradiction here between Haeckel's evolutionary theory and Strindberg's. Haeckel saw man's subconscious as formed out of previous phases of existence on earth that the human being repeats or recapitulates as he grows from the moment of conception, while Strindberg saw man's subliminal self as formed out of higher planes of existence. He reconciled the conflicting views by entertaining the idea that man had descended not from the lower forms of life, as Darwin and the natural scientists argued, but from some ideal existence,[18] as Plato and the modern occultists would have it. In his great project Strindberg accommodated both views. As a naturalist he held on to the evolutionary theory while as an occultist he inverted it. There is, he said, a phylogenesis of the mind as well as one of the body, and in our dreams, in our myths, in our fairy tales we catch glimpses of our previous existences (SS, 27:604).[19]

Strindberg's method of studying the inner workings of the mind or spirit was consistent with the principles underlying his great project. Just as the organic and inorganic had been united in the monistic philosophy, so now the material and the immaterial were to be considered as sharing the same ground.

When everyone was recognizing the homogeneity of matter, all proclaiming to be monists without being so in fact, I went a step further, drawing the final conclusion from this doctrine and eliminating the frontier separating matter from what was called mind (SS, 28:35).[20]

If matter and spirit were conjoined, and if the physical world were accepted as a reflection of the inner world, then the observer would have something more tangible to work with than mere thoughts. "I am a naturalist-occultist," said Strindberg. "I want to see first with my outer eyes and then with my inner eye."[21]

In order to see with his inner eye it was necessary for Strindberg to place himself in a receptive frame of mind. There are artificial techniques for doing this, but Strindberg had a natural aptitude for it. "If only I do not harden my inner sense," he said, "much is revealed, and in the visible images of nature."[22] It is a generally accepted fact that emotion precedes thought or distinct memories. Ideas do not recall ideas; rather, a state of soul sets in motion a chain of associations.[23] Strindberg writes of the state of soul in which he found himself in 1895, "a jumble of sensations more or less condensed into ideas" (SS, 28:33).[24] When he was in the proper emotional state, the chaos began to condense into patterns of meaning, matter began to reflect his spirit, and the world became filled with signs and haunted by indefinable powers.

It is this state of soul that invests the evocative first scene of To Damascus. Strindberg's alter ego remarks that where he once saw only "objects and actions, forms and colors," he now sees "thoughts and meanings"; where before he saw only chance, he now sees purpose and plan (SS, 29:10).

5

The more one examines Strindberg's writings, especially his letters, the more apparent it becomes that not only was the study of religious man intended almost from the first to form the culmination of his great project but that he was determined to establish so solid a continuity between matter and spirit that the evolution of religious man would appear as logical as the evolution of land creatures from sea creatures. The most delicate part of the project was the forging of the links between the material world and the immaterial. The great speculative minds of the past had devoted themselves to this problem. Strindberg's approach, however, was to be experimental rather than speculative. When he said that he wished to be "the Zola of the occult," he meant that he was going to make the connection between mind and matter as clear as Zola had made the connection between individual behavior and heredity. "It is up to me to bridge the gap between naturalism and supranaturalism by proclaiming that the latter is only a development of the former" (SS, 28:214).[25]

To effect the transition between natural science on one side and occultism and religion on the other, he resolved to continue and enlarge on the work of Charcot, Ribot, Carl Du Prel, Sir William Crookes and others whose studies involved psychic phenomena. "I am not a spiritualist," he wrote in 1896, "but I have discovered that my researches went beyond routine science and formed the transition to scientific occultism." [26] Having already reconnoitered certain areas of the dark continent of the mind through experiments in derangement of the senses and free association, he now set out to explore far more forbidding territory. He submitted himself to a study of mental obsessions, of baseless fears, of the sick conscience, and of the persecution complex.

The psychological exploration that Strindberg embarked on was as perilous as it was illuminating. About two weeks after he had set forth on it he wrote that he was "not afraid of the madhouse. . . . I would take it as an education toward a new life." [27] His purpose was to surpass by the use of the experimental method those who knew madness only at one remove. Just as he had criticized Zola for inventing too much, so now he criticized the psychiatrists who studied madness without having experienced it.

Nothing is more crucial to an understanding of Strindberg than his conception of his work as a series of experiments. Both as a creative writer and as a would-be scientist he followed a procedure of examining a variety of theories and philosophies, rejecting what did not satisfy him, and holding on to whatever would serve his deeper purposes. Strindberg's description of the writer Arvid Falk in *Gothic Rooms* is a frank revelation of his own methods.

[Falk] experimented with points of view, and like a conscientious worker in a laboratory set up control experiments, adopting tentatively an opposed position . . . and when the experiment turned out negatively, he returned to the tested assumption. You don't understand that. But Falk would have made everything clear if he had used Kierkegaard's method. Kierkegaard invented fictional authors and gave himself a new pseudonym each time. . . . [The fictional authors] taken all together constitute Søren Kierkegaard. Falk was a vivisectionist who experimented with his own soul, always suffered from open wounds, until he gave his life for science—I don't want to employ that misused word "truth." And if his collected works were to be published, not a word should be altered, but all the contradictions left to be resolved in the comprehensive Kierkegaardian title: Stages on Life's Way. [SS, 40:45–46]

When, in his great project, he came to consider occult and psychic phenomena, he "abandoned all the resistance" he felt toward such things as a naturalist and, "by way of experiment," adopted the viewpoint of a believer (SS, 28:399).[28] He threw himself recklessly into the experiment as he gathered more and more evidence through the natural sciences that the soul or spirit was the substance of the universe, that the material world was only an accidental guise, and that human beings and their actions were part of a large and comprehensive design. To confirm this hypothesis he withdrew, he said, "into solitude"[29] in July 1896.

6

It was time for him to carry out the experiment that was to lead to the final subject of study and complete the great design: *homo spiritualis*. If he waited any longer, he might be anticipated by others. A new cosmos was in the making, and he wanted more than anything else to be one of its makers. He was perfectly mindful that the juncture he had reached in his great work coincided with a crisis in European culture, a crisis that could be sensed in both science and literature. The sudden blossoming of Symbolist poetry and drama in Paris was only a portent of things to come. The poet Stéphane Mallarmé sensed that the air was disturbed by "the trembling of the veil of the temple" and knew that the age was "seeking to bring forth a sacred book."[30] In the spring of 1894, Maeterlinck published an essay on the tragic element in daily life ("A propos de Solness le Constructeur," in *Le Figaro*, 2 April 1894) in which he advocated a drama with virtually no outward action, a drama in which we might see man as he is in daily life, subject to subtle influences and not to mighty passions. "Let us not forget," he wrote, "that our soul often appears in our feeble eyes to be but the maddest of forces, and that there are in man many regions more fertile, more profound, and more interesting than those of his reason or his intelligence."[31] In the fall of 1894, Strindberg, who had certainly read this essay, heaped scorn on Maeterlinck and declared that naturalism was not dead. Maeterlinck and his school, jeered Strindberg, have never made "a discovery in the realm of the psyche."[32] It was also in 1894 that Hamsun predicted that Strindberg was about to make his greatest psychological discoveries. And it was in 1894 that Strindberg plotted his journey toward the inferno. A strange coincidence? Or the calculated response of a man determined to keep himself in the vanguard?

Three years later Strindberg could read how matters stood between himself and Maeterlinck, as far as the critics were concerned. Leo Berg (who was published by Strindberg's publisher), found that no one surpassed Strindberg in dramatic power—except Maeterlinck. Strindberg's

great sex trilogy (*The Father, Miss Julie*, and *Creditors*) is in regard to dramatic psychology and the art of making an immediate impact perhaps unique in all contemporary literature. Apart from the drama of Maeterlinck, who in this respect still far surpasses him, it is not easy to find other works in which . . . passion and mental strife are so nakedly presented.[33]

If this critic offered a tacit challenge to Strindberg to outdo Maeterlinck, another German critic, Edgar Steiger, in one of the finest discussions of the drama to appear at the end of the century, opened new perspectives. "What is drama," he asked, "if not a continual, ever repeated development of the ego of the author. . . . a continuing transformation of the soul and a transmigration of the soul?"[34] Steiger's book was published in 1898, when Strindberg wrote To Damascus, in which the development of the author's ego is pictured both metaphorically and literally as a pilgrimage.

Steiger also recommended that chance be allowed to alter the course of events in a play. To shake the chain of strict causality would not only heighten the impression of reality, argued Steiger, it would also provide opportunities for symbolism and for the spiritualization of the action by lifting it out of the purely mechanical. He went on to say that Maeterlinck had found the dramatic form for presenting inner anguish and the conflicts of the soul.

If we did not know what Strindberg had gone through from 1894 to 1898, it would be perfectly reasonable to argue that he created To Damascus and opened the portals to the twentieth-century drama merely by responding to the challenge of Maeterlinck and certain advanced critics. Much of the psychological experimentation of those years may have been prompted by the Maeterlinck craze and by the desire to make those discoveries in the realm of the soul that Maeterlinck never made.

The gist of all this is that the great crisis in Strindberg's life, the Inferno crisis that formed the strait gate to a new artistic life for him, was part of a plan. Without the experiment in the psychology of the unconscious, he could not complete his scientific magnum opus. Without it he could not maintain his position in the literary vanguard. Without it he could not "bridge the gap between naturalism and supranaturalism." The crisis was as carefully planned as anything in life can be. Although he could set up the conditions for the experiment, he could not predict the results. If he could have foreseen the consequences, he would not have needed the experiment. That unpredictableness makes Strindberg's art as fascinating as life itself.

Nothing was more important to Strindberg in the middle of his life than his scientific work. It meant more to him than family, friends, or literary fame. When his sex trilogy, *The Father, Miss Julie,* and *Creditors,* was performed in Paris and his notoriety rivaled that of Ibsen, a reporter who interviewed him was astonished to hear that the dramatist valued his chemical studies[1] more highly than his plays.

CHAPTER FIVE

THE GUINEA PIG

A few years later, in 1902, he was almost happier about the publication[2] in a popular German magazine of one of his scientific essays, "The Sighing of the Stones," than about the Berlin production of one of his recent plays, *Crimes and Crimes.* Although Max Reinhardt gave him the success that had previously eluded him in the German theatre, Strindberg was more concerned about the constitution of matter than about the casting of his play. In his essay, he outlined his general theory of monism, rhapsodized about the vital spirit, and contended that the transmutation of the elements occurred continually in nature and that the transition from inorganic to organic matter was part of universal history.

"The great Pan," he proclaimed, "is indeed not dead, though he has been ill. And now an Orpheus must go down into the underworld to sing life into the stones, which are not dead, only sleeping" (SS, 27:234–35).

This was more a poet's than a scientist's prophecy. "I was the rival of Orpheus," he said of himself, "and it was my role to bring back to life an inanimate nature that had died in the hands of the scientists" (SS, 28:81).[3] He knew that the atom was not the irreducible building block of the universe and that all nature was infused with a vital force. He had written "The Sighing of the Stones" in 1896 when the physical sciences were in an explosive state. The years 1895 through 1898, recognized now as the four golden years that opened the heroic age of physics, saw the discovery of X rays, radioactivity, the electron, and radium, discoveries that revolutionized man's conception of the structure of matter. In the first months of 1896, Strindberg, sensing that monumental discoveries were in the making, worked feverishly trying to put his thoughts on paper and into print. Strindberg had followed closely the work of the eminent British chemist William Crookes, who in the late 1880s in his *Gene-*

sis of the Elements had insisted that hydrogen could not be a primordial element and argued that it contained some undiscovered substance, which he called protyle. A group of French chemists, led by Pierre Berthelot, had proved that certain organic compounds could be formed synthetically and had demonstrated that chemical processes are subject to the laws of physics and mechanics. Strindberg saw that it was only a question of time before scientists would score a major breakthrough and accomplish the transmutation of the elements (SS, 40:113–14). He knew his theories were fundamentally right, but he was unable to substantiate them in the laboratory. His chemical experiments, conducted for the most part in his lodgings with the equipment of a medieval alchemist (he carefully studied Berthelot's volumes on the history of alchemy, published from 1885 to 1893), had produced no evidence that would convince professional scientists; his observations in other fields, which he had been collecting since 1884 on thousands of slips of paper, bundled together in a green carpetbag—he called it his "Green Sack"[4]—remained in a confused and chaotic state; and the scientific essays that he was able to publish—about eighteen between December 1895 and July 1896— were but fragments of the great design he had conceived and only a small portion of the two-thousand-page manuscript he lugged about.

To add to his desperation, he had been shamefully neglecting his family responsibilities. Unproductive as a writer, living off contributions, often anonymous, from friends whose generosity must soon be exhausted, and falling ever farther behind in the payments supporting the children from his first marriage, he would soon be compelled to abandon his crucibles and take up his pen or to find some other employment. "One spring morning," he said,

I wake up to reality and see unfulfilled duties behind me in the form of uncared for children. See the necessity of a compromise with life. I must do . . . as most people do: divide myself in two, living exoterically at a trade and in a job, scrubbing and drudging, while keeping my inner development to myself.[5]

When his supporter, the publisher Torsten Hedlund, rejected the manuscript of his scientific magnum opus, Strindberg was frantic. "I become epileptic," he wrote, "when I see my work strewn about in pieces."[6] Parts of it he had printed at his own expense.

2

There was, however, another alternative. He could temporarily abandon his studies of the physical world and resume his studies of the mental life of man. In the field of psychology he felt confident of his powers, and he did not require a vast laboratory with expensive equipment. All he needed was his own mind. In February 1896 he began looking for some way to continue part 2 of his magnum opus "so that like Aristotle I might transfer my thoughts to metaphysics, man and God, and the secrets of creation."[7] In 1895 he had expressed his eagerness to end his exploration of the world of physical matter and prepare himself for the study of spiritual matters. For his magnum opus was to conclude with the transmutation of the physical into the spiritual, and the great plan of the work consisted in having it end in the heavens. The ascension from the physical to the spiritual could only be conceived of as occurring in the *homo spiritualis*, spiritual man, who represented the highest form of earthly life. And what was the distinguishing characteristic of spiritual man? It was not necessarily ratiocinative or even vaticinatory powers, but simply the moral sense. Emanuel Swedenborg, having mastered all the physical sciences and arriving finally at the study of the seat of knowledge, the human brain, and seeking there the connection between body and soul, saw visions that were exclusively of moral import. Similarly, when Immanuel Kant pondered the world beyond appearances, he invented the categorical imperative. In their explorations Strindberg saw the direction that his own must take. But Kant's approach was dogmatic and dualistic, and Swedenborg's information—obtained in conversations with angels and lesser spirits—did not, at first, impress Strindberg, who wanted to lift himself by his own bootstraps.

He may have remembered and taken to heart Nietzsche's comment that religious people have never been absolutely conscientious about their experiences. They have

a thirst for things that are *contrary to reason*, and they don't want to have a hard time satisfying this thirst. So they experience "miracles" and "regenerations," and hear the voices of little angels! But we who are different, we who thirst for reason, want to look the experience straight in the eye as if it were a scientific experiment, hour by hour, day by day. We ourselves want to be our experiments and our guinea pigs.[8]

Strindberg's method of carrying out his experiment was suggested by certain French poets, like Baudelaire and Rimbaud, who had wanted to explore the unknown. Rimbaud revealed his purpose and method in letters he wrote in 1871.

I am debauching myself as much as I can. Why? I want to be a poet, and I am working to make myself a *Seer*. . . . The first task of the man who wishes to be a poet is to learn to know himself. . . . The poet makes himself a *Seer* by a slow, prodigious, and calculated *disordering of all his senses* [*dérèglement de tous les sens*]. All forms of love, of suffering, of madness—he searches himself, he consumes within himself all the poisons in order to retain only the quintessence of them. Ineffable torture for which he needs the greatest faith, the greatest in superhuman strength, and by which he becomes the great diseased one, the great criminal, the great outcast—and the supreme Knower!—Because he has attained the *unknown!*[9]

These ideas were part of the credo of the Decadent school of poets, and when Strindberg came to Paris he allied himself with them by writing an essay "Sensations détraquées," published in 1894 and 1895 in *Le Figaro littéraire*. This delightful essay is the propylaeum to the temple of a new world[10] that he was about to enter. Letting ideas and impressions associate freely, he describes Versailles as experienced by a man whose nerves and senses have been "sharpened by sleeplessness and dissipation" to the point where the ordinary seems strange and the fantastical, perfectly logical. Faced with the prospect of crossing the vast Place d'Armes, he is seized by an inexplicable fear. He overcomes his agoraphobia to the extent of getting halfway across, at which point he clutches a lamp post and wonders how he can navigate the rest of that ocean of stone. Passing clouds give him his answer. Their shadows become ships. "What does it matter, when all is said and done, that they are only shadows, like everything else? I am a poet, a magician. I choose the steadiest; I make my way aboard carefully; and then cast off!—Beautiful! the crossing is completed" (SS, 27:539, 543).

This says as much about Strindberg's way of looking at the world as anything he wrote. But this sort of fancifulness and imaginativeness did not satisfy him because it added nothing to his knowledge. It was only a *jeu d'esprit*. He could not learn much from Baudelaire, Rimbaud, and Verlaine because they were voluptuaries, seeking new stimuli for their jaded nerves, and unconcerned whether they found heaven or hell because their heaven and hell were places of sensual delights and torments. Fleeing a desert of middle-class boredom, they sailed waters familiar to any dissipated soul in a drunken boat looking for *l'Inconnu*— by which they meant a thrill they had not yet experienced. Still, the poeticizing of existence through a disordering of the senses suggested to Strindberg the means for a deeper exploration of the psyche.

If the derangement of the senses through alcohol and drugs allowed the French Decadents to break down the palisades of convention in the mind, letting their thoughts run free, then it might have the same effect on the spiritual man. In the case of the latter, a purposeful unbalancing of the mind might elevate part of it to a higher and possibly unworldly level beyond the physical senses. The part of the mind to be affected was the conscience, since it is conscience that distinguishes man from the creatures beneath him. The more delicate the conscience, the closer it is to the divine. Further, since it was known that a guilty conscience often manifests itself in the form of persecutory paranoia, a mental illness that alienists were studying with increasing attention and interest in the 1890s, the connection between insanity and divinity had been given a psychological basis. It was on the swaying bridge of conscience that Strindberg intended to cross from the physical to the spiritual, from science to religion, from naturalism to supranaturalism, while beneath him lay the abyss of madness. To achieve the transition, the persecutory fears would be allowed to express themselves freely without the restraints ordinarily imposed on them by the practical or social self. These fears lived in that part of our being that psychiatrists in the pre-Freudian era called the somnambulistic self or the second consciousness. Just as Baudelaire had deliberately sinned in order to identify himself with the sinner and to suffer the ultimate humiliation, Strindberg intended to feed his subconscious fears in order to experience the sharpest pangs of conscience.

Social isolation, sleeplessness, a reduced intake of nourishment, a mixture of drugs, both stimulants and depressants, and possibly absinthe were the means by which Strindberg the experimenter inoculated himself with madness. He could have found in the scientific literature of the time suggestions as to how he might proceed. Direct inspiration may have come from a book by the philosopher and psychologist Carl Du Prel, *Die Philosophie der Mystik*. Strindberg possessed a copy of the Swedish translation, which bore the attractive title *Det dolda själslifvet*, "The Hidden Life of the Soul." Starting with the common idea that there are two egos in man, two levels of mental life, and that the unconscious level is basic, Du Prel called for experiments[11] in which the activities of the psyche might be studied, experiments that would lower the threshold of consciousness to the level reached in somnambulism or deep sleep and that would thus bring the hidden life into view. He pointed out that the transcendental or unconscious level reveals itself more readily when the body is ill because the inner life withdraws itself then from contact with the exterior world, and he noted that great hunger and thirst can cause an extreme lowering of the threshold of consciousness, producing visions. In the same vein, Francis Galton in his *Inquiries into Human Faculty and its Development* (1883) had described how hallucinations could be produced even in normal persons by isolation, fasting, and lack of sleep. The psychiatrist Emil Kraepelin, in his *Ueber geistige Arbeit* (1894), had shown how lack of sleep could seriously harm a child's mental health. (Experiments conducted in America in the 1960s revealed that a sleep loss of fifty to sixty hours produces visions and hallucinations in absolutely normal and sane persons and that after one hundred hours of sleeplessness psychotic delusions inevitably appear.)

Whether Strindberg used alcohol, particularly absinthe, during the July experiment is a moot question. In the midst of the experiment itself he wrote that he had lost weight and "abhorred food and liquor."[12] The absinthe episodes in *Inferno*, recorded as having occurred in May and June 1896, suggest that Strindberg swore off absinthe for some time (SS, 28:68–71).[13] He was, however, notoriously a heavy drinker, and in *Inferno* he had already begun to poeticize the facts. Later in his life, he stated flatly that some of the visionary experiences he recorded in *Inferno* occurred while he was under the influence of alcohol. "Alcohol," he said, "possesses, as do certain poisonous herbs, the satanic power of exteriorizing one's sensibilities" (SS, 48:889).[14]

The evidence that Strindberg used drugs in 1896 is fairly clear. If he is to be believed, he sometimes even inhaled the fumes from cyanogen (SS, 27:208; 28:280–81).[15] At various times in his life he relied on sedatives to get to sleep, and at least at one point during the 1896 experiment, in August, he took sulphonal, which was a common soporific, while at the same time a doctor was giving him doses of strophanthin, a cardiac stimulant. The doctor was Anders Eliasson, a rather eccentric personality with an interest in chemistry and the transmutation of elements. Strindberg's stay with this sympathetic fellow-scientist at his house in Ystad in southern Sweden during the summer of 1896 is the basis of those stories, repeated over and over in encyclopedias and handbooks of literature, that Strindberg spent some time in a mental institution. He never did anything of the sort. He went to Eliasson partly because he used him, as he used other acquaintances, for free lodging and food (he had spent a month with Eliasson the previous summer), and partly because he needed treatment for his heart and lungs,[16] which had been affected by excessive smoking and by the chemicals he worked with. (See figure 4.)

His strange behavior while at Dr. Eliasson's house,[17] described by Strindberg himself in *Inferno*, is usually cited as evidence of his persecution complex. The copper coils of the bed springs became in his imagination the induction coils of an electric machine designed by the diabolical doctor to torture him. One night, fearing that his life was in danger, he climbed out of his bedroom window in his nightshirt, walked the streets, and woke up another doctor. Recounting the episode in *Inferno*, Strindberg adds some dramatic touches and pictures himself as being on the verge of insanity. From his letters, a different image develops. There we learn that Dr. Eliasson was giving Strindberg large doses of sulphonal, three grams at a time when one gram was considered adequate. A few months later, Strindberg learned from a Danish doctor of the dangerous effects of sulphonal.[18] One of this doctor's patients who took the medication awoke from a drug-induced sleep quite mad and leaped out of the nearest window. Overuse of sulphonal was known to produce a morbid state of mind known as sulphonalism; combined with the cardiac stimulant its effect would be unpredictable and Strindberg's susceptibility to the drug would have been increased by his run-down condition. In typical fashion, Strindberg gives a physical explanation for his irrational acts in writing to Dr. Eliasson, while in the poeticized version in *Inferno* the cause is entirely within his mind.

3

Living in Paris, where he was not a well-known figure (his notoriety as a misogynist and playwright was short-lived), and cutting himself off from his circle of Scandinavian friends, Strindberg planned to devote two or three months to this psychological experiment. He could not afford to continue the experiment beyond September 1896 because the stipends sent to him,[19] at fairly regular intervals, by a benefactor in Sweden would probably cease at that time, and Strindberg would be compelled to return to the practical world and earn his living, working "exoterically at a trade." The benefactor's almoner, Torsten Hedlund, a theosophist who hoped to enlist Strindberg in Mme. Blavatsky's brotherhood and who had found him a patron, was also to serve unwittingly as assistant in the experiment. As Strindberg lowered himself into the depths of his subconscious, he sent up reports to Hedlund in the form of a series of letters with the pages numbered consecutively from one letter to the next, a series that may be said to form the first rough draft of *Inferno*.

Indeed, Hedlund probably gave Strindberg the spur that finally goaded him into the psychological experiment when, in a letter in May 1896, he remarked that Strindberg was suffering from a persecution complex and from megalomania. Strindberg replied to this in both an article and a letter. In the article, he said that from his observations of his dreams he had become convinced that

man lives a double life and that fantasies, imaginings, and dreams possess a kind of reality. Thus we are all of us sleepwalkers in spirit and perform in our sleep acts that, according to their nature, accompany us into our waking state, giving us either a feeling of satisfaction or a guilty conscience, out of fear of the consequences. And for reasons that I reserve the right to set forth at some other time I believe that the so-called persecution complex often has a solid basis in the qualms of conscience that follow a bad deed committed in one's "sleep," the hazy memory of which haunts us. [SS, 28:280][20]

In the letter, he responded to Hedlund[21] by describing different types of persecution with which he was personally familiar. A man may feel persecuted because he actually does have enemies who are attacking him. His work is destroyed by others; he is threatened with legal prosecution, falsely accused of being an anarchist, plagued by debts, and insulted in public. If one is treated like this, the persecution is obviously not a delusion or a mental aberration. A second type of persecution occurs when a man has committed a venial sin but fears the consequences and comes to believe that the party he has offended will punish him. If he is not persecuted, his own imagination will devise a punishment to fit the crime. It may happen, however, that he fights off his guilt feelings, arraigns the witness who made him feel guilty, and sees that person succumb to insanity.

Strindberg had three specific people in mind, and just who they were is made clear in the ensuing correspondence. The man with real enemies is Strindberg, of course, and his persecutor, who is spreading malicious rumors about him, is Willy Gretor. Gretor had been Strindberg's patron for a while in 1894 and had undertaken to sell some of his paintings. But Gretor, who was a confidence man, the model for the hero of Frank Wedekind's play *The Marquis of Keith*, was now suspected of being a forger and art thief, and, since Strindberg was a potential witness against him, Gretor was letting it be bruited about that Strindberg was an anarchist. The second type of persecution involved Strindberg and Stanislaw Przybyszewski, the neurotic Pole who had revered Strindberg in Berlin and had married Strindberg's former mistress. Strindberg now felt extremely guilty about his part in the affair and had reason to believe that the Pole's admiration had turned to jealousy and hatred. Finally, the misleading witness who is punished with insanity is Ossian Ekbohrn, the customs inspector who had won Strindberg's hatred by testifying on behalf of Strindberg's wife in the divorce proceedings in 1890 and 1891 (SS, 28:84–86).[22] While Strindberg was subsequently conscience-stricken over his treatment of his wife, it was Ekbohrn who had become subject to attacks of insanity.

It would strain the laws of probability to assume that—through sheer coincidence—Strindberg received information about Gretor, Przybyszewski, and Ekbohrn between June 9 and June 20, when he was preparing for the experiment in madness. Yet that is what happened. It is more logical to assume that Strindberg sought information about them as part of his preparations. All three had invaded Strindberg's conscience, and each was associated with a woman who had played a part in his life. Ekbohrn was a reminder of his first marriage, Przybyszewski of his mistress, and Gretor of his second wife. Any one of the three might serve as the punishing self that his experiment in persecutory paranoia required. The one with whom Strindberg came to identify most strongly and to fear most intensely was Przybyszewski, who figures in *Inferno* as Popoffsky. Przybyszewski had abandoned his common-law wife and children and had taken a mistress. Strindberg, who had divorced his wife after treating her badly, who had had more than one mistress since the divorce, and who was unable to support his children, could charge himself with the same behavior. And, since the Pole's mistress had formerly been Strindberg's, the emotional bond between the two men was made even stronger, combining guilt with jealousy. The decisive factor in Strindberg's thinking was the news that reached him,[23] evidently through the painter Edvard Munch on June 18: Przybyszewski had been arrested in Berlin for the murder of his wife and children.

Just before this, at the point when Strindberg was about to set up in the real world a working model of the tensions and conflicts within him, events took a bizarre but dramatically inevitable turn. Precisely when he was ready to lock himself in his laboratory for his three-month experiment, there appeared on Strindberg's doorstep his sister Anna and her husband Hugo Philp. They had journeyed from Stockholm to Paris, arriving there June 9, to confirm rumors that had reached their ears to the effect that Strindberg was mentally incompetent. Surely a man who devoted himself to alchemical experiments in the transmutation of elements, who lived frugally on the generosity of friends and on money siphoned through theosophist channels while doing nothing to support his own children when he could have been making money writing novels like *The People of Hemsö*, his popular success of the 1880s, or at least cashing in on the reputation as a playwright he had recently won in Paris, must be mad. That was the judgment of the bourgeois mentality confronting that of the bohemian, of the materialistic and practical mind confronting the rigorously artistic or inquisitive mind, a judgment often reflected in the writings of psychologists who analyze Strindberg. (Four years later, he turned the tables on the Philps by using them as models for the married couple in *The Dance of Death* and judging them.)

Naturally, Strindberg was furious.

Sister and brother-in-law dropped in on me here, [he wrote to Dr. Eliasson, a soul more kindred than his sister] without announcing they were coming; then began to examine me, and finally expressed their joy at finding me actually—sane!

I tell you it was enough to drive me crazy! [24]

Subjected to the daily scrutiny of the Philps, he had to be on his best behavior. He played the helpless, impractical dolt to his patronizing brother-in-law, "a man who has solved all the mysteries of the universe without even exerting himself," [25] and got the Philps to leave the city convinced that they had persuaded him to be sensible, to return to Sweden and his writing. They departed in the middle of June, having spent less than a week in Paris, [26] but their visit brought home to Strindberg the realization that if he carried out his experiment he would always be in danger of being legally certified as incompetent. And the more successful the experiment, the greater the danger. As he explored the abysses of the psyche, he would be as vulnerable as a deep-sea diver whose lifeline could be cut at any moment. To guard against this peril, it was necessary for Strindberg to have available at a moment's notice evidence that the persecutory symptoms had a basis in fact and were not the delusions of a diseased mind. Since most of us have seldom found ourselves in such circumstances, it is difficult to tell how even the most sane among us would arrange matters. Strindberg's solution, bizarre as it is, seems the only feasible one. He had to improvise quickly, and he took advantage of the means at hand. An article he had written a number of months previously, "Etudes funèbres," [27] was to be printed in the next issue of *Revue des Revues*, which was due to reach the public on July 15, when Strindberg would be deeply immersed in his experiment. He inserted into this essay some peculiar paragraphs which have nothing to do with the rest of the piece and which are supposed to represent the rambling thoughts of an insane person. In 1970 Sverker Hällen explained the nature of the allusions in these paragraphs [28] and thereby revealed Strindberg's reasons for inserting them. One paragraph is in effect a cryptogram implicating

Willy Gretor in art forgeries and in murder. Strindberg was not letting his imagination run riot; he was only making use of rumors that were circulating about Gretor. The allusions had to be provocative without being libelous; they had to point to Gretor in such a way that only he and his circle would understand them. It was a kind of reverse blackmail. If Gretor responded to the intimations and revived the rumors of Strindberg's anarchism or accused him of being insane, Strindberg could point to these attacks as evidence that he was not suffering from persecutory paranoia but was being persecuted in reality. (Notice that a private letter to Gretor would not serve Strindberg's purpose because it could be destroyed, leaving Strindberg without any evidence if matters ever reached the point at which someone would ask why Gretor was persecuting Strindberg.)

At this point Strindberg's situation begins to resemble one of those optical illusions in which background can become foreground. Here we have Strindberg pretending madness in order to insure himself against being certified as mad. One cannot help thinking that the ingenuity displayed in these protective measures, that the nature of the experiment itself, that the convolutions of a mind that seeks madness and simultaneously the appearance of sanity can only be interpreted as madness itself. Be that as it may, it was madness with method in it. Like Hamlet, he knew a hawk from a handsaw.

July was the crucial month of the experiment. As he descended into his subconscious, he could write on July 6 that "fantasies possess a complete higher reality," and on July 11 that he was not afraid of the madhouse, that he would take madness as "an education for a new life." On July 20 he mocks psychiatric textbooks, those "madhouse manuals written by idiots who lack the wit to go mad." In the following days the persecutory attacks reach their acme, and a week later the experiment begins to come to an end, and he can write, "My mission is over and I have served out my sentence." The statement comes jointly from his conscious mind and his subconscious. Two weeks later he announces that he is abandoning the natural sciences. Now he must finish his great design, incorporate in it the results of his experiment, make his study of religious man, and, like a scholar at the end of his leave, think about returning to the workaday world. On August 20, he writes that his "state of grace is over,"[29] a reference to the fact that the monthly payments from his patron in Sweden are coming to an end. Having for some time enjoyed the luxury of carrying out his researches without having to earn a living, he now had to take the first steps, as he said, toward reconciling himself with life by submitting to the yoke, becoming a breadwinner, and supporting his children. As Goethe said, "When money begins to matter, Buddhism ceases to."

4

It remained for Strindberg to make sense of his experiences, but this was to be the work of many months. The first efforts at comprehension are to be seen in *Inferno* and *To Damascus*. To organize his thoughts, convey what he had observed, and guide the reader or spectator through the depths of the psyche, he had to invent new techniques. In the evolution of the novel, the gap between *The Idiot* and *Ulysses* is filled by *Inferno*, and in the evolution of the modern drama, the gap between Ibsen and the expressionists is filled by *To Damascus*. Through the narrow channel of Strindberg's experiment in madness in July 1896, the main currents of the late nineteenth century disembogue into the twentieth.

Strindberg quickly understood that through this perilous experiment his life had taken on new meaning and his genius had found new wells of inspiration. "I suffered," he later said, "but it was a time of joy; and it was [then] that the great subject matter of my life took form." [30]

The experiment exacted a physical as well as a mental toll. His health declined, and in September he suffered an attack of angina pectoris. Nietzsche had insisted that the scrupulous experimenter in religion must maintain his objectivity and listen always to the voice of reason. Strindberg learned that when the vivisector operates on himself it is difficult to tell whose hand guides the knife—the doctor's or the victim's. "I thought I was experimenting with points of view," he said, "but I soon found that I was not the experimenter but the guinea pig." [31]

One of the paradoxes of the stage is that what happens on it is often believable to the extent that it is unfamiliar. The great, classic plays deal with events that few people have experienced. For most people, the events that changed their lives, or the moments when the veil was lifted and they saw the world for what it is, occurred without shedding an innocent man's blood, fighting a duel for a woman's hand, falling into a foaming fit of jealousy, or discovering that

CHAPTER SIX

THE UNDER-WORLD

one's wife is one's mother. Even the number of husbands who have thrown lighted lamps at infuriating wives must be far smaller than the number of husbands who go to the theatre. The telling moments in real life are often so quiet that no one except the concerned party notices what has happened. Such moments have been the subject of lyric poetry in all ages, but in the drama they were, until fairly recently, confined to soliloquies set in the midst of violent actions.

In the 1890s more than one writer attempted to make these quiet moments of revelation central to the drama. Chekhov wanted his plays to be as simple as life itself. "People eat their dinner," he said (in 1889), "just eat their dinner, and all the time their happiness is being established or their lives are being broken up."[1] For Maeterlinck it was a simple fact that "the true tragic element of life only begins at the moment when so-called adventures, sorrows, and dangers have disappeared." He believed that

an old man, seated in his armchair, waiting patiently, with his lamp beside him; giving unconscious ear to all the eternal laws that reign about his house, . . . motionless as he is, does yet live in reality a deeper, more human and more universal life than the lover who strangles his mistress, the captain who conquers in battle, or 'the husband who avenges his honor.'[2]

Many serious writers have recognized the truth of this and have for that reason shunned the drama, believing that the cardboard conventions of the theatre must coarsen reality and inevitably compel the dramatist to see life as a reporter for a tabloid sees it: all crime, scandal, and sensation. Maeterlinck made his mark in the history of the drama by challenging this idea. He believed he could create a static drama, a drama in which there was virtually no intrigue and no violent physical action, on or off stage. In his early one-act plays, he succeeded in doing just that. But he quickly exhausted the possibilities of the form, and in his longer efforts, he found he had to fall back on the conventions of the older drama. In his most memorable play, *Pelléas and Mélisande*, a jealous husband stabs his wife's lover to death.

It remained for Strindberg to cultivate the seeds that Maeterlinck had planted. He even began his first static drama as if he had taken his cue from Maeterlinck. The protagonist of *To Damascus* is, at the beginning of the play, seated on a park bench, lost in thought, writing in the sand. While he is ruminating, a woman appears. He falls in love with her and takes her away from her husband. Together they visit her parents, who express their disapproval of their daughter and her new mate. Feeling increasingly guilty, he suffers a nervous breakdown and finds himself in the sick ward of a monastery. After receiving spiritual advice from a priest, he decides to face the man whom he has made unhappy, the former husband of his wife. After that confrontation, he meets his wife again. The meeting takes place where the play began. He is sitting on his park bench, lost in thought, writing in the sand, when she reappears.

This is not the kind of story that would have been considered dramatic material before 1900, although it might have filled out the pages of a short psychological novel. The fragile plot unfolds in seventeen scenes that carry the hero from a park bench in Paris to a monastery in the mountains by way of the seashore, a ravine, and the house of the woman's parents. The journey represents the hero's attempt to find himself, and he wanders aimlessly because his soul is in disarray. Life has lost any meaning it might once have had for him, and seeing no purpose to his existence, he is driven only by whim and acts only on impulse. Middle-aged, virtually destitute, with a broken marriage behind him and no prospects for success as a writer before him, the hero, who remains nameless throughout the play, no longer knows which way to turn. All he knows is that he has reached a turning point in his life, symbolized by the street corner at which the play begins. His travels are less geographical than spiritual, and the whole drama may be construed as taking place entirely in his mind.

Before Maeterlinck and Strindberg there were precedents for internalized dramas of the soul, notably the morality play *Everyman* and Ibsen's verse drama *Peer Gynt*, the last act of which is in the morality play tradition. In these dramas, however, the way to salvation and wholeness of soul is clearly indicated. By means of Knowledge, Everyman can proceed to Confession and Salvation on a direct and meaningful course. Old Peer Gynt, in anguish and despair, learns that the path to the salvation of his soul is straight and narrow and not roundabout. But the hero of *To Damascus* is on a pilgrimage without a Mecca. Although Strindberg appropriates the form of station drama—a drama that uses movement from place to place to suggest the hero's progress and development— there is little sense of direction. The lines connecting the stations seem to be entirely haphazard.

The reason for this is that Strindberg was departing from the conventional drama in which the protagonist exerts his will and suffers the consequences. Strindberg's hero does not exert his will; rather, he submits to unknown forces. He does not know where he wants to go or what he wants to do. When he does act, he is moved by intimations too subtle to be expressed in words, by forces that can be only dimly sensed. He is like Maeterlinck's old man in the armchair, "giving unconscious ear to all the eternal laws that reign about his house, interpreting, without comprehending, the silence of doors and windows and the quivering voice of the light, submitting with bent head to the presence of his soul and his destiny."[3] Strindberg's hero acts capriciously and, like Maeterlinck's, he may ignore a tempest and tremble at a breeze.

During 1894 and 1895, Maeterlinck published a series of essays dealing with the mystic life of the soul. There is a difference, he said, between *esprit* and *âme*, between the reason and the transcendental consciousness, between what goes on between people and what goes on in the realm beyond reason. To anyone who has acquired the habit of seeing into that more profound area, every event, however insignificant, may have spiritual meaning. A new awareness, a new conscience, is about to be formed in humanity, a superior conscience that is as unfamiliar to us as the other side of the moon. In the new emergent morality will be discovered marvelous laws that we are now

perhaps constantly disobeying, laws of whose existence our conscience is ignorant, though our soul has been warned. Whence comes the shadow of a mysterious transgression that at times creeps over our life and makes it so hard to bear? What are the great spiritual sins of which we can be guilty? Will it be our shame to have striven against our soul, or is there an invisible struggle between our soul and God?[4]

These oracular utterances can now be seen as presaging the analytical psychology of Jung and, to a lesser extent, the teachings of other psychologists who have explored man's unconscious life. Oddly enough, Strindberg, whose passion was psychology, missed the significance of

Maeterlinck's writings, though his own essays written in 1894 and 1895 were clearly pointing in the same direction. In "Des arts nouveaux" (1894), which deals with the role of the unconscious in artistic creation, Strindberg mentions Maeterlinck rather disdainfully as a poet who "puts rhymes in the middle of his prose."[5] Strindberg thought then that the Symbolist would contribute nothing to the study of psychology.

Not until he had passed through his Inferno was Strindberg able to appreciate Maeterlinck. Toward the end of 1900, when he read these mystical essays of Maeterlinck, collected under the title *The Treasure of the Humble*, he was so entranced that he rendered long sections of them into Swedish[6] for his fiancée. Praising the book to a friend, he noted that it was published in 1896, the year of his Inferno, and said, "It deals with the discovery of a supersensuous psychology, a transcendent psychology that concerns itself with the direct connections existing between souls."[7]

Strindberg failed to understand Maeterlinck in 1894 because he saw that the Symbolist's theories were only literary exercises without any basis in fact and experiment. Maeterlinck was like an armchair explorer who describes places he has read about but has never actually visited, the very vagueness of his descriptions making Strindberg wary and suspicious. When Maeterlinck wrote about the unexplored mind, he drew on Jakob Boehme, John Ruysbroeck, Novalis, and Ralph Waldo Emerson. When Strindberg ventured into the dark continent, he described what he himself saw and heard: soot in his absinthe, a pendulum clock, Schumann's "Aufschwung," a drunken tramp. His transcendental world was as solid and real as a scientist's laboratory and just as cluttered. Maeterlinck entered the underworld by following the Symbolist stream, and all he found was a bluebird.

Strindberg, on the other hand, had prepared for his psychological experiments by studying Charcot, Pierre Janet, and Bernheim—the teachers of Freud. Through their investigations of somnambulism, hypnosis, and hysteria, he knew that the human mind was divided and that more than the instincts were at work in the part beyond the threshold of consciousness. Strindberg knew that, logically, there had to be some organizing principle operating in the mind, governing the way in which the unconscious worked. At first he ascribed the workings of the unconscious to chance, but when he began to discern hazy patterns of meaning, he had second thoughts. The change is discernible in the two essays he wrote on the subject of nemesis. In the first, written in 1887 when his point of view was that of a naturalist and atheist, he argued that what pious people take to be God's punishment of the sinner is nothing but chance at work. In the second essay, written in 1894, he assumed a different attitude. Describing the punishment that had recently been inflicted on his enemies, he noticed that chance and his own wishes appeared to be collaborating with each other. On the day he received a libelous letter, the sister of the sender went mad. "Chance," he said, "was more devastating than my boldest wishes" (SS, 22:163ff.).[8] Divine retribution no longer seemed illogical and random in its operations, and Strindberg began to perceive beneath the surface of events a web of connections as complicated as the tissues in the human brain. He was moving rapidly toward the position that Goethe reached in his sixties. Looking back over his life, the German poet saw a kind of system or order running through all things, material and spiritual, an order that

was not divine, since it seemed irrational; not human, since it had no mind; not satanic, since it was beneficent; not angelic, since it often manifested itself as a joy at other's mishaps. It resembled chance in showing no signs of logical sequence; it was like Providence in that it suggested that there was a connection.[9]

This extradivine, extrahuman order of things, which Goethe labeled "the demonic," with reference to the ancient Greek concept of demons or tutelary spirits, became the theoretical basis for Strindberg's psychological investigations in the following years. In 1894 he "abandoned on principle his skeptical atitude, which threatened to make havoc of all intellectual life, and began, by way of experiment, to take the stance of a believer" (SS, 28:399).[10] A year later, in the essay "Etudes funèbres," he was beginning to glimpse purpose and meaning in apparently random thoughts, thoughts that in his case circled around the idea of previous existences and the rebirth of the soul. When he wrote this, Strindberg had adopted the position that there was a single principle governing events in the material universe. In his study of the physical world he turned his back on conventional chemistry and embraced alchemy because the alchemists believed that there was a single primitive form of matter of which all the so-called elements were only variations. When Strindberg turned his attention to the science of the mind, he also sought there for the equivalent unifying principle, the law that lay behind the seemingly haphazard workings of the irrational mind in the same way that alchemical transmutation lay behind the chaos of the elements. If there was a *prima materia* in the physical world, there could be a transcendental self in the realm of the psyche. Strindberg avoided the use of any such term at first because he did not set a goal for himself. He did not know what he would find. In retrospect it is clear that what he was looking for was pushing him forward. Like Cromwell, he soared high because he did not know where he was going.

2

The main problem in studying the mind is that what is being observed is doing the observing. This is true even when there are two minds involved, as is usually the case, but the difficulty is compounded when only one mind is involved, as in self-analysis. Nothing at all could be accomplished in this area unless it was assumed that the mind was divisible, which would make it possible for one part to observe the other part. This assumption had always been made, and nineteenth-century psychological studies of second existences, that is, of hysteria, hypnotism, and somnambulism, had amply demonstrated that not only was the mind divided but that the barriers between the parts of the mind could at times be almost impenetrable. The science of the mind consisted essentially in having the rational, ordering part of the mind, which was regarded as being in the light, observe the other part of the mind, variously thought of as being in the dark, over the threshold, or on the other side.

For Strindberg, the trick was to devise a scheme or method for registering what was going on in the darker part while it was actually occurring. He tried all sorts of techniques from rhabdomancy to the I' Ching (SS, 46:27, 29, 67),[11] which he discovered in a book on Leibniz; from familiar techniques such as the inkblot test (SS, 46:190–91),[12] which seems to have enjoyed a vogue as a party game after the publication of Justinus Andreas Kerner's book *Klecksographien*, to techniques of his own devising, such as the crumpled paper test. This consisted in wrinkling a piece of paper or tinfoil which could not be wrinkled on purpose, or the test would fail to record the subconscious thoughts.

You receive a letter or a package that makes you feel one way or the other. You crunch the paper and throw it into the waste paper basket without thinking. Don't you suppose the hand that crushed the paper was acting unconsciously and expressed the passions you felt—perhaps in a whole series of pictures?[13]

During the 1896 experiment, fortunately, he decided to rely principally on two other means of access to the unconscious: dreams, which have always been thought of as emanating from the inner chambers of the mind, and trivial incidents that for no obvious reason are disturbing and unsettling. Maeterlinck's soul could ignore a storm but tremble at a breeze. And Kierkegaard, in *Repetition: An Essay in Experimental Psy-*

chology, remarked that at a certain instant a mere mote, a speck of dust in his eye, hurled him from the peak of joy into the abyss of despair. What the speck of dust in his eye was to Kierkegaard, a flake of soot in his absinthe was to Strindberg. These trivialities, magnified out of all proportion, so insignificant in themselves, so powerful in their effect on the mind, moments that everyone has experienced, were the ones that Strindberg wanted to explain. Early in 1896 he began recording such incidents, along with his dreams, in a large folio volume he called *The Occult Diary.*

In April he noted that he saw a skull and heard Schumann's "Aufschwung." The next day he found a playing card in the street, the nine of spades, signifying death. In the following month he noted that on one particular day soot fell in his absinthe, a drunkard approached his table at a sidewalk café, and someone died in his hotel. The concurrence of these incidents struck Strindberg as being "more than a mere matter of chance." Among the entries for June is this: "Thursday, the 18th. Word that Przybyszewski arrested for murdering his wife. Soot in absinthe." These few examples show that Strindberg was operating on the principle of the association of ideas. The drunkard and the death in the hotel were omens regarding the dangers of absinthe, which Strindberg at this time was drinking habitually. Schumann's "Aufschwung" was a piece of music associated with Przybyszewski, the Polish writer who had been Strindberg's sexual rival in Berlin and who was the center of a complex of emotions touching on Strindberg's guilt. Strindberg subconsciously feared Przybyszewski because he represented nemesis. The judgment visited on him could be visited on Strindberg. The flake of soot that spoiled his happy hour at the café on a spring afternoon brought his feelings of guilt to the surface. It was the equation mark between Przybyszewski and Strindberg.

Freud knew that there was a psychopathology of everyday life that explained the remarkable coincidences he heard about (his book on the subject did not appear until 1904), and Strindberg knew that there was a psychic explanation for what he noted as meaningful coincidences in his daily life. For neither Freud nor Strindberg was there such a thing as a psychic accident. The nameless hero of *To Damascus* remarks in the first scene that for some time everything has been significant to him.

For some time I've been noticing everything. But not as before, when all I saw was objects and actions, form and color. Now I see meanings and connections. Life, which was all nonsense before, now begins to make sense, and now I discern a purpose where before I saw only chance.

To the psychiatrist, Strindberg's state of mind in the 1890s appears to be paranoia. Strindberg would have partly agreed. His own diagnosis was that he suffered from paranoia during his Inferno period, when he perceived things that went unnoticed in normal life. He also noted that the ability to bring together ideas that seem remote from each other is the essence not only of paranoia but of poetry, and he knew, having read it in Maudsley's standard work on the pathology of the mind, that the distinction of genius consists in the tendency to "new and copious suggestions of analogy."[14] Furthermore, the monistic philosophy, as he pointed out, necessitated the discovery of likenesses and analogies. "I know very well," he said, "that psychologists have given a Greek name to the tendency to see likenesses everywhere, but that does not frighten me, because I know that likenesses are everywhere since everything is part of the all everywhere" (SS, 47:779).

His monistic philosophy was in harmony with his idea of poetry, the essence of which, he said, lay in finding correspondences between different planes of being (SS, 27:262; 46:207, 218). As an artist, he was always trying to participate in the creation of a monistic universe by transforming life into poetry. It was the artist in him who said,

I don't hold any views; I only improvise. Life would be pretty monotonous if we thought and said the same things every day. We've got to keep it new and fresh. Life itself, after all, is only a poem, and it's much more fun to float over the swamp than to stick one's foot in the mire looking for firm ground where there isn't any.[15]

As a poet and paranoiac, he converted life into a dream, and as actor and dramatist, he converted the dream back into palpable reality. His work in the laboratory paralleled his work at his desk, the alchemist distilling the universe into spirit, while the dramatist took the stuff dreams are made on and made it into a pageant.

During the Inferno period Strindberg was, in effect, carrying out a prolonged free association test on himself by making the physical world of his daily existence into a vast inkblot. In the Talmud Strindberg read, "If you wish to know the invisible, observe with open eyes the visible," words that serve as epigraph to his *Occult Diary*. Out of the thousands of impressions coming from the outside world there were those few that collided with something in his mind, setting off a tiny flash, and that flash was evidence of a deeper interior life, a second existence. He knew that in artistic creation the association of ideas was governed by an unconscious purposive urge. In the general life of the mind there must be a similar operating principle. The disturbances occasioned by small events were the Brownian movements in the chambers of the soul, evidence of activity so subtle as to have escaped notice heretofore and inexplicable now without a new science of the mind.

3

Claude Bernard, the author of the classical *Introduction to the Study of Experimental Medicine*, the basis of Zola's naturalism, quoted with approval the poet who told him, "Art is I; science is we" ("L'art, c'est moi; la science, c'est nous").[16] Art is a creation of the mind and a reflection of the artist's personality, but in science, the study of natural phenomena, the mind must create nothing. Generally that is true, but in the science of the mind, the reverse may apply. In this no man's land between science and art, Strindberg was the perfect forager and reconnoiterer.

Independently of each other, Strindberg and Freud were drawing the same chart of man's unconscious life. To indicate how true this is, let me quote a recent summary of Freud's impact on the modern mind. His influence had to do with three things, we are told:

his attention to and reinterpretation of the ordinary (the psychopathology of everyday life, as he chose to call it), his deeply puzzling examination of the relation between the intended and the unintended, and finally his interpretation of the nature or meaning of "significance." . . . For Freud, the ordinary conduct of everyday life was the starting point. Neurosis was not a blemish nor a disease, but a continuation of ordinary living. The ordinary, for Freud, was as much in need of interpretation as the extraordinary. One did what one intended to do, yes, but there was a hidden reason, a latent content as well as a manifest one.[17]

Strindberg's approach was exactly the same, only he called the manifest content the exoteric and the latent the esoteric. In 1896, before Freud had published his works on dreams and the psychopathology of everyday life, Strindberg commented that life had begun to take on a different appearance for him,

that an intrusive hand occasionally reveals itself, and that behind the so-called natural explanations, and along with them (!) another one exists.

I have been keeping a diary (and also a record of my dreams) for almost a year, noting everything. . . . The natural causes I recognize as exoteric explanations for the public, but behind these lie the esoteric causes, and they should not be divulged to the public.[18]

(In 1897 Freud wrote to his confidant, Dr. Wilhelm Fliess, "Since I have started studying the unconscious I have become so interesting to myself. It is a pity that one always keeps one's mouth shut about the most intimate things.")[19]

An even more striking resemblance between Strindberg and Freud manifests itself when the modern critic explains Freud's revolutionary idea of significance.

If the ordinary is not what it seems, what is it? Here is where Freud's literary genius took charge. Beneath the ordinary is a drama. Each of us is a cast of characters, acting out a script. Looked at carefully, our reactions to the world could be seen as an enactment of the script. It is in terms of these scripts that the surface of experience has systematic meaning or significance. . . . The ordinary, in a word, was to be understood as explicable in terms of its symbolic, coded value; coded values were to be understood in terms of the way in which the world was organized in secret thought below the surface.[20]

Working as a dramatist, Freud explained the significance of the ordinary; working as a scientist, Strindberg dramatized it. The fact that Strindberg was a scientist and explorer of the mind using methods similar to those of Freud and following a parallel avenue of inquiry puts a work like *To Damascus* into a special category: art as science. Freud was inclined to believe that creative writing was closely akin to neurotic fantasy and that the artist, like the hysteric, created imaginative works to shield himself against the consequences of his darkest impulses. The psychoanalyst views men as fantasts and poets as hysterics. Given that approach, a writer like Strindberg is an anomaly. If Strindberg's theories of the mind are to be taken as hysterical or neurotic imaginings beneath which lurks a real truth, then Freud's theories, identical with Strindberg's in so many respects, must also be taken as neurotic imaginings beneath which lurks a real truth. The difference between the two is that Freud could present his findings with the authority of a lecturer on nervous diseases, while Strindberg could get a hearing for his theories only by presenting them in the guise of fiction. That is probably one reason why he put aside plans for a natural philosophy of the occult[21] in late 1897 or early 1898 and returned to playwriting. Freud could make the interpretation of dreams into a science or pseudoscience, but Strindberg had to make his science or pseudoscience into a kind of dream. Where many artists fear that psychoanalysis will dry up their creative channels—Rilke, for instance, refused to be analyzed by Freud for just that reason—Strindberg's self-analysis ushered in a new creative phase in his career, just as Freud's self-analysis resulted in some of his most provocative and imaginative theories.

4

Strindberg's task as an artist was to transform his real experiences into a drama that would directly involve the spectator in the action while at the same time adumbrating the significance of what was happening from moment to moment. He had to create on stage an equivalent of the world of intimations and vibrations that he had lived in, a world in which the spectator's mind would be buffeted, jostled, and nudged along by forces too subtle to be defined. Ideas would have to be associated and combined in various ways while the meanings behind the associations would remain half hidden. He had to convey the sense of a life without purpose while simultaneously giving it an obscure sense of direction.

Much of this he had accomplished in his novel *Inferno*, his first effort to unscramble all the material he had collected during his psychological experiments. His task as a dramatist was enormously more challenging. A subtlety that could be given point in the novel by a sentence or two of commentary would lose its point in the bright light of the stage. He had to make the most physical of the arts deal with the most intangible of subjects. He had to dematerialize the stage while theatricalizing the spirit. To make a play out of his experiences he had to condense some of them, eliminate most of them, change the chronological order of many of them, invent a few of them, and transmute all of them. Because the unconscious life is life striving to be a drama, the reinvented world of *To Damascus* revealed a more profound level of truth than the novel. The further he got from the original experiences and the more he refined and reshaped the material, the deeper he descended into the psyche.

This expedition to the center of the soul begins innocently enough. The hero finds himself at a street corner in Paris and at a crossroads in life. He is middle-aged, bored, and troubled. Confronting him are a café, a Gothic church, and a post office, representing the alternatives with which he is faced. The registered letter in the post office does not entice him because he is certain it contains a legal summons or something of the sort. It is a reminder of the past that he wishes to forget. The wine and absinthe of the café offer an escape from the humdrum world. "Wine makes my soul leave its casement, fly out into space, see what no one has seen, hear what no one has heard" (SS, 29:22). But this derangement of the senses is ultimately unsatisfying. Something—is it the liquor?—is causing his mind to work differently than before. He feels the presence of undefined forces, knows that these forces are contending with each other deep in his mind, and dares to hope that something new and exciting is about to happen to him. The woman who will figure prominently in his story now appears, as if conjured up by his thoughts, as if she were one of these still undefined forces. She suggests that the church offers the solace he needs.

This opening scene, haunting, evocative, quivering with delicate and unsettling intimations, captures Strindberg's state of mind immediately before the Inferno venture. In the introduction, probably written in 1896, to *Jardin des plantes*, a collection of scientific essays, he described how he felt then.

Arrived at the middle of my journey through life, I sat down to rest and ponder. All that I had daringly dreamed and earnestly desired had come to me. Having had enough of fame and scandal, pleasure and pain, I asked myself: "What's left to do?"

Everything repeated itself with deadly monotony. Nothing changed. There was nothing new. The older generation had said, "The universe holds no secrets. We have answered all the riddles, solved all the problems." . . .

But a generation that had had the courage to rid itself of God, to demolish state and church, society and morality, still knelt before science. In science, where freedom should rule, the watchword was: believe the authorities or perish. . . .

In other words, nothing remained to be done in this world, and feeling I was useless, I decided to vanish from it.

The spirit lamp was already lit under the retort. . . . Cyanogen, the generator of the blue color, born of yellow salts, began to form and develop—the most innocent of all combinations, pure carbon joining with neutral nitrogen in a terrible alliance, one without parallel, one that has compelled science to admit its ignorance of this sort of miracle.

The fumes rose from the receptacle and soon tightened the muscles in my throat. . . . My arm muscles felt numb, and there was a growing pain in my spine.

I cut short the experiment when the odor of bitter almond became noticeable. Without knowing why, I thought I saw an almond tree in bloom in a garden and heard the voice of an old woman saying, "No, child, do not believe it!"

And I no longer believed that the secrets of the universe had been unveiled. And I have gone my way, now alone, now with others, to ponder the great chaos in which I was able nevertheless eventually to discover an infinitely coherent order. [SS, 27:207–08]

The melodrama of this half-hearted attempt at suicide is a little too reminiscent of Faust to be convincing. Having advanced to the frontiers of knowledge, Faust puts a vial of poison to his lips and is only saved from death, the last great experience, by the voices of angels, and he sets off on new adventures. In the first scene of his play Strindberg handles the same moment much more honestly and poetically than in his essay.

The melodrama is transformed into irony tinged with melancholy. The wish to die is muted and subdued, while the boredom of the old ways and the same old thoughts and the desire to find something new, to find oneself again and be reborn, are brought to the fore and heightened.

This scene not only renders Strindberg's state of mind at the turning point of his life; it also sets his personal history within a larger frame of reference. The hero seated on the park bench at the beginning of *To Damascus* corresponds to Dante at the beginning of *The Divine Comedy*. At the midway of this our mortal life, Dante found himself in a dark wood, having wandered from the right road. His dark wood is the wood of sin, and how he got there he cannot say because he was dull with sleep when he left the narrow road. Strindberg, too, is halfway down the road of life. His dark wood is his own troubled mind, and he finds himself in a dreamlike state. When he put his experiences into the form of a novel, he called it *Inferno*. In the play, the experiences are winnowed out, sorted and arranged to suggest the nine circles of Dante's Inferno. There is no direct correspondence between the scenes of the play and the circles of hell: all that Strindberg offers is the hint of a connection.

This is typical of his method, which creates a stage world of vibrations and hidden associations in which the audience can participate. The associations brought out in the psychoanalyst's consulting room are too private to be shared until they have been explained. It was incumbent on Strindberg as an artist, especially as a playwright, to create a shared experience, one in which the viewer would feel that something was significant without knowing why, could sense the vibrations without, at first, understanding what caused them. To accomplish this, Strindberg resorts to different degrees of association, ranging from the obvious to the willfully obscure. In the theatre, the allusion to the circles of hell is likely to escape the spectator unfamiliar with the play, although the increasing torment of the hero should make itself felt. Even more subtle is the link between the woman's husband, the doctor—jestingly referred to as the werewolf—and the beasts who appear in Dante's opening verses as images of sin.

The funeral march that pursues the hero affords a clearer example of Strindberg's technique. In reality, it was not Mendelssohn's funeral march that haunted Strindberg; it was Schumann's "Aufschwung." As mentioned above, he associated the Schumann piece with Przybyszewski and with a whole complex of emotions. That complex of emotions, a very private one, could not conceivably be evoked on stage without an enormous amount of preparation. So he replaced the Schumann piece with the Mendelssohn funeral march, which had been part of a small poetic incident recorded in *The Occult Diary* on August 19, 1897, one of those revelatory moments which James Joyce would think of as "epiphanies," sudden spiritual manifestations arising from the trivialities of life, of which Strindberg recorded hundreds in his diary. The funeral march establishes a sense of foreboding and presents the theme of spiritual death, which is so vital to the story that it had to be made prominent at once. With the dramatist's sense of economy and the musician's flair for variations, Strindberg elaborates the death theme, counterpoints it with the rebirth theme, and lets it swell out into the theme of guilt. At first the funeral march is heard in the distance; shortly afterwards pallbearers actually appear on stage. The fact that they are dressed in brown, not black, disturbs the hero; certain resemblances between him and the dead man are pointed out; simultaneously the ominous ticking of an unseen clock is heard; and this sound is associated with the ticking of the deathwatch beetle, whose sound presages death. By these means Strindberg creates a true poetry of the theatre, fusing language, visual images, and aural effects into a theatrical whole that is greater than the sum of its parts. (See figure 14.)

(Ingmar Bergman in his film *Wild Strawberries*, which was modeled on *To Damascus*, imaginatively translated Strindberg's stage images into cinematic ones; the hearse with the broken wheel, the casket falling out of the hearse and breaking open, the dead man's hand protruding from the casket and clutching the hand of the dreamer, the clock without hands.)

Shortly before the entrance of the pallbearers, the rebirth theme is heard briefly when the hero thinks of himself as chopped up and boiling in Medea's cauldron, from which he will either go to the soap factory or else rise up reborn by Medea's—the woman's—magic. In the next scene, at the doctor's house, the death theme is elaborated further. The doctor actually has on hand pieces of dead bodies that he uses in his experiments. The funeral march is heard again, played on a piano by a neighbor who works at the post office. Virtually none of this is recorded in *The Occult Diary* or comes from life. Strindberg invented these images in order to adapt his private mental associations to the demands of the stage.

Even more enlightening as to Strindberg's artistic methods is the figure of the Doctor. When he first comes within range of Strindberg's dramatic vision, he is Doctor Eliasson, the somewhat eccentric general practitioner of medicine who befriended him during the Inferno period, and the Doctor's house and garden in *To Damascus* are exactly like Eliasson's. As a doctor, Eliasson could be assigned the necessary role of counselor in the drama, and this role was strengthened dramatically and psychologically by making him the embodiment of Strindberg's conscience. In *The Occult Diary* and in *Inferno*, Przybyszewski is the person onto whom Strindberg projects his feelings of guilt. Since the complicated Przybyszewski story would have been too distracting (Strindberg saved it for another play, *Crimes and Crimes*, which he composed a year later), he dropped it and drew instead on his marriages to Siri von Essen and Frida Uhl. By that means, the association of ideas that constitutes the infinitely complicated pattern of the novel *Inferno* was eliminated and the story line straightened out, with the Doctor being introduced to tie the threads of guilt together. By centering his guilt feelings on one person, Strindberg could deal with them summarily at the end of the play, and by making that one person a doctor, he could give a symbolic validity to the healing process. Also, by combining all the elements of his guilt in the Doctor, the dramatist performed the function of the analyst who effects a synthesis of the disturbing factors in the unconscious and reveals them to the patient.

5

To Damascus is primarily a study of guilt and the workings of conscience. That sets it apart from most Symbolist works, gives it a significance that Maeterlinck's plays lack, and brings it into line with Dostoevski's novels. Dante created an inferno in which he could delight at seeing his enemies tortured; Strindberg fashioned an inferno out of his own guilt and "placed himself alone among the glowing coal heaps" (SS, 28:391).[22] He endeavored to trace his feelings of guilt to their source, hoping in that way to rid himself of them.

His first thought was to write a play based on Robert le Diable, the legendary hero who was the subject of a French miracle play and of a popular Meyerbeer opera. Robert, son of the duke of Normandy, is a brigand and murderer whose crimes force his father to outlaw him. Robert seeks out his mother and, feeling some shame for his crimes, asks her why he is so evil. She informs him that in order to get herself with child she had prayed to the devil. Robert now knows that he is cursed and damned, the devil's offspring. He appeals to the pope for absolution; the pope sends him to a holy hermit, and the hermit, instructed by God, imposes a penance on Robert. He must play the madman, be a laughingstock, and eat the food of dogs. Subsequently, an unknown knight performs feats of valor when the country is invaded. Refusing to admit that he is the heroic knight, Robert assumes the role of a madman. Inevitably, the hermit identifies him and declares that Robert's penance has come to an end. It is easy to see what attracted Strindberg to this legend: the curse, the humiliation, the assumed madness. The bare bones of this story form the skeleton of *To Damascus*.

Strindberg also found his own situation depicted in Bulwer Lytton's novel *Zanoni* (1842), which he read early in 1897. Zanoni is a reincarnated spirit who aspires to rise above the materialism of the nineteenth century, with the effort made considerably easier for him than for ordinary mortals by his knowledge of alchemy, which enables him to produce precious metals through transformation of baser ones. He is also able to produce an occult child, apparently through normal methods. Nevertheless, the mother of the child flees from Zanoni out of fear of the "unknown" in him.[23]

When Strindberg finally hit upon a solution to the problem of putting the workings of conscience on stage, he took the unknown in Zanoni and made it the central figure in the drama. This was an audaciously simple and theatrically revolutionary stroke. The unknown element in the personality, the demonic, the darker side, had heretofore either been mysteriously hinted at without being defined or else had been shadowed forth in the form of the hero's double, a favorite device of romantic writers. Strindberg's innovation was to put it boldly on stage as the hero himself, with the other characters representing other components of the personality, the stage representing, consequently, not the physical world but the interior mental world. This step could not have been taken until the end of the nineteenth century, when the idea gained ground that the darker area of man's mind, which appeared to be a chaos of impressions and instincts, of feelings and images, all jumbled together without any plan, was actually a realm with its own laws and logic. As a scientist, Strindberg had attempted to find the design inherent in the great disorder of the physical universe; as a psychologist, he now sought to discover the principles that underlay the chaos of the unconscious. He was much more successful as psychologist than as chemist because the mental life of man had the characteristics of drama.

More than one writer on the subject of the unconscious drew an analogy between the mind and the theatre. Hippolyte Taine, for instance, in his widely read and often reprinted book *De l'intelligence*, pictured in theatrical terms the way in which some images and memories push themselves forward and endure while others have only fleeting existences.

One can compare the mind of man to a stage of indefinite depth. The apron is very narrow, but the stage increases in width in proportion to the distance from the footlights. On this lighted apron there is hardly room for one actor. He enters, gestures for a moment, and leaves. Another actor appears, yet another, and so on. [These represent the strong and forceful images in the mind.] Beyond them, on various sections of the stage, are other groups, appearing less and less distinct the farther they are from the footlights. Still farther away, standing in the wings and at the backdrop, are a multitude of obscure shapes who will sometimes be suddenly called on stage, even led up to the footlights. And within this swarm of actors of every kind, unknown tactics bring forth the stars who one after the other, as in a magic lantern, parade before our eyes.[24]

Similarly, Du Prel in his book *The Hidden Life of the Soul*, to which I referred earlier in connection with Strindberg's experiment in madness, devotes an entire chapter to the dreamer as dramatist, and half of that chapter is concerned with the splitting up of the ego in dreams.[25]

What was lacking in these theatrical metaphors of the unconscious life, was the one thing that was most needed: a plot, a story, an action, the soul of drama. Because of his Inferno experience Strindberg was able to supply it.

The character whom I have referred to as the unnamed hero of *To Damascus*, sometimes calling him Strindberg, is actually listed among the dramatis personae as the Unknown (*Den okände*). The play is an intricate set of equations in which the protagonist is the algebraic x. The plot consists in making the unknown known, not so much by having the unconscious become conscious as by having the viewer descend into the depths where his view of things becomes that of the Unknown. The world above is distorted by the medium in which he finds himself. Everything appears different to him. Above the surface the Woman resembles Strindberg's second wife; seen from the depths, she bears some resemblance to his first wife. The Doctor when seen from below is a refraction of all those who trouble Strindberg's conscience. The Beggar, an educated man but a drifter and a sponger, takes on the appearance of Strindberg himself. They are all seen as creatures of the deep and are compelled to act in accordance with the laws that prevail there. The effect is that of a dream. Events and people of the real world are distorted and brought into strange conjunctions with each other. The result is, in Strindberg's words, "a fiction, but with a terrifying reality behind it."[26]

Nothing like this had ever been achieved before in the drama or in literature. Countless writers had deliberately descended into the depths of the mind, but they either represented what they had seen from the viewpoint of reality, carefully observing the line that divides one realm from the other, or else they pictured the unconscious as a clutter of images without much order. Where they only recorded their impressions, taking snapshots here and there, Strindberg drew maps, took soundings, and charted the reefs and shoals.

The exploration of the unconscious is also, inevitably, a journey into the past. To make this point poetically, Strindberg sketches into his drama a parallel between the hero's pilgrimage and Aeneas's descent into the underworld. To enter the kingdom of the dead, Aeneas was instructed by the Sibyl to pluck the golden bough, which conferred special powers on him. In the first scene of the play the Woman offers the Unknown One a Christmas rose, the hellebore, which is reputed to cure insanity. Armed with it, the Unknown One enters Hades and encounters in the following scenes the monsters of death, impoverishment, and guilt. Between the sixth and seventh scenes the Woman and the Unknown One cross a river to reach her childhood home. Here he becomes Aeneas crossing the river Styx. The last coin that he possesses, which he contemptuously throws into the river in defiance of the gods, is the obol that Charon demands. Once across the river, the Unknown One meets the Woman's mother, who takes on the role of his own mother. He attempts to resist his growing sense of remorse; he wrestles with it as Jacob wrestled with God; and, suffering a fall in the mountains, he is wounded in the thigh as Jacob was. He becomes delirious, either from his wound or from his mental torments, and ends up in the sick ward of a monastery known as the Helping Hand. Here he reaches the bottom of his descent. The ninth circle of Inferno in the Dantean parallel corresponds to the Elysian fields in the Virgilian parallel, and where Aeneas met the virtuous souls, including his father, the Unknown One meets all those people whom he feels he has offended, including his parents. These figures are merely the other patients being cared for in the monastery hospital, but they appear to him, in his fevered condition, as ghosts from his past: the brown pallbearers, the Beggar, a lady in mourning with two children (Strindberg's first wife and the children he was not supporting), the Woman, the Doctor, and, finally, his mother and father, silently reproaching their prodigal son. The Father Confessor reads the curse from Deuteronomy, and the Unknown One takes it as a judgment pronounced on him.

Structurally, this scene is the central one in the drama. Strindberg can plumb the depths no farther, and from this point the journey of the Unknown One proceeds upwards, the last eight scenes in the play reversing the order of the first eight. The geographical journey from place

to place now describes both an ascent from the depths of the unconscious and a coming to terms with the conscience.[27]

As soon as the curse from Deuteronomy has been read, the spirits of
the Unknown One begin to rise. When the Unknown One leaves the pit
of the inferno, Strindberg abandons Dante for Kierkegaard. At this point,
let me exchange the appellation "the Unknown One," which is awkward
in English, for "the Stranger," which is less accurate but more convenient. The reversal of scenes is meant as a dramatic metaphor for Kierkegaard's Repetition, as Strindberg explained in one of his more helpful
moments. The psychological explanation is that the Stranger can only as-
suage his conscience by reexperiencing the past and meeting his "victims." He returns to the Doctor, who is the embodiment of guilt feelings
that can be traced back to the Stranger's childhood. For a moment he
fears that the Doctor has taken the ultimate revenge of marrying the
Stranger's first wife and becoming father to the Stranger's children. But
that thought is only the product of his conscience, as he learns from the
Doctor, who also informs him that the Helping Hand is an insane asylum. When he asks for the Doctor's professional help, he is told that guilt
for a single misdeed must be considered as only one entry in a complicated set of accounts.

"For a long time I hated you, as you probably know, because an unforgivable
act of yours gave me a bad reputation, which I didn't deserve. But as I grew older
and wiser, I saw that although my punishment that time wasn't deserved, I still
had it coming to me for other pranks I had got away with. Besides you were just a
child. And you had a conscience that would punish you. So that matter need not
bother you."

"I see," says the Stranger. "Will you give me your hand?"

"No. I can't do that. I mustn't. Besides, how can my forgiving you be of any
help if you haven't the strength to forgive yourself? . . . Some things that we have
done can only be helped by being undone. This is beyond help."

"'The Helping Hand'?" asks the Stranger, thinking of his illness, whether
mental or physical, as punishment.

"Not bad!" says the Doctor. "You challenged fate, and you lost. No shame in
a battle well fought." [SS, 29:131–33]

To be aware of one's guilt and to be unable to do anything about it
can drive one mad. To plunge so deeply into the unconscious that the
rational mind no longer exercises any control over the personality is
madness itself. From his experience in the asylum, the Stranger learns
that the two madnesses are one and the same. At this time Strindberg
could not sink any more deeply into his unconscious. His personality
could not stand the pressure. His ego demanded a hearing against the

accusations of the conscience. The journey upwards marks the steps in the process of reintegration of the personality. In the first scenes of the play the various characters appear to be fragments of the hero, having split off from him as he sits on the park bench. In the last scenes he encounters these parts of his personality, gathers them to himself, and becomes reasonably whole again, incorporating into himself first the Mother, then the Beggar, then the Woman, and, finally, the Doctor.

6

Because of the hero's changing outlook, his desire to wipe the slate clean and start a new life, and his increasing awareness of a moral order different from the old law of retribution that he once accepted, his journey in the last half of the play is likened to that of Saul on the road to Damascus. The play in its entirety now takes shape in the spectator's mind as a drama of conversion, with the Stranger reenacting the experience of Saul on the road to Damascus. As Saul had been a believer in the Torah and a persecutor of the Christians, so Strindberg had been a believer in the laws of natural science and a mocker of religious mysticism. As Saul had come to realize that his obedience to the law had only brought him confusion and despair, so Strindberg had come to see that his reliance on the materialist philosophy of the nineteenth century had led him into a blind alley of boredom, hostility, and artistic frustration. As Saul was struck on the road to Damascus by a blinding light and heard a voice asking, "Wherefore persecutest thou me?" so the Stranger is struck by the realization that it is not the world that has been persecuting him but that it is he who has behaved dreadfully toward others. As Saul died and was reborn spiritually on the way to Damascus, so Strindberg died and was reborn on his journey into the unconscious. As Saul, through strict exercise of the law, died unto the law that he might live unto God, so Strindberg pursued natural science to the point where it became mysticism and he, its apostle.

The moment when Saul saw the light is elaborated in Strindberg's treatment into a series of scenes. Saul found it "hard to kick against the goad" within him; the goad within the Stranger is his conscience. In the first scene, when he is still the skeptical man of the world, he can talk lightly about "the lovely pangs of conscience," regard them as the aftereffects of a night of drinking and carousing, and find a perverse joy in his hangover, when his soul seems to take leave of his aching head and float like a cloud around it. As his journey progresses, however, the lovely pangs become increasingly unpleasant. In the hotel room with his new bride, he sees the face of the Doctor, her first husband, in the design of the tablecloth and in the pattern of the wallpaper. In the mountain ravine, the cliff forms the Doctor's profile. In the asylum, the patients become the silent incarnations of his sins. When he tries to sleep, he has nightmares, and all his past transgressions unroll before his eyes in an unending panorama. By confronting his past and admitting his misdeeds, he puts himself among the elect, among those who were born to be reborn. The agonizing review of the past is a necessary antecedent to regeneration. When the torments of conscience reach a certain excruciating point, the spirit dies—but only in order to be reborn. The death of spirit for the Stranger occurs in the second kitchen scene, in which Strindberg concentrated in a few lines all those incidents, involving unexplained sounds in his ears and unaccountable pains in his chest, that constituted a large part of his Inferno experience. Sleepless, plagued by nightmares, and haunted by the sounds of a horse restless in its stall, the Stranger leaves his bed in the middle of the night and goes to the kitchen, where he meets his mother-in-law. Seeing how troubled he is, she asks what happened when he went to his room.

"I—I really don't know. I didn't actually see anything. But when I walked into the room, I felt there was someone. I looked around with the lamp. Didn't see anyone. So I went to bed. Then—someone began walking with heavy steps right over my head. . . . Do you believe in spooks and ghosts?"

"No. And it's against my religion. But I do believe that our sense of right and wrong creates its own form of punishment."

"Of course. Anyway, after a short while, I felt an ice-cold draft on my chest, probing around until it got to my heart. Then my heart turned cold. And I had to get out of bed."

"Yes?"

"I had to stand there in the middle of the floor and watch the whole panorama of my life roll past. All of it. Everything. . . . There's nothing worse."

"I know what you mean. I've been through it. There's no name for that illness, and there's only one cure."

"What's that?"

"You know. What children have to do when they've been bad."

"What do they have to do?"

"First, say they're sorry."

"And then?"

"Try to set things right."

"Isn't it enough that you suffer as you deserve to suffer?"

"That's only revenge."

"Of course. What else should it be?"

"Can you repair a life you've ruined? Can you undo a bad deed? Undo what's been done?"

"No, that's true. . . . But I tell you I was forced to do what I did, forced to take, because no one would admit I was right. What about the one who forced me? Blame him!"

He suddenly gasps in pain, and his hand clutches his heart. "Oh, my God, he's here, here in this room, and he's tearing my heart out!"

"Bend down."

"I cannot."

"On your knees."

"I will not."

"Christ have mercy on you. The Lord have mercy. . . . On your knees before Him who was crucified. Only he can make things right."

"No, not before him. Not him! If I'm forced to, I'll take it all back—later."

"Kneel, kneel, my son."

"I can not kneel. . . . I cannot. . . . Help me, Almighty God!"

While the Stranger stands there in agony, the Mother mumbles a prayer. "Is it better now?"

He recovers somewhat. "Yes. . . . Do you know what that was? Not death. Annihilation."

"Yes, annihilation of the divine. It's called death of the spirit."

"Is that what you're getting at," he says, without his usual mocking tone. "I'm beginning to understand."

"My dear boy, you have left Jerusalem. You're on your way to Damascus. Go there. It's the same road that took you here. And plant a cross at every station, until you get to the seventh. You don't have fourteen, as He did."

The scene ends with dawn breaking. The Mother looks out the window and says, as if to herself, "You beautiful morning star! Why have you fallen so far from heaven?"

After a pause, the Stranger asks, "Have you noticed how, just before the sun goes up, a shiver runs through you? Are we children of darkness that we tremble before the light?" [SS, 29:107–11]

In Strindberg's parable, the morning star substitutes for the light that blinded Paul.

From this point on, the Stranger's sufferings, instead of being a burden, actually lighten his conscience and speed him on his way, for, as Meister Eckhart said, "Suffering is the animal that bears you fastest to perfection."[28] Since Jesus is the type of sufferer, the Stranger's stopping places are thought of as stations of the cross, but the scenes are brief, the suffering light and the journey back much briefer than the journey out. Soon the Stranger finds himself once again at the street corner, sitting on a bench, writing in the sand with his cane.

7

The crowning touch to this parable comes at the end of the play and like everything else in it, has both a latent and a manifest meaning. At the gentle urging of the Woman, the Stranger picks up at the post office the registered letter he had refused to claim at the beginning of the play, convinced that it contained a subpoena, a summons, or something equally unpleasant. Now he finds it contains a check, the very money he had been looking for when he was on his honeymoon with the Woman. In a sense, the whole journey, all the poverty, shame, and humiliation, could have been avoided if the Stranger had gone to the post office in the first scene. But without the journey, the Stranger would not have put off the old man with his deeds and put on the new man. On the symbolic level this letter is the good news that Paul brought, the glad tidings of the New Testament. As Saul, he had made the law his command, and, under that dispensation, "sin sprang to life and I died." But, kicking against the goad within him, he came to see the light, turned away from the law with its doctrine of sin and punishment, and passed beyond good and evil. Out of his spiritual need, Paul interpreted the resurrection in a symbolic sense as meaning a rebirth here on earth, a new life in which love and the spirit of Christ would replace the law. An evil deed could not be undone, certainly, but in Paul's teachings the doer of the deed could still be emancipated from sin. The power of the spirit of Christ could annul the moral past. This was Paul's good news for mankind, and it is the news that the Stranger hesitantly accepts at the end of the play.

If one takes into account only the beginning and end of the play, Strindberg seems to be saying that the world is good or bad depending on one's attitude. The message is then much like the one the psychologist William James delivered in *The Will to Believe* a year before Strindberg wrote *To Damascus*: "Believe that life *is* worth living, and your belief will help create the fact." But Strindberg was never one to swallow the placebo of positive thinking. His question was, What creates the belief? Not in a young person with money and a happy family, but in a middle-aged person with no money and no family. The answer he gives in *To Damascus* is twofold. There has to be a predisposition to believe and the belief has to be brought out by a purgative process. The world cannot appear good and just until it has first been revealed as cruel and unjust. The play is a demonstration of the power of negative thinking. The new outlook is possible for the Stranger only because it was present in him from the beginning, just as the letter with the good news lay in the post office from the beginning. It has been lying there the whole time, just as the new attitude toward the things of this world has been part of the Stranger's innermost thoughts, his unconscious, the whole time. The play reveals how the latent thought manifests itself.

The post office, rather than the café or the church, is the focal symbol. The café offers a naturalistic or scientific explanation for the Stranger's experiences; the church offers a religious interpretation. But in the post office lies a third alternative. It is the home of the indefinable forces that govern our inner lives. Strindberg called them the Powers and regarded them "as one or more concrete, living, individualized beings directing the course of the world and the careers of men consciously and hypostatically, as the theologians say" (SS, 28:82).[29] That is how he described them in the spring of 1897 when he was writing Inferno and attempting to give a meaning and an order to his recent experiences. In 1894, when he wrote on the subject of nemesis, he had concluded that chance could not account for the way in which certain events were linked together any more than cause and effect could. His view then was, as he later called it, "mechanistic." "Human destinies balance each other out and, in the abstract, result in a sort of nemesis" (SS, 28:82).[30] In the course of the Inferno experiences, the idea of the Powers supervened upon that of nemesis. When the Doctor absolves part of the Stranger's guilt by explaining that unmerited punishment is balanced against unpunished pranks in the ledger of justice, the Doctor is expressing the view that Strindberg held in 1894. But the Doctor does not have the final word. That comes from the Powers, and they speak through the post office.

These Powers do not differ essentially from the beings that constituted "the demonic" in Goethe's pantheism. In Goethe's time, however, at the high tide of romanticism, these beings lived too far from the shore and too deep in the sea to be observed and studied. Eighty years later, at the ebb tide of romanticism, scientists and psychologists could venture far from the old shore line and observe at least the traces left by these beings from the depths. A psychoanalyst might think of them as operating in the unconscious; that is how Strindberg thought of them. It is these Powers that persecute the Stranger and send him on his way to Damascus. When he hears the funeral march at the Doctor's house, he is told that it is being played by the girl who works at the post office. The Powers are tutelary and guiding spirits that work with a purpose and that constitute a second intelligence operating with the means at their disposal to make themselves felt and to direct the ego—"a superior intelligence," in Freud's words, "outside the patient's consciousness." [31] They make those connections that transform chance into purpose, nonsense into meaning, and the ordinary into poetry.

To Damascus can be interpreted either as religious drama or as psychiatric drama, and it makes perfect sense either way. The Stranger is seeking the redemption of his soul and the reintegration of his personality. Cut off from the rational and social world, he discovers his true self and a world of higher meaning. In the religious view, the world is ultimately governed not by physical forces but by spiritual ones, and they generate a moral order, a scheme of justice, in which man is compelled to find a place. In the psychological view, man's quest is for a proper balance between his inner and outer selves. "True sanity," writes a modern psychiatrist in a passage that might have been composed with Strindberg's hero in mind,

entails in one way or another the dissolution of the normal ego, that false self competently adjusted to our alienated social reality; the emergence of the "inner" archetypal mediators of divine power, and through this death a rebirth, and the reestablishment of a new kind of ego-functioning, the ego now being the servant of the divine, no longer its betrayer. [32]

Strindberg consistently maintains both the religious and medical points of view throughout the play, from the opening scene, in which the café and the church incorporate the two alternatives, to the final curtain, when the Stranger agrees to pass through the church in order to hear some "new songs" (an allusion to Revelation [33]) before proceeding on his way. The Helping Hand may be either an asylum for the insane or the sick ward of a monastery. The Stranger may have been half insane when he fell and injured his hip, or, alternatively, the injury he sustained may have been the cause of his fever and delirium. The attack of angina pectoris in the kitchen scene certainly has its physical causes, but it occurs at a time when other causes seem more relevant and more immediate. The Doctor is a general medical practitioner offering commonsense advice, but he functions as a healer of souls. Always there is a double motivation for what happens, a physical and somatic explanation as well as a psychological one, a manifest cause and a recondite one or, to use Strindberg's terms, an exoteric cause and an esoteric cause. The mystical and spiritual constructions of Strindberg always have a solid footing in concrete reality.

8

This ambiguity extends even to the tone and manner of the drama, which is neither tragic nor comic nor even tragicomic. In the dark of the unconscious, all genres are grey, but this ambiguity of mood is a perfect reflection of Strindberg's personality. He could never be completely depressed by sorrow, he said, because

he entertained a vague idea that life was not entirely real, that it was a level of dream life, and that our deeds, even the worst of them, were committed under the influence of some outside, highly suggestive force. Accordingly, he felt himself, to a certain extent, not responsible. He didn't deny his meanness, but he knew also that there existed deep within him a greatly striving spirit that suffered the degradation of being invested in the body of a human being. This inner personality possessed the tender conscience and could at times, much to his alarm, have its way with him and become sentimental, crying over his—or its—deplorable behavior, which of the two it was hard to determine. Then the latter laughed at the former's silliness, and this laughter, which he called the divine frivolity, served him much better than any heavy-hearted grubbing about in his miseries.[34]

When Strindberg was asked what was the principal trait in his character, he replied, "A strange mixture of the deepest melancholy and the most awful frivolity."[35] A typical expression of this mixture of melancholy and levity, or of the alternation of moods, is Strindberg's reaction to *Inferno*. When he received a copy from his publisher and reread what he had written half a year before, he said, "This is really horrifying. It frightens me; I'm astonished that I could laugh at this."[36] A good friend found that the essence of the man was revealed in his enigmatic smile, "half skeptical and self-mocking, half resigned and melancholy."[37]

Although the years of crisis in the 1890s were a time of hardship and suffering for Strindberg, they stimulated his imagination and enabled him to create a poor man's poetry. He was, as he said, "enough of a child at heart, and miserable enough, to extract poetry from the most common and the most natural incidents" (SS, 28:174).[38] It was a poetry made up of found objects, of *objets trouvés*, of things that came his way without his looking for them. Collected in his *Occult Diary*, his book of little revelations, they were transmuted by the alchemy of genius under the pressure of adversity into a new genre of art, beyond realism and naturalism, and beyond tragedy and comedy.

Nowhere is the Strindberg temperament more apparent than in the first scene of *To Damascus*, one of the most sublimely poetic scenes in dramatic literature; its wayward humor, gentle irony, and abrupt transi-

tions from banter to serious talk make it as unmistakably Strindberg's as
the moods of Hamlet are unmistakably Shakespeare's. Although love is
not mentioned in it, it is also one of the great love scenes that the drama
has to offer, with the infatuation of the Stranger and the Woman growing
as they josh each other and play various roles for each other's benefit,
like two young people teasing each other for hours at some street corner,
both reluctant to leave and both afraid that a serious and solemn word
will make the speaker vulnerable. Strindberg wanted the part of the
Woman played with a certain amount of roguishness and puckish humor,[39] and she helps to build and sustain the mood of the scene almost
as much as the Stranger does. When she kisses him at the end of the
scene—lowering her veil and kissing him on the mouth, which means
she is giving herself entirely to him—even the elements are astonished.
The tree shakes, the heavens frown, the rose window darkens, and a
shriek is heard from within the church.

In the Stranger's world the borderlines between the serious and the
comic, the real and the imaginary, the sophisticated and the naive are
quickly blurred. Momentous events are trivialized, and trivial events become momentous. The undetermined and fluctuating tone of the play accounts in part for the casual, often playful, manner in which legends and
myths are employed to sketch the Stranger's inner life. The Woman is
seen as Eve when the Stranger desires a return to innocence, and as
Medea when he thinks of being remade and reborn. She is one of the Par-
cae spinning his fate, only here she crochets and does not run out of yarn
until two scenes from the end of the play. The Stranger is Adam to her
Eve, and the book she reads about the Stranger's first marriage is the fruit
of the tree of knowledge. As social rebel, he bears the mark of Cain, actually a scar on his forehead caused by a blow delivered by his brother. He
is Polycrates, who did not know what to do with his good fortune; he is
Aeneas descending into the underworld; he is Virgil in Dante's Inferno;
he is Jacob wrestling with an unseen adversary; he is Saul, who used the
law until it shattered; and he is Christ, who suffers that the law may be
replaced by a larger understanding. The fabric of the play is shot with
these allusions, which diminish the hero as often as they magnify him.
(See figure 15.) The result is a mock epic of a different sort. The hero
stands in the light of legend and myth in order to enjoy the giant shadows his little figure casts. And what holds together this assemblage of
public and private symbols, of musical motifs and mythical allusions, is
a solid framework in three dimensions, Dantean on one side, Pauline on
the other, and Kierkegaardian in depth.

Because of the novelty of Strindberg's method and his disinclination to write lengthy explanatory notes, critics have been slow to recognize the artistic merits of *To Damascus*. Instead of studying it as a work of art, they have read it as personal confession. After Strindberg's pioneering drama, the method he used became familiar mainly through the works of James Joyce and his followers. Joyce complicated the system of allusions and parallels without adding anything essential to the method. *Facile est inventis addere.*

In devising a technique for giving a literary and dramatic equivalent of the mental underworld of private associations, inchoate thoughts, and inexplicable tremblings of the soul, Strindberg created a thoroughly innovative and imaginative work of art. A work of such complexity of design and richness of meaning could not have been written—and written in less than two months—if it had not grown out of life itself. The seeds of his psychological experiments had to be planted in *The Occult Diary* and the letters he wrote to Hedlund in 1896; these had to blossom into the novels *Inferno* and *Legends*; and only then could *To Damascus* fall from the artist's hand like ripe fruit from the tree.

Although Strindberg is generally thought of as having a tragic view of life, he was actually much less doleful and pessimistic than the popular image of him as a gloomy Swede would suggest. As a young man, he was too combative and too obstreperous to lose himself in elegiac and melancholy moods. "I find the joy of living," he asserted in his preface to *Miss Julie*, "in the fierce and ruthless battles of life, and my pleasure comes from learning something, from being taught something" (SS, 23:101). In the 1890s, life taught him a hard lesson, and the middle-aged Strindberg who climbed out of the inferno saw life as a divine comedy. The paradox of his career was that the worst of times became the best of times. Out of his sufferings and tribulations a new life began.

CHAPTER SEVEN

THE TURNING POINT

He quoted with approval Voltaire's pert remark that "resurrection is a quite natural thing; it is no more astonishing to be born twice than once" (SS, 27:605).[1] No more astonishing, perhaps, but certainly much more unusual. No matter how awe-inspiring the first and physical birth may be, the second parturition is an event of much greater rarity. When Strindberg quoted Voltaire in 1895, he was seeking rebirth, and in his eagerness to create a new life, he discounted the travails that lay ahead. He had no idea then how difficult the spiritual labor of rebirth could be. When it was all over, the dramatist was as fascinated as the psychologist by the whole process—especially by those moments when it seemed that the new man was conceived. In those miraculous moments lay the heart of a psychic mystery.

Inferno contains the first vivid description of one of these critical moments. "Have you ever heard," Strindberg asks his readers, "that rumbling in the ears that sounds like the noise of a watermill?"

Have you noticed in moments of solitude, during the night or even in broad daylight, how memories rise from the past, one by one, two by two? All the mistakes you have made, all the crimes you have committed, all the follies, come and make the blood tingle in your ears, the sweat break through your scalp, shivers run down your spine. You relive your whole life, from the day you were born to the present moment. You suffer again all the sufferings you once endured. You drink again the bitter dregs of the cups you have drunk so often. You crucify your bones because no flesh remains to mortify. You immolate your soul because your heart is already in ashes.

You know what I am talking about.

These are the mills of God, and though they grind slowly they grind exceedingly small. You are reduced to powder and think that it is all finished with. But no, it will begin again, and you will be ground yet again between those millstones. Be happy! It is hell here on earth. Luther recognized it, Luther who esteemed it a particular sign of grace to be ground to powder this side of the empyrean.

Be happy, contented, and grateful. [SS, 28:193][2]

Those moments of solitude and silence in which Maeterlinck could feel the tremblings of the soul were for Strindberg the moments when the soul was shattered. He learned to accommodate himself, masochistically, to these tribulations of soul and agonies of body by taking them as a sign that he was someone special, one of the elect, one man picked out of ten thousand. After thirty days of torment, he felt born again.

I awoke at last from my bad dream, and I understood the benevolent will of the stern Master who had been punishing me with a hard and knowing hand. Now I understood the obscure and sublime words of Job: "Happy is the man whom God correcteth."

Happy, because for the "others" he does not trouble himself at all. [SS, 28:120][3]

The logic behind this is familiar to theologians. To others it would seem that if Strindberg is tormented inwardly he must be guilty of something. The theologians make a virtue of suffering and argue that, since we are all guilty in one way or another, the susceptibility to inner torments is evidence of being among the chosen ones of God. "The elect are those who have had a conscience," said Strindberg, paraphrasing Swedenborg, "the condemned are those who have lacked a conscience" [SS, 46:77]. Our qualms of conscience may count for more in the Book of Life by which we are finally judged than our transgressions.

Shakespeare may be making a similar point in *Macbeth*. At the beginning of the play Macbeth is a man of great heart who must be goaded into criminal acts by his apparently conscienceless wife. After the murders, after the ghost of Banquo appears at the supper table to haunt him, Macbeth inures himself to the pricks of conscience. He becomes an amoral being, a nihilist, for whom life is a tale told by an idiot, full of sound and fury signifying nothing. In contrast, Lady Macbeth acquires a conscience as her husband loses his. Her tortured soul allows her no sleep; the blood on her hands is beyond the power of man to remove, and she dies a victim of her remorse.

What I am presenting here is essentially Strindberg's perceptive interpretation of the play (SS, 50:164–76). Lady Macbeth, says Strindberg, infuses her husband with her own evil will and desire. But having done so, she is free of the evil that was her strength; she weakens, declines mentally and physically, suffers agonies of conscience, and dies, while Macbeth takes on her evil will and develops it into a bestial ferocity.

Macbeth remains a somewhat melodramatic villain, and one of the difficulties in producing this tragedy is that the viewer is likely to find Lady Macbeth the more interesting character. Unfortunately, Shakespeare did not delineate the change that takes place in her. We can follow with our ears and eyes Macbeth's degradation step by step. Not so with Lady Macbeth. At the end of act 3, she is still the remorseless woman supporting her ghost-ridden husband. At the beginning of act 5, she abruptly appears as a deeply perturbed woman, walking in her sleep, ceaselessly washing her hands. What happened to her during act 4 when she was not present to our eyes? Shakespeare does not tell us.

Now it is precisely here, where Shakespeare fails us, that Strindberg makes a unique contribution to dramatic art. Shakespeare, with his insight into all forms of human nature, could certainly have offered some explanation for the collapse of Lady Macbeth. He must have hesitated to do so because his explanation would not be theatrically effective. When the conscience is working, the body is still. "Those who act never have a conscience," said Goethe. "The only ones with a conscience are those who contemplate."[4] Shakespeare could picture Macbeth overcoming his conscience by throwing him into battle against his enemies. It is different with Lady Macbeth. Her enemies are within her, and when she fights against them, there is no clatter of arms, only the silent washing of her hands. The fact that nothing much happens outwardly poses a problem for the dramatist. But there is a second and greater problem: how to explain why this hard-hearted woman, who would willingly dash out the brains of the babe at her breast if that would further her ambitions, should ever feel the qualms of conscience. Shakespeare gives no answer.

2

What Shakespeare avoided, other dramatists shunned too. As with Lady Macbeth, heroes who undergo a profound change of heart and soul are shown before and after the conversion, not in the midst of it. Even Hamlet has to be transported to England and removed from our sight in order to return a changed man who has learned that there is a divinity that shapes our ends and a special providence in the fall of a sparrow. An exception is the peasant guilty of infanticide in Tolstoy's *The Power of Darkness*. Interrupted in the business of hanging himself in a barn, he regains his lost soul as he listens to the rambling mutterings of a drunken hired hand. This scene of a conversion is remarkable because it is so rare.

Strindberg's great achievement was to bring off-stage conversions onto the stage and to disclose exactly what was happening within the convert's mind. He did not accomplish this simply by describing his own experiences during the critical year 1896. He would not have been able to find a suitable dramatic expression for the process of conversion if he had looked only to the dramatic masterpieces of the past. Instead he delved into mysticism and philosophy, and what he needed he found in Swedenborg and Kierkegaard.

The most troublesome point in Kierkegaard's philosophy was the leap of faith that was necessary to attain the religious stage of life. Inclined to avoid metaphysical thinking and determined to build his great scientific project upward from the material world, Strindberg had to find some firm ground between psychological man and religious man. In 1896 Swedenborg came to his aid.

It is astonishing that up to that time Strindberg had been virtually ignorant of the works of the greatest Swedish mystic and visionary, except for the book recording his dreams and fantasies, and it is ironic that he was introduced to them by occultists in France. Although he could hardly have reached middle age without some awareness of his great compatriot's accomplishments, there is no strong reason to doubt him when he says that Swedenborg did not become of significance to him until some time in 1896. What made the poet and psychologist ripe for the mystic and divine at that particular time? Briefly, the answer is that Strindberg's magnum opus had reached the same critical juncture that Swedenborg's own scientific project had reached 150 years earlier. Strindberg was trying to bridge the gap between natural man and spiritual man, and Swedenborg had faced the same problem. Eminent as an engineer and inventor, absolute master of the physical sciences, Swedenborg in the middle of the eighteenth century had endeavored to find the point at which nerve endings, becoming ever finer, evanesce into thought and ideas. Peering ever closer at ever finer filaments of matter, he suddenly plunged through troubling dreams into an other-worldly space in which he found himself conversing familiarly with angels. From them, he learned of the doctrine of correspondences, learned that matter and spirit are as intimately connected as water and wave and that any mental activity manifests itself in the physical world. Does not a happy frame of mind, for instance, reveal itself in a beaming countenance? With respect to matter and spirit, the doctrine was only a revival of a Neoplatonist principle: "as above, so below." However, when Swedenborg applied it to analyzing the unconscious sphere of mental life, which he called the inner or spiritual memory, he opened up a whole new area of speculation.

This is what made the doctrine of correspondences irresistible to Strindberg. In the spring of 1896 he was fumbling his way into the unconscious, grasping at all sorts of strange ideas in the hope that one of them might light the way. When he heard from the Parisian occultists about the concept of double existences, according to which the "other self," the unconscious, takes its abode in another body, he immediately put it to the test. The psychological experiment that he carried out in July 1896 was intended to summon forth his other self. Still, though Strindberg had encountered some of Swedenborg's ideas in May 1896, the doctrine of correspondences made no impression on him until after the July experiment.[5] It was then that he required a method or scheme for dealing with the other self, the second consciousness, in order to make it serve as the link in his great system between psychological man and religious man. What he got from Swedenborg was the idea of direct correspondences between two levels of existence. This improved on and replaced the older theory of double existences, which was too easily controverted by his own observations even when he was most disposed to believe. Now he could affirm with less fear of contradiction that "parallel with our earthly existence we live a second life on the astral plane, but unconsciously" [SS, 46:22].

In adapting this doctrine of correspondences to the theatre, Strindberg resolved, probably encouraged by the success of Maeterlinck's symbolic plays, to let the stage represent that borderland between reality and dream that he had inhabited during the Inferno crisis. Using the Swedenborgian idea of correspondences between the natural world and the world of spirits, that borderland was made to serve as the area in which the subtle and unseen tremors of the soul would manifest themselves in the visible and palpable things of the physical world.

Kierkegaard offered the dramatist a different kind of assistance.

Strindberg found in the religious thinker a scheme for reducing to order the chaos of the Inferno experiences, of arranging them in a pattern that revealed meaning, Kierkegaard explained the sufferings of Job as a trial of probation in which Job is placed in a relationship with God that transcends poetic justice or workaday morality. At the end of his ordeal, which Job does not know is a probation, he gets back what he thought he had lost. To Kierkegaard, the meaning behind this story that seems to end where it began lies in the fact that Job receives not only what he had lost but also something he had never had before. Having wrestled with God and lost, he takes back from the experience a new self, a religious self that was not his before the trial. The repetition of the outer situation accompanies a profound change in the inner man. Kierkegaard terms the process Gjentagelsen, which means both taking back and repetition.

Strindberg employed this idea to direct the events of To Damascus, Part One. "The trick to the whole thing," he explained,

lies in the composition, which symbolizes the Gjentagelsen that Kierkegaard writes about. The action unrolls toward [the central scene in] the Asylum, turns at that point, kicks against the prick, and is spurred back to the beginning—a pilgrimage, a being made to do one's lessons again, getting paid back in spades. Then something new begins at the place where the game ends and where it began.[6]

In sending his hero back along the road to repeat all the encounters of the first half of the journey, Strindberg may appear to have appropriated the manner of Kierkegaard's essay Repetition: An Essay in Experimental Psychology without its matter. But a careful scrutiny shows that the dramatist understood what was involved in the philosopher's concept. Kierkegaard defined recollection and repetition as movements in opposite directions, recollection taking one backwards into temporality and the physical world, repetition carrying one forward into the transcendent and providing a springboard for a leap into religion. If To Damascus were acted on the purely realistic level, the hero, Strindberg's other self, would accomplish no more than Kierkegaard's experimental self did on his sentimental journey to Berlin. Since the action of To Damascus takes place above and below the realistic level, however, the journey through the stages of life becomes in its last half an ascent of the spirit toward its source, even though Strindberg leaves him suspended in skepticism and ready for more experiments at the end. Still, it is clear that the hero has come to recognize at least the possibility of the kind of rebirth comprehended in Kierkegaard's Gjentagelsen, the new life that the New Testament holds out to man.

3

Now both the peregrinations of the hero and the structure of the play conveyed the idea of spiritual renewal. Another problem remained to be solved, however, a problem of motivation. What causes the action to reverse itself at one particular point and not at another? Or, to put the question with regard to Lady Macbeth: at what point does she cease being a villainess and become the victim of her crimes? What thoughts occur to her while she is out of our sight in the fourth act that cause her to feel true remorse and to come back into our vision a radically changed woman? A number of easy answers may suggest themselves, but the dramatist must find one that works on stage, and in a drama of conversion it must be one that is so dramatically right and psychologically sound that the action of the whole play can pivot on it.

Again Strindberg found an answer in Swedenborg. The concept of double existences, or double consciousnesses, was all right as far as it went, but it did not go far enough. As long as each existence held its course and kept its own counsel, no discoveries could be made. Strindberg was looking for the mystical point where the parallel existences might meet. For Swedenborg, there was such a point. It lay in the dark night of the soul, in that anguishing experience he called vastation, and when Strindberg read Swedenborg's description of it, he recognized his own Inferno. Vastation simply means, said Swedenborg, "being let into one's internals, that is, into what is the spirit's own."[7] It means seeing one's spirit divested of the masks and trappings that society and convention make it wear, seeing the goods and evils of one's life neatly separated and weighed. By being vastated, man enters, at least temporarily, another level of existence.

For the psychologist, vastation opened a door to the unconscious. For the playwright, it provided the central or climactic scene, because the divesting or disrobing of the spirit is inherently dramatic. It was the Strindbergian equivalent of what Aristotle called recognition (*anagnorisis*), a prime ingredient in the Greek formula for effective drama. Strindberg probably could not have returned to the writing of plays until he had seen that in vastation lay the key to a drama of the psyche. Aristotle also points out that the very best kind of dramatic plot combines the recognition with a peripety, a sharp reversal in the hero's fortunes. When Oedipus learns the truth about himself, he is simultaneously and instantly transformed from the most fortunate of men to the most unfortunate. A comparable moment is lacking in *Macbeth*. Shakespeare's tragic hero marches on from crime to crime until his enemies overcome him. After his first crimes, he does not change in any fundamental way: he only becomes more of what he was before. Lady Macbeth, however, does undergo a radical change. She is vastated; she sees herself as she really is and, unable to bear the sight, collapses.

It is obvious that a reversal in a drama is no reversal unless there are events leading up to it and events leading away from it. (Fifth act conversions are not reversals but catastrophes.) Swedenborg's vastation becomes for Strindberg a powerful dramatic device because it is part of a meaningful sequence of events with a beginning, a middle, and an end. Swedenborg tells us that when men die, their souls first enter a state of exteriors where they are rather like what they were here on earth except that they have lost their fleshly incasement. Next the soul or spirit enters a state of interiors where it sees itself as it truly is. Here, Swedenborg says, "hidden things [are] laid open and secret things uncovered."[8] For many, if not most, spirits this amounts to vastation, with the truths and goods being separated from the falsities and evils. After this, a good spirit will move to heaven, but a thoroughly evil spirit will cast itself into hell in pursuit of congenial company, thinking nothing but what is false and doing nothing but what is evil.

None of this would have much moral import, however, unless what happens to the soul after death corresponds to what occurs in its earthly existence. And such is the case. Swedenborg's hell is surprisingly like Sartre's: it epitomizes one's life on earth. Swedenborg rejected the redemption theory and saw that man's acts are his fate. Moreover, since the whole natural world corresponds to the spiritual world, and since "no man can live . . . unless he is conjoined . . . with the world of spirits, nay, with hell, through the spirits that are within him," it is possible for man to experience vastation and see hell while in the life of the body.[9] Drawing on his own experiences Strindberg described vastation as a summing up of the past.

The debit side shows a horrifying plus. Scenes from one's past life, unrolling as if on a panorama, are seen in a new light. Forgotten things are dug up; the smallest incident is brought to light. . . . It is Judgment Day. . . . Swedenborg calls this natural process vastation of evil. The pietists call it the "awakening" before conversion. [SS, 46:33–34]

Only those who have a conscience and who can hear the voice of the soul suffer the agonies of vastation while here in the life of the body. For the man of action, remorse for what is done is idle and useless. But for the Swedenborgian man of conscience, to be tortured here by memories of his misdeeds and follies is to turn from hell to heaven. To be vastated here is to be reborn spiritually.

The process, which is obscured in the novel *Inferno* by the wealth of details and by Strindberg's inability at the time he wrote it to separate the significant details from the insignificant, is brought into relief in *To Damascus*. In the novel Strindberg is like a scientist who is only halfway toward discovering the formula that is implicit in the data he has collected. In the play he has found it. During the first scenes the Stranger manages to suppress his feelings of guilt. But in the sixth scene, set in the ravine, they break out, threatening him on all sides. The profile of the Doctor looms ominously in the crags. A blacksmith shop emits a red glow in intimation of hell. The mill suggests the mills of God. The inexplicable sound of a hunting horn makes the Stranger feel he is the prey of unknown forces relentlessly pursuing him. Crossing the river, he descends into his past. In the central scene of the play, the ninth, the inmates of the monastery asylum are transformed in his eyes into the ghostly doubles of those he has hurt and offended.

This is the first of Strindberg's many attempts to put on stage that moment of crisis he described in *Inferno*, the reliving of one's life, especially the cruelties and stupidities that trouble the conscience, the moment when the mills of God grind the conscience-stricken soul to powder. A drowning man is supposed to see his whole life flash before him; the guilty man, when he sees himself for what he is, sees only his misdeeds and errors. The review of life or, more fittingly, the review of guilt,[10] this panorama of transgressions, forms part of the process of vastation, which is the prerequisite to spiritual rebirth.

That is why this scene in *To Damascus* is not as melodramatic and as emotionally charged as one might have expected. Encountering the ghosts of his past, and hearing the curse from Deuteronomy pronounced on him, the Stranger's response is cool and subdued: no wailing and lamenting, no writhing in agony, no praying for forgiveness. Instead of admitting his sins and trespasses, instead of being reduced to fear and trembling by the ghosts, the Stranger reminds the prior that Deuteronomy also offers a blessing. Two factors determine the Stranger's attitude. On the one hand, his self-esteem has not yet been entirely crushed; his ego can still find strength to banish the ghosts from his sight. Significantly, Strindberg's stage direction calls for the Stranger to sit with his back to the inmates, the ghosts. On the other hand, he evidently has a presentiment that his tribulations are not a punishment for his sins but a presage of a different life to come. This moment in the play is the counterpart to that moment of recognition in the novel when Strindberg understands the meaning of Job's words: "Happy is the man whom God correcteth." Knowing he is one of the chosen, the Stranger can find a means of accommodation with his conscience. His besieged ego consents to the invasion of the ghosts when his sense of sin confers on the ego the honor of being one of the elect.

The process of rebirth, muddled and confused as presented in *Inferno*, is clearly delineated in *To Damascus*. Each step by which the new man comes into the light is set forth. The vastation of the old spirit does not end in the asylum; it continues three scenes later in the kitchen. In that scene, the Stranger can no longer turn his back on the ghosts that haunt him. There his real agonies are externalized and displayed. Elsewhere, Strindberg lists the symptoms of vastation:

constrictions of the chest, shortness of breath, feelings of suffocation, pains in the heart, horrible attacks of anguish, sleeplessness, nightmares. . . . The angina pectoris and the insomnia, all the nocturnal horrors . . . are nothing other than the work of the invisible ones. [SS, 28:293][11]

Because it is the easiest to represent theatrically, Strindberg shows only the angina pectoris; but it is enough. The Stranger's pride is broken, if only for a moment. He is almost brought to his knees in agony of body, if not in humility of spirit, the esoteric and exoteric causes being conjoined, as always, in Strindberg. There, in the kitchen, the Stranger learns that the darkest hour is nearest the dawn; there he sees the light of the morning star; and there his substitute mother presides over his rebirth.

4

Structurally, the vastation brings about a reversal of events, a peripety. When the Stranger seems most damned, he is closer to being blessed than he ever was before. This kind of reversal, in which opposites meet, as in Sophocles's treatment of the Oedipus story, is the essence of drama.

But however dramatic it might be, a spiritual vastation is not the essence of theatre. It is too subjective, and nowhere is Strindberg more theatrically inventive than in his efforts to convert spiritual drama into stage drama. On some occasions he succeeded so well that no one noticed what he had accomplished, it was all so theatrical.

There is, for instance, the extraordinary reversal that occurs in *The*

Dance of Death, Part One, a play that is often misunderstood as being a naturalistic play like *The Father*. On the surface it is, but with Strindberg, appearances are deceptive. It is true that the setting and the characters are more solid than those in *To Damascus*. The characters even have names. And it is true that *The Dance of Death* does point forward to plays like O'Neill's *Long Day's Journey Into Night* and Albee's *Who's Afraid of Virginia Woolf?*, which are naturalistic insofar as the dialogue is concerned and the fullness with which the characters are drawn. *The Dance of Death* also has the unpleasant atmosphere of the two American plays. In all three plays, the characters spend most of their time accusing each other of various assortments of venial and deadly sins, and beneath all the viperous talk lies a mutual guilt that seeks an outlet in the accusations.

There is also a similarity in the plots of the Albee and Strindberg plays. While the middle-aged spouses are abusing each other as failures, another man enters their home, and he becomes the instrument by which the wife hopes to offer the ultimate insult to her husband. Intruder and wife make love, but things do not work out quite as the wife had expected. The man leaves, and the middle-aged couple find themselves alone again, now with a better understanding of each other. The wife in Strindberg's play finds that her husband is a man after all, and the wife in Albee's play learns that the husband she ridicules and savages is the only person who can give her what little happiness she will ever get from life.

The tone of these two plays is also very much alike. The intruder in *The Dance of Death* says the husband "would be comic if he weren't so tragic" (SS, 34:70). The audience has the opposite point of view: the characters on stage would be tragic if they weren't so comic. The result is *Schadenfreude* on both sides of the footlights. The situation is absurd because these people insist on making things as unpleasant as possible for themselves. Their laughter is either a cruel weapon or a howl of despair. In either case it comes from the abyss.

So it should in a play set in hell. Reading Swedenborg, Strindberg found that the visionary, in describing hell, might as well have been describing life on earth. In a sense he was. The Swedenborgian hell is not so much a physical place as a society of like-minded people who like the things of this world and will do anything to get what they like. The governors of Dante's inferno and Brueghel's hell employ an army of expert torturers. Swedenborg's hell is run much more economically: the inhabitants of hell are their own tormentors, who need not even be taught their trade because they simply continue to behave as they did on earth, only

more intensely, since they have nothing else to do. The dwellers in hell
are spirits, and by spirits, Swedenborg means ourselves as we are inwardly, as we would be if we did not live in a society in which good and
evil are mixed together. In the world of spirits the good and bad are
sorted out. An evil person in hell is in the company of kindred spirits, all
freely exercising their evil wills. They merely continue their earthly behavior without the moderating influence of good people. Though Swedenborg's heaven and hell may seem medieval, his moral universe is
very modern. Jean-Paul Sartre's existential version of hell as other people is very Swedenborgian and completely Strindbergian. In Strindberg's
entire dramatic production, said Sartre,

there are only characters in situations, who in the midst of these situations are
nothing but what they make of others and what others make of them. . . . All
those who nowadays think that man is not something other than his life can
profit from a study of Strindberg's drama.[12]

The two plays that Sartre specifically referred to were *Creditors* and *The
Dance of Death*, and Sartre's *No Exit* is their offspring.[13] Like *Creditors*,
No Exit is a ninety-minute one-act play in which the essential lives of
three characters are revealed in the situation in which they find themselves, and that situation is strictly the result of what they have done in
the past.

In *No Exit*, hell is a Second Empire parlor. In *The Dance of Death*,
hell is an island fortress, known locally as Little Hell, in which an army
captain, Edgar, and his wife, Alice, live in virtual isolation. Twenty-five
years earlier, when they married, he had planned a career as a commanding officer, and she had dreamed of a career on the stage. He never got to
be a major; she never got to be a great actress. Now they live in an army
post in the provinces, passing the time playing cards and deriding each
other as failures. Originally built as part of a prison, the round room that
serves as their parlor is a visual metaphor of the sameness and monotony
and inescapability of their lives. Outside on the battlements, a sentry
paces back and forth, his figure appearing at regular intervals with clock-
like precision, the sound of his boots on the stones unremittingly fading
away and returning, his crested helmet enhancing his ominous appearance, while his unsheathed saber, held at a slope to his shoulder,
glitters now and then in the opening scene of the play as it catches the
red glow of the setting sun. This sentry, whose endless pacing provided
one of the memorable effects in Max Reinhardt's famous production[14] of
the play, is part of the hell imagery. He is the monster that Swedenborg

says guards the gates of hell, a monster "that represents in a general way the form of those within." [15]

The Captain is one of the great virtuoso roles in the modern theater, a part fashioned for the stage and for acting on the grand scale. Giving advice to the young actor (too young) who played the part in 1909, Strindberg described the Captain as "an exquisitely cruel devil." Acting out the part as he spoke, Strindberg said the Captain's

eyes shine with evil, and sometimes a glint of satanic humor flashes in them. His face is puffy from alcohol and dissipation, and he takes such delight in saying nasty things that he practically sucks on them, savoring them, licking them, before he spits them out. Of course he thinks he is clever and better than others, but like all stupid people, he becomes at such times only a pitiable, choleric wretch. [16]

What makes him such a devil is his materialism and his atheism. He thinks he is completely self-sufficient, and he believes only in himself and his physical powers.

"When the machinery breaks down," he says, "you take what's left, put it in a wheelbarrow, and haul it out to manure the garden. But as long as the gears are turning, you've got to use them, use your hands and feet, keep slugging and kicking as long as the parts hold out! That's my philosophy" (SS, 34:34).

The movement into the world of spirits, into the state of interiors, begins with the arrival of an old acquaintance, Curt, whom Edgar and Alice have not seen in fifteen years. Life has taught Curt that there are other powers in the world besides the physical ones. To act out his own philosophy to Curt and to demonstrate his physical vigor, the Captain dances wildly, overexerts himself, suffers a stroke, and nearly dies. Having been "on the other side of the grave" (SS, 34:119), he returns to the living with intimations of immortality—his own. "I exist," says this monumental egotist, "therefore there is a God" (SS, 34:69).

Willing to accept the idea of eternal life, he still rejects the idea of good and evil, of heaven and hell. "You don't believe in hell?" asks Curt, incredulously, "You who are in the midst of it" (SS, 34:67).

Actually, they are in the midst of their interiors on their way to hell. Plotting against each other to win the affection of Curt, Edgar and Alice behave exactly like those spirits without conscience that Swedenborg describes.

When such in the other life enter into the state of their interiors, and are heard speaking and seen acting, they appear foolish; for from their evil lusts they burst forth into all sorts of abominations, into contempt of others, ridicule and blasphemy, hatred and revenge: they plot intrigues, some with a cunning and malice that can scarcely be believed to be possible in any man. For they are then in a state of freedom to act in harmony with the thoughts of their will, since they are separated from the outward conditions that restrained and checked them in the world. In a word, they are deprived of their rationality, because their reason while they were in the world did not have its seat in their interiors, but in their exteriors; and yet they seemed to themselves to be wiser than others.[17]

This state of interiors is intermediate between heaven and hell. Once their interiors are revealed, the souls move on toward their destination. For Edgar and Alice, this movement is shown in the third scene, in the full light of the sun of the world, which, according to Swedenborg, "implies both the salvation of the good and the damnation of the wicked."[18] As Edgar rushes toward hell, his face glows phosphorescently like that of a devil.[19] The natural or exoteric explanation for his appearance is that he is still suffering the effects of his stroke. Hell is the place of deceit, self-love, and physical lust, and no part of it is omitted in this scene. To revenge himself on Curt, the Captain has used his influence in the army to take Curt's son from him, and to revenge himself on Alice, he announces that he has begun divorce proceedings against her. She responds to this by embracing Curt lustfully and unbuttoning her bodice. Curt lifts her up, bites and kisses her throat, then hurls her down and runs out of the room. That Dracula bite on the throat shows how far Curt has descended into the hell of Alice and Edgar.

In the notable productions of The Dance of Death, this has always been one of the great acting scenes. In the 1920 Danish staging,[20] Bodil Ipsen made the scene a tour de force. After Curt fled from her, she laughed; the laughter changed to sobbing; she hid her face in shame; and to her soft crying, the curtain fell.

The next scene is perhaps the most theatrical scene in the play. In the book, it consists of a page of stage directions without any dialogue. In performance, it invariably affords a great actor a chance to display his genius. The Captain, alone, plays solitaire for a while, then impatiently gives it up and throws the cards out the window. Then he throws out his whiskey bottles, his cigars, and his spectacles. He closes the lid of the piano, locks it, and throws the key out the window. He lights the candle on the piano (figure 16). He tears up the picture of his wife and takes the pictures of his two children and puts them in his breast pocket. He sits at his desk, clutches at his heart, stares as if seeing some horrible vision. He takes a package of old letters and throws it on the fire. Suddenly, the telegraphy apparatus makes a single clicking sound. Startled, he waits for it to continue. It does not. A noise at the door now attracts him. He steps out and comes back with a cat. He strokes it, and with the cat in his arms, he leaves the room.

"Naturalism," says the ordinary viewer and critic. "A picture of a man in utter desolation."

"Supernaturalism," says the Swedenborgian. "A picture of a man undergoing vastation."

The portrait of his wife and the letters represent his past life, which is now passing in review in his mind. In throwing away his whiskey and cigars, he is rejecting the natural man. In throwing away his spectacles, he is rejecting the outer world and turning inward to things of the spirit. The candle he lights signifies spiritual light as opposed to the natural light of the sun, which represents the passions. The terrifying single unexplained click of the telegraph is a signal from the spirits that the accounts have been added up. At that very point, the direction of the Captain's spiritual life is reversed. Having been vastated of evils and falsities, he is in a state to be brought back into the order of heaven by means of mediating spirits. The cat is the mediating spirit. Man is born into evils, says Swedenborg, and must be brought into the divine order, but animals are born into the natural order and are governed by the general influx from the spiritual world.[21] The cat represents the influx of spirit into the Captain's life and signifies his conversion.

5

Although Alice and Edgar are in hell, they are also in the natural world, in the life of the body. The world, says Strindberg, "is a reflection of your inner self and of the inner selves of others, from which it is probable that each man carries his heaven and hell within him" (SS, 46:30). This conception of a hell of the living is less pessimistic than it seems because it contains the possibility of change, and The Dance of Death is another one of Strindberg's conversion dramas. The egocentric and utterly materialistic Captain of the first scene learns to see himself and others in a new light, and how this happens determines the shape of the play. In its structure, it resembles To Damascus, with the central scene, the third, bringing Edgar, Alice, and Curt farthest along the road to hell. The Dance of Death is more Swedenborgian than To Damascus, however, since each scene corresponds to a stage in the Swedenborgian progress of souls. The first scene shows the state of exteriors; the second, the state of interiors; the third, the preparation for heaven or hell; the fourth, the purgation or vastation; and the fifth, the return to the state of exteriors.

In the last scene, the Captain reveals that he never tried to separate Curt from his son and that he never began divorce proceedings against Alice. He invented those lies to hurt those who were hurting him. Now he asks Curt's forgiveness. When Alice embraces Curt again, Edgar rushes at her, swinging his saber but hitting only the furniture. His bumbling bravado drains what little strength was in him, and he falls to the floor.

"Hurrah, he's dead!" exults Alice.

He isn't. He struggles to his feet and sheathes his sword. Alice runs to Curt. He throws her to her knees.

"Down, back to the abyss you came from!" he says to her, and leaves (SS, 34:115).

Edgar's collapse in this scene matches his stroke in the first scene, as the action of the play continues to reverse itself. Abandoned by Curt, Alice must make her peace with her husband. Unfortunately, in plotting her revenge on him, she conveyed to the authorities evidence that he was embezzling army funds. When the telegraph begins to tap out a message, she is certain she will lose Edgar. She implores him not to listen, falls on her knees, and prays to God. A long ticker tape (the counterpart of the letter in *To Damascus*) has been emerging from the telegraph. She reads it, raises her eyes to heaven in gratitude that the tape contains nothing of importance, and kisses Edgar. Like him, she has had a foretaste of hell itself and is the better for it.

They settle down to the bickering and gibing that has become habitual with them. But there is a change. Out of fear and loneliness, the Captain has exchanged his completely materialistic philosophy for a belief that man consists of body and soul and that there is a life of the spirit as well as a life of the body. "When I fell the first time," he says, "I went more than a piece beyond the grave. What I saw I have forgotten, but the impression remains. . . . That this is life itself, I've never really believed that. This is death. Or something even worse" (SS, 34:119).

Everything that happens has a natural explanation, but what gives the events a special flavor and raises the play above naturalistic drama are the Swedenborgian correspondences between the physical and spiritual planes. The water that surrounds Little Hell signifies the boundaries of heaven and the separation of natural man from spiritual man. When Curt *casts* (Strindberg stresses the word) Alice into a chaise lounge after kissing her on the throat, he is casting her into hell. When he kisses her foot in the last scene, he does so because spirits are cast into hell head foremost and because hell is beneath the soles of the feet. These correspondences are all to be found in Swedenborg,[22] but the telegraph is Strindberg's own and represents Anschluss mit Jenzeits, contact with the beyond. It keeps Little Hell in touch with the mainland, and it puts the Swedenborgian angels and spirits in touch with Edgar and Alice.

None of these correspondences can be made explicit in staging the play. On the other hand, they should not be ignored. Strindberg's mysticism enhances the theatricality of his drama, just as Yeats's mysticism inspires the imagery of his poetry. The Captain speaks (in the last scene) of seeing life from a different angle, and the spectators should feel that they are seeing reality from a different angle. The success of Max Reinhardt's production of The Dance of Death was due in part to the blending of the coarsest naturalism with an obvious otherworldliness. The acting did more than any other element in the production to bring together the two planes of the drama. It was a kind of acting that was new to the modern theatre, as a German critic noted.

Behind the sharply etched figures, symbols are projected, and the light from them is thrown on the events. The actor seems lit by a searchlight, and he may not step out of the cone of light. This limits indeed his freedom of action, but it endues his performance with a spiritual quality and raises it occasionally to the transcendental.[23]

Reinhardt, however, did not understand that the transcendental element was supposed to change the outlook of Edgar and Alice. To judge from his management of the last moment of the play, he did not see The Dance of Death as a conversion drama. In a bit of directorial business that was much admired, Reinhardt ended the play exactly as it began,[24] with Edgar and Alice sitting far apart from each other, their backs toward the audience, staring out into nothingness. This violated Strindberg's stage direction, which says that the Captain rises from his chair to speak his last line. Still, when the play was produced at his own theatre in 1909, Strindberg approved his director's ending, in which Edgar goes to the liquor cabinet and pours himself a shot of whiskey as he had done at the beginning of the play (SS, 34:217).

The point of Strindberg's cyclic arrangement is to show that, though the outward situation is the same, the inner state has changed. The ending, he said, proclaims "the great resignation without which life is impossible."[25] This necessitates a return of the physical action to its origin while at the same time there must be a suggestion that the spirit has moved forward. In England and America, parts 1 and 2 of The Dance of

Death have often been cut and combined into one play, destroying the cyclic structure of part 1. Even Laurence Olivier's production suffered from this fault. Part 1 has the same structure as *Waiting for Godot*, another twentieth-century play for which *The Dance of Death* is the paradigm. Strindberg is less pessimistic than Beckett, however, and the ending that Reinhardt contrived, which prefigures the image of Beckett's two tramps motionless in undefined space, is wrong for Strindberg. Edgar and Alice may still needle each other as they did at the beginning of the play, but their barbs penetrate less deeply. An unromantic, unmawkish attachment is formed between them, much more common in reality than the sentimental love that the theatre has always preferred to depict. The lesson they have learned in hell is that even demons need spiritual support, a love of some kind, to carry them through the day and that, as far as they are concerned, neither angels and good souls nor sweetness and light will serve that purpose. Like Martha and George in *Who's Afraid of Virginia Woolf?* and like Gogo and Didi in *Waiting for Godot*, Edgar and Alice need each other because each other is all they have.

In the last minutes of the play, they see themselves for what they are and make the best of things. Having been vastated, having caught a glimpse of the other side, and knowing that the machinery, his body, may fail him at any moment, Edgar is disposed to make the first conciliatory gestures.

ALICE. And now I suppose you think I'm going to be your nurse.
EDGAR. If you want.
ALICE. What else should I do with myself?
EDGAR. I don't know.
ALICE. (*sits down apathetically. Looks crushed.*) This must be the everlasting fire. Is there no end?
EDGAR. There is, if we have patience. Maybe when death comes, life begins.
ALICE. Would it were so!
    (*Pause.*)
EDGAR. So you think Curt was a fake and hypocrite?
ALICE. Of course.
EDGAR. I don't believe it. The trouble is that anyone who comes near us becomes like us. Then off they go. Curt was weak, and we were too strong for him.
    (*Pause.*)
    Still, it's all so boring nowadays. There was a time when men fought with their bare fists; now they only shake them at each other. . . . Tell you what I do believe, though. In three months I'm pretty certain that you and I will be giving a party—our silver anniversary. With cousin Curt giving you away—again, like he did twenty-five years ago. And the supply officer will be toastmaster, making pretty speeches. And my staff sergeant will lead the singing:

"For they are jolly good fellows. . . ." And if I know my man, the Colonel will pop up too. Uninvited.

(ALICE *laughs.*)

You think that's funny? What about Adolf's silver anniversary? You know, Adolf in the combat engineers. His bride of twenty-five years had to wear her wedding ring on her right hand because Adolf in one of his tender moments had chopped off her left ring finger with a machete.

(ALICE *puts her handkerchief to her mouth to suppress a giggle.*)

EDGAR. I know. It's enough to make you cry.—Ah, ha, you're laughing. Well, my precious, sometimes we laugh, sometimes we cry. I don't know which is right. . . . I read in the paper the other day about a man. Been divorced seven times. Consequently married seven times. Finally ran away—ninety-eight years old—and remarried his first wife! If that isn't love, what is? . . . Whether life is a serious business or simply a big joke, that's something I've never been able to figure out. As jokes go, it's rather sick. Better to take it seriously. Makes it more peaceful and pleasant. . . . However, just when you've made up your mind to be serious, along comes somebody who puts you on. Like Curt. . . . Well, what do you say? A party for our silver anniversary?

(ALICE *is silent.*)

EDGAR. Oh, come on! Say yes. Sure, they'll laugh at us, but what the hell! We'll laugh with them. Or be very solemn. Whatever we feel like.

ALICE. All right. Why not?

EDGAR (*seriously*). Right. A silver wedding anniversary.

(*He stands up.*)

Wipe out and move on. So—let's move on. [SS, 34:120–22]

Strindberg approached the problem of putting the inner life of man on stage in two ways. Sometimes he painted a grossly realistic picture over a symbolic one, with the latter determining the form of the over-painting. This was the method used in *The Dance of Death*. Sometimes he created a representation of the inner life entirely out of symbols and let it be acted out through a shimmer of reality. This was the method of *To Damascus*, Part One. That play, with its

CHAPTER EIGHT

THE CHASTISING SPIRITS

perfect blending of method and matter, seemed to accomplish all that Strindberg had set out to do. But he felt otherwise, and a second part of *To Damascus* followed hard upon the first.

To anyone who expects more of the same, Part Two is an alarming disappointment. The tone is bitter; the humor, cruel and scathing; the people, vicious and demonic; and what happens to them, unfathomable. The Woman, no longer roguish, saucy, and seductive, is as burdened with guilt as the Stranger; and the Stranger, who now fully believes in the occult powers, carries on like a mad scientist in a melodrama. Having passed through the chapel at the end of Part One, he appears to have descended into a realm far more hellish than the inferno he had left behind. Nor do his new adventures carry him much beyond the point he had reached earlier. At the end of the second part, he leaves with a priest to enter a monastery, spurning both wife and newborn child. In contrast to the conciliatory note sounded at the end of the first part, the Stranger's final words here strike a jarring discord. "Look, she's afraid I'll wake the child, that little monster who took her from me! Come, priest, before I change my mind" (SS, 29:235).

From the technical point of view, too, the play is disconcerting. Instead of a simple plot embroidered with poetic symbols and resonant with literary echoes, Part Two offers a maddening plot made doubly bewildering by an illogical time scheme and character relationships that defy analysis. On the estate of his wife's family, the Stranger has set up a laboratory to conduct experiments in the transmutation of the elements. By producing cheap gold, he hopes to undermine the economic systems of the leading nations, reduce civilization to chaos, and write the last chapter in the history of mankind. Reading from the Zohar, surrounded

by other occult books, by galvanizers, batteries, an iron stove with crucibles, bellows, and all the other paraphernalia of alchemy, he could be
mistaken for Faust at work in Frankenstein's laboratory. In order to accomplish the transmutation of the elements, he must, like the alchemists
of old, be absolutely pure in spirit. The purification of the elements parallels the perfection of the spirit of the experimenter, an alchemical concept that is the opposite of the modern scientific one. The function of the
Stranger's wife is to rid him of impurities.

"I have to make another person my double," he says,

a double who can absorb all that binds my spirit. So that my soul might find
again that pure fire and air with which it can soar toward the ether, rise above the
Dominations, to reach the throne of the Eternal One, there to place at his foot the
complaints of mankind. [SS, 29:175]

While the Stranger is in the process of making gold in order to
"smash the golden calf and overthrow the tables of the moneychangers,"
his wife is about to give birth to his child (SS, 29:175). The two major
motifs of the play are suggested by the Stranger's alchemical pursuits and
the Woman's pregnancy. He seeks perfection through knowledge, and
once he has achieved his scientific goal, he will rid the Woman of her
sick conscience and raise her, too, above the earthly mire. Knowledge
will accomplish everything. But the unborn child holds down his soaring spirit; the demands of society and family make their claims on him;
and when he receives a letter informing him that he is to be honored at a
banquet for his scientific achievements, he must choose between the way
of godlike knowledge and power and the way of family affection, between forbidden wisdom and sanctified love.

"Faced with the choice between love and learning," Strindberg says
of himself at the beginning of Inferno, "I had decided to attain the sum-
mit of knowledge, and the sacrifice of my affections made me forget the
innocent victim I had immolated along with them on the altar of my ambition, or of my calling" (SS, 28:8).

The Stranger does not hesitate for a moment. Feeling that his marriage to a woman with an unsavory past is a stain on his honor as a man,
he goes to the banquet to establish his honor as a scientist. His first duty,
he says as he departs, is not to provide for his family but to shield his
personality from destruction.

The testimonial dinner is held in a restaurant, where the tables are
laden with pheasant, lobsters, melons, grapes. The guests are formally
attired, many displaying medals of merit and badges of honor. An or-

chestra is playing softly. Everything is as it should be. Except that the orchestra is playing the Mendelssohn Funeral March. As the ceremony honoring the Stranger proceeds, the restaurant, right before his eyes, dissolves bit by bit into a low tavern frequented by the dregs of society, including his old acquaintance, the Beggar. The Stranger is presented with the bill. He cannot pay it and is sent off to jail. There, in the company of the sympathetic and understanding Beggar, he hears the funeral march, the sound of a hunting horn, and the chanting of a rosary. In the next instant he is transported to the Woman's Rose Room, where he finds that his wife is still in labor. This sequence of transformation scenes—banquet, jail, and Rose Room—comprise one of the most brilliant effects in the modern theatre. A Swedish critic has rightly said that these scenes, unsurpassed in their theatricality, form the fountainhead of all expressionistic drama.[1]

Like everything else in the play, the tavern banquet had its origin in reality. In December 1894, Strindberg was to be honored in Paris as the author of The Father with a banquet arranged by the editor of the Symbolist journal La Plume. In July 1896, an international congress of chemists met in Paris, and Strindberg hoped that two or three of the participants would present papers demonstrating the possibility of producing minute traces of gold using methods akin to his own. And there were taverns and cafés in which the highest and lowest classes mixed, especially in the small hours of the night. Strindberg was familiar with them from his nightly wanderings. Nothing came of the banquet, and the following month, Strindberg had to enter a hospital to be treated for psoriasis, a perennial ailment with him now made serious by his chemical experiments. Nor did Strindberg attend the chemists' meeting. But with his theatrical imagination and his genius for combining ideas, he fashioned the banquet-tavern scene out of these elements.[2]

Upon his return to the Rose Room, the Stranger receives another letter, the second in the plot, telling him that his first wife has remarried. What the Stranger has feared most has now come true: his children have another father and are lost to him. The distraught Stranger goes back to the tavern, to take a mud-bath, as he puts it, and to harden his skin against life's stings. In the following scene, he finds himself in a ravine in the company of the Beggar. The three children of his first marriage appear with their mother and stepfather. So does the Doctor, the ex-husband of the Stranger's wife, now quite mad, pursued by his homeless and distraught sister. The final scene of the play takes place in the Rose Room. The child has been born, but the Stranger takes no interest in it.

He is now prepared to enter the church, and the Confessor of Part One presents himself.

The Stranger learns that this priest, who earlier had been identified for the viewer as being the same person as the Beggar and the Dominican, was the Woman's first husband, who entered the church when she deserted him. This news is supposed to ease the Stranger's conscience, since he should be able to see himself as the punisher of his wife's former infidelity. He refuses to do so, and he even doubts that what he has been told is true. Nor does he believe the news that comes to him in a third and final letter, the news that the congress of chemists has arranged to honor him at a banquet.

In spite of the murkiness of the play, the moral of the story manages to shine through. In the first scene, the Dominican enunciates the Swedenborgian theme. Because the Stranger seeks power over the elements instead of receiving the love of truth that is offered to him, God will send strong confusion upon him that he shall believe what is not true. Sure enough, at the end of the play, the Stranger does not believe the good and comforting news that comes to him. "There is the divine punishment," says the Confessor-Dominican. "He shall believe the lie because he would not have the truth" (SS, 29:232).

If this outline does nothing else, it makes one wonder why Strindberg ever bothered to write the play. He himself said that the play was "spawned in hatred and deals with hateful people." [3] As I have sketched it, the play reduces the hero to a spiritual level lower than the pit of the inferno of Part One, and the ending does not seem to lift him much above that level. At the end of Part One, the Stranger receives good news and accepts it as a sign of his spiritual progress. At the end of Part Two, he receives good news and believes it is a lie. He had hoped to redeem his past by achieving fame as a scientist, while the Woman apparently finds some balm for her conscience in becoming a mother. At the end, the Stranger is left no solace but that of the church, even though he feels that his sufferings have been sufficient to atone for the pain he has caused others. He is left with his pride; the Woman, with her baby.

Still, this way of trying to understand the play—describing the characters, outlining the plot—which is the common approach, can be entirely misleading when symbols and allusions, mood and aura, carry as much of the weight of the play as plot does. What is left out of the outline, because it is never clearly stated in the play, is that the whole play is a dream. In the note he prefixed to A Dream Play Strindberg referred to To Damascus as his "previous dream play." He must have had particu-

larly in mind Part Two, whose strange plot does indeed reflect the workings of the dreaming mind. The characters have a preternatural understanding of each other; some of them merge into one another as persons
do in dreams; and the laws of real time and space are violated again and
again. But why did not Strindberg oblige the reader with an explanatory
note, or the viewer with a framing scene, so that they would at least feel
at ease in their bewilderment? Apparently, Strindberg wanted his audiences to find out for themselves. Even the most obtuse or most inatten-
tive person would be made to realize by the transformation scenes that
he was participating in a dream. The gala banquet degenerates into a low
tavern scene, and at the end of it, the stage grows dark. In the dimmed
light, wings and flats are thrust on and off to create a confusion.

Landscapes, palaces, interiors are raised and lowered, while the persons and furniture of the tavern scene disappear, until only the Stranger is seen, standing as if
in a trance, asleep. Finally, he too is hidden from sight, and out of the chaos of
scenes emerges a prison cell. [SS, 29:196]

A similar transition occurs at the end of the prison scene, and out of that
confusion emerges the Rose Room. When the Stranger enters it, he in-
quires about his wife's condition and learns that no time has passed
since he left the room to go to the goldmakers' banquet. He seizes on the
hope that the nightmarish tavern scene was only a dream.

2

By means of this technique, Strindberg involves the viewer directly
in the Stranger's nightmare. A nightmare without an explanation, however, would be utterly confusing and chaotic. What Strindberg presents
is a dream made coherent, an artfully arranged nightmare, a dream with
its analysis built into it. The dream can be interpreted in terms that
Strindberg might have used, terms drawn from the occult sciences, or it
can be recounted in terms familiar to students of modern psychology. Because of what happens in the next to last scene, the vocabulary and theories of Jung seem especially applicable.

In that scene, the Stranger settles accounts with his conscience. The
guilt he felt when a curse was pronounced on him in the first scene
of the play is canceled out by the sufferings and disillusionments he
has endured. He sees that the Doctor, the embodiment of his guilt and
transgressions, is half mad, but the Doctor's plight scarcely touches the
Stranger because he has just seen his own worst dream come true: the

children are lost to him and have come under the charge of a stepfather. That his conscience no longer pains him is suggested by the setting. The old mill in the mountain ravine, the mill of conscience, now lies in ruins. Overhead is the constellation Orion, a symbol so full of import that Strindberg, becoming unusually helpful, diagrammed it in a footnote.

Jung had been led, through his research and clinical experience, to distinguish several components in the human personality. The first of these is the ego, which is the center of the field of consciousness. It develops over the years out of the conflict between the inner and outer worlds of the individual. The first part of To Damascus is perplexing because the psyche is viewed at an uncustomary angle, with the ego in a submerged position. The psyche is turned upside down, as if an iceberg had tipped over and revealed the 90 percent of its bulk that is normally invisible. In Ibsen's plays, the subliminal self is revealed in glimpses through rifts in the realistic surface. In To Damascus, Part One, the subliminal self, the Unknown One, is on the surface, fully in view, while the ego, the public self, the Strindberg one might have accidentally encountered in Paris, appears in a minor role in the person of the Beggar, who frequents the cafés, scrounges for money, scorns his social responsibilities, concerns himself with the physical, outer man ("What's inside is absolutely pure—muck."), and thinks the Stranger with his troubled conscience is "goldarned comical" (SS, 29:115). The Beggar functions as the ego of the dreamer in Parts One and Two of To Damascus, calling him back to reality and preventing him from succumbing to complete despair.

The second component in the personality is the shadow, which represents, says Jung, "a moral problem that challenges the whole ego-personality." It is of the same sex as the subject, and "to become conscious of it involves recognizing the dark aspects of the personality as present and real."[4] Since the shadow involves the personal unconscious, as distinct from the deeper collective unconscious, its contents can be made conscious fairly easily. In To Damascus, the Doctor provides a more nearly perfect example of a shadow than anything Jung himself offers. With insight, the shadow, the adverse representative of the dark chthonic world, can "to some extent," says Jung, "be assimilated into the conscious personality."[5] Part Two of To Damascus is a demonstration of how the shadow is assimilated.

A third component of the personality is the anima, which is embedded more deeply in the psyche and which cannot easily be made conscious. It is an imago or archetype formed out of all the experiences of man with woman through the ages. The Woman in Strindberg's play is both mother and sexual mate: woman, in Jung's words, as "solace for all the bitterness of life" but also the seductress who draws man into life, "not only into [its] reasonable and useful aspects but into its frightful paradoxes and ambivalences where good and evil, success and ruin, hope and despair counterbalance one another."[6]

Basic to Jung's theories was the process by which an individual realizes himself. Unless this process is carried through to the point at which the different components are brought into some sort of harmony, the individual will be disturbed, neurotic, or insane. The process of individuation is a lifelong process and may be thought of as occurring in two parts. In the first half of life, the individual adapts to his environment and provides himself with an outer aspect, his persona, with which he makes his mark on the world. In the second half of life, half way down the road of life, the individual seeks the inner reality and turns back to those aspects of his being that have hitherto remained unconscious. To accomplish this, the psyche must be thrown off balance. The individual must cut through the layers of the psyche and penetrate "to the centre that is the source and ultimate foundation of our psychic being, to the self." The first step in this soul-shattering process is to encounter the shadow, which is projected upon an outside object. The second step is to encounter the anima, the Eve within man. The activation of these images is an "event of fateful importance, for it is the most unmistakable sign that the second half of life has begun." The third step consists in the realization of the self, the bringing into balance the two psychic systems, the conscious and the unconscious. That the process has reached this point is made evident by the appearance of a symbol of completeness and totality, a mandala.[7]

In dreams, the self is frequently represented by a child or by a Christ figure, while the mandala usually takes the form of a circle or of a four-sided figure or a quaternion. This is because the assimilation of the shadow and the anima by the conscious mind is not enough to complete the individuation process. There must be a transcendent harmony of the various components, including the ego. Consequently, wholeness of personality is suggested or symbolized by a fourth element that encompasses ego, shadow, and anima. The triad must be absorbed by a quaternion. In religious iconography, for example, the four evangelists or the Virgin must be added to the Trinity.

In the process of individuation, the personality establishes a new center between the conscious and the unconscious. The self includes both systems and is the center of the totality "as the ego is the center of consciousness, for it is the function which unites all the opposing elements in man and woman, consciousness and unconsciousness, good and bad, male and female . . . and in so doing transmutes them." This new state of being cannot be reached without struggle and suffering. When it has been attained, the concept of self consists

in the awareness on the one hand of our unique natures, and on the other of our intimate relationship with all life, not only human, but animal and plant, and even of inorganic matter and the cosmos itself. It brings a feeling of "oneness," and of reconciliation with life, which can now be accepted as it is, not as it ought to be.[8]

This description, by one of Jung's explicators, of the emergence of the self in the process of individuation could serve as a gloss on the ravine scene in Strindberg's play. The mill is in ruins; the constellation Orion is visible in the clear sky; there is snow in the foreground and the green of spring in the background. The ruined mill, along with a reference to the flood waters that have wiped out the Woman's estate, which was built by mulcting others, signifies that the Stranger has canceled his spiritual debts. When he sees that his children are lost to him, he can come to terms with his shadow, the Doctor, who has avenged himself so completely that the Stranger no longer feels any ache of conscience.

At this point the upheaval within his soul is so violent that he falls to the ground. Rising, he says to the Beggar,

Where am I? Where have I been? Is it spring, winter, or summer? Which century is this? Which universe? Am I a child or an old man, man or woman, god or devil? Who are you? Are you you, or are you me? Are these my entrails I see around me? Are these stars in the heavens or phosphenes in my eyes? Is this water or only my tears? Quiet! Now I just shot forward a thousand years in time, and I'm beginning to shrivel up, to condense, to crystallize. Wait, wait. In a moment I shall be made over, recreated, and out of the dark water of chaos the lotus will stick its head into the sun and say: "This is I." I must have been sleeping a thousand years. I dreamed I exploded and became ether, felt nothing, suffered no pain, relished no pleasure, had entered into peace and found equilibrium. But now—! Now! I suffer as if I were all of mankind. I suffer and have no right to complain. [SS, 29:225–26]

The division of the stage set into winter and summer conveys the division in his psyche, the conflict between the conscious and the unconscious, while the constellation Orion symbolizes the temporary resolution of that conflict as the Stranger attains a new plateau of existence. The three stars forming the belt of Orion represent the Beggar, the Dominican, and the Confessor, according to Strindberg's note[9] on a drawing of the constellation in his manuscript, and those three figures are versions of the ego, the shadow, and the anima. They have a less tangible existence than the other characters, and they merge into one another, becoming one character by the time the play is over. The Dominican's function, like the Doctor's, is to make the hero suffer for his sins, while the Confessor's role is ultimately to lessen his burden of guilt. When the Confessor appears for the first and only time in the play, he is revealed as the Woman's first husband, whom she deserted. What she did to him is then to some extent balanced out in the larger scheme of justice by what the Stranger may have done to her.

The three stars in the center of Orion, even though they represent a union of three components of the personality, do not represent an integrated personality. But the four stars forming a trapezoid enclosing the three stars of the belt do just that. They suggest the self, the circumference that encloses the conscious and the unconscious; they raise the trinity into a quaternion, a symbol of wholeness. Furthermore, since Orion is the great hunter of myth, he is to be associated with the motif of the hunting horn that is heard through Parts One and Two of *To Damascus* and with the unknown huntsman whom the Stranger has fled down the labyrinthine ways of his own mind. Strindberg referred to himself at the time he wrote this play as the quarry in the wild hunt[10] of medieval legend, the antichrist who is pursued. In the individuation process, the self is both the pursued and the pursuer. The perfect image of the new self is seen at the end of the play: the Woman sitting at the crib of her newborn babe.

3

All the elements in the ravine scene become comprehensible when given a Jungian interpretation. But the play in its entirety—in fact, the whole *To Damascus* trilogy—provides a complete illustration of the individuation process. The correspondence is so exact that a cultural historian of a future age, given only a synopsis of Jung's teachings, the dates of his writings, and Strindberg's play, would assume that Jung had written a commentary on Strindberg, making obscure what was already clear.

When Strindberg endeavored to explore his unconscious, his first step was to make the contents of that underworld of fantasies and imaginings perceptible and tangible by seeing those contents as reflected in the physical and material world. As Jung explained, "activated unconscious contents always appear at first as projections upon the outside world."[11] This meant that not only were *objets trouvés* given a significance they would not have to the rational mind but that people in the exterior world were made to play roles in the underworld assigned to them by the "other" intelligence. As Strindberg proceeded with his self-analysis, the people who were part of his outer life became less real or objective and more a part of his inner life. As they sank into his unconscious, they lost their individuality and became types. The change is apparent if one compares the novel *Inferno* with the *To Damascus* drama. Strindberg's self-analysis amounted in fact to a dramatization of his inner life. Once this inner life had been organized as a drama, the analysis was over. In Part One, Frida Uhl, Strindberg's second wife; Dr. Eliasson, who offered Strindberg refuge; and Torsten Hedlund, who tried to convert Strindberg to theosophy, who reproved him for his pride, and to whom Strindberg sent long letters describing his Inferno experiences, become respectively the Woman, the Doctor, and the Confessor,[12] archetypes gathering to themselves all past events, great and small, that would be related to them. This method of making people in the exterior world serve as bins for sorting out the elements of his conscious and unconscious life explains why Strindberg gave them designations rather than names.

In Part One, the Woman acquires many of the qualities of Strindberg's first wife, who had left her husband to marry the dramatist, as the Woman does in the play. In Part Two, the Doctor bears a greater resemblance to Ossian Ekbohrn than he does to Eliasson. Ekbohrn,[13] the customs inspector in the Stockholm skerries, had been meant to play a part in Strindberg's psychological experiment of 1896. For siding with Strindberg's wife during the divorce proceedings, Ekbohrn had earned Strindberg's hatred, and when madness broke out in Ekbohrn's sister and brothers, Strindberg saw that nemesis had struck down his enemy. In *Inferno*, Strindberg concludes his account of the affair by saying that every time he has told this story of just retribution he has been punished for it. In *To Damascus*, the punishment precedes the event. The Stranger sees that he has lost his children and immediately thereafter sees that the Doctor and the Doctor's sister have lost their wits. It is no longer a case of nemesis divina but of one event from the past serving to cancel another seemingly unrelated event as the personality attempts to find its true self.

To the extent that the characters are projections or, as Strindberg would say, spiritual extensions of his inner life, they become part of himself and are his doubles. He described how this happens with regard to a woman whom one loves. "We begin to love a woman by depositing bits and pieces of our souls with her. We duplicate our personality, and the loved one, formerly indifferent and neutral, begins to assume the guise of our other self: she becomes our double" (SS, 28:279).[14]

4

Once the contents of the unconscious have been activated and projected, the process of self-realization begins in earnest. Not only is this process as detailed by Jung exactly like the process that Strindberg dramatizes, but Jung's own development, the path by which he came to understand the methods of the unconscious, is remarkably like Strindberg's. Without knowing it, Jung became Strindberg's double.

As a student of nineteenth-century psychology, familiar with diseases of the personality, Jung investigated the phenomenon of double consciousness and set about exploring the depths of the psyche by means of association techniques. By 1896 or 1897, he recognized that the principal task of psychology was to demonstrate that the soul exists as an intelligence independent of time and space. He sensed that psychic illness results from a division within the psyche and that psychic health means a harmony of the conscious and unconscious mental lives. He was convinced that the mental life of the insane or mentally disturbed reveals what is hidden in the normal or balanced psyche. He also knew that it was not enough to read about the psychic experiences of others in order to understand them; one must experience them. Consequently, in the middle of his life, when he had already acquired an international reputation in his field, he embarked on a period of self-examination during which he withdrew from the world. He put himself in a receptive frame of mind, banished, as much as possible, all preconceptions about the psyche. When he ventured into his own psyche, he discovered that an image of woman loomed up from within. He soon realized that he had to differentiate himself from these unconscious contents by personifying them and bringing them into a relationship with the conscious life. As a result of this self-exploration, he saw that life is a series of metamorphoses and that the process of self-realization is in part a regression into the land of the dead, analogous to the journeys of Virgil and Dante into the underworld. The balance between the conscious and the unconscious is achieved by reversing the direction of the journey. The whole of this journey is inevitably erratic and full of danger because of the possibility that the conscious and the unconscious will become irrevocably separated. Only gradually did the journey reveal its import, but the coherence of events made it clear that there was a meaning. There was a unifying agent at work. What had seemed to be mere coincidence turned out to be especially significant. When he emerged from this period of self-discovery, this healing illness, he realized that a message had come through with ineluctable force. The spiritual development of the individual did not consist in a straight advance toward some predetermined goal but in a continual circumambulation around the core of the personality and that while in the first half of the life of the individual the conscious mind was allowed to assert itself often at the expense of the unconscious, in the second half the unconscious must be allowed its say. Because of what he learned about the psyche, this period of illness, which provided him with material for his writings and teachings from that time on, led to genuine creativity.

This account of Jung's career corresponds in every single aspect to Strindberg's. What is left out is the interest both men took in alchemy, which they saw as a way of making contact with the absolute that formed the ground for all phenomena, material and spiritual. Jung came to study the writings of the alchemists after his period of self-analysis. Only after his theories had been formulated did Jung discover that the experiences conveyed by the alchemists in symbolic terms were his own experiences as reflected in his dreams and that the individuation process paralleled the alchemical process. Strindberg took up alchemy before he undertook his self-analysis, and undoubtedly, his delving into the mystic writings of the alchemists affected his view of the progress of the soul. (Strindberg also dabbled in the I'Ching around 1903; Jung became interested in it around 1920.)

The difference between the two psychologists is that Strindberg went through his creative illness and formulated his findings all in a space of three years. Jung's creative illness lasted from 1914 to 1919, and it took him several more years to bring order and meaning to his experiences. All the principal theories of Jung were anticipated by Strindberg and were enunciated by him between 1897 and 1901. If Jung's analytic psychology marks a major breakthrough comparable to the great discoveries in the physical sciences, if it is not to be thrown on the scrap heap of discarded notions along with the medieval heaven and hell, spontaneous generation, phlogiston, the flat earth, the crystalline heaven, and the luminiferous ether, then Strindberg's *To Damascus* trilogy must be regarded as an intellectual and creative event of equal magnitude.

The fact that, so far, Strindberg has not been given proper credit for his achievement is due in part to the psychologists themselves: Freud and Jung treated Strindberg as ungraciously as Newton treated Leibniz and perhaps for the same reason. It is also due to the special vocabularies the psychologists of the leading schools invented to describe the operations of the unconscious and to set forth the rationale of the irrational. For decades Freud and Jung carried out a campaign, conducted with large numbers of troops, to win ground for their theories, and the extent to which they succeeded can be measured by the extent to which their special terms have become part of the language. Strindberg, too, had to devise a special vocabulary, but he spent little time trying to sell his theories of the psychic life to the public. Developing a new science of the mind was an astounding accomplishment. Freud and Jung followed it up with another, equally astonishing: making people believe it. Strindberg followed up his discoveries by transmuting them into art.

Strindberg's vocabulary tends to be closer to Jung's than to Freud's, possibly because the dramatist's conception of the second intelligence resembled Jung's more than Freud's and certainly because the dramatist delved into the kind of literature that was to attract Jung. Strindberg studied the cabala, Gnosticism, alchemy, spiritualism, magic, and religion on the assumption that the mystics of all ages had been exploring the same subcontinent of the mind. To take one example: Jung got his concept of the quaternion from these occult works, and so did Strindberg. Eliphas Levi, a nineteenth-century mystic whom Strindberg is known to have read, described the significance of the tetrad:

The philosophical triad, emanating from the antagonism of the duad, is completed by the tetrad, the four-square ground of all truth. According to the consecrated dogma, there are three persons in God, and these three constitute only one Deity. Three and one provide the conception of four, because unity is required to explain the three.[15]

Strindberg may not have seen the full significance of the Orion constellation until after he had read this or a similar explanation of the tetrad.

5

To Damascus would be immediately comprehensible to a large number of readers nowadays if it were rendered in Jungese,[16] with the Doctor appearing as the shadow, the Woman as anima, the Beggar as ego, and so on. But there is a vital difference between the development of the personality as Jung sees it and as Strindberg sees it. Jung is concerned mainly with the need of the individual to achieve a balance between the conscious and unconscious, while Strindberg is concerned mainly with the problem of guilt. The analyst repeatedly describes the individuation process as one in which there is a descent into the unconscious and then a reversal, the reversal being necessary in order to achieve the balance between the two realms. The dramatist focuses his attention on that moment of reversal, and asks: Why is there a reversal? When does it occur? Under what circumstances? Jung's answers to these questions relate to the normal development of the individual. In middle age there should be a readjustment within the psyche. Strindberg would agree with that only to ask how that readjustment comes about. If it were merely a matter of age, a glance at the calendar or a look in the mirror would suffice to initiate the crucial phase of the process. To Strindberg the answer is ultimately moral and not chronomantic.

In Part One the turning point is fragmented and acted out in a series of scenes rather than analyzed. Strindberg wanted to go beyond this, and he wrote Part Two to examine those nightmares in detail, to plunge even more deeply into the psyche, to see exactly what it is that impels the conscience, and to depict as concretely as possible the actual twistings and turnings of a conscience in agony. No wonder he found the characters distasteful; no wonder the play made him ill; no wonder he found it difficult to finish.[17] To write it was to relive his own worst nightmares.

In Part One, Strindberg had devised a way of putting on stage a mind responding to subtle intimations and associations, of showing the interplay between the inner and outer worlds. In writing Part Two, Strindberg responded to an equally difficult challenge: to show the mechanism itself when the mills of conscience begin to grind. The older way of dramatizing the uneasy conscience was to have the ghost of the villain's victim appear, as in Shakespeare, or to put the villain's dream on stage, as happens in Lewis's *The Bells*, a nineteenth-century melodrama made popular by Henry Irving. Lewis's villain kills a Jew for his money, and years later, when he is prosperous and respectable, a pillar of society and safe from the law, his remorse expresses itself in a dream in which he is brought to court and tried for his crime. In a Strindbergian version of this, the troubled hero would dream that he killed a Jewish friend for his money and would awake from his dream to read in the paper that the Jew had gone bankrupt. The first case raises no moral, psychological, or dramatic problems. The second does.

Anyone who reads through Part Two hastily will not believe that

Strindberg found a solution to these problems. The scenes resemble the scattered pieces of a jigsaw puzzle. Yet Strindberg said that the play had "a sound armature,"[18] and this armature stands out boldly when the scenes are grouped in sets of three coiling around the Rose Room.

1. Cottage Exterior	2. Laboratory	3. Rose Room
4. Tavern	5. Prison	6. Rose Room
7. Tavern	8. Ravine	9. Rose Room

The middle three scenes, Tavern, Prison, Rose Room, linked together by *changements à vue*, form a distinct unit. These are the most nightmarish and most subjective scenes in the play, and no time seems to have elapsed between scenes 3 and 6. When the Stranger enters in scene 6 to inquire about the birth of his child, his mother-in-law tells him that things are just the same as when he asked a few moments ago. Having just heard him bid a brusque farewell at the end of scene 3, she asks why he has not left for the alchemists' banquet. These middle three scenes depict the Stranger undergoing vastation in accordance with a description that Swedenborg gives.

Some are kept in a middle state between wakefulness and sleep, and think very little, only now and then arousing and recalling what they thought and did in the life of the body, and again relapsing into a middle state between being awake and being asleep. In this way these are vastated.[19]

In another passage, which so impressed Strindberg that he copied out parts of it and inserted them in the Swedish version of his novel *Legends*, Swedenborg deals with two kinds of extraordinary visions that he himself had had on only a few occasions. In the first kind,

the man is brought into a certain state that is midway between sleep and wakefulness, and when he is in this state he cannot know but that he is wholly awake. . . . This is the state of which it is said [in the Bible] that they are *withdrawn* from the body, and that they *do not know whether they are in the body or out of it.*[20]

The other kind consists in being transported by the spirit to another place. "I had walked for hours," says Swedenborg, when

suddenly I was in sight of the body, and became aware that I was in another place. Greatly amazed at this, I perceived that I had been in such a state as they were in, of whom it is said [in the Bible] that they were *led away by the spirit into another place.*[21]

In such states, whether they are devastating or merely visionary, man is in communication with the spirits, and the whole of To Damascus Part Two takes place in the Swedenborgian world of spirits, which, in the romantic and in the pre-Freudian construct of the mind, is the unconscious or the subconscious. Man's external is governed in the world of spirits, which is Swedenborg's way of saying that what we do in the outer or natural world is determined by what we think. What determines our thoughts? Only the activity in a deeper part of the mind. This continuous activity takes place below the level of consciousness, and our feelings and thoughts are merely the evidence of the underlying process. "The greater part by far of our mental activity goes on unconsciously and unfelt by us," said Nietzsche.[22] Swedenborg's model of the mind differs from that of the romantics since, being a visionary, he tended to see the irrational as flooded with light, and instead of conceptualizing the operations of the mind in terms of ideas and thoughts that are repressed or discharged, he saw individual spirits working with and against each other. Although the model was different, the formula was the same. "The natural man who has the spiritual degree opened," says Swedenborg, "does not know that he thinks and acts from his spiritual man, for it seems as if he did this from himself, when yet he does not do it from himself but from the Lord.[23]

It is the Lord who governs the interior of man's mind, but he does this indirectly by means of mediating spirits. When a man dies and leaves the body, he is brought into this world of spirits. Under certain conditions, he can enter this world of spirits while alive. He withdraws from the body and is "brought into a certain state that is midway between sleeping and waking, and when in that state he seems to be wide awake; all the senses are . . . perfectly awake." [24]

While in the state of interiors, a man may catch a glimpse of heaven and hell, which are specific spiritual realms and, as such, distinct from the general world of spirits. They are states of soul rather than the general unconscious life. In undergoing vastation, man enters this other world and leaves the body. The interior life, his innermost thoughts, the ones he has shunned and repressed, take possession of him. In the first part of To Damascus, the moments of vastation were represented with a degree of objectivity in the asylum scene and in the second kitchen scene. In Part Two, Strindberg opens up those moments, lets us into them completely, and pictures them in subjective detail.

When the Stranger attends the alchemists' banquet, he finds himself in hell. Swedenborg describes hell (SS, 28:141)[25] as a place in which all seems beautiful at first, but gradually the beautiful palace turns into an ugly hovel. "Those in the hells, because they have no truths, appear clothed in garments, but in ragged, squalid, and filthy garments, each one in accordance with his insanity."[26] In the second tavern scene, scene 7, the Stranger finds himself among the dregs of society and feels that he is dead. "One is said to be dead whose mind is a hell,"[27] says Swedenborg.

STRANGER. We've sunk pretty low. But I know that the lower I sink, the closer I am to the goal, to the end.
BARMAID. Don't talk so loud. There's a man dying in there.
STRANGER. I thought I smelled dead bodies.
DOCTOR. Maybe they're ours.
STRANGER. Can you be dead without knowing it?
DOCTOR. The dead say you won't know the difference.
STRANGER. Frightening! Is it possible? All these shadowy figures, whose faces I seem to recognize from memories of the school room, swimming lessons, gym class—.
(Clutches his heart.)
No, No! He's coming, the awful one who sucks my heart from my breast.— He's coming, the invisible one who has haunted me for years.—He's here!
(He is beside himself.)
(The doors are opened. A choir boy, carrying a lantern with blue glass that casts a blue light on the tavern people, rings a silver bell. Everyone howls like a wild animal. The DOMINICAN enters with the sacramental vessels. The BARMAID and the PROSTITUTE fall to their knees; the others howl. The DOMIN- ICAN lifts the monstrance; all fall to their knees. The choir boy and the DO- MINICAN exit into the room at the left.) [SS, 29:216–17]

(Some of the striking dramatic touches in this scene—the blue faces, the smell of death, the belief that he was already among the dead—came from the experiences of Axel Herrlin (SS, 28:234),[28] docent in philoso- phy at the University of Lund. He believed in the reality of what he saw and simultaneously knew that it had a symbolic meaning.)

The triadic division of the play represents three stages in the Strang- er's progress in accordance with Swedenborg's description of how man can be reborn spiritually. In the first three scenes, the Stranger is in a state of damnation, delving into the occult, seeking to attain the ultimate scientific knowledge, and shirking the divine truth and love. In the mid- dle three scenes, his reformation commences. He recognizes his sins and refrains from willing them. The last three scenes are devoted to his re- generation. From being natural man relying on his rational faculty, he be- comes spiritual man. He becomes spiritual, however, only so far as he is "in truths," to use Swedenborg's language. The fact that he will not ac-

cept the truth in the last letter that he receives suggests that his regeneration has only just begun. He still believes the lie because he will not have
the truth.

6

Swedenborg's mediating spirits are very roughly analogous to Jung's
components of the personality, with the great difference that Swedenborg's spirits are defined in terms of good and evil, heaven and hell,
while Jung's components are not. The individual has within him "at least
two spirits from hell, as well as two angels from heaven,"[29] and qualms
of conscience are nothing but the conflict between these spirits. Among
the spirits at work in the interiors of the mind, said Swedenborg, are
chastising spirits, instructing spirits, contradictory spirits, and angelic
spirits. These spirits, especially the first two, appealed to Strindberg, and
in 1897, he found that they provided a better means of explaining what
goes on in the interiors of the mind than did the vaguely defined occult
powers. At the end of *Inferno* he wrote, "Karma will become God, and
the mahatmas will reveal themselves as regenerated powers, as corrective spirits (demons) and instructive spirits (sources of inspiration)."[30]
Later in the same year he wrote,

The occultists say that man's soul has the creative power to project its passions in
the form of demi-beings, which they call elementals and elemental spirits and so
on, and that the guilty conscience emits or radiates punishing spirits that can
only be exorcized by the patient himself through remorse and better behavior.[31]

The Woman, no longer the helpful companion she was in Part One,
is a contradictory spirit who destroys what the other spirits have done.
The Doctor is, of course, a chastising or correcting spirit, reproving the
Stranger for evil deeds and thoughts drawn out of the past, and the
Mother is an instructing spirit who tells the Stranger what he must do.
The Beggar, the Dominican, and the Confessor exist on another plane and
are, it would seem, all angelic spirits, whose function is to keep the other
spirits in line and to moderate, if need be, the punishments inflicted by
them. If this sounds medieval, it can be brought up-to-date by recalling
that the Woman is akin to the anima as seductress, the Mother to the anima as protectress, the Doctor as the shadow, the Beggar as the ego, the
Dominican as animus or logos, and the Confessor as Jung's Wise Man or
representative of the self.

The angelic spirits, according to Swedenborg, inhabit the cerebellum,[32] which is in a wakeful state when the cerebrum, the center of consciousness and voluntary actions, is asleep. In other words, they constitute what we would call the unconscious, and the principle governing these spirits is in keeping with the theory that the unconscious is the ultimate source of our being and of our actions. Communication between the angels, the spirits, and natural man can only be from the higher to the lower. The influx, to use Swedenborgian language, "proceeds from the Lord through their heavens to the lowest, and not contrariwise,"[33] which is to say that the conscious mind does not dictate to the unconscious. The opening of the mind to true love and wisdom is by degrees, which are like the atmospheres between the sun and the earth except that the degrees are sharply demarcated. The three degrees correspond to will, understanding, and results; that is, to the end in view, to the cause by which the end may be achieved, and to the effect. "The end begets the cause, and, through the cause, the effect, that the end may have form."[34] The angels of the third or highest degree perceive in the will of the individual the end for which he acts, and man searches in his understanding, his rational part, for the means to attain this end. The will in modern terminology is equivalent to the unconscious thought that seeks expression through the conscious mind.

Swedenborg was using the language of religion and ancient philosophy to explain the relationship of brain to mind, of mind to soul. By itself, the notion of three degrees is no more helpful in explaining the mind than the theory of four elements is in explaining the constitution of matter, but when combined with the idea of chastising spirits and spirits of other sorts, the Swedenborgian scheme offered possibilities almost as rich as the constructs of Freud and Jung.

Strindberg found that he could use this Swedenborgian scheme to construct the plot of his play. He spoke of certain compositional tricks he employed, and one of the oddest has to do with the letters[35] that in at least three instances give a new direction to the plot. He hit upon the device because letters came to have a fateful bearing on his life during the 1890s when he was constantly hoping that the post would bring money from a publisher or benefactor and constantly fearing a threatening letter from his first wife demanding payment of subsistence money for herself and the children. Employed discreetly and symbolically in Part One, letters become the mainspring of Part Two. In scene 3, the Stranger takes from the Woman's green dress a letter inviting him to the congress of chemists. (Green is the color[36] of the clothes of the enchantresses of hell, says Swedenborg, who saw them.) In scene 6, he takes from a green jacket that is hanging next to the green dress a letter informing him that his children are lost to him and belong to their stepfather. (The green jacket belongs to the Stranger's father-in-law, who left his wife for another woman. In that respect he is like the Stranger. Hence the letter saying his children have a new father comes appropriately from the green jacket. That is how the dreaming mind works.) In the last scene of the play, the Woman hands him from the green dress a newspaper and a diploma establishing the correctness of his scientific theories.

Coming at the end of each triad of scenes, the letters are intended as the results of what has gone before. The first scene in each triad discloses what the unconscious wants, and the second scene shows how the unconscious finds in the conscious mind the means by which to attain the required end. It seeks a reason acceptable to the waking mind (the understanding, in Swedenborg) while screening the actual submerged reason (the will, in Swedenborg).

	End	Cause	Effect
Damnation	1. To be punished for harm done to Doctor	2. Stranger's pride in his intellectual achievement	3. Invitation to the banquet
Reformation	4. To be punished for his arrogance in the past	5. The fear that he will lose his children	6. Letter saying his children have a stepfather
Regeneration	7. To be punished for having had false values	8. A division within himself	9. Good news that he refuses to believe

The ends and the effects are not directly related because a mind divided against itself works in devious ways. Only in the overall design is there direct relation, which is brought out in scenes 1, 5, and 9, the diagonal triad. In the first scene, the Dominican says that, because the Stranger did not embrace the truth but has instead sought scientific or rational knowledge, "God will bring great confusion on him so that he will believe the lie" (SS, 29:143). In the fifth scene, the Stranger is jailed as a charlatan, and in the last scene, the Stranger tears up the newspaper and the diploma without even looking at them, convinced that they are only meant to deceive him as he was deceived before. He refuses to believe the truth even when it is good.

The central scenes 4, 5, and 6, are the most dreamlike because they picture the Stranger inventing punishments to inflict on himself. To the dreamer they are as real and as painful as the events that occur outside himself: in his nightmare the Stranger sees his true inner self. These scenes are central to the vastation process, the confrontation with one's conscience. Strindberg states the theme explicitly in the opening scene, firmly restates it in the last scene, and on both occasions joins it with the main theme of Part One. "When a secret sin has been committed," says the Dominican in scene 1, "the curse from Deuteronomy is pronounced on the suspected one. If he is innocent, he is untouched by it. But if it strikes home, then, as Paul says, his body is delivered over to Satan to be tortured that he may be bettered and his soul saved." In the last scene, the Confessor explains what has been happening to the Stranger. "You foreswore yourself to me once—when you lay sick and felt madness approaching. You swore then to serve the powers of good. But when you regained your health, you broke your promise, and therefore you were made uneasy in spirit, and have wandered without peace of mind, tormented by your conscience."

"God does not rule over slaves," says Strindberg, paraphrasing Swedenborg, "and therefore he has let mortals enjoy freedom of will. There are no powers of evil; those that seem to be so are servants of the good acting as chastisers. The punishment is not eternal. Everyone is free to atone for his sins patiently" (SS, 28:293).[37]

The suffering soul is in despair until it knows why it is suffering. When this awareness dawns on the sinner, the worst anguish is tinged with joy. This is the paradox of vastation and of the remorseful sinner. Strindberg, just before he began writing To Damascus, put it this way: "Swedenborg in sketching hell has simply pictured earthly life so that what is down there is up here. The state of affairs is therefore all for the best, that is to say, the more of the bad, the more of the good, and the worse things get, the better they are."[38]

An obscure sense of this paradox, so well expressed in the French proverb A force de mal aller tout ira bien ("By dint of going wrong, all will go well"), evidently precedes the final scouring of the mind in the vastation process. In scene 5, the middle scene of the play, when the Stranger's fortunes are at their nadir, the light of the Lord enters his mind. Having been unable to pay his bill at the banquet, he finds himself in a prison cell, and from the Beggar he learns that he is being ridiculed in the papers as a charlatan. A beam of sunlight shines through a small window, striking a crucifix on the wall. The Stranger, wearing his brown cape (brown is the color of those who are yearning to come into heaven; they are like caterpillars waiting to be "changed into chrysalises and thus into butterflies"),[39] sits at a table contemplating the spot of sunlight. The imagery suggests that the Stranger is only subconsciously cognizant of what is happening to him, for, as Swedenborg says, the truths of faith rarely manifest themselves in such an immediate way that the rational mind is excited; rather, only a vague and general idea of such things as agree with the truth is produced, and this operation "is effected by imperceptible influx; which when presented to the sight appears as light flowing in."[40]

What is imperceptible to the Stranger in his cell is made perceptible to the reader and viewer by the symbolic light and crucifix and by the three musical themes, which are brought together in this central scene for the first and only time in the play. The Stranger hears the chanting of a rosary, the winding of the hunting horn, the playing of the funeral march, while he stands in a hypnotic trance. The rosary is associated with the birth of the child and with original sin; the funeral march with the death of the spirit; and the horn, with God or conscience. Together they reveal the state of soul of the Stranger *before* he inflicts the worst punishment on himself, the news that he has lost his children, which comes in the next scene simultaneously with the midwife's announcement that a child has been born. When in the depths of his mind, in the nightmare that his conscience stages for him, he recognizes his sins, reviling himself as a lost soul who "slew his brother" and refusing to see or touch his newborn and innocent child lest he contaminate it, and makes his punishment worse than anything in reality, then the process of vastation can continue to the next stage, in which the spirit will be regenerated.

7

Not only do the angels or guardians come into conflict with the spirits, but the spirits fight among themselves. In the Swedenborgian economics of the spiritual life "evil punishes itself," and the "Lord turns all the punishment and torment to good, and to some use."[41] The Stranger and the Woman live together like angels half the day and the other half like devils torturing each other. From the beginning the Woman is a corrective or disciplinary spirit to the Stranger. In the master plot her part is to chastise him for his past errors. "When it comes to plaguing me," says the Stranger, "her powers of invention leave my own most infernal ideas far behind. If I escape from her clutches alive, I'll come away as pure as gold from fire" (SS, 29:147).

To humiliate him and to test her powers, the Woman has tricked him into wearing the clothes of her previous husband. Since evil punishes itself, her craftiness redounds on her, and the Stranger becomes like the Doctor not only in appearance but in spirit. Just as the Doctor incorporates the Stranger's guilt, so the Stranger comes to incorporate the Woman's guilt, becoming her corrective spirit. In the process, her case comes to resemble the Stranger's more and more. She had deserted her first husband (who is not the Doctor) to have an affair with a married man; subsequently she seduced the Doctor and got him to marry her (scene 7). Whether what we are told about her past is true is beside the point. The psyche must arrange matters in accordance with its needs, often bending the truth, which always proves to be pliable since it is never found in its pure state in the real world. It creates its own truths, for fictions become facts in the life of the mind. "Man lives a double life; fantasies, imaginings, dreams possess a kind of reality" (SS, 28:280).[42]

In order to find peace, the Stranger must exorcise the Doctor from his mind. He cannot undo what has been done. Even God cannot change the past; all He can do is settle accounts by keeping an elaborate ledger. The guardian spirits or angels are the actual bookkeepers; the others are the debtors and creditors. In the last moments of the play, the Woman absolves the Stranger by telling him that his function has been to punish her for leaving her first husband. Her first husband was the Confessor, in whose hands the Stranger now places himself. The Stranger and the Woman cannot remain together since their marriage will always remind them of the pain they have caused the Doctor. By undergoing vastation and by torturing himself mentally, the Stranger has settled accounts with the Doctor, while the Woman has her baby to give meaning to her life. The banishment of the Doctor, and the absorption of the Beggar and the Dominican into the figure of the Confessor at the end, imply that the personality of the Stranger is being restored to wholeness. The discordant ending intimates, however, that his journey to perfection is far from over. He is still in the state of falsities, to use Swedenborg's language, when the curtain falls on Part Two.

The necessity of a third part to complete the Stranger's journey must have been apparent to Strindberg even as he outlined Part Two, if not earlier when he was composing the first part. The novelized form of his spiritual odyssey was intended to form a triptych: *Inferno*, *Legends* (*Inferno II*), and a third part, left unfinished. This third part, entitled alternatively "The Inferno of Love" and "Coram Populo" in the manuscript, was published under the title

CHAPTER NINE

PARADISE

Jacob Wrestles. *Inferno* afforded a detailed description of his experiences during the great crisis of his life. *Legends* drew on the experiences of others to show that the author's experiences were not unique and that Western civilization was turning a corner and moving toward a revival of religious feeling. After the personal document and the general evaluation, the third part was meant to be a metaphorical assault on heaven itself. But the direct confrontation with the spiritual powers only brought confusion to Strindberg's thoughts, and he found himself slipping down the mountain of heaven back toward his inferno. The assault was abandoned, and a new project begun, the *To Damascus* cycle, in which the approach was consistently personal and psychological.

The galley proofs of *Legends* were sent to him shortly after he had finished writing the first part of *To Damascus*, and rereading *Legends* may have made him see the obvious: that after inferno comes purgatory. Following Dante, he would write of that second domain where the human spirit is purified and becomes worthy of the ascent to heaven. Swedenborg's spirits and angels could be seen as purging the Stranger's soul of all attachments not of God, and as in Dante, the principal subject would be love, the power that moves the world. The nine levels of Dante's purgatory could easily be accommodated to Swedenborg's triads. And to make everything nearly perfect, the world of spirits in which Strindberg set his nightmare is, in the Swedenborgian universe, situated between heaven and hell, as is Dante's purgatory.

Ironically, Strindberg gave up the writing of *Jacob Wrestles* when he saw that the mystic Swedenborg who had the enviable power of communing with angels also had a small soul and was dogmatic in his opinions, petty in his judgment of others, and revengeful toward those who opposed him. Yet it was Swedenborg who, with all his faults, furnished the ideas that Strindberg needed to work his way out of the impasse he had reached as a writer and thinker. After 1898, the artist never again lost faith in the mystic.

2

Since Strindberg had been able to bring the Stranger through purgatory while still leaving certain issues unresolved at the end of the second part of *To Damascus*, the third part of the cycle should have followed of its own accord. During the summer and autumn of 1898, he jotted down notes for a third part[1] in which the Stranger would be reconciled with himself by learning that he was not the primary cause of the unhappiness and sinfulness of others. The scene for this drama would be a monastery representing the first stopping place of the soul after the body died. At that point, the Stranger's journey was aborted because there was no material for drama. Strindberg usually drew on life for the raw material of his art and on books for the form. Parts One and Two of the cycle take their main substance from his Inferno crisis and from his first and second marriages. By the end of 1898, this vein of material was almost exhausted. Two and a half years later, however, he could gather his old notes together and add to them because he had fallen in love again.

During rehearsals of the first part of *To Damascus*, a young Norwegian actress named Harriet Bosse had captivated him. He began to hope that through her he might take a more optimistic view of earthly existence. Half his age, she became the focus of his thoughts and passions. He felt he stood in telepathic communication with her. He even copulated with her in spirit ("Possessed her when she sought me out").[2] Her sexual attraction made him wonder at times if she was an incubus, a demon, while at other times an angel revealed itself in her exotic beauty and innocent smile. "What I am going through now," he wrote in his diary on February 12, 1901,

is both horrible and wonderful. I sit as if waiting for the final sentence to be pronounced. Sometimes I think she loves me, sometimes not. . . . So far there have been as many signs for as against. At her last visit I thought an angel was in the room, and I made up my mind to believe the good, hoping for reconciliation with woman, through a woman. For three days now I have felt her in my rooms and experienced an elevating, ennobling influence—which could not very likely come from a demon.

She became for him the incarnation of woman in nearly all aspects: wife and mother, sister and seductress, temptress and angel. To his diary he confided,

All my thoughts concern Bosse, but coming to me as kind and loving, and restoring my faith in the goodness of woman and of mankind. Bosse is like: 1. my second wife (whom she acted in *To Damascus*); 2. my sister Anna; 3. my mother; 4. Mlle. Lecain, the beautiful Englishwoman who tried to snare me in Paris, and who was like all the others; often made a motherly impression. . . . But she was a demon, said Gauguin, and she enticed men—and women; 5. She smiles like my boy Hans when he was four—like an angel.

Later in the day on which this is recorded, February 14, Strindberg waited for Harriet Bosse to keep an appointment they had made.

I waited the whole morning in deathly anxiety. The clock struck the half hour. I collapsed as if my whole life ended with the thought: she's not coming—Shortly thereafter she arrived! Simple, kind, gentle, not so resplendent as last time. Talked warmly, sincerely, conversed about trifles. I came to life, but was so gripped by my happiness at seeing her that I cried. Finally I kissed her hand because she had cared enough to come. . . . [Afterwards] at four o'clock I had an attack of crying—over nothing in particular—over my miseries and everybody's, crying without reason, a dim sense of happiness, of pain at not being happy, in premonition of misfortune.

Only two days previously he had received a letter from the monastery in Belgium that he had visited in 1898, entertaining thoughts then of withdrawing from the world. Now the issue was joined: either reconciliation with mankind through a woman or retirement from the world in the company of monks. Although the question was more theoretical than real, it did provide dramatic material of the sort that Strindberg stood in need of at this time. He had written the first two acts of Part Three and did not know which direction the action should take. He gave Harriet what he had written, so that he might ask her opinion.

"Should I let the Stranger end his days in a monastery?" he asked when she returned the manuscript.

"No," she replied, "he has more to accomplish in life."

Three days later, on March 5, Strindberg and Harriet Bosse were engaged to be married, and Strindberg did not return to his *To Damascus* manuscript until after the marriage, which took place on May 6, 1901. A few days of bliss were given to him. Then came the inevitable quarrels between the middle-aged writer who had had enough of the bohemian life and the ambitious actress who wanted to display herself and to mingle with others in her profession. Within a few weeks, husband and wife were separated. The failure of the marriage was, however, the making of the play. The last half of it, which was evidently written in June,[3] pictures the Stranger making one last effort to find happiness in marriage, and when that fails, he enters a monastery.

Coming after inferno and purgatory, the third part of the cycle had been sketched out as a Swedenborgian fantasy of the ascent to heaven. If a man "suffers himself to be reformed," says Swedenborg, "he is led out of hell, and is led up into heaven, and there he is transferred from one society to another, and this even until death."[4] In the first scene, the Stranger, as rebellious as he was at the end of Part Two, wants no more of life, and in the company of the Confessor, he bids farewell to the Woman and to his daughter of his previous marriage. He is then ferried across a river to begin the ascent to the monastery, located at the top of a mountain. In Buddhistic thought, crossing the river[5] means crossing over from worldly ignorance, fleshly desire, and physical decay to transcendental wisdom, divine love, and the spiritual life.

The second scene takes place on the other side of the river and one-fourth of the way up the mountain. The presence of the worshippers of Venus[6]—syphilitics taking the cure—provides the occasion for disquisitions on sexual love and, since the Stranger feels that his former liberal views on sex had led many young people astray, for yet another essay on the origin of guilt. This long scene is a play in itself, with the Woman putting in another appearance, more motherlike than before, to offer solace to the Stranger.

The next two scenes, higher up the mountain, consist in further expatiations on the themes of sex and guilt brightened by the wit and skepticism of a figure known as the Tempter, who is the Beggar in another guise and whose function is to entice the Stranger back among the living by making light of all that weighs heavily on him. The lively discourse, almost Shavian at times, leads to the bewildering conclusion that sin and punishment may not stand in the presumed relationship of cause to effect and that vice may in itself be a punishment. Take the case, says the Confessor, of the man who as a youth was a teetotaler fanatically opposed to the sale and consumption of alcohol and who died an alcoholic.

In the meantime, the Stranger, pursuing the image of his mother, is easily enticed into considering a remarriage with the Woman,[7] though rematch is the better word for it, since he and she once again find themselves sparring with each other. Physical eros inevitably turns out to be a mockery of spiritual *caritas*. After this decisive exposure of the delusions of love, the Stranger unhesitatingly enters the monastery at the top of the mountain.

To ascend the mountain means to come to terms with one's past and one's conscience. The Tempter exculpates the Stranger by tracing the source of all wrongdoing back to Adam and Eve and thence to the Creator; the Confessor offers the absolving notion that the crime is the punishment, which would leave the conscience with nothing to gnaw on; and the first lesson the Stranger learns in the monastery is that the truth has many faces, that the lives of great men are filled with error, that they all ended by denying what they once affirmed and affirming what they once denied, and that the discords of life are best resolved in the harmonies of Hegel. The Stranger's life, of which the last half has been a contradiction and a gainsaying of the first half, is not unusual. Luther and Voltaire, Schiller and Goethe, Boccaccio and Kierkegaard, Bismarck and Uriel Acosta—all traveled the road to Damascus.

"You spent the first part of your life saying yes to everything," the Stranger is told. "After that you took to saying no to everything on principle. Now finish up by comprehending all. Don't be exclusive. Don't say, 'Either—or;' say, 'Both—and.' In a word—or two: Humanity—and Resignation" (SS, 29:359).

3

Part Three is the weakest play in the trilogy. Strindberg no more than Dante could make heaven as stimulating as hell or purgatory. Strindberg's heaven, like Swedenborg's, turns out to be a place where there is much talk, some thought, and no action. As so often happens in the theatre, celestial delights prove more painful than the torments of hell.

As philosophical drama the play brings the Damascus journey to a fitting end by summing up all the arguments on sexual conflict and the origin of guilt that were explicitly or implicitly expressed in the first two parts. As religious drama the play takes the hero to the threshold of heaven, following the course that Swedenborg describes. Like the first two parts of the trilogy, the play has nine locales, and in conformity with Swedenborg's chart of the spiritual world, it has four acts. (The act divisions are indicated by blank spaces in the Swedish edition.) Act 1, at the river bank, corresponds to the world of exteriors. Act 2, at the crossroads halfway up the mountain, corresponds to the world of interiors. Here the Stranger sees things as they are when stripped of their external husks.

Act 3, which includes scenes 3, 4, 5, and 6, corresponds to the preparations that the soul must endure to determine whether it is to enter heaven or hell. Here the Stranger remarries and reexamines his conscience. The fourth act, comprising the last three scenes, is set in the monastery. In the final moments of the play, the Stranger is draped in a black pall to signify his entrance into the spiritual world.

On the psychological level, the play completes the Stranger's journey in a way that is entirely consistent with Jung's theories. In the individuation process, the integration of the shadow with the total personality must precede the recognition and the disarming of the anima, which extends deeper into the unconscious. The Doctor, representing the shadow, was dealt with at the end of Part Two, but the Woman remained a disturbing factor. In act 3, the scenes showing the preparation of the voyager for the Swedenborgian heaven, the Woman is transformed into the archetypal mother who comforts and heals and makes all things right. In the first part of the trilogy, the Stranger had put himself in her hands because he made her over into a mother figure. Now, in the realm of spirit, she becomes entirely the mother she could not be as wife. When the Stranger tries to embrace her, she vanishes into the clouds.

After this last effort to find happiness with a woman, the Stranger enters the monastery at the top of the mountain. In the language of the psyche "the mountain," says Jung, "stands for the goal of the pilgrimage and ascent; hence it often has the psychological meaning of the self." [8] Having confronted Mother as part of the preparations for heaven, the Stranger must now, as he enters heaven, confront Father. The last wound in his soul is healed when the prior of the monastery, a majestic father figure, introduces the Stranger to another father who is revealed to be the Doctor. Here the end of the trilogy links up with the beginning. Early in the first part, the Doctor recognized the Stranger as the person who, when they were both children, had falsely blamed him for a trivial wrong. Now, at the end of the pilgrimage, the secret that the Stranger had repressed is revealed by the Doctor who himself had been guilty of a prank or two for which others were blamed. It is significant that Strindberg cannot bring his hero's pilgrimage to an end until the guilt feelings have been traced back to an origin in childhood and have been ameliorated by a father figure who may be regarded as equivalent to the superego in Freud's psychology or to the animus in Jung's.

The prior, described as having a Zeus-like head with long white hair and beard, is a representation of G. E. Klemming,[9] who appears several times in Strindberg's works, always as a venerable and rather awesome figure. The prior is able to call to mind thoughts that the Stranger had long suppressed. Klemming exercised a similar power over Strindberg. As a young man, Strindberg worked at the Royal Library in Stockholm, where his chief was Klemming, and under Klemming's spell, the young librarian was able to read virtually indecipherable manuscripts at first glance. Klemming, a professed spiritualist, was also a link between Swedenborg and Strindberg (SS, 28:319).[10] Swedenborg's dream diary, which records the dreams and hallucinations that the scientist had just before and during his religious crisis in the mid-1740s, was first published by Klemming in 1859. Strindberg in all probability read the dream book when he was working under Klemming; he certainly read it in 1896 at the time of his own mental crisis, when he discovered how similar his symptoms, physical and mental, were to those described by the mystic in his dream book.

Once he has squared his past with his conscience, the Stranger's pilgrimage is ended. The images in the final moments of the trilogy are simple and vivid. Stage center is a coffin. The Stranger appears dressed in the white robes of a novice. A woman carrying a child about to be christened crosses the stage, followed by a young couple about to be married. The Tempter vanishes, and the Confessor drapes a black pall over the Stranger.

4

Looked at from Jung's point of view, Part Three augured a happier existence for the dreamer, the warring elements in his soul having been brought into concord. Nothing could be further from the truth. If anything, his soul was more frayed and torn after the pilgrimage than before, and since he could not get himself a new one, all he could do was brush up the old one. The positive result of his journey was that the warring elements within him had been energized, and out of the conflict he could create drama. Desolated as a human being, he was stimulated as an artist. Part Two of the cycle is much more successful than Part Three in nearly all respects because it is a nightmare full of real fears, whereas Part Three is a daydream offering false hopes. Strindberg's infatuation with Harriet Bosse and his unavoidable disillusionment furnished the stimulus he needed in order to finish Part Three, but all he had succeeded in doing was to veil his deepest feelings with words like Humanity and Resignation. Artistic convention, religious tradition, and simple human weakness demanded that the pilgrim's progress end with despair defeated and the world overcome. But Strindberg knew that the Stranger's journey was not over, that the monastery on the mountain top was a mirage. The Stranger had advanced to the point at which deceptive woman, who gives with one hand and takes with the other, is transfigured into Mother, whose only shortcoming is that she does not exist; and he had traced the dark stream of conscience to its source in a small lie told by a little boy. To go beyond this, to explore the underworld of the psyche in another direction, if not more deeply, Strindberg had to abandon the Stranger and dream another dream. Even as he worked on Part Three, he shuffled old notes and scribbled new thoughts that would suddenly and magically coalesce into another dream play, which a Swedish critic has rightly called *To Damascus*, Part Four.[11]

11. *Miss Julie.* From the motion picture directed by Alf Sjöberg, 1951. Anita Björk as Julie, Ulf Palme as Jean, and Märta Dorff as Christine. Production Sandrew Film and Teater AB.

12. *Miss Julie.* Staged by the Department of Drama, Vassar College, 1969. Directed by Clinton Atkinson. Meryl Streep as Julie. (Photo by Arax-Serjan Studios.)

13. *The Father*, act 3. The Royal Dramatic Theatre, Stockholm, 1953. Directed by Bengt Ekerot. Lars Hanson as the Captain and Elsa Carlsson as the Nurse.

14. *To Damascus*, Part One, act 1, scene 1—at the street corner. Staged at the Royal Dramatic Theatre, Stockholm, 1937. Directed by Olof Molander.

15. *To Damascus*, Part One, act 4, scene 3—by the sea: "The three un-rigged masts of a foundered ship resemble three crosses." Staged at the Royal Dramatic Theatre, Stockholm, 1937. Directed by Olof Molander. Lars Hanson as the Stranger and Märta Ekström as the Woman.

16. *The Dance of Death*. The "vastation" scene. Staged at the Dagmar Theatre, Copenhagen, 1920. Directed by Henri Nathansen. Poul Reumert as Edgar.

17. The growing castle. Set for the world premiere of *A Dream Play* by Carl Grabow. Staged at Svenska teatern, Stockholm, 1907.

18. The theatre corridor in *A Dream Play*, as staged by the Royal Dramatic Theatre, Stockholm, 1935. Directed by Olof Molander. Sets by S. E. Skawonius.

19. Fairhaven in *A Dream Play*, as staged by the Royal Dramatic Theatre, Stockholm, 1935. Directed by Olof Molander. Sets by S. E. Skawonius. Projections by Isaac Grünewald.

20. Harriet Bosse as Indra's Daughter in *A Dream Play*.

21. *Master Olof.* The revolutionary and his disciple. The Royal Dramatic Theatre, Stockholm, 1951. Directed by Alf Sjöberg. Per Oscarsson as Olof and Anders Henriksson as Gert.

22. *Gustav Vasa*, act 3. The meeting of the fathers. The Royal Dramatic Theatre, Stockholm, 1939. Directed by Rune Carlsten. Lars Hanson as Gustav and Georg Blickingberg as Herman Israel.

23. *Erik XIV.* Partners in politics. Directed by Alf Sjöberg. Ulf Palme as Erik (at left) and Lars Hanson as Göran Persson.

24. *The Ghost Sonata.* The Malmö State Theatre, 1954. Directed by Ingmar Bergman. Benkt-Åke Benktsson as Hummel, Folke Sundqvist as the Student. Courtesy of the Swedish Information Service. (Photo by Skåne-Reportage.)

25. *The Ghost Sonata.* The Royal Dramatic Theatre, Stockholm, 1942. Directed by Olof Molander. Set by S. E. Skawonius.

26. *The Ghost Sonata*, scene 2. The Royal Dramatic Theatre, Stockholm, 1942. Directed by Olof Molander. Lars Hanson as Hummel and Märta Ekström as the Mummy.

27. *The Pelican*. Deutsches Theater, Berlin, 1914. Set by Ernst Stern. Directed by Max Reinhardt.

28. *The Pelican*. The final moments: "Hold me close, dear brother." Theater am Kurfürstendamm, Berlin, 1959. Directed by Oscar Fritz Schuh. Hanne Hiob and Peter Broglé. (Photo by Heinz Köster.)

Although *A Dream Play* incorporates many of the features of a dream, it is first of all an artfully constructed play. It begins like a Hans Christian Andersen fairy tale, develops into an anxiety dream, and ends like a nightmare. An officer in uniform is held prisoner in a strange castle with a dome that resembles a huge flower bud. A young maiden magically releases him from his prison, which is nothing more than his childhood home and all the disquieting memories associated with it, and together maid and man run off to conquer the world. He is transformed into lawyer and poet, she into woman and mother, as if they were characters in an English pantomime, and their adventures on life's way flash by like sketches in a musical revue. If Beckett turned a clown routine into *Waiting for Godot*, Strindberg turned the variety show into *A Dream Play*.

CHAPTER TEN

THE WORLD OF DREAMS

It resembles in form "the jumble and confusion of a dream," said Strindberg,

but still with a certain logic in it. The impossible becomes the probable. The characters flit by, with a few traits sketched in, the sketches merge, a single character dissolves into several characters, who again merge into one. Time and place do not exist; a minute is as long as many years; the snow lies on a summer landscape; the linden tree turns yellow, then green; and so on.[1]

To duplicate the transitory nature of dreams, their insubstantiality, the mixture of the vague and the precise, Strindberg contemplated the use of projections and fragmentary set pieces. At one rehearsal, Strindberg suggested to the designer that a limelight might be helpful and was rebuffed. Limelight, he was told, was only proper in a variety show. "So what if it is," replied Strindberg (SS, 50:288–89).

The sequence in which the Officer ages from a breezy, well-dressed young man, with a bouquet of roses for his beloved, to a decrepit and doddering old man in rags, with a bouquet of thorned twigs in his hand, is a vaudeville number in itself, as is the ballet of Plain Edith, the sad young woman who never gets asked to the ball. The whole play is compounded of such numbers—comic skits, dances, pantomimes, poetry readings—put together with incomparable adroitness to form a structure that is vastly larger than the sum of its parts.

Regrettably, the form and method of A Dream Play, so different from that of conventional literary drama, has often led critics and directors to see in it only the chaos of disconnected scenes and not the logic of poetry and dreams. Like the designer who was put off by Strindberg's suggestion that a spotlight be used, the critics have all too often been disconcerted and put off by the sheer theatricality of Strindberg at his imaginative best. Bernhard Diebold, that fine early German critic of Strindberg, distinguished poetry of the theatre from poetry in the theatre and valued the former as high art when it was an integral part of the play. But the end of A Dream Play disappointed him. Chrysanthemums instead of enlightenment: the poet gives up, and the prestidigitator takes over.[2] The visual richness of the play makes it extremely difficult to stage adequately and almost as difficult to read. No other play in world literature contains so many pictures and images, scenes and characters that are quickly and lastingly imprinted on the mind. But the literary critic tends to overlook the pictures or refuses to examine them with care, preferring to look for meaning where he has always found it before: in the words, in the plot, in the characters.

There is, of course, the semblance of a narrative in A Dream Play, but as Strindberg implies in his preliminary note, the narrative sways rather wildly and threatens at times to plunge completely off the road. In the prologue, Indra's Daughter descends from heaven to hear the complaints and grievances of mankind. Incarnated as Agnes, she appears on earth talking to a glazier in front of a growing castle. They enter the castle to release an army officer who is held prisoner there. The Officer is seen next in his parents' home and then at the stage entrance to an opera house, waiting in vain through the seasons and years for his beloved Victoria. A mysterious door with a cloverleaf vent-hole makes him feel uneasy, and when the police forbid him to open it, he goes to an attorney to obtain an injunction. Now the Lawyer meets Agnes and tells her that he is about to be awarded his degree as doctor of laws. In a mimed and danced scene at the church where the ceremonies are held, the Lawyer is denied his degree because he has been the advocate and defender of suffering humanity. The church organ, emitting the sound of human voices, is transformed into Fingal's Cave as the Lawyer and Agnes decide to unite their destinies. The next scene is a domestic one showing the Lawyer and Agnes married and wrangling bitterly over trifles. The Officer comes to release her from this domestic hell and carry her off to the seaside. Scenes at Foulstrand and Fairhaven present a broad view of society, with the tone varying from the satiric and humorous to the melancholy.

The next scene finds Agnes back in Fingal's Cave talking to a poet who had made his first appearance at Foulstrand. To the music of the wind and the waves, Agnes reads the Poet's complaint to the gods, and she confesses to him that she has had her fill of earthly life and desires to return to heaven. The scene shifts to the theatre corridor for the ceremonial opening of the cloverleaf door that is supposed to conceal the secret of the universe. The learned faculties are gathered there to learn the secret. The door is opened by the glazier and reveals nothing. In the last scene, outside the castle once again, the Daughter bids goodbye to her companions in life. The castle begins to burn. The whole cast parades by to throw their illusions on the fire. The Daughter enters the castle, and as she ascends to heaven, the golden crown of the castle bursts into a huge chrysanthemum. (See figure 17.)

There are at least three important motives threaded through this plot. First: "People are to be pitied." Life on earth is generally pretty miserable and someone should let the gods know. Second: "Love conquers all!" Perhaps love can find the way out from this vale of tears. Third: "The secret of the universe." Concealed behind the mysterious door, it must reveal the origin of human suffering or the meaning of it or the way to end it.

Tracing these three motives through the play reduces to order some of the apparent chaos of the play. Another pattern emerges from a consideration of the structure of the play. Although Strindberg, trying to capture the fluidity of a dream, designates neither acts nor scenes, there are obviously three separate acts, an act division occurring when there is a distinct break in the flow of merging scenes. (White space marks the divisions in the printed playscript.) Within each act or sequence, Strindberg has welded the scenes together by transformations, lighting effects, and other stage tricks to give the effect of dissolving views and uninterrupted action. Lights are dimmed, a wall is lifted away, a bed becomes a tent, an office a church, an organ a cave, and so on, but the flow of the action is unimpeded. (The prologue and the coalheavers scene on the shores of the Mediterranean lie outside the original design of the play. The latter was inserted after the final scenes had been written;[3] the former was written in 1906 when plans were being made for the first production of the play.) The first act or sequence begins at the castle and ends in Fingal's Cave with the Daughter and the Lawyer united. The second act begins in the home of the newly married couple and ends with the Daughter resolving to return to heaven—or with the contrast between the rich and the poor on the Riviera, if the coalheavers scene is kept. The third act begins in the grotto with the Daughter and the Poet seeing visions of drowning humanity and ends at the castle with the Daughter ascending to heaven. A diagram, using Strindberg's own scene designations (as given in a draft outline), may be of some help.

Acts	Scenes
I	1. Castle in the hollyhock forest
	2. Officer's room in the castle
	3. Mother's room
	4. The theatre passageway
	5. Lawyer's office
	6. Church with organ
	7. Fingal's Cave
II	8. Lawyer's parlor
	9. Foulstrand
	10. Fairhaven
	11. The schoolroom
	12. By the Mediterranean
III	13. Fingal's Cave
	14. The theatre passageway
	15. Castle in the hollyhock forest, with backdrop of human faces.

In the third act, Strindberg has repeated some scenes from the first act. His original intention was to duplicate the form of Part One of *To Damascus*, in which the last eight scenes reverse the order of the first eight. According to Martin Lamm, Strindberg abandoned the scheme.[4] If the scenes in *A Dream Play* are grouped as in the diagram—my reasons for doing so will become apparent later—it can be seen that Strindberg has simply made subtler use of cyclical structure.

This arrangement of scenes in both *To Damascus* and *A Dream Play* enhances the effect of sinking into a dream and awaking from it. Since, in Strindberg's view, earthly life is an illusion, the deeper the dreamer sleeps, the farther the Daughter sinks into the slough of human existence, achieving complete incarnation as a human being in the kitchen-bedroom scene that opens the second act. Her explorations at the bottom of life occupy this act, and in the third act, her ascension begins. This ascension represents an escape from suffering. When she finally shakes the clay of human existence from her feet and enters the burning castle, are we not to understand that the dream of life is over and that death is an awakening to the higher life promised by the burgeoning chrysanthemum? Such a view, after all, accords rather well with the quasi-

Buddhistic philosophy expressed by the Daughter in the last act. It is also explicit in the thoughts Strindberg recorded in his diary in the days before he wrote the final version of *A Dream Play*.

I feel how my soul is tied to the lower spheres where my wife now keeps company. This love affair, which was so great and extraordinary for me and which dissolved into a mockery of itself, has fully convinced me that life is an illusion and that the most beautiful affairs, which burst like the bubbles in dishwater, are designed to fill us with a loathing for life. We are not at home here; we are too good for this wretched existence. My soul loved this woman, and the brutality of the marriage bed disgusted me. Moreover, I have never really understood what the higher love for the beautiful soul of woman has to do with the not so nice reproductive system. The love organ is the same as one of the excremental organs. Isn't that typical![5]

The Daughter's revelation to the Poet at the end of the play carries the same burden. Strife is inevitable here on earth, and there is no meaning to the strife. Human beings only delude themselves by imposing a meaning on it and on their aspirations.

2

There may be another explanation. Since this play duplicates the workings of a dream, why should we not regard the Daughter's disclosure as an example of what Freud called secondary elaboration? When the dreamer is about to wake up, he tries to impose on the disorganized material of the dream a meaning acceptable to his consciousness. Such attempts invariably represent the last efforts of the dream censor to disguise the true meaning of the dream. Significantly, it was not until Strindberg had shaped and fashioned nearly all of the play that he sought to articulate to himself and to the Poet what it might mean. On November 18, 1901 he read a book on Indian religion and adapted some of its ideas to his own use in the final dialogue between the Daughter and the Poet. But Brahma has little to do with the rest of the play. It is much more helpful to invoke Schopenhauer and especially that awakener of modern times, Freud.

Although Strindberg never read a word written by Freud, both men were products of the same century and pupils of the same teachers. Both men followed in the wake of Schopenhauer and Hartmann, and both were guided by the pioneering works of Ribot, Charcot, Bernheim, and the host of other philosophers and medical men who were probing the inner life of nineteenth-century man while the followers of Marx and

Darwin were exploring his outer life. Strindberg was on the track of the Oedipus complex by 1887. In 1888, while Freud was translating Bernheim's *De la suggestion et de ses applications à la thérapeutique* and adding an introduction in which he elaborated on the distinction between hypnotic suggestion and autosuggestion, Strindberg was using Bernheim for the ending of *Miss Julie* and exploiting the same distinction. Freud worked out his "free association" method between 1892 and 1895, while Strindberg sketched his theory of *l'art fortuite* and automatic art in 1894. Both men began taking notes on their dreams about 1895. And if the fact that Strindberg's dream plays, *To Damascus* (1898–1901) and *A Dream Play* (1901), and Freud's central work, *The Interpretation of Dreams* (1898–99), were written at virtually the same time is not evidence for the existence of a zeitgeist, it certainly suggests that great men think alike.*

Freud describes at least five techniques by which the reprehensible thoughts of the unconscious are disguised and are allowed to slip into the conscious mind: secondary elaboration, symbolism, condensation, displacement, and dramatization through regression to visual concepts. The last is not so much a method to disguise thoughts as it is the natural method employed by the primitive, unconscious mind to express itself. Pictures and images are employed rather than abstractions and words. For instance, causal connections rendered by the conscious mind with such words as "therefore" and "because" are indicated by the unconscious in the succession of two apparently unconnected scenes.

The visual element is almost as strong in Strindberg's play as it is in our own dreams, and if we listen to the dialogue with our eyes closed,

---

*It is unlikely, but not impossible, that Strindberg had heard of Freud's theories in 1901; it is inconceivable that Freud would not have heard about *A Dream Play* during those years when *The Interpretation of Dreams* went through numerous revisions. Freud, who had wide cultural interests and who read Ibsen, would certainly have been attracted to a work with the title *A Dream Play*, especially in the period 1910–20, when Strindberg was one of the most talked about writers in Germany. But Freud was extremely jealous of his reputation as a pioneer and innovator and particularly anxious not to accord priority for his theories to anyone else. (See Frank J. Sulloway, *Freud, Biologist of the Mind* [New York, 1979], pp. 467–76. In the many volumes of the *Standard Edition of the Complete Psychological Works of Sigmund Freud*, Strindberg is cited only once, and *A Dream Play* is not mentioned at all. Although Freud gives the impression that he has read almost nothing by Strindberg (even the one passage he quotes was called to his attention by another doctor), he does not hesitate to aver that the dramatist suffered from a "grave mental abnormality." (*The Psychopathology of Everyday Life*, in *The Standard Edition of the Complete Psychological Works of Sigmund Freud*, trans. James Strachey, 24 vols., [London, 1953–74], 6:212.)

we shall never comprehend the play. Let us look at the first few scenes. The Daughter and the Glazier refer to a prisoner in the castle. The scene changes to a room in the castle where the Officer, rocking in a chair, is striking a table with his saber. The Daughter tells him not to do so and removes the saber from his hands. Sixty years after Freud, the symbolism of this scene is elementary. The daughter of the gods is a mother figure in the eyes of the Officer, who describes her as the embodiment of the harmony of the universe, and like a good nineteenth-century mother, she is telling her son, rocking in his crib, not to masturbate. This vision of childhood plus associated thoughts of injustice and the impossibility of escaping from the prison motivate the next change of scene, which reveals the nature of the Officer's prison. In one sense, his prison is his childhood home from whose formative influences he can never escape. He remains a child in spirit throughout the play. The motive of injustice is developed when the Officer's mother, evoked by the presence of the Daughter, reminds him of a childhood theft for which the wrong person was punished. Now a brewing quarrel between the Officer's parents suggests the disharmony of earthly life, but the Daughter declares that, although living is difficult, love can smooth the way. This optimistic declaration is the open sesame to the following scene in the theatre corridor where the Officer waits with unfaltering hope for his beloved Victoria. (See figure 18.)

Imagine this sequence of three scenes as a silent film. The daughter Agnes and fatherly old man outside fantastic castle—close-up of bars on windows—Agnes entering room—Officer rocking—close-up of Agnes removing saber from his hand and shaking her finger at him—pout of displeasure on Officer's face changing to look of admiration and devotion—Agnes urging Officer to escape—Officer shrugging shoulders hopelessly—Officer's mother and father fading in while Agnes and Officer remain on screen—and so on. Filmed this way, the scenes would link together more clearly than they do on the page, for the dialogue often diverts our attention from the basic level on which the play operates. The dialogue is an outgrowth of the visions, not vice versa. That is as it should be, for the play is no more about ideas than the best music is. Hence Strindberg could suggest his *Dream Play* to a composer-friend who was looking for a good musical subject. "But shortened!" wrote Strindberg. "A musical chamber play, with all the philosophizing cut out and only the 'scenes' left. . . . Dramatic-lyrical music, not theatrical-recitative-argumentative."[6] The words function like music to gild the pictures and conceal their meaning, but without the inner tension and the beauty they provide, the play would be all the poorer, all depth and no surface.

The visual links are more apparent in the next sequence of three scenes: the theatre corridor, the Lawyer's office, the church. Here Strindberg has artfully made the stage properties remain the same throughout while serving different purposes. The linden tree becomes a hat tree and then a candelabrum; the doorkeeper's room becomes the Lawyer's desk and then a pulpit; while the mysterious door becomes the Lawyer's files and then the door to the church sacristy. These three scenes are rigidly grappled together as far as the eye is concerned, and to understand their significance we should think of them as superimposed on one another so as to form one. This is a perfect example of condensation of scenes.

Condensation of characters or its opposite, decomposition of character, is another dream technique that Strindberg consciously and deliberately employs. In his prefatory note he says, "The characters split, double, multiply, dissolve, thicken, fade away, coalesce." The three chief male characters—the carefree, eternally hopeful Officer who wins the laurel wreath; the harrassed Lawyer, who knows only life's pains and responsibilities and who is given the crown of thorns; and the Poet whose moods alternate between enthusiasm and skepticism—are manifestly aspects of one person. Similarly, the Daughter subsumes the characters of the Officer's mother and of the Doorkeeper, whose place she physically takes and whose shawl, incorporating thirty years of disappointment, she wears. It is only one step more to see that Strindberg intended that all the men coalesce into one male and all the women into one female. He seems to have thought of his play as basically a two-character drama, and in an early version, he listed the dramatis personae under two headings: the Man and the Woman.[7] Finally, remembering the bisexual nature of man, the subjective nature of the play, and the egocentric nature of dreams, we must allow the two characters ultimately to fuse into one; and it is absurd to ask, as some caviling critics have, which of the thirty characters in the play is the dreamer.

3

The story line of the play takes us on a journey through life in which the Man grows up to his responsibilities, while the Woman sinks into the mire of earthly existence. In the last part of the play, as the Woman ascends and shakes the clay from her feet, the Man becomes a poet seeking a meaning to the strife of existence. This journey starts at the castle, proceeds through the theatre corridor where the cloverleaf door is the center of attention, and reaches its first stopping point in the cave. The castle, theatre, door, and cave are the dominant symbols in the play by virtue of their position in its structure.

The theatre introduces us to the notion, basic to the thought of the whole play, that the world is an illusion and a dream. The idea is conveyed symbolically here by having us enter the adult world of law, religion, and learning through the theatre. The fact that the mysterious door which opens on nothing is first encountered in the theatre enforces this view.

In the office and in the church the Lawyer[8] is pictured as a Christlike sufferer, who takes upon himself the cares and crimes of the world and receives in return only the contempt of the right-thinking people. The Daughter offers him a crown of thorns and the consolations of love and marriage. Love is to conquer all. At this point, there occurs another symbolic transformation. In the church, the organ, at which the Daughter has been playing and from which the voices of mankind have welled up in a profoundly moving kyrie, is transformed into a sea grotto as the Daughter and the Lawyer decide to marry. As symbols, water and church are associated with woman; the grotto is a common simulation of the female sex organ, notoriously in Wagner's *Tannhäuser*; and the union of organ and cave here is an obvious symbol of sexual intercourse. The association of organ and cave occurs earlier in Strindberg in his long short story "The Romantic Organist at Rånö," written in 1888, in which the dreamy organist thinks of the musical instrument (SS, 21:216–33) as a gigantic organism which has taken thousands of years to grow and compares it first to a cave and finally to his loved one. The prototype for this feat of imagination is found in an even earlier story, "Rebuilding," written in 1884. There, the repressed heroine intoxicates herself with perfume and, in a remarkable rapture, imagines herself in church, the organ pounding out a *Dies Irae*, voices of angels and titans lifting the roof, while flashes of lightning illuminate the words "Crucify the Flesh." After a sudden bolt of thunder, the organ grows quieter, its pipes become syrinxes, its tunes become the melodies of Pan, Saint Francis becomes Apollo, "and from the graves beneath the floor could be heard the pounding of the imprisoned beings who wanted to get out, and they shouted, 'The Word is made Flesh!'" (SS, 15:22).

Another source for the transformation of the organ into cave is to be found in Samuel Butler's *Erewhon*,[9] which appeared in a revised edition in 1901. Butler describes a dream in which an organ turns into Fingal's Cave, precisely as in Strindberg's play. Butler's vitalism and his stinging animadversions on the Darwinists would have attracted Strindberg to the English writer. Having read him, he would have wanted to know more about Fingal's Cave. Strindberg had never visited the famous grotto (though he might have seen Turner's painting of it, Turner being the painter whom he most admired at about this time), and any grotto could have been made to serve his symbolic purpose. But none so well as Fingal's Cave. When seen in a drawing where there is no sense of scale, it is an excellent representation of the vulva.[10]

The second act begins in the kitchen and bedroom of the Lawyer's home, where Strindberg treats us to a miniature drama of married life. From this domestic hell Agnes is rescued by the Officer, just as she had once rescued him from his imprisonment at home. As the Officer takes her out to enjoy life, the kitchen-bedroom apartment is transformed into Foulstrand and Fairhaven. (See figure 19.) The small world gives way to the large in a kaleidoscopic series of scenes.

When Agnes has ranged over all of earthly life and has seen how fleeting happiness is, how illusory are our hopes, how unceasing the conflict between pleasure and duty, she is ready to begin her ascent to her heavenly home. She must start at the bottom, work her way up, and undergo the final test of existence as a human being: the repetition of all one's miseries. Here we have another reason for the cyclical structure of the play.

She returns to Fingal's Cave where the flowing waters, the broken silver cord, the drowning people, and the song of the wind, which is likened to the cries of newborn babes, all suggest that the scene signifies birth, probably in two senses: the complete coming into the world of the Daughter, that is, her utter separation from heaven, and the beginning of her rebirth as a goddess. At the time that Strindberg was working up his notes for *A Dream Play*, he painted a seascape with a distant shore line entirely framed by foliage so that the picture looks like a sea grotto. He called it "Baby's First Cradle."[11]

Now the scenes carry us quickly back to our starting point, back through the world of illusion, back through the theatre corridor and the pageantry of the door-opening ceremony, and back to the reality of the castle. I say the reality of the castle, for if my line of thought is correct, the theatre must divide the illusory world from the real.

It takes no doctor come from Vienna to tell us what this castle stands for, with its ability to grow and raise itself, with its crown that resembles a flower bud, with the forest of hollyhocks that surrounds it, and the manure piles that lie below. It takes all the imagination of a poet to conceive of it as a castle and only an adolescent's knowledge of anatomy to recognize it as a phallus.[12] The castle and its surroundings are the optical equivalent of Strindberg's perception that the sex and excremental systems are joined. As Yeats would say in his "Crazy Jane" poem, "Love has pitched his mansion in / The place of excrement." For the male dreamer the fundamental reality is that represented by the castle. By extension, that reality is equivalent to the id, which Freud postulated as the reservoir of the libido and the basis of the personality. When Strindberg in his preliminary note describes the mind that presides over the dream as having no secrets, knowing no inconsistencies, no scruples, no laws, and neither judging nor acquitting but only narrating, he is giving a beautifully precise definition of the id. Since the id represents the mind in its pristine state before civilization has made its imprint, the castle lies outside society, and the Daughter on her return trip must go into the desert to reach it. As the id is the wellspring of all mental life, so the castle is the source of all the action of the play, which flows from it and returns to it. This is yet another reason for the cyclical structure.

The fact that the Officer is a prisoner in the castle points in two directions. If the castle is a phallus, the Officer represents the soul or spirit imprisoned in the body from whose peremptory demands it cannot escape. The conception of the body as a prison where the soul is punished for sins committed in previous existences is a basic doctrine of Gnosticism and Neoplatonism. "The soul was cast into the body's prison," and similar statements are common in Strindberg (SS, 28:316; 40:127; 46:23; 48:1022).[13] But as mentioned before, the Officer is also the prisoner of his home and his parents, those agents which inhibit the id and which eventually contribute to the formation of the conscience or superego. The transformation of the castle to home and the simultaneous introduction of the theme of injustice show the first step in a process that culminates with the appearance of the duty-obsessed Lawyer.

If we allow the castle to stand for the idea that the only reality is the sensual and unconscious life and that all else is illusion, we can come to a better understanding of the secret of the universe, the search for which is one of the three main motives in the play. Three times it is almost completely revealed: when the door is opened, when the Daughter reads the Poet's lamentation in the grotto, and when the Daughter is about to ascend to heaven. The opening of the door reveals the futility and super-ficiality of organized knowledge. In the grotto scene, the Poet almost stumbles on the secret when in his complaint to Brahma he asks:

Why are we born like animals,
We the progeny of God, the family of man?
Our spirit demands other vestures
Than these of blood and filth.
Shall God's image cut his second teeth—

"Shush!" interrupts the Daughter. "No one has yet solved the riddle of life" (SS, 36:304). Why such a reaction to the mere mention of teeth? Either the Daughter is an informed Swedenborgian who knows that in the doctrine of correspondences teeth are a symbol of sensuality or a Freudian analyst who believes that the second dentition coincides with the beginning of direct sexual expression or a Strindbergian poet who associates innocence with the milk teeth of childhood: "those pearls without any apparent purpose other than to light up a smile." [14]

In the last scene, the Daughter herself tries to explain the riddle of the universe to the Poet. Brahma, the original power or potency, was se-duced by the world mother Maya, and out of this sinful union the il-lusory earth was born. For the dreamer, only the male principle is real; the conjunction of male and female ends in illusion. The very structure of the drama supports this view. The castle contains the whole play, while the castle and cave together flank the first and last acts, fencing in both the world of illusion represented by the theatre and the social world of the kaleidoscopic second act.

This gives rise to a further thought, a refinement on what I have sug-gested so far. May not the grotto, the scene of symbolic birth, be the uterus? And may not the theatre corridor which separates the castle from the cave be the vagina? We must not hedge in our thoughts with scruples when dealing with the unconscious, which is always more concrete and tactile than the analytical mind. At one time Strindberg seems to have thought of the corridor as having an underground aspect, for in an early version of his play, he pictured mushrooms growing out of the walls of the corridor. [15] Mushrooms are relevant to a vagina symbol since the Swedish word for mushroom is the same as the word for sponge, and sponge in the slang of the time denoted a common form of female con-traceptive. Freud, in 1897, reported the case of a young girl [16] who, be-cause of a similar confusion in German, had developed an irrational fear of mushrooms (Schwamm). Freud traced the origin of the fear to the stern warnings of the girl's religious mother against the use of preventives in sexual intercourse, sponges (*Schwamm*) having been specifically mentioned.

If the corridor is a vagina symbol, we might expect to find in it some male symbol or the intimation of a union of male and female symbols. We do not have to look far. Dominating the scene is a single gigantic aconite. With its flowers in a long stiff spike, this is probably a male symbol, providing a reminiscence of the towering hollyhocks of the opening scene and a harbinger of the profusion of aconites that will surround the castle in the last scene, though its immediate function in the theatre corridor is to keynote the scene, its combination of beautiful flowers and poisonous root symbolizing the deceptive hopes and illusions with which life lures us on. The linden tree and the nearby cellar window are intended, I believe, as a visual echo of the castle and cave. The early version of the play ends with the Officer, after having spent his life waiting for his beloved, falling down dead at this cellar window.[17]

4

The pageant of human suffering that the play offers requires some kind of explanation, and toward the end of the play, an attempt is made to provide one. From the unfortunate union of male sexual energy with maternal matter there arise all the contradictory strivings that plague mankind. "To free themselves from earthly matter," says the Daughter,

the progeny of Brahma seek deprivation and suffering. . . . But this yearning to suffer collides with the craving for pleasure, or love. . . . [The result] is conflict between the anguish of joy and the pleasures of suffering, the torments of remorse and the delights of sensuality. [SS, 36:324]

The conclusion reached by the Daughter is only slightly different from Empedocles' view of life as based on the ceaseless oppugnancy of love and strife and is perhaps even closer to Freud's dualism of Eros and the death instinct. The idea of recurrence expressed by the Lawyer, connected as it is in the play with moral masochism, guilt feelings, and the conception of death as the only liberator, provides an illuminating analogy to Freud's repetition compulsion, from which he derived the death instinct.

In this struggle, the woman plays the double role customarily assigned her by Christianity and by the Oriental religions. As the embodiment of the reproductive instinct, she is the temptress. But once she has satisfied her instincts and filled her womb, she becomes the redeemer with the power to lift man to heaven on the wings of the hope that he, too, can be reborn. Sinking down into earthly existence, the Daughter is primarily the temptress; ascending, she is the redeemer.*

The end of the conflict of male and female principles can come only with death. But death in this play has a double meaning, too. As the Lawyer and the Daughter were united through the agency of the organ and the cave, so now the Poet and the Daughter are united by fire in the final moment. The fire suggests sexual excitement, dying signifies orgasm ("The intensest moment of love resembles death," wrote Strindberg, "— the closed eyes, the corpselike paleness, the cessation of consciousness" [SS: 47:776]), and the bursting chrysanthemum on top of the castle is ejaculation poeticized.

In the finale, all the characters pass in review to throw their illusions on the purging fire. Only the old sensualist Don Juan has nothing to toss into the flames. When Christina, the girl who spends her time sealing windows—a perfect representation of the inhibitive forces, as is the Officer's mother who is continually trimming the lamp (notice, by the way, how both have the same significant name)—comes to continue her work at the castle, she is informed that there is nothing there for her to seal up.

"Shall I never learn how to mortify the flesh?" wondered Strindberg in 1895. "It's still too young and fiery. But then it shall be burned up! And will be indeed! But what of the soul? Perhaps up in smoke too!" [18]

So the play ends and the dreamer awakes. For a moment, the irreconcilable opposites have been reconciled. If the play had gone on, we would have seen only the scorched hills and the charred tree stumps that greet the Daughter after her marriage to the Lawyer.

5

Harriet Bosse's exotic, somewhat Javanese beauty inspired the creation of the Daughter (figure 20) and gave Strindberg's dream an Oriental cast, but Harriet's leaving him after only a few weeks of marriage became the wellspring from which the play gushed forth. Alone in the rooms where he had enjoyed a few precious days of inexpressible joy with her, he was torn by conflicting thoughts about this woman who gave him

---

*The basic plot of A Dream Play may have been suggested by Empedocles. In his Purifications, a divine spirit, after being incarnated, sets about purifying the world and having done its best, is redeemed, allowed to shed its fleshly encasement and to re-enter the realm of spirit.

happiness and took it away with her. He saw her alternately as an angel and as a demon. At times he could, because of her, believe that "woman comes from a higher source but has fallen farther down than man." At other times he saw her as a spirit from the "dark underworld."[19] His ambivalence provided the conflict his dream play needed. The downward movement of the Daughter in the first act of the play, in which she becomes a creature of flesh and blood, and the upward movement in the third act, in which she becomes etherealized, represent the two contradictory aspects of woman.

There were also moments when Harriet was a woman in both flesh and spirit at once. Before he married her, his thoughts of her were so intense at times that he both saw and felt her come to him. He copulated with her in spirit. To him these masturbatory fantasies were direct and simple verifications of Swedenborg's belief that the human being "is so created as to be in the spiritual world and in the natural world at the same time. The spiritual world is where the angels are, and the natural world where men are."[20] Strindberg took dreams to be the element in which natural man and physical man were equally present. A Dream Play, which Strindberg called "my best-loved play, the child whose birth gave me the greatest pain"[21] because he poured into it all his unrequited longing for Harriet, fuses together the physical and the spiritual by making the things of the spirit as physical as possible and by converting the fundamental physical things into symbols. The fire at the end is both sexual ardor and spiritual purification. The golden chrysanthemum is at one and the same time a symbol of the phallus and an image of peace and harmony. The religious imagery, which often seems obtrusive, is necessary to maintain the transcendental aspect.

It is this psychophysical parallelism that makes A Dream Play difficult to stage effectively, not the large cast or the meandering plot. Too much stage machinery and the spirit vanishes; too much symbolism and religious talk and the audience vanishes. It is not true, although one often hears it said in America, that the play has never been staged successfully. There have been several fine productions in Sweden and a few elsewhere in Europe. Strindberg's own ideas on mounting A Dream Play[22] inclined toward the starkly simple: a few props, some painted flats if needed, some projections if possible. He believed that the audience's imagination should do most of the scene designer's work.

In masturbatory fantasies and in wet dreams, matter and spirit come together, and the bursting chrysanthemum conveys that well enough. The door, on the other hand, is a more deceptive symbol because of all the talk about finding the solution to the riddle of the world behind it. In the Freudian doctrine of correspondences, the door is a female symbol, and not surprisingly, the Daughter guards it. (And in German slang at about that time "the great secret of the world" meant one's first experience of sexual intercourse).[23] An entry in Strindberg's diary[24] made when he was writing *A Dream Play* links together Daughter, door, castle, and riddle:

Read about the teachings of the Indian religions. The whole world only a sham. The divine original force (Maghavan-Atma, Tat, Om, Brahman) let itself be seduced by Maya, the reproductive drive. In that way the divine element sinned against itself. (Love is sin, therefore the pangs of love are the worst hell.) Thus the world exists through sin—if it exists at all, since it is only a dream image (hence my Dream Play an image of life), a phantom, whose annihilation is the purpose of asceticism. But this purpose comes into conflict with the sex drive, and the final result is a ceaseless vacillation between sensual orgies and pangs of repentance.
That seems to be the answer to the riddle of the world.
I got the above from a history of literature just when I was about to finish my dream play "The Growing Castle." That was the morning of the 18th. But that morning I saw the castle (the cavalry barracks) illuminated, as it were, by the rising sun.
Indian religion gave me the explanation of my Dream Play and the meaning of Indra's Daughter, the Secret of the Door:—Nothing.

Nothing is the answer to the world riddle because sexual desire and sexual remorse cancel each other out. The world itself is nothing, a mirage, because it, too, is the result of a sexual union. The Daughter's own words in the play (quoted earlier) refine this idea and provide a poetic and philosophic commentary on the action of the play.

One thing they definitely do not do: that is, reveal the secret behind the door. Strindberg's note in his diary was written after he had worked the scene of the door opening into his scenario. He hit upon the explanation for the scene after he had conceived it. This, of course, is typical of dream work: first the image, then the rationalization. It was also characteristic of Strindberg's poetic vision. The physical fact or event came first; subsequently, he sought an occult or spiritual explanation for it. That was the operating principle behind *The Occult Diary*. What Freud calls secondary elaboration was the poet's attempt to escape from the thralldom of matter and the prison of the body.

In this instance he found what he wanted in a history of world literature. Earlier in the process of giving shape and coherence to his dream play, he had certainly got some help from Carl Du Prel's *Det dolda själs-lifvet* (The Hidden Life of the Soul), which was in Strindberg's library. Du Prel, whom I have mentioned before (page 67) in connection with Strindberg's psychological experiments, stands midway between Schopenhauer and Freud in the development of theories of the unconscious. Starting with the premise that there was a double consciousness in human beings, an empirical self and a transcendental self, Du Prel accumulated evidence, much of it from the behavior of somnambulists, showing that a conflict exists between these two selves and that the final arbiter is the transcendental self. The empirical self, which is much like the ego in Freud's system, deals with the external "real" world while the transcendental self, which is the individual unconscious, is the gray eminence behind the scenes. The transcendental self (or subject), hidden from observation most of the time by the busy external self (or object), reveals a bit of itself in the inspired creations of the artist, in the strange workings of the conscience, and in sexual infatuations that flout convention and defy reason. It reveals even more of itself in the actions of the somnambulist and in the images of the dreamer. It will reveal itself fully only when we die, since death is merely an awakening in the transcendental sphere.

There is nothing new in all of this, but when Du Prel discusses dreams, he takes a giant step towards Freud's position. "That brilliant mystic Du Prel," Freud said of him, "one of the few authors for whose neglect in earlier editions of [*The Interpretation of Dreams*] I should wish to express my regret, declares that the gateway to metaphysics . . . lies not in waking life but in the dream." [25] Du Prel devotes an entire section to the dreamer as dramatist, who sketches out a plot that can only be fully perceived and understood on the transcendental level, and he implies that the dream arises from the conflict between the divided selves. (He even touches briefly, in a passage that Freud noted, on the phenomenon of condensation of ideas and characters in dreams.) [26] The transcendental self leads our thoughts; it is the secret director and stage manager of our dreams, but it cares only for our well-being and has no concern for the wishes and demands of the empirical or physical self. Since the dream weaves together elements of the two selves, Du Prel thought of the dream work as a reconciliation rather than as a conflict, and he emphasized what the dream reveals about the transcendental self rather than what it conceals. Thus the concept of repression eluded him. He saw that the dream was the portal to the "dark realm where we shall find man's metaphysical roots,"²⁷ but he did not see the censor who stood at the portal. What need was there to censor the metaphysical, which cared only for our well-being?

Du Prel comes closest to the idea of dream censorship and of repression when he offers an explanation of the telescoping of time in dreams.²⁸ In some of the most perceptive pages of his book, he shows that the cause of a dream is equally the cause of the awakening. A sleeping man hears a shot. He then dreams of being recruited into the army, of deserting, being caught, court-martialed, condemned to death, haled before the firing squad—and is awakened by the real shot. The whole dream occupies only the time it takes the sleeping man to wake up. It is almost a case of the effect preceding the cause. Du Prel says that the only acceptable explanation for this phenomenon lies in the existence of two selves in the mind. The transcendental self or consciousness either foresees the cause and teleologically directs the events of the dream to that end, or it deliberately arranges matters so that the disturbed sleep of the dreamer may be soothed. Either way, the final occurrence in the dream is "only the cause of the awakening in fantastic guise."²⁹

In A Dream Play, the opening of the door and the bursting of the chrysanthemum are the fantastic guise assumed by the real cause, and to suggest as strongly as possible that the dream is caused by what ends it and makes the dreamer wake, Strindberg places the castle at both the very beginning and very end of the play, like the sound of the gunshot in the dream of the firing squad.

6

The dramatist could also have found in the mystic philosopher the germinal idea for the riddle that provides an element of suspense in A Dream Play. Du Prel wrote that thinking man is confronted by two great mysteries, the mystery of the world and the mystery of man, the first having to do with the ultimate composition of the physical world and the second having to do with the transcendent world, with man's psyche. "Just as the natural world shall provide the explanation for the riddle of the world [verldsgåtan], so the dream world shall provide the explanation for the riddle of man [menniskans gåta]."³⁰ Strindberg changes the riddle of man to the riddle of life (livets gåta), which sharpens the contrast between the two riddles and then combines them to form a single strand in the plot of A Dream Play. The Daughter refers to the riddle of life when she objects to the Poet's comments on children's teeth, while the solution to the riddle of the world is supposed to lie behind the door. When the old man with the glass-cutter (Haeckel) opens the door and finds nothing behind it, the world riddle is disposed of. But this non-revelation leaves the riddle of life unsolved. Like the learned men of the graduate faculties, we feel cheated.

THE CHANCELLOR OF THE UNIVERSITY. Will the Daughter of the gods be so good as to tell us what her intentions are? What is the purpose of this door opening?

THE DAUGHTER. No, good people. If I were to tell you, you would not believe me.

DEAN OF THE MEDICAL FACULTY. It's nothing! Nothing at all!

THE DAUGHTER. You are right. But you have not understood. [SS, 36:318]

The Daughter seems to be addressing herself to us as well as to the dean. Why does no one see anything behind the door? In the church that door led to the sacristy; in the office it was the door to the Lawyer's files; and in the theatre, where it was first seen, the Officer was struck by its resemblance to the pantry door of his childhood. It is manifestly not true that there is nothing behind the door. Everything seems to be behind it.

Telling us that the door contains nothing is a perfect example of displacement, the dream technique by which the ego diverts our attention and shifts the emphasis from what is truly important. That door is the last portal to the dark realm, and it is guarded by the Daughter. When we first hear of it, the dreamer in the guise of the Officer associates it with pantries and with food. For the dreamer, the door connects with mother, the provider of nourishment and the source of physical satisfaction and contentment. But the cloverleaf ventilation hole in the door stamps it unmistakably as an outhouse door, and consequently the door must be taken to represent the food of life in its passage from pantry to privy, from ingestion to excretion. On the most basic and earthy level the castle is phallus and the door is anus. In more general terms the two symbols can be equated with the two main biological concerns, sex and food. One of them is more easily sublimated than the other, and whereas the castle in its upward growth aspires to spiritual significance, the door remains imbedded in the physical world. The secret it reveals is the secret of matter, and the riddle it solves is Haeckel's world riddle. The other riddle remains to be solved. The one has to do with how we live; the other with why we live.

In the guise of the Poet the dreamer seeks union with the Daughter in the grotto scene where the birth symbols are so prominent. The journey back to the mysterious door from Fingal's Cave is effected through a series of images. If Strindberg had written his play a decade or two later, he would probably have made use of projections and created a cinematic montage. As it is, some of the images have to be verbalized. The fabled ghost ship *The Flying Dutchman* turns into a vessel in distress in a howling gale. Its crew calls for help, and in response Christ appears walking on the water. Instead of welcoming him as their saviour, the endangered sailors scream in terror at the sight of him and hurl themselves into the storm-tossed waters. The mast of the ship now becomes a telephone communications tower, and the tower is transformed into a church spire—or rather into the shadow of one cast on a snow-covered military drill field. Finally a cloud sweeps over the field, blotting out the vision.

This montage crowds together the principal statements of the play, producing a stretto effect in the fugal structure. The captain of *The Flying Dutchman* hopes to be redeemed by love but is doomed to roam the seven seas forever. Christ offers redemption through sacrifice, but drowning mankind not only shuns the salvation he offers, it executes him. The telephone tower is a modern tower of Babel, an image of modern man's futile efforts to attain heaven by means of science and invention, while the church that should carry man upwards appears only as a shadow without substance. The image of the cloud sweeping across the field and blotting out the sun contains all these contradictions and presents the basic polarity of Strindberg's vision. "The light of the sun," explains the Poet, "created the dark tower, but the dark shadow of the cloud smothered the dark shadow of the tower" (*SS*, 36:309). At the end of the play, the Daughter will define the opposed forces as male and female, and here the vision of a platoon of soldiers marching across the shadow of the spire seems to carry a sexual significance, with fire and water symbolizing the male and female principles. "The wet cloud put out the sun's fire," is the Poet's comment (*SS*, 36:309).

Condensing the major themes of the entire drama, this montage of images reveals that man's efforts to resolve the discords and contradictions of earthly life through love, devotion, and redemption are unavailing because they have their source in, and are energized by, the irremediable tensions between the male and female principles, between Brahma and Maya, spirit and matter.

While these visions are passing before the eyes of the Poet and the Daughter, the scene of action changes from the grotto to the theatre corridor, where the Daughter sets about making arrangements for the opening of the door. This event is not particularly disturbing to the dreamer because it has to do with the world riddle and not the riddle of life. The knowledge and learning of the scholars turns out to be as worthless as excrement when the outhouse door is opened. In contrast, the immolation scene at the end confronts the dreamer with the riddle of life, and for him it is both excruciatingly beautiful and excruciatingly painful because this death by fire intimates that the riddle of life can only be solved by a violation of a basic taboo—a physical union with mother. At first this realization, the thought on the verge of becoming deed, is as sublimely beautiful as the aconites in bloom outside the castle. But, like the aconite, the thought has a poisonous root. The Daughter enters the castle—an example of dream inversion—and the submerged oedipal thought breaks to the surface at the moment of orgasm and death. The veil is rent, and for a fleeting second the soul finds release, for a brief moment the eye is blinded by a vision of life without contradictions; and then the dreamer awakes in anguish, feeling but not understanding the enormity of his guilt.

All those questioning, sorrowful faces seen in the burning castle may be condensed into the face of the tormented dreamer. And behind all the irreconcilable feelings that the play presents lies the first one that we experience, the one that casts us out of paradise.

"Yes, my friend, the universe does have secrets," says Esther to her lover Max in a novel Strindberg wrote in 1904.

But people go about, not like the blind, because they do see, but not understanding.

Who you are, who I am, that's what we don't know. But when we were together, I felt as if I were embracing a corpse, which wasn't yours, but someone else's—I won't say whose.

And you, you seemed to be my father, and I felt ashamed and disgusted! What is this frightening, secret thing we have stumbled on to?

Now for the first time perhaps mankind will get to know the unsolvable riddles. Suspect them anyway! [SS, 40:243–44]

7

Vague but inescapable feelings of guilt compelled Strindberg to embark on his journey to Damascus in 1898. If he could come to terms with his conscience, he would be a new man. But his conscience, imbedded in his unconscious, held secrets his ego refused to face. The second part of the To Damascus trilogy disclosed how the unconscious conceals its primary motives behind secondary ones that are more acceptable to the ego. In the third part, the long road to Damascus ends in the blind alley of childhood, where a small lie had warped the hero's moral universe.

Strindberg made this lie the starting point of his deepest exploration of the unconscious, the journey undertaken in *A Dream Play.*

The examination of the moral sense had been a fairly simple business in earlier times. When Rousseau was sixteen and serving as a footman, he stole a pretty pink and silver ribbon, and when it was found in his possession, he lied and said a maid servant had given it to him. That lie festered in his soul, and years later he tried to rid himself of it by writing his confessions. Why had he lied in the first place? Because he feared shame and dishonor more than death itself, as the old novels used to say.

For Strindberg, such an answer only raised more questions. He saw that the demon of guilt lurked in the unconscious, in what Du Prel called the dark realm. Yet was it conceivable that it lay in wait year after year, ready at any moment to pounce on the ego, simply because of a childhood prank? Could so many accusing devils be made to stand on the point of one little lie? If so, why would not confession exorcize them, one's own confession and the confession of others, all canceling each other out, as at the end of the *To Damascus* trilogy? The conclusion of the trilogy is a false conclusion, and in *A Dream Play* the admission of guilt only leads to more anguish.

If conscience is the presence of God in man, why did it not manifest itself before the lie rather than after? If not, if it was not innately in man, what gave birth to it? In the first part of *To Damascus* all such questions were referred to the Higher Powers. In *A Dream Play* the Higher Powers have vanished through the door that conceals the secret of life and the meaning of dreams. And the poet-dramatist, the explorer of the soul, is no longer traveling down the road to Damascus waiting for the blinding light to strike him; he is making his way gropingly towards that portal to the dark realm, the modern man's gate of horn, in order to see once and for all what lies behind it.

There, the revelation that should make the dreamer blissfully happy is seen to be the source of all his agony of soul. "When the pain is most excruciating," says Strindberg in his prefatory note to the play, "the moment of waking comes and reconciles the dreamer to reality, which, however agonizing it may be, is a joy and a pleasure at that moment compared to the painful dream" (SS, 36:215). The journey that began with a Jungian search for the self ends in a Freudian consummation with mother. The dream tetralogy that opened with prospects of rebirth and intimations of immortality culminates in the little death of orgasm. The dreamer's union with mother is a union of Eros with Thanatos, of love with destructiveness. Strindberg's dream cycle, the gateway to the twentieth century as surely as *Faust* is to the nineteenth, ends with the most representative single image of the century of the id and the age of anxiety. As the Daughter enters the burning castle, the flames light up a "wall of human faces, questioning, sorrowful, despairing. As the castle burns, the flower bud at the top bursts and blossoms into a huge chrysanthemum" (SS, 36:330).

Between Parts Two and Three of the *To Damascus* trilogy, Strindberg wrote fourteen other plays, averaging a full-length play every twelve weeks or so. Five of these are history plays, and it is characteristic of Strindberg's working methods that he should turn to history for dramatic material before he had quite finished exploring his psyche. Perhaps he grew tired of drinking water out of his own cistern, but there may also have been a commercial motive. Strindberg knew that the *To Damascus* plays were too abstruse in thought and too revolutionary in technique to attract a large audience. By exploring Swedish history he could establish an immediate rapport with his audience and give his new view of life a wider hearing than it could possibly receive in the subjective form of the dream cycle. There was another reason, too. As a compulsive writer Strindberg always kept more than one iron in the fire. While the material for one drama was being tempered, another was being hammered into shape. In this way he kept his interest from flagging; and for his own well-being, if for no other reason, his psychological self-analysis needed the balance and objectivity that history could provide. In writing history plays, the artist could put away his mirror and let others sit for their portraits. In September 1901, while he was working on *A Dream Play*, "the child whose birth gave me the greatest pain," he wrote *Queen Christina*, one of his most sparkling plays, and both plays reflect his relationship with Harriet Bosse.

By turning to history, Strindberg was in fact returning to old hunting grounds. He had always been interested in Swedish history, not so much in its kings and their conquests, however, as in the life of the common people through the ages. In 1880 and 1881 he had written, in collaboration with Clas Lundin, a history of the customs, manners, and daily life of the people of Stockholm, richly illustrated and containing chapters on such subjects as the Christmas and Easter holidays, street songs and popular entertainment, trade guilds, flora and fauna, slang and dialect, and superstitions and old wives' tales. What Bertall did for France in his monumental *Comédie de notre temps* (1874–76) and what Eilert Sundt accomplished in his pioneering sociological studies of Norwegian peasant life, Strindberg did modestly and spottily for Stockholm.

CHAPTER ELEVEN

THE WORLD OF POLITICS

Not surprisingly, *Old Stockholm*, as it was called, sold quite well, and because of its success, Strindberg was asked by a publisher to write a popular cultural history of Sweden on the model of Johannes Scherr's best-selling history of Germany, *Germania: Zwei Jahrtausende deutschen Lebens* (Stuttgart, 1877–78) (*SS*, 19:179). The chauvinism of Scherr's book, which exploited the nationalistic fervor produced by Germany's victory over France in 1871, repelled Strindberg, and he resolved to write a more temperate and objective history of his country, even though he knew there was no such thing as an objective history. Confronted by the enormous amount of material he had collected, he had to find a way of sorting it out, of deciding what was significant and what was not. This meant, in effect, finding a principle that manifested itself in the record of man's deeds. But was there any logic to history? Did some Hegelian meaning lie buried in the data and documents, waiting to be brought to light by some insightful researcher? The sceptical Strindberg of the 1880s doubted it did.

Perhaps history was only one incident *after* another instead of *because* of another. Was not history a capricious hodge-podge, a constant recurrence of events? Civilizations rose and fell; new societies emerged only to vanish; religions changed; while mankind remained as unwise and as unhappy as ever. Certainly those who had once believed that they saw a logic in history had only been acceding to the organizing demands of the brain's machinery, which insisted on putting things in a causal order; and if some phenomenon or other did not fit in, it was left out. [*SS*, 19:180]

On the verge of abandoning the project because he could not find a meaning in history, he decided to lower his sights. If he could not write a new philosophy of history, he would settle for a history with a new point of view. Heretofore, history

had been looked upon as produced by personal wills of varying strength. . . . Providence had been regarded as operating through God-chosen individuals, and the historical record had been written by God-chosen members of the privileged class. Now someone from the lower classes would conduct the inquiry. Now one of the unprivileged would picture history as seen from below and describe how those monuments, the great personalities of history, looked when lit from underneath. [*SS*, 19:180–81]

The result of his prodigious researches and lower-class outlook was an engagingly written, two-volume opus, published in 1882 and entitled *The Swedish People on Holiday and at Work, in War and Peace, at Home and Abroad, or, A Thousand Years of Swedish Culture and Customs*. Although this informal history, a kind of sociocultural journalism, did not give Strindberg a standing among Swedish historians, it helped him as a creative artist. Studying the history of Swedish habits, manners, dress, speech, and entertainments gave him that easy familiarity with past epochs that a writer needs in order to bring them to life again in stories and plays.

Ten years before publishing *The Swedish People*, Strindberg had written another historical work that was even more important to his career as an artist. In fact, it was the making of him as a dramatist—and almost the unmaking. This was the drama *Master Olof*, written when Strindberg was a student at Uppsala (see figure 6), or, more precisely, just after he had dropped out of the university, having decided to be a writer rather than an academician. The central figure in this play is the preacher and religious reformer Olaus Petri who in the sixteenth century endeavored to free the Swedish people from the dominance of the Catholic church.

In the play, Olof is an idealist; he believes that liberty means practicing what the Bible preaches. For him political freedom should go hand in hand with spiritual freedom. He soon learns that the interests of the state speak with a louder voice than the Bible. To his right stands Gustav Vasa, the king of Sweden, who is eager to rid his country of foreign influences. Gustav turns to the fearless reformer and plausibly suggests that they work together since their aims are similar. To Olof's left stands Gert Bookprinter, a social revolutionary, who has been excommunicated from the church for printing the works of Luther. He tells Olof that to liberate the country from Catholicism by making Gustav master is only to substitute servitude under the crown for servitude under the church. Gustav is determined to create a unified nation out of a loose confederation of provinces by reducing the power of the nobles and making them all subservient to a central authority. Gert, a socialist ahead of his time, wants to put the people above both church and crown. Living at a time when nationalism was on the rise, however, Gert can offer Olof nothing but a vision of what true political freedom means, whereas Gustav can offer Olof a position as chancellor. Olof takes it, and the rest of the play is a masterful depiction of a young man seduced by politics into betraying his ideal.

Olof soon realizes that he has been serving Belial instead of God and seeks to redeem his errors. But it is too late; the wings of the idealist have been clipped, and his soaring spirit, caged. His mother, on her deathbed, implores him to take up his old faith again, and when he refuses, she dies cursing the hour she gave him birth, convinced that because of him she will be cast into hell. Having sacrificed his mother's happiness for

his beliefs and seeing how he has compromised those beliefs by supporting Gustav's politics, he tries to make things right by joining Gert's conspiracy to assassinate the king. The conspiracy is discovered, and Gert
and Olof are arrested. Gustav sentences the political revolutionary to
death, but he shrewdly gives Olof, who has a strong following among the
people, the alternative of dying on the scaffold or of publicly confessing
his sins against the crown and swearing complete allegiance to the king.
Gustav knows his man. Olof takes the oath to serve his king faithfully. As
his wife and friends embrace him, he asks to be left alone for a moment,
alone with his God. Instead of God's voice he hears the voice of one of his
followers who has arrived late on the scene and does not know that Olof
has been spared.

"Before you die," he says,

I want to thank you for the good you have done us. . . . Why you are going to die
is something we don't know. You could never do anything but what is right. And
if you are going to die because you gave help to some oppressed people, as they
say, that should not pain you, even if it does hurt us very, very much. You once
told us how they burned Huss at the stake because he dared to speak the truth to
those in power. You described how he stepped onto the pile and joyfully com-
mended himself into the hands of God. . . . I've seen you going to your death like
that, your brow untroubled and your eyes raised to heaven while the people
shout, "So dies a witness to the truth!"

Crushed by these words, Olof hears another voice from far off, the
voice of Gert shouting, "Traitor!" (SS, 2:184)

2

There are only a handful of plays written by authors under twenty-
five years of age that can compare with *Master Olof*. Schiller's *The Robbers* comes immediately to mind not only because Schiller was still a
student when he wrote it but also because of the rebellious spirit in the
play. And then there is *Danton's Death*, written by Büchner when, like
the author of *Master Olof*, he was only twenty-three. Büchner's extraordinary drama of the French Revolution seems much more worldly-wise
and cynical than Strindberg's drama of the Reformation, but that is
largely because the young German writer combined sex and politics
while the young Swede mixed religion and politics.

Although Strindberg may have been influenced by Schiller, he knew
nothing of Büchner. For guidance, Strindberg turned to Shakespeare,
after having read Georg Brandes's essay on *Henry IV* in which the critic

demonstrated that Shakespeare's characters spring so vividly to life before one's eyes because they are seen at home as well as in the forum.[1]
They sound real because one hears their most intimate small talk as well
as their public orations. Strindberg took the lesson to heart. He also
learned from reading Shakespeare the dramatic value in giving a cross
section of an age and in showing all classes of society. *Master Olof* has a
cast of over thirty characters, nobles, churchmen, burghers, farmers,
prostitutes, many of whom are clearly etched with the dramatist's instinct for the telling detail and all related to each other in the total composition by the moral of the piece: that he who would serve both Caesar
and God ends by serving the devil—and politics is the very devil. It was
a moral that derived from Kierkegaard's either-or philosophy and the all-
or-nothing demands of Ibsen's *Brand*. If the university had done nothing
else for Strindberg, it had brought him under the spell of the uncompromising idealism of the Danish philosopher and the Norwegian poet
(SS, 18:355–56, 428).

The most admirable person in *Master Olof* is Gert Bookprinter, who
dies for what he believes; and the supreme irony at the end of the play
is that the people offer their sympathy and understanding to the backsliding Olof and leave their true spokesman, Gert, to die alone and
unlamented.

In making Gert the hero of the play and in picturing Gustav Vasa as a
shrewd politician, Strindberg was almost as tactless as Gert. It was not
the way to win the approbation of the critics. *Master Olof*, the first Swedish drama to merit a place in the international repertoire, was censured
by the very people who should have been the first to see its greatness.
The readers for the Royal Theatre in Stockholm objected to a historical
drama that was written in prose and not in verse. Strindberg then obediently recast the play in rhymed verse and submitted it to another theatre. Again it was rejected, this time with the stricture that the author had
failed to place the great and familiar figures of Swedish history on the
exalted level that was theirs by right and custom. These charges were
true without being entirely honest. Strindberg had resented seeing the
ordinary man made a figure of fun in the historical drama while the nobleman was idealized, so he had deliberately "knocked the high heels off
the highborn and elevated the shoes of the lowborn" (SS, 50:240) by giving the courtier, at times, the vocabulary of the man in the street.

This was precisely what the critics were objecting to when they
spoke of verse and lofty characters. In their eyes the underlying fault of

the play was that its political bias was democratic and socialistic, though they could not say so frankly and straightforwardly without letting the cat out of the bag and admitting that esthetics and taste are matters of politics and class preference. Young as he was, Strindberg knew this, and when he prepared the second version, he prudently played down the politics, made Gert a dolt, and converted his original uncompromising drama into a philosophical disquisition on the relativism of truth. Still no theatre would stage it; the dramatic life of the play had been drained out of it along with the politics. So he rewrote it once again. By this time, he had found employment in the Royal Library. He had been tamed, like Olof, and had learned to be just as accommodating. In the final rewriting, Gustav Vasa, the great antagonist, disappears entirely, and the feckless Olof, instead of being crushed by the accusation that he is a traitor to the people's cause, humbly compliments himself for having learned how to make his way in the world. Strindberg should have known that compromise is for politicians, not for artists. All this rewriting served no purpose, not even the politician's. When the play finally reached the stage, in 1881, the original version was used. By that time, the political atmosphere had changed. Bjørnson and Ibsen had ventilated the Scandinavian theatre with the fresh air of the social problem play, the workers at the sawmills had organized the first major strike in Sweden, and Strindberg himself had become the literary leader of the young radicals.

Looking back on recent history, Strindberg in 1884 described his struggle against religious superstition and political lies.

I cried out as early as 1872, in *Master Olof*, but I was silenced until 1882. Then, after ten years, ten terrible years, Gert Bookprinter could speak out, and the mighty voice of [the actor] Emil Hillberg gave strength to my voice, weakened as it was by privation, hardship, sorrows, in roaring out what had been silently thought during those long twilight years.

And still they pretended not to understand what I was saying. The whole matter was wrapped in the veil of the beautiful, and the estheticians took charge of it. [SS, 54:227]

3

In *Master Olof*, Strindberg was not writing the conventional history drama that allows the spectator to escape from the present and relive the past as a great adventure story. Like all good history plays, *Master Olof* recreates the past in order to make us understand the present better. Part of that understanding has to do with an increasingly skeptical attitude toward such concepts as fate and character when applied to history and progress. If Emerson is right, and history is only biography, all the writer of historic drama has to do is fit the crowded life of his chosen hero into the two or three hours' traffic of the stage. Plays written on this principle are easy to grasp because for centuries Western man has been schooled to see action as flowing from character. A strong and determined king like Henry V invigorates his people and spurs them on to magnificent achievements; a weak king like Richard II saps the moral fiber of his people and must be deposed. Very logical and very simplistic, it could account for only a small part of what actually happened in history. Great men are often complicated creatures, impelled by ideas that contradict their actions and interacting with other men who are equally complicated. Immediately after writing *Henry V*, Shakespeare dealt more honestly with the moral muddles of history by taking up the case, in *Julius Caesar*, of a ruler who refuses to abdicate for the good of his country and who must be assassinated. He did not return to English history until the very end of his career when he wrote *Henry VIII*, a play in which he made the contradictions of history and human nature the main point of interest.

But such contradictions, when presented as fundamental and irresolvable, however fascinating they may be to talk about, can be disastrous in the theatre. Henry is shown falling in love with Anne Bullen and prepared to divorce Katherine. But when he deposes his reasons for considering a divorce, he says that his concern is with the legality of his marriage: if the church views it as incestuous, the legitimacy of his daughter Mary is called into question. Nothing in this speech suggests that Henry is being deceitful. Both selfish motives and a concern for the welfare of the state are present, and since they can both be made to work toward the same end, all that is called into question is the basic decency and noblemindedness of the king. The vectors of character and circumstance become hopelessly intricate because of the machinations of Cardinal Wolsey, whose personal ambition sometimes works for the interests of the state and sometimes against them. When at the end of the play, Shakespeare (or Fletcher) had to make sense out of the mixed motives and the double intentions, he brought on the infant Elizabeth to be eulogized as the harbinger of a time when "God shall be truly known, and those about her / From her shall read the perfect ways of honor" (V, 5, 36–37). The final speeches, politically tactful and complimentary to rulers past and present, no more resolve the issues raised in the play than the Pope's prayers for peace put an end to war. All that is asserted is that behind the contradictions of history lies a divine plan and that this plan manifests itself in the divine right of kings.

This royalist premise was soon called into question by the constitutionalists, and by the time that Robespierre had finished what Cromwell had begun, it was apparent that the divine plan was untrue and would have to be discarded. What was to take its place? Schiller struggled with the question in his *Wallenstein* trilogy, which was begun during the French Revolution and finished when Napoleon was on the march. Although Schiller set his drama in the Thirty Years' War, he is obviously trying to comprehend the political turmoil of his own times by lifting himself above it to gain the perspective that 150 years of history affords. As generalissimo of the imperial armies, Wallenstein was in a position to put an end to a senseless war by surrendering the troops under his command to the enemy. But in doing so he would be foreswearing his oath of loyalty to the emperor and gaining for himself the throne of Bohemia. To the realist Wallenstein, the situation can only be analyzed in terms of lives that can be saved and a crown that can be won. To the idealist (Schiller had to improve on history by inventing one for his play, since his sources pictured all the leading figures of the war as being as hardheaded, politically minded, and power-hungry as Wallenstein himself, if not more so), the situation can only be comprehended in terms of the eternal truths and the highest spiritual bonds, meaning the bonds between man and God and between man and his country. If God is denied or an oath of fealty broken, the basis of civilization is threatened. That is how the idealist views the problem, and the upshot is that the idealist, for whom deceit and disloyalty are the worst of crimes, sends his troops off to be slaughtered, while the realist—whose selfishness and ambition might have spared thousands of lives, introduced religious freedom, and established a German confederation of states ahead of its time—is assassinated by men loyal to a despotic and intolerant emperor whose only claim to the throne is a hereditary one.

Schiller's dramatic presentation of the discrepancy between morality and power politics, between what should happen and what does happen, is admirable. But what can he do to bring the one into line with the other? In conventional esthetic theory, tragedy is meant to heal this breach in the moral universe by a process as mysterious as that of transubstantiation. In his essay on the tragic art, written before *Wallenstein*, Schiller asserted that the difference between ancient and modern tragedy is that in the former, morality was subordinated to fate, while in the latter, the discontent with destiny is effaced and resolved in a clear consciousness of a teleological concatenation of things, of a sublime or-der, of a beneficent will. . . . The thing that seemed to militate against this order, and that caused us pain . . . is only a spur that stimulates our reason to seek in general laws for the justification of this particular case, and to solve the problem of this separate discord in the center of the general harmony.[2]

One of these general laws held that a defect in character, a vicious mole of nature, in Hamlet's words, would prevent the individual from being in harmony with the sublime order. In his notes on Shakespeare's history plays, Coleridge borrowed Schiller's idea and expressed it more succinctly. "In the drama, the will is exhibited as struggling with fate, . . . and the deepest effect is produced when the fate is represented as a higher and intelligent will, and the opposition of the individual as springing from a defect."[3]

This defect of character became the shibboleth of the romantic un-derstanding of tragedy, so much so that Aristotle's *hamartia* had to be mistranslated to mean either an error of judgment or a moral flaw in or-der to bring classic theory in line with romantic theory. Making a trait of character the cause of the hero's fall worked well enough as long as the focus was on the individual. But when the individual was woven into the fabric of history, it became apparent that a defective character often contributed more to social progress and to the development of the nation than did a perfect one. It was a paradox of history that Wallenstein, the man who served a good cause, was defeated. To make moral sense out of this, Schiller could no longer ascribe Wallenstein's downfall simply to ambition, because it was this ambition that promoted the good. So he had to raise Wallenstein from the political arena, where morality and efficacy were hopelessly ensnarled, to the cosmic realm, where everything was straightened out and set to rights. The doomed Wallenstein meets his death with quiet dignity, surrendering himself to fate, while his assassins are shown to be conniving opportunists, petty in their aspirations where Wallenstein was majestic. "Nothing is common in the paths of my des-tiny," he says in a final proud assertion.[4] His moral faults fade and vanish as he takes his place in the great design of history.

Schiller and Coleridge assumed that this great design was woven by a beneficent will, an intelligent will. But why assume anything of the sort when confronted by the injustices and disasters of history? Even He-gel, who was so adept in finding reason and purpose in the historical process, found nothing in *Wallenstein* but death and meaninglessness. The destiny to which Wallenstein falls victim is silent and indifferent to the moral plight of man, and that silence, that indifference filled Hegel with horror.⁵ Anyone who chose to look at the darker side of history and of human existence could argue persuasively that the universal will was neither intelligent nor beneficent. Schopenhauer perceived that those who thought like Schiller and Coleridge were clutching at a straw and pointed out that that straw existed only as an idea in the minds of men more desperate for goodness and beauty than for truth. After Schopenhauer came Hartmann, who mitigated the pessimism of Schopenhauer by attending to the discoveries of science. Physical evolution gave a direction to life and pointed toward a meaning in the universe. By the exercise of his reason, man could discern this meaning or purpose, and by devoting himself to a cause larger than himself, he could be saved from drowning in the whirlpool of oblivion and nothingness.

4

It was at this juncture that Strindberg wrote *Master Olof*. As first conceived, this was to be a play about a young man who learns that it takes a long spoon to sup with a politician. Olof, the religious reformer, strikes a bargain with Gustav only to realize that he has sold his ideals for a title and a promotion. Disillusioned, he joins the conspiracy against the king and escapes death only by swearing allegiance to him. In the early notes for the play, Strindberg seems to be replying to Ibsen's *Brand* by saying that the tragedy of the idealist does not lie with the man who turns his back on society when it will not measure up to his standards but with the man who succumbs to the disease of compromise that he had hoped to cure.

This familiar and unremarkable conception of the tragic fall was enriched by bringing in some nineteenth-century ideas. First, there was the example afforded by the Paris Commune of 1871 of a people who rebelled against both church and state. When Strindberg worked on *Master Olof*, the Franco-Prussian War and the Paris Commune were fresh in everyone's mind. The spectacle of the people of Paris holding out against the Germans after the French government had surrendered astounded the world and made it abundantly clear that two wars were being fought and that the second was much more significant than the first. The war between the French and the Germans was fundamentally a conflict of business interests, settled in a businesslike manner by the payment of an indemnity and the transfer of some territory. The real war was a class war in which the antagonisms were so violent and so deep that the extremists among the Communards did not hesitate to execute a president, some

priests, and even a few journalists, while the extremists on the government side did not hesitate to kill women and children—and to go on trying, condemning, deporting, and executing Communards for eight years
after the fighting had ceased and for five years after the French government had paid the entire indemnity of one billion dollars to the Germans. While Strindberg was writing his play, the situation in Paris was
still so inflammatory that the National Assembly continued to meet at
Versailles. All the European governments were frightened by the specter
of communism.

Since it would have been folly to write a play dealing directly with
the uprising, Strindberg resorted to the stratagem of mirroring the present in the past. The German peasant insurrection of the Anabaptists under Thomas Münzer in the sixteenth century was the first significant political revolution of modern times, and Strindberg pictured it obliquely
by showing its repercussions in Scandinavia at the time when the Swedish nation was being formed. A play about Gustav Vasa's accomplishments was outwardly as safe a subject for Swedish conservatives as a
play about George Washington would be to the Daughters of the American Revolution.

Strindberg's sympathies lay wholly with the Communards, but the
debacle of May 1871, in which 17,000 Communards were executed by
government troops, only proved that the oppressed people were no match
for their oppressors. He was faced with the thousands who had laid
down their lives for freedom, whereas his play showed only a man who
preferred not to die for any reason. The Communards represented a third
force, opposed to both church and state, and that third force needed a
voice in his play. So Strindberg made the revolutionary Gert Bookprinter
the second most important character in the drama, the idealist who dies
a martyr to the cause of freedom. An Anabaptist in sixteenth-century
Sweden, he sounds like a nihilist or communist of the nineteenth century. Those who read Strindberg's play in manuscript recognized the
voice and were determined that it should not be heard in the land. Incor-
ruptible and fearless, Gert provides the standard against which Olof is to
be judged.[6]

In his farewell to Olof (figure 21), Gert says,

It's right that you should live on after me. You're young. I am dying a happy man:
the name of every new martyr becomes the battle cry for a new army. Never believe that lies can fire men's hearts. Never doubt the pain that sears your soul
when you see spiritual and physical suffering. Even if the whole world says
you're wrong, believe what your heart tells you—if you have the courage for it.

Once you deny the spirit within, you are dead. Eternal damnation is mercifulness itself for those who deny the Holy Ghost. [SS, 2:179]

For Gert, the Holy Ghost is the spirit of the proletarian revolution. In the Christian calendar, Pentecost is the day on which the Holy Spirit descended on the disciples, and *Master Olof* begins at Pentecost with Gert infusing Olof's soul with revolutionary fervor. At the end of the play, Gert, as he is arrested by the king's soldiers, reminds Olof of the meaning of the Holy Spirit. His parting words are: "Remember the great Pentecost!" In the Communist calendar, Pentecost marks the day, May 28, 1871, when General MacMahon and his government troops marched into Paris to slaughter thousands of Communards, French soldiers doing what German soldiers did not do, and spelling out in blood that the real war was the war of classes and not the war of French and Germans. Gert's reference to Pentecost combines Christian and Communist lore and yokes the end of the play to the beginning.

The Christian allusions are so appropriate in a play about a religious reformer that some of the more significant ones fail to stand out. It is easy, for instance, to overlook the fact that Olof and Gert themselves play biblical roles. Up to the end, Olof is presented as a Jesus figure, the bringer of revolutionary change, willing to sacrifice himself for his people. The numerous parallels between Olof and Jesus underscore the irony of the last moments of the drama. This latter-day Jesus lets the cup pass from him without drinking, rejects the cross, and accepts Pilate's offer. Strindberg had even intended to entitle the play "What Is Truth?" but had rightly feared that this pointed allusion would harm its chances of being accepted by the theatres (SS, 19:28). Gert, as John the Baptist, emerges as the true martyr. He is the prophet with a strong following— the Anabaptists!—among the people, and he is the first to recognize Olof as the man who can usher in the millennium. When he plays mad, he calls himself Satan and Huss, Lucifer and Luther; this only underscores his symbolic role as the perennial radical.[7]

5

Once Olof and Gert had been set up as progressivists who could improve the circumstances of the working people, the whole question of political and social progress had to be considered. Why was it that the majority of the common people who stood to benefit from Olof's reforms and Gert's revolution threw stones at the reformer and let the revolutionary be executed? Why was it that Gert who went among the people to liberate them was cursed by them as an antichrist, while Gustav was adulated by the masses even as he was leading hundreds of them to their deaths in one war or another. The phenomenon is as old as recorded history, though it has seldom been examined by historians.

One historian who did set himself the task of dealing with this phenomenon and with the whole matter of the relationship of the people to their rulers was Henry Thomas Buckle. In his ambitious *History of Civilization in England*, he was determined to write a different kind of history, not a saga of kings with chronicles of battles, deliberations of parliaments, and summaries of treaties, but a history that would bring to light the underlying factors that governed the development of civilization. He hoped to make history into a science by formulating the principles that regulated the evolution of human society, by studying the political and cultural life of nations in the same way that Darwin studied the flora and fauna of the Galápagos Islands. The fact that the first volume of his *History of Civilization* appeared immediately before Darwin's *Origin of Species*, and the second immediately after, was just the sort of fact that Buckle would have found more enlightening than anything in the acts of Parliament. It was his conviction, based on historical evidence, that lawmakers do not effect any profound changes; they only swim with the current of their times. The people are the innovators of genuine change, and without their cooperation and support, there can be no significant development of society. This conviction of Buckle's clashed with another of his convictions, also based on historical evidence: that the people resist change and happily submit to those who tyrannize over them. When Charles III of Spain liberated his people from the oppression of the church by greatly reducing the power of the Inquisition, he won neither their love nor their appreciation. They saved that for his successor, Charles IV, who restored the power of the church and made the Holy Office once again a feared tribunal.

On the one hand, Buckle was saying that the people are the source of change; on the other, that they resist change. He resolved the contradiction by arguing that superstition and ignorance are the main obstacles to progress and that lasting change can come about by raising the general intellectual level of the nation. This is accomplished by new ideas, discoveries, and inventions, which irresistibly make their way into the lives of the people. The revelations of thinkers like Adam Smith, the discoveries of scientists like Hutton, and the new machines of inventors like

Watt alter the material circumstances and the mental attitudes of a continually growing number of people, who eventually become a force that impels the lawmakers to enact new laws. All this takes time, and the prophet or politician who tries to rush things will be no more successful than Charles III was. Instead of furthering the development of the people, he is more likely to produce a reaction and set back the clock of progress.

However ordinary and obvious Buckle's ideas may seem now, to the nineteenth-century mind they implied a new and thoroughly materialistic conception of history. For Bernard Shaw, who read Buckle in 1894, the *History of Civilization* was "a book as epoch-making in the minds of its readers as *Das Kapital*."[8] Buckle did for history what Darwin did for biology: he found God unnecessary and cashiered him. Like Marx, he turned Hegel's universe upside down and let the Absolute Spirit drain out of it.

To the young Strindberg this unmystical way of seeing history as completely the work of man came as a revelation. Buckle, he said later, "was the pathfinder for a new *Weltanschauung*, which puts to one side heavenly affairs and puts forward our duty to earthly existence" (SS, 17:212). Buckle was published serially in Sweden in 1871 and 1872, perfectly timed to provide the young radical with a convincing explanation for the periodic defeats and setbacks of the forces of progress. It accounted for the massacre of the Communards in Paris in 1871, for the otherwise inexplicable return to power of the conservatives (SS, 19:27)[9] in the Swedish elections of 1872, and for Gustav Vasa's total triumph in sixteenth-century Sweden, along with Olof's compromise and Gert's martyrdom. Olof's mistake was to suppose that he could, by means of legislation, liberate a people so superstitious and so ignorant that they reverenced the very king who was leading many of them to their deaths.

"Poor children," says Olof at the end of act 4. "They're dancing to his pipes and marching to his drums—marching to their deaths. Why should all die that one may live?"

To which Gert replies, "One shall die that all may live!" (SS, 2:133–34).

Buckle said that

to seek to change opinions by laws is worse than futile. . . . This has always been the error of the most ardent reformers, who, in their eagerness to effect their purpose, let the political movement outstrip the intellectual one, and, thus inverting the natural order, secure misery either to themselves or to their descendants.[10]

Gert hopes to accomplish by violence what he knows cannot be accomplished by law. As a communist, he knowingly and willingly pays with his life the price of being so far in the vanguard that only a small group of conspirators support him. Gustav is victorious because he recognizes that there is a tide in the affairs of men, and he instinctively catches it at the flood. He does not carry out the Reformation in Sweden, but as a realistic politician, he is shrewd enough to take credit for it (*SS*, 19:29).[11]

6

In spite of Olof's compromised position at the end of the play, there is a sense of progress, largely owing to the presence of Gert. But as Strindberg rewrote the play, the prospects of revolutionary change in society grew dimmer, and to the third and last version of *Master Olof* he appended an epilogue in which his pessimism reaches Schopenhauerian depths. In this epilogue, Olof witnesses a medieval mystery play entitled *De creatione et sententia vera mundi*, in which Lucifer appears as the bringer of light who tries to make human beings understand that God created them simply in order to entertain himself and that he is otherwise utterly indifferent to them. God is revealed as the wayward will of the universe, practically identical with the Immanent Will in Hardy's monumental trilogy on the Napoleonic Wars, *The Dynasts*, in which the Will weaves without concern for man's welfare or its own improvement the random, haphazard, and pointless patterns of history.

This epilogue was written in 1877,[12] shortly before Strindberg would come before the public with his novel *The Red Room* and establish himself as the leading writer of the realistic school in Sweden. Twenty years later, when the realist had taken his journey through the unconscious and emerged as a mystic, Strindberg made the *Master Olof* epilogue serve as the prologue to *Inferno*, the journal of his incursions into the realm of the irrational. But he added a couple of scenes to clarify the link between Schopenhauer's universe and his own newly discovered one. In these scenes, God, seeing that men are becoming stronger than he is, attempts to destroy what he has created only to find that he has unleashed forces beyond his control. In his frustration, he goes mad, runs amok, and prostrates himself before the suzerain of all, the overlord, the Eternal One, the Supreme Being, to pray for his blessing.

These brief scenes encapsulate the modern history of God. In the middle of the nineteenth century, the anarchist Bakunin had avowed that it was necessary to abolish God. Taking the necessity for the truth, Nietzsche had reported that God was dead, and the naturalist Strindberg had taken the news in his stride. Now, at the end of the century, Strindberg realized that the actual truth of the matter, the horrible truth, was not that God was dead but that God was insane. It was a point that Bernard Shaw was to make in his speech "On Christian Economics" in 1913, ten months before the outbreak of the First World War.

During the decadent 1890s, the *fin de siècle*, when most of the advanced poets and artists were succumbing to their senses, Strindberg took up physical science, psychology, and history, pretty much in that order, looking for a design in the chaos of nature, a direction in his own broken career, and a purpose in the contradictions of political history. What had happened to him seemed, at first glance, as senseless as what had happened to nations. He could not understand why he should suffer humiliation and poverty in the middle years of his life after having spent the best part of it as a crusader trying to free the people from religious superstition and political demagoguery. Why should his conscience trouble him, why should his sleep be haunted by nightmares, when his transgressions were much more remittable than the sins of those who prospered in the world? Casting his eyes beyond his own life down the reaches of history, he could ask why it was that the most virtuous souls, who had devoted themselves to the betterment of mankind, were condemned to the cross or the stake, while the monsters of history, whose victims were numbered in the thousands, died peacefully in their beds. His own life, as he wrote in the concluding pages of *Inferno*, seemed a practical joke played on him by the Almighty. Not content to leave it at that, he wrote the *To Damascus* plays to find the intention behind the hoax. As his own life began to take on new meaning, so did the life of mankind. His own madness had proved to be the entrance to a deeper level of knowledge. Was it not likely, then, that the apparent insanity of God was only a distortion set up in the minds of men, caused by their viewing a vast moral cosmos from the wrong angle?

Even before he had finished his journey to Damascus, Strindberg had embarked on an odyssey through history, hoping to find the divine agent there as he had found it in the individual psyche. Not surprisingly, he went first to the Swedish Middle Ages for subject matter and found it in the life of Magnus the Good, a Christ-like ruler who was despised by his people. Strindberg pictures the martyrdom of this saintly man, who must be sacrificed for the sins of others in order that peace might prevail in the country, against a background of civil war and the Black Plague,

CHAPTER TWELVE

MAKING SENSE OF HISTORY

and fills in the foreground with half-naked flagellants, a hooded hangman, and a possessed woman with Cassandra-like powers of prophecy. Visually and theatrically, *The Saga of the Folkungs* is a succession of stunning scenes that call for cinematic treatment. (Ingmar Bergman was inspired by it when he wrote and filmed *The Seventh Seal*.) Thematically, the play blends classical and Christian sentiments about the scapegoat who suffers for the sins of others and vivifies the superstitions of the Middle Ages with Strindberg's first-hand experience of imagined fears (SS, 50:241).

The next historical subject to attract Strindberg was radically different: Gustav Vasa, the king who had ensnared Master Olof. Certainly not a scapegoat, Gustav Vasa was, in contrast to the Christ-like Magnus the Good, a robust soldier and a stern sovereign, with a formidable constitution and an untroubled mind, whose energy, political astuteness, and formidable self-assurance overwhelmed all opposition and enabled him to hammer the Swedish provinces into a nation. In a word, he was a king very much like his English coeval Henry VIII with respect to physical appearance, patriotic ambition, intolerance to opposition whether from the secular arm or the church, sanguineness of temper, and even plurality of wives (though Gustav had only three, Sweden being a much less populous country than England). Here, one would suppose, was precisely the kind of man who would be utterly immune to any disease of the conscience and completely resistant to Strindbergian treatment. Yet Strindberg probably admired him the most of all the Swedish kings, and what one admires one either imitates or recreates in one's own image. A dazzlingly successful career like Gustav's, which consisted only of battles won and difficulties overcome, seemed to offer no scope for Strindberg's views on sin and suffering. But it was his conviction that no man climbed the heights of greatness without first having wandered in the shadowed valley and having known desolation. So he transformed Gustav Vasa's success story into a story of defeat and humiliation by concentrating on that one moment when fortune seemed to go against the king, and all Gustav could do was bow his head.

To give the plot a dramatic contour, Strindberg first shows the king triumphant and arrogant. The middle-aged Gustav, having forged an independent Sweden by ridding the country of the Danish invaders, negotiating with an implacable pope for bishops who would defend the rights of the Swedish crown, bending the Romanist peasants to his will, dealing with the Hanseatic League for financial aid, and educating the remnants of the old feudal aristocracy in the business of government, looked upon what he had created and saw that it was good. This is the strong-willed, self-confident king whose godlike presence is felt in the opening scenes of the play. In a fascinating exposition, a marvel of economy and deftness, rivalling the best things of this kind in Shakespeare, Strindberg gives us a king who is master of all he surveys. And he does it without bringing the king on stage. He pictures the king as he is reflected in the minds and actions of others, in their fear and awe of him. In this way, which is Molière's way in *Tartuffe*, Gustav Vasa appears as a force in the lives of men rather than as a physical being. Through his soldiers, he metes out harsh punishment to the men of Dalecarlia, who have rebelled against his administration more than once. Now he feels that he has finally brought them into line. Gustav does not actually appear until the third act, and the inner drama, the drama of a proud man brought low, occupies the last three acts of the play. Here is the Strindbergian drama of a man who must settle accounts with his past.

In *Master Olof*, Strindberg had drawn on Buckle's theories for a materialistic interpretation of the Swedish Reformation. When he returned to the subject after his Inferno, he brought spirit back into the matter, and in portraying an older Gustav Vasa, he drew largely on his own experiences. The Gustav that we get to see is no self-assured *Realpolitiker*, though he seems a giant to those around him, but a troubled man with blood on his hands. Ever since he had to execute a man who had been his friend from childhood to quash a rebellion in Dalecarlia, he has had no peace of mind. This was part of the price he had to pay to make Sweden a united nation. And there is more. Still outstanding are two large debts, a financial debt to Lübeck, the Hanseatic town that loaned him money for his wars, and a debt of gratitude to Dalecarlia, the province that provided him with the men who fought the Danish invaders. To prevent Sweden from becoming the thrall of Lübeck, Gustav wants to discharge the monetary debt immediately. To accomplish this, he exacts contributions from the Dalecarlians. By this time, however, the farmers and miners of Dalecarlia feel they should be the recipients of favors from the king rather than the subjects of further exactions.

At this moment a peasant uprising in another province in Sweden, in Småland, imperils the king's position. The Lübeckians want to abet the rebels since a king in need is a king deeper in debt to Lübeck, while the Dalecarlians, who resent the king's impositions on them, look upon the rebels as their allies. The king is caught between the rebellious peasants in Småland to the south of Stockholm and the disaffected Dalecarlians to the north. There it is, a typical political crisis, the testing of old alliances and friendships calling for strength and discretion. A single miscalculation, a small error of judgment, or a bit of bad luck and all that Gustav Vasa has built up will be destroyed.

One of the marvels of this play is the skill with which Strindberg has joined the political drama to the psychological drama, picturing the complexity of the immediate causes that determine the course of history while adumbrating an underlying design. In his anguish, Gustav turns to Master Olof, who as a young man had come within the king's gravitational field and who now circles obediently around him. Bluntly and fearlessly, Olof tells him that there are powers to which even kings must submit. He urges Gustav to humble himself by writing to the peasant who is the leader of the rebels in the south. The king does so, and now, no longer the mover and shaker, he must wait for events to take their course. Like Strindberg during his Inferno, Gustav feels at one moment that he is the plaything of the capricious gods and at the next that he is being punished for having harmed others. While he is counting on his fingers and naming those he has had to execute, he hears soldiers enter the palace. To his surprise they are not the rebels from Småland; they are the Dalecarlians, who have come to help Gustav put down the southern rebels. Once again the gods have smiled on Gustav, who lifts his hands in recognition of the god who imposed these tribulations on him to test him. His whole career has been guided by some higher power or destiny. It began when a messenger named Engelbrekt brought to the young Gustav the news that he had been chosen to lead the Dalecarlians against the usurping Danes (an item of information carefully planted by Strindberg in the first moments of the play) and is rounded off dramatically when Engelbrekt, drunk and a little unsteady, enters the palace in Stockholm to inform the middle-aged Gustav that the Dalecarlians have arrived to help him suppress the insurgents.

Although this is a very personal interpretation of the historical chronicle, the character of Gustav as Strindberg drew him rings true. The historians criticized Strindberg for diminishing the stature of Sweden's greatest monarch, but the dramatist knew that by including the king's weaknesses and failings in the portrait, he had made him a more believable king than the one that strutted through the history books. "Time will tell whether they [the academic critics] or I am right," said Strindberg (SS, 50:248), and time has told against the critics.

2

The story of the testing of Gustav Vasa, which is a relatively simple one, provides the burden of the composition. But Strindberg almost always composes contrapuntally, and in *Gustav Vasa*, a second subject dominates the second act and is subsequently joined with the first subject in the central, the third, act of the play. The first act tells of Gustav as father of his country. The second act concerns the sons, and there are several of them in the play. There is, first of all, Erik, the crown prince, who has hated his awesome father ever since childhood. There is Erik's boon companion Göran Persson, who regards himself as sired by perjury out of fornication, since his father was a monk who foreswore the oath of celibacy and married. There is Reginald, the son of Master Olof. Having once sown the seeds of skepticism among the people, Olof must now reap the harvest in the form of his son's religious disbelief and filial disaffection. And finally there is Jacob Israel, son of Herman Israel, councillor of Lübeck. The father has been serving as financial advisor to Gustav in mutual trust since Sweden and Lübeck have a common enemy in the Roman church. When Gustav decides that Lübeck's business interests are encroaching on Sweden's independence, the two men come reluctantly to a parting of ways. Herman's son has a different sort of interest in Sweden, being in love with a Swedish girl. He is so reluctant to leave that he betrays his father.

Strindberg gives Gustav Vasa and Herman Israel the same part to play, both being stern fathers who must sacrifice loved ones for the sake of a higher cause (figure 22). The father motif and the son motif are combined in the complicated intrigue of the third act, the outcome of which is that Gustav must order the execution of two Dalecarlians who have joined the rebels, and Herman Israel must condemn his own son for defying him. A thematic outline of the play:

Act I.   King Gustav as father of his country and as tyrant to the Dalecarlians.
  II. i. The sons, Prince Erik and Jacob Israel, opposed to their fathers.
       Småland in rebellion against Gustav.
    ii. Erik and Göran as comrades in misfortune.
  III.   The father figure as the man of conscience.
       The father of the family versus his son Erik.
       The father of his country versus the rebels.
  IV. i. The king in the tavern. Humiliation.
    ii. The king learns to humble himself.
  V.   The Dalecarlians come to his support.[1]

In the middle act, all the major themes are combined as the father is seen in his religious, psychological, and political aspects.

Strindberg worked out the religious drama, which places Gustav Vasa between the Dalecarlians and the Higher Powers, by using the *Damascus* method, suggesting through verbal allusions, sound effects, and visual devices the inner conflict, the conflict between the terrifying power of the king that dominates the first two acts and the spiritual forces that subdue him in the last three acts. The psychological and political drama is worked out by bringing on stage a host of secondary characters. Their presence has the additional effect of giving a panoramic view of Swedish society on all levels in Shakespeare's manner. In fact, the tavern scenes in *Gustav Vasa* seem to have been inspired by those in *Henry IV*.

The technical dexterity involved in varying the father-son theme so that it can sound throughout the score on the religious, psychological, and political levels is admirable in itself. The question is, does the cleverness serve any other purpose? When Shakespeare has Falstaff and Prince Hal exchange roles, he is after something more than laughs. When Strindberg draws parallels between the various fathers and between the various sons in the play, he is doing more than bringing a host of characters into a tidy arrangement. The ultimate piece of legerdemain is to make the parallels meet, and Strindberg does this by seeing in the antagonisms of father and son, in the conflict of generations, the reflection of larger forces.

The father theme is brought to a full and harmonious close at the end of the play. The nation appears united once again under the weight and authority of Gustav. But this impression is modified by the pervasiveness of the opposing force, represented by the sons and the rebels. As character drama (and the play is almost always discussed as character drama), the play is about Gustav as father of his country and of his family; as a history play it is about forces larger than individuals. Strindberg kept Gustav off stage during the first two acts in order to endue him with the qualities of a force at work in history and in the lives of men. For the same reason, he populated the stage with Erik and Göran and Reginald and Jacob, with rebels and conspirators and unhappy sons, all of whom, though never acting together, become the embodiment of another force.

3

Parallel lines appear to meet when drawn in perspective, and to gain the necessary perspective, Strindberg made *Gustav Vasa* the middle play in a trilogy, with lines extending from it in both directions. The first play, *Master Olof*, shows how Gustav consolidates his power by getting rid of the radical political opposition (Gert) and assimilating the church (Olof). In the second play, Gustav is in full command, his power sanctioned by a god who seems to take a personal interest in his career. In the third play, *Erik XIV*, the power is transferred to Gustav's son. Strindberg wanted these three plays published together in one volume because, as he said, they "belong together and explain each other. . . . The three make a monument—if joined together. Separated, they collapse."[2]

Erik, the eldest son of Gustav, is the most romanticized figure in Swedish history. In Strindberg's version, Erik hated his domineering father ever since, as a child of four, he had seen his mother struck by the king in a rage. This hatred was nourished by the king's affection for his new queen, Erik's stepmother, and while Erik was being educated, trained, and disciplined as heir to the throne, his young half brothers were being coddled by a loving father. In awe of his Odin-like parent and unloved by him, disdained by his stepmother and despising her, Erik developed into an unhappy and unstable young man who disliked and feared the nobility and most of all, and most rightly, his two half brothers. He preferred to choose his friends from the lower classes. He met the pretty Karin Månsdotter, the daughter of a soldier, when she was selling nuts in the marketplace, fell in love with her at first sight, and took her as his mistress. His closest friend was Göran Persson, the son of a Lutheran priest and an outspoken enemy of the nobility. Instead of learning the art of government as his father had, Erik, this handsome prince, educated by the best tutors, schooled in the social graces, adept in music, trained in sports, in every outward respect the Renaissance man of virtu, spent his time carousing with a reprobate who had barely escaped the hangman's noose and with a wench who at best was the betrothed of an ensign in the royal guard and at worst a soldier's whore. The death of Gustav could only come as a relief to Erik. But one heavy hand was lifted from his shoulder only to be replaced by another, that of the nobility who distrusted him as much as he distrusted them. One calamitous confrontation led to another, and finally Erik had several nobles arrested, imprisoned, and eventually executed. He may even have taken a personal hand in killing one of them. After the massacre, by a kind of Alice-in-

Wonderland logic, the lords were tried and found guilty as charged. The response to this was inevitable. The half brothers John and Charles formed an alliance with other nobles to raise an insurrection against Erik. They finally succeeded in deposing him, and six years later, he was poisoned in his prison cell.

On the surface, Erik's life was too sensational and too full of incident for a playwright who concerned himself with the life of the soul. But Strindberg knew as well as Napoleon did that the history one finds in books is an agreed-upon fable, and what Strindberg saw in Erik's career was not what the historians saw. To him, Erik was more than a mad king whose excesses would have brought his country to ruin if he had not been deposed. It was to be expected that the dramatist who was consistently accused of debasing his country's heroes should cast a sympathetic eye on one of its scapegraces, especially on one who was either totally insane at times or half-insane at all times. What was not to be expected was that the dramatist who had a profound understanding of disturbed personalities and who had just passed through a religious crisis should have neglected to take full advantage of the opportunities for the drama of madness, murder, and remorse that Erik's life offered. It was so little to be expected that critics have persisted in seeing Erik XIV as essentially a character study of a seriously disturbed young man and of the effect he has on others and have failed to see how it differs from Strindberg's previous history plays.

4

Strindberg feared that Erik XIV by itself would be "unsatisfying and incomprehensible."[3] His fear was only half-justified. Erik XIV can stand by itself, and of all Strindberg's history plays, it has been the most attractive to actors and directors outside Sweden. Still, it is true that unless it is seen in relation to the other two plays it cannot be fully appreciated. As the capstone of the trilogy, it was obviously meant to resolve an issue raised in them. Shakespeare's Henry V, for instance, takes on added significance when seen as the culminating play in a tetralogy. Richard II, the two plays about Henry IV, and Henry V were almost certainly not planned from the start as a unit, but before Shakespeare had finished them, they had become the four acts of a greater drama. The first play shows England disunited and compelled to rid itself of an ineffective king. In the last play, all of England is united under an ideal ruler and triumphant over its enemies.

By insisting on the unity of the plays in his Vasa trilogy, Strindberg is asking us to see a meaning in them that overarches all three plays. At first glance that meaning appears to be the opposite of Shakespeare's. In *Master Olof* Sweden becomes a nation united under Gustav; in *Erik XIV* it is in danger of disintegrating. The trilogy ends with the half brothers of Erik determined to fight each other for the crown (SS, 31:399).

"God, it's beginning again," says Erik's chancellor.

"I think the world's gone mad," says one of the brothers.

"That's what Erik thought, too," says the other. "Who knows?"

These ominous words and the prospect of internecine war have confirmed most commentators in their view that the play vividly expresses the senselessness of history. Why else is the hero of the play a madman? Why else are the scenes as disconnected as they are? There is no more logic in the sequence of events than there is in Erik himself, and the madness of the man who sits on the throne reflects the meaninglessness of the world.

This was a view that Strindberg might have shared in the middle of his naturalistic period when the history of man appeared to him to be a series of happenings governed by chance, a view that led him to get rid of a god who no longer had a function (SS, 19:244, 248). But it was certainly not the view of the Strindberg who had moved beyond naturalism. For the reborn Strindberg, purpose had replaced chance, and significance and meaning were everywhere present, in the history of man as well as in the life of the individual, if one only had the inner eye with which to see them.

The brothers Charles and John are too close to the events and too obtuse by nature to see any meaning in the history they are helping to make. Erik and Göran have more insight but not much more perspective. As they are about to be carried away by the current of history, the doomed Erik asks, "Should we laugh at life or cry over it?"

"As well one as the other, I guess," replies Göran. "It's all nonsense to me. Which doesn't mean there might not be a meaning hidden in it" (SS, 31:390).

This is the playwright's way of inviting us to look for the meaning. Obscured by the welter of events, it is gradually revealed in the trilogy as Olof yields to Gustav and Gustav to Erik. In the first play, Olof is persuaded to serve the state under the illusion that he is liberating the people from the oppression of a corrupt church. From the point of view of Gert Bookprinter, however, Olof has sold out the people and secured the position of Gustav as tyrant. In the next play, Gustav is seen at the apogee of a career that seems blessed by providence. Then the tide turns against him, and he is temporarily overwhelmed by doubts. As nationalistic drama, both *Master Olof* and *Gustav Vasa* show how Gustav created a united political state. On the level of personal drama, Olof is pictured as a man who loses faith in himself and in his belief in progress when he decides to serve Gustav, while Gustav is shown as a ruler who learns that no man is worthy to rule unless the inner man has been tested as well as the outer man, and that the god who makes the good man prosper is also the god who brings calamities on that man's head. In this Job drama, Gustav's success is due to the men of Dalecarlia; his afflictions are embodied in the rebels who march on him from Småland; and his ordeal comes to an end when the Dalecarlians, whom he thought were forever lost to him, arrive to aid him.

Strindberg might have ended the Vasa story at that point. Like Job, he might have been silenced by the voice from the whirlwind. But a question larger than that of Gustav's successes and sufferings still remained in Strindberg's mind. There was sense and meaning in what happened to Gustav, but what was the meaning of the subsequent events? After Gustav had consolidated the country, it fell apart under Erik. Shakespeare faced the same situation at the end of his tetralogy. After Henry, those who governed England "lost France and made his England bleed." Instead of examining the deeper implications of this, Shakespeare chose to see history as the endless chronicle of ambitious men who rose and fell, meteors of fortune momentarily lighting up the dark and inscrutable heavens. Eventually, his pessimism reduced the pageant of history as well as the life of the individual to a tale full of sound and fury, signifying nothing. Strindberg, coming out of his inferno, rejuvenated in mind if not in body, had a completely different view. He did not see the course of history as determined exclusively by the commands of autocrats and the clash of arms. As a child of the revolutionary nineteenth century, he saw the panorama of the past as the history of the people; and where Shakespeare saw only the rise and fall of heroes, the ebb and flow of political power, Strindberg saw the gradual progress and advance of the people through a dynamic process akin to the methods nature employs in transforming the physical world.

In *Gustav Vasa* he pits fathers against sons in order to show how the forces of history operate. The king, who dominates the first two acts purely as a force and not as a corporeal presence, is the power that gathers and builds. The sons and the rebels constitute the opposing force, which divides and tears down. The process is never-ending, and the two tendencies are simultaneously at work, with first one and then the other temporarily dominant.

At the beginning of the Vasa trilogy, Sweden is in a disorganized state. Gustav takes advantage of the Danish oppression and the religious turmoil to build an empire, while Olof seeks to unite the various religious sects into one church. In the second play, Gustav's work is accomplished, but Olof realizes that his own dreams have been defeated, that he himself was actually a schismatic who has left his own son with nothing to believe in.

Like Olof, those who dissolve the social aggregates usually do not realize what they are doing. The results of their efforts are quite different from what they expected. Hegel attributed the divergency of aim and accomplishment to the "cunning of Reason." An individual may be gratifying his own selfish passions, but in the process, something else is accomplished which is latent in the actions of the individual and of which he is not conscious. The middle-aged Olof is aware of this when he talks to his estranged son.

At your age I foresaw as if in a vision my whole frightful future. Foresaw the cup and the pillory, and still had to move toward them. Had to go into the fog and mist; I myself had to chase that will-o'-the-wisp that was meant to lead mankind astray. I even foresaw this moment when my son would stand here and say, "Look at me. Look at what you have made me." [SS, 31:254]

Olof has come to understand that his mind was working on two levels, and by pointing this out, Strindberg connects the cunning of Reason or the ruse of history with the individual unconscious. For Strindberg, the contradiction between what man proposes and what society disposes provided clues to the workings of history, just as irrational behavior in the individual provided clues to the workings of the psyche.

To the neurotic Prince Erik, history is all contradictions, and for the best evidence of that, he points to his father.

He's sound as a bell, full of horse sense. But he carries on like a madman. First he liberates the country from the invaders, then he lops the heads off the liberators. So now he's freed the country from foreigners, what does he do? He brings in foreigners and sets them over the lords of the land. If that's not crazy, what is? Then he decides the church is not going to cheat its faithful believers out of their money—not on his life, oh no! So he turns around and extorts money from the church for his government. And death to anyone who opposes him! This champion of freedom is the greatest despot in the world. This tyrant is the greatest living freedom fighter. [SS, 31:182–83]

Strindberg does not allow this view of Gustav to dominate the play. The major theme is the success of a man with a noble purpose to fulfill. Erik's belief that men are irrational and history illogical is heard only in the bass. But in the last play of the trilogy, the play that bears Erik's name, the bass theme moves into the upper part. *Gustav Vasa* ends with a tableau in which the king greets the Dalecarlians, and standing with the Protestant king are his Lutheran queen, his Catholic mother-in-law, and his Catholic son John—a picture of solidarity. Significantly, Erik is missing from the group, having been shoved aside by his father a few moments earlier when Gustav rose to meet the Dalecarlian advance man.

5

In the last play of the trilogy, in the story of the alienated son who is in love with the memory of his mother and who is convinced that his father killed her, Strindberg found the material for one of his most consummately drawn portraits, the Swedish theatre's Hamlet (SS, 50:75–76)[4]. The very fascination of this character has proved, however, to be a stumbling block to an understanding of the play. Critical attention focuses on Erik, and once his form and feature and mental constitution have been revealed, the rest of the play serves merely as background. "After the first act we recognize all of Erik's eccentricities," writes one of the foremost Strindberg scholars, "and we know that no outer events can change his mental state, that no failure or success can, for more than a moment, transform him." Consequently it is pointless to follow Erik's career through to his dethronement. This same scholar could write with extraordinary discernment about Gustav Vasa because Gustav is a man noticeably transformed by events. Erik merely oscillates from one extreme mood to another, and even his direct participation in the execution of his enemies does not make him a different man. Although this way of depicting Erik is psychologically sound, it is dramatically harmful because it does not allow Erik to develop. His experiences lead nowhere. The actions of the half-mad prince only reflect the half-mad world that he inhabits. And therefore, concludes the scholar, the play has no governing idea and even lacks artistic organization. It merely reveals that "life is without meaning."[5]

The fallacy in this approach lies in the premise—in the drama at least as old as Menander—that character is fate, and in its corollary that the deeds of great men settle the destinies of nations. The view that a man did what he did because he was what he was served the dramatist well enough as long as his concern was with the individual. This simplistic view, which was enormously helpful to the dramatist, was contravened by the historical records, especially if one read them for a moral meaning, and by a growing awareness of the complexity of human nature. When the individual was placed in a social situation, it was difficult to establish a relationship between character and action. The results of the great man's decisions were often different from what he intended, and his intentions were often ambiguous from the start. Shakespeare's Henry VIII had both political and personal reasons for divorcing Katherine (SS, 50:210–218);[6] and Schiller's Wallenstein, who believed in the equivalency of fate and character and who read his destiny in the stars and in the lines of his hand was to his amazement defeated by forces he was not aware of. When his dream of ending the war left the realm of his imagination and became a factor in the lives of others, he could no longer control it. It was swept up by the dreams and ambitions of others; his star-willed destiny lost itself in the ambitions and destinies of others. Schiller hesitated to see the consequences of this view of destiny. Hebbel did not hesitate, and for him, the individual became a droplet in the great current of life. The question then became, What determines the direction of the current? If great men at their best and worst are not the makers of history but only the rocks in the stream, what then makes the current change its course at certain times?

The Vasa trilogy recapitulates the history of the history play from the traditional kind in which character is dominant to a new kind in which the hero is submerged in the flow of events. *Master Olof* pictures the achievements of Gustav and the failures of Olof, and their deeds are directly related to their characters. In *Gustav Vasa*, the new view counterpoints the old. The great man still dominates the upper part, though he is buffeted by forces he does not understand, while in the lower part, men are the playthings of the gods. When Gustav is seen from this level, as Erik and Göran see him, his actions are inconsistent and contradictory. The world of Erik and Göran is one in which the right deed is done for the wrong reason and the wrong deed for the right reason, in which wise decisions have dreadful results and rash, impulsive acts are crowned with success. The last play of the trilogy belongs to these two men, whose lives are nothing but a series of mishaps and miscalculations, of ironies and inconsistencies, of thwarted intentions and defeated expectations. So much do men and things appear to be leagued together in a conspiracy against them that they would be the first to agree with those critics who say that Erik XIV reflects a universe without meaning, design, or purpose.

All this seems to support the interpretation that Erik XIV shows a half-mad king adding to the madness of the world. But this impression is the result of seeing the play as character drama. If Strindberg's intentions had been those attributed to him by the critics, he would have portrayed Erik as mad as he is in the traditional accounts. Instead, he toned down Erik's madness and drew, as he himself said, "a character sketch of a man without character" (SS, 50:248). He did this in order to open up the play to other concerns and to provide a vista beyond portraiture. At that point where Erik ceases to develop as a character, that point where the ordinary critic sees the play dissolving into meaninglessness, there Strindberg lets us glimpse the deeper significance of events. Because playwrights and critics still thought of drama in pseudo-Aristotelian terms, it was extremely difficult in Strindberg's time to move beyond a drama in which plot was not welded to character. Afterwards, Piscator, Brecht, and others succeeded in creating a new non-Aristotelian form in which social conflicts replace psychological conflicts. "Aristotelian dramaturgy," said Brecht, "takes no account . . . of the objective contradictions in any process. They have to be changed into subjective ones, located in the hero."[7]

Perfectly aware of the dramaturgical problem and writing before epic theater had been offered as a solution, Strindberg hit upon the strategy of nullifying the hero and of severing the bonds between character and action by showing that, as often as not, the hero's intentions had nothing to do with the results. He moved the fulcrum of the action from the hero to a spot outside the court, beyond the battlefield, even beyond the marketplace. From that point he could move the whole weight of man's history. But to the viewer who still saw the hero as fulcrum and the hero's decisions as the lever of action, the sequence of events in Erik XIV was illogical and incomprehensible.

There is probably no more cogent, and certainly no more readable, critique of traditional philosophies of history than that given by Leo Tolstoy in his two epilogues to War and Peace, written in the 1860s. Before his time, says Tolstoy, the chroniclers wrote either of chosen men who led the masses, usually to destruction, or of nations more or less consciously pursuing some noble end, such as Prussianizing Germany, Frenchifying Europe, or Christianizing the world. What the chroniclers failed to explain was the nature of the force that impelled the masses. To say that one man like Napoleon could by himself set hundreds of thousands of men marching toward Moscow made no sense at all. Nor did it satisfy reason to say that a nation was driven by an idea, such as egalitarianism in politics or consubstantialism in religion. Buckle's demonstration of the effect of new concepts and new inventions on the people was no more convincing to Tolstoy than the established theories averring that great men were the source of the motive power in history. It was clear to Tolstoy that the cause of "an event in which millions of people fought one another and killed half a million men cannot be the will of one man." It was equally clear to him that there is a "law of predeterminism"[8] that guides history. Ruefully accepting the fact that the ultimate aim of human activity is beyond mortal comprehension, Tolstoy declared that the task of the historian was to examine the incredibly complicated social relationships that underlay the deeds of historic characters and the so-called destinies of nations. To accomplish this, it would be necessary to accumulate an infinite number of small and seemingly insignificant events and sum them up—to devise, in a word, an integral calculus of history. The fifteen books of *War and Peace* were Tolstoy's attempt at such a calculus. In the climactic scene of the novel, the battle at Borodino, the random killings on the field of carnage along with the small happenings at headquarters, such as Napoleon's coming down with a cold, are all recorded as part of the data to be summed up. The unorthodox description of the battle represents *in nuce* the method employed by Tolstoy in the novel as a whole.

Having the same general understanding of history but working within the limitations of dramatic form, so much more strict than those of the epic novel, Strindberg, writing some thirty years later, invented his own calculus for dealing with the amorphous material of history. Like the Russian novelist, Strindberg saw that there were three factors to be considered. First, the masses who furnished the steam power of history; second, the heroes who appear to direct and control this energy; and third, the tracks on which the locomotive traveled. Strindberg made Erik represent the aggregate of individual wills—energy without apparent direction. The irrational king rules without attempting to rule; he seems only to respond to the acts of others and exercises power without having a consistent aim. His political partner, Göran Persson, is the spokesman for a moral purpose and a higher idea in history, yet all his plans go awry. Göran assumes that there is design and meaning in history but learns that the design is continually being scratched out or modified by the perverse imps of the unforeseen and the unexpected. Using Erik and Göran as symbols of two vast conceptual fields—power and purpose—Strind-berg was able to advance a step or two beyond Tolstoy in describing the internal mechanism of history.

6

At the beginning of *Erik XIV*, the personable but unstable king enter-tains unrealistic hopes of marrying Queen Elizabeth of England. Expect-ing at any moment her acceptance of his proposal, he approves the request of his half brother John for permission to marry Catherine of Po-land. Erik has no more than done so when word comes that Elizabeth has rejected his offer of marriage. Immediately afterwards, Göran, his closest friend, tells him that his best political move would be to marry Catherine of Poland.

This quirk of events establishes the pattern that is to be followed in the rest of the play. In the hope of avoiding such blunders in the future, Erik appoints Göran as his special advisor, giving him extraordinary powers. From then on the two men are inseparable—"No Göran without Erik," as Prince John says. They complement each other perfectly. Erik is prepossessingly handsome; Göran, repugnantly ugly. Erik is weak and vacillating, Göran, strong and firm. Erik is unthinking, impulsive, and emotional; Göran, logical, calculating, and cold. Erik was born to wear the crown and has been trained to rule; Göran is untutored but was born to rule. Strindberg has lavished as much care in delineating Göran as Erik. Together they form a double portrait, and together they constitute the protagonist of the play, the throne and the power behind the throne (figure 23).

"Since I can rule only through my king," says Göran,

> he is the sun that gives me life. When that sun sets, I'll fade and die. No regrets. . . . We're chained to each other by invisible bonds. As if we were born in the same litter and under the same stars. What he hates, I hate; what he likes, I like. Your hates, your loves, those are the ties that bind." [SS, 31:315]

The second scene concerns the efforts of Erik and Göran to secure a strong base of power for the throne against the nobles. The king is sup-ported by the populace, not by the lords, and to strengthen the bond be-tween the king and his people, Göran wants Erik to legitimize his rela-tionship with the flower-girl Karin Månsdotter by publicly taking her as his bride. Although Erik is deeply devoted to Karin in his own erratic way, the marriage plan meets with two obstacles. First, the lords intend to embarrass the king by formally charging him with adultery. Second, Karin's former lover, now an ensign in the king's guards, is betrothed to her and insists on marrying her. The first obstacle can be circumvented by bringing the lords into disrepute. The second obstacle can simply be removed by having the naive ensign put out of the way.

In the third scene, Göran moves against the lords. Prince John has married Catherine of Poland without getting Erik's permission to do so. Göran construes this as an act of treason and arrests and imprisons the nobles belonging to John's faction for conspiring with a foreign power against Sweden.

The next scene, the fourth in a total of seven, is the pivotal scene. Göran has prepared the speech in which Erik will present the crown's case against the traitors. Erik's children come to play with him, and one of them inadvertently picks up the speech and walks off with it. Erik addresses his parliament and blunders his way through an improvised speech that presents the case against the nobles so badly that the charges against them are dropped. Then Karin learns that her former lover, the ensign, has been killed. Stricken with terror, she flees the court and takes refuge with the nobles who are seeking to depose Erik. While Erik protests against the god who allows loved ones to be taken from a man who has done them no harm, Göran inveighs against the god who permits political traitors to go unpunished. "I don't understand," says Göran, "how what has happened could have happened. It's against all logic, all expectation, all that's just" (SS, 31:363).

In a world in which everything seems to be going wrong, only one thing remains right—for the moment: the traitorous lords have not yet been released from their prison in the vaults of the castle. Taking justice into their own hands, Erik and Göran order the execution of the lords, and Erik goes down into the cellars to witness the bloodbath.

When he comes up, nervous and tense, with blood on his hands and conscience, he realizes that he has not put an end to the consequences. He has only added another link to the chain of retribution, for now he fears Karin and his children will be killed in retaliation. "Can you untangle this mess?" he asks Göran.

"No, I can't," replies Göran. "None of this makes any sense to me. Events just unravel themselves, and there's nothing we can do. Don't you see that? I'm struck dumb, paralyzed. Can't lift a finger. Can only wait and ask, 'What next?'" (SS, 31:367)

When he appears in the following scene, Erik is a different man. Reunited with Karin, he forgives her for running away from him and decides to make her his queen. In the next scene, Erik's half brothers respond to this politically shrewd move by determining to remove Erik from the throne and to claim it for themselves.

These two short scenes prepare for the complications of the final scene. To celebrate his marriage to Karin and to make peace with the nobles, Erik is giving a great banquet in his castle. As a token of his good will, he restores the honor of the slain lords by exculpating them from the charge of treason. In the meantime, Göran has assembled the estates and produced the evidence that was missing at the trial because of Erik's carelessness. While they are being declared innocent by Erik, they are being pronounced guilty by parliament. Once again in this tragicomedy of errors Erik and Göran have undone each other.

And worse is to follow. The scheming half brothers have prudently stayed away from the wedding festival, warned by Karin that Göran was reopening the case against them. Erik chooses to regard Karin's action as condign punishment for his having sought to compose his quarrel with the nobles. When he persecuted them, Karin left him; when he relents, she betrays him. Whatever he does is wrong. Such is the way of Erik's world, a world that from his point of view is without rhyme or reason, without point or purpose. As Göran says, however, that does not preclude the possibility that there might be a meaning hidden in it.

The wedding feast turns into a fiasco. None of the lords arrives, and Erik, enraged and humiliated, opens the banqueting hall to the rabble who have been standing outside. Göran remarks that their manners are no worse than the nobles,' and Erik admits that he feels right at home among these people. They have no time to mingle with their new guests, however. The two half brothers John and Charles see to it that Erik and Göran are caught. John enters to claim the crown for himself, and the crowd hails him. Charles contends that he was to share the throne. While John tells his followers that order and peace have been restored to the country, Charles announces that he will make war against John. The play ends as civil war begins.

7

It is not customary to end a history play, especially the last one in a trilogy or tetralogy, in the midst of the struggle and with the state on the verge of chaos and dissolution. Exceptionally, Schiller achieved a tragic effect in *Wallenstein* by declining to resolve the discords of history, although Hegel thought the effect more disturbing than tragic because Schiller's ending did not point upward to a higher stage in the evolution of man and society. But Strindberg's ending does. While Schiller raised his eyes to heaven in the hope that there was a divine plan even if he could not discern it, Strindberg looked at the world around him and saw that the resolving force, what Montesquieu called "*l'allure principale*," lay in the common people. The decisive factor in history was ultimately not the sovereign but the populace, not Alexander or Caesar or Attila or Napoleon, those imposthumes on the face of history, but the laboring masses who constituted the blood and muscle of history. In Shakespeare's view the great man makes history; in Strindberg's view history makes the great man. And what makes history? The desires of the people; and all that the great man can do is give voice to those often unformulated desires. Strindberg would have agreed with Mao Tse-tung that "the people, and the people alone, are the motive force in the making of world history."

Gustav Vasa succeeds in building a nation because he has the support of a people who wish to rid themselves of their Danish oppressors. Olof's position is more questionable since Gustav uses him as a stalking horse. The majority of the people regard him as a heretic and a destroyer of old values. Still, he has enough followers to make him valuable to Gustav. The consequence is that he stays alive and compromises his ideals. In the second play of the trilogy also, the people are the prime movers. When Olof tells the troubled Gustav that he must humble himself before a higher power, it is specifically the "justifiably discontented" and rebellious farmers of Småland who represent that higher power. The extent to which Gustav's whole career has been dependent on the people is underscored by Strindberg at the end of *Gustav Vasa*. The drunken soldier who brings the despairing Gustav the news that the Dalecarlians have come to aid him is the same man who years earlier brought the same kind of news to the young Gustav and put him on the throne of Sweden.

The impression of a monarch who manages to rule by responding adroitly to the movements of the populace is radically different from the impression that Shakespeare creates, even though Strindberg's history plays deal with roughly the same period of national development. Strindberg's rulers lead in the same way that a dog does when it takes its master out for a walk. In Shakespeare the question is only, Who is fit to wear the crown?, while in Strindberg the question is, In which direction is the mass moving?

The question is not easy to answer since the populace is not a homogeneous mass, except at those epochal moments in history when something causes the swirling mass to flow in one direction. In all parts of his trilogy, Strindberg shows the people as divided into groups[9] inimical to each other, and the tension between these groups channels the energy that develops nations, extends frontiers, and impels great men to do what they do. In *Master Olof* there are the superstitious, ignorant, unthinking masses who, as Buckle described them, fear change as they fear the devil and who look upon the man who would free them from their oppressions as an antichrist. They stone Olof. Then there is another large group who want change as long as somebody else does the dirty work. These are the followers of Olof. Finally, there is a small group of active revolutionaries, the conspirators led by Gert Bookprinter.

In *Gustav Vasa*, most of the Dalecarlians strongly support the despotic king even when he expropriates their wealth, while the farmers of Småland are up in arms against his unjust treatment of them. The lower classes are not motivated simply by a desire for food and for freedom; there are many people who would prefer a mere subsistence level of existence to a loss of order and discipline in society. Most of the time people adore their tyrants. Consequently, the behavior of the mass as a whole seems irrational, illogical, and unpredictable. To Strindberg, that confused mass, which formed the wellspring of history, was like the unconscious part of the mind, apparently unformed and inchoate yet always determining the direction of the individual's inner life. On the basis of this similarity between the mass mind and the individual psyche, Strindberg attempted to depict how scattered events align themselves as if they were iron filings in a magnetic field, for the "powers" are at work in the destinies of nations just as they are in the individual unconscious. The Vasa trilogy is the objective complement to the dream tetralogy. A couple of years after finishing *Erik XIV*, he contemplated writing a cycle of plays[10] that would show the conscious will in world history (conscious in the sense of purposeful and teleologically directed, not in the sense that the people were conscious of it). By that time, however, his concept of a social force that determined the course of Swedish history had been abstracted into a world will not much different from Hegel's Spirit of History.

In *Erik XIV*, Göran and Erik are emphatically identified with the lower classes. Erik, who learned in his childhood to hate his father, has developed into a young man who hates all rulers and masters and is most at home in taverns among the ordinary people. This "lord-loathing peasant king" (SS, 50:76)—Strindberg's appellation—is significantly missing from the group gathered around the triumphant Gustav at the end of *Gustav Vasa*, and he chooses to make a flower girl his queen. While the nobles dislike and distrust him, he is loved by the people. (There is a subtle indication of the people's attraction to Erik at the end of *Gustav Vasa*: the messenger from the Dalecarlians mistakenly greets Erik as the king.) Similarly, Göran, who is a reincarnation of Gert Bookprinter, represents the populace. He refuses to be ennobled, and he regards the crown as entrusted to Erik by the people, not conferred on him by the lords.

Although Erik and Göran are yoked together as spokesmen for the common people, Erik works for the people impulsively, his actions governed almost entirely by his emotions and by his conscience, while Göran is the man of reason and intellect, without much conscience. He is Erik's brain, but he cannot exist without the irrational Erik, who possesses the power to do what Göran thinks. Erik represents the populace as the unknowing, unthinking, inarticulate mass; Göran is the mind, the scientific theoretician above the populace, seeking to direct it. If the people are thought of as a psychic entity, Erik stands for the unconscious, Göran for the ego. Yoking together Erik and Göran is an artifice by which the playwright can indicate in theatrical shorthand the contradictory nature of the populace. It is a means for representing what Trotsky calls the "dynamic of a revolutionary process, which creates thousands of contradictions only in order accidentally and in passing, as though in play, to resolve them and immediately create new ones."[11] Often the populace defeats its own purposes and is hostile to its own best interests. What Göran does, Erik undoes, and vice versa. Yet progress is made in spite of their defeat—or rather because of it. The final irony is that, out of the turmoil created by Erik and Göran, the people have made an advance. At the end of the play, they are occupying the palace, invited by Erik to partake of the feast that the nobles have scorned, and the nobles are about to reduce their own ranks in a civil war. The visual effect of the stage being filled with laden tables and ragged guests speaks more clearly than words.

The complexity of the forces at work in history is also intimated visually by a child's doll that is an indispensable stage property in the play. In the opening scene, Karin, pitying Erik, calls him Paleface because he is so much like a doll she played with as a child. Always thwarted by forces beyond his control, Erik does seem as helpless as a doll. The point is driven home in the central scene when the document itemizing the evidence against the lords disappears just as Erik is about to read from it to the assembled estates: one of Erik's children has used it as a blanket in which to wrap his doll—a doll named Paleface,[12] of course. The audience sees this happen and subliminally understands that the innocent doll is the emblematic focus of all those circumstances, like the length of Cleopatra's nose, or the sudden death of the Empress Elizabeth in 1762 that kept Frederick great, those convergences of the twain, those intricate lines of influence, fields of forces, "vast congeries of volitions, interests, and activities," that are variously and collectively referred to for convenience' sake as chance, fate, national destiny, historical necessity, general providence, and the World Spirit "coming to itself and contemplating itself in concrete actuality."[13]

In the next scene, the doll continues to work its spell. Unaware of the part it has already played in Swedish history, Erik picks up the doll and is reminded of a happier time in his life when he played with his children. These memories provoke his rage against the lords who have taken his wife and children from him and determines him to execute the nobles he still holds in prison. Thus the doll embodies both the forces impinging on him from outside and the forces prompting him from within, both the circumstances that set him back and the powers that thrust him forward on the path of progress.

Although the doll is easily overlooked in reading the play, in the theatre it would, if properly managed, make a sharper impression than an actor descanting on the philosophy of history, the inextricability of cause and effect, and the interpenetration of psychological and political motives in determining the course of events. Like the Belshazzarian banquet that finishes Erik's career, like the flame-lit chrysanthemum at the end of *A Dream Play*, the doll shows how a master artist can make a comprehensive statement succinctly and memorably by utilizing the unique resources of his medium and by leaving to critics the task of translating it into another medium.

8

If Strindberg had lived long enough to write about the Russian Revolution, he would have seen in Lenin a reincarnation of Göran. Lenin was convinced that the revolution had to be brought to the people by dedicated communists who would work out the strategy for replacing the autocracy of czar, church, and capitalist with a dictatorship of the proletariat. In 1902, in his essay "What Is to Be Done," Lenin the theoretician asserted that "all worship of the spontaneity of the working-class movement, all belittling of the role of 'the conscious element,' . . . means . . . a

strengthening of the influence of bourgeois ideology upon the workers."
Yet Lenin's carefully thought-out plans all seemed to go wrong. The Bolsheviks came to power in spite of Lenin's scientific socialism, not because of it. It was the same on the other side. The reactionary forces were
defeated because in trying to quell the revolution they only succeeded in
opening the way to it. The German imperialists and capitalists sent the
exiled Lenin to Russia in 1917 to provoke political dissension and to
compel Russia to lay down its arms before the German soldiers. In Russia, the moderate forces, who took power after the Czar abdicated, fought
among themselves, and in the economic disorganization that ensued, the
Bolsheviks were carried to power on the tidal wave of discontent that
temporarily united working man and peasant. In the next decade, power
was again consolidated in a central authority under Stalin. Strindberg's
play about Stalin would portray him as the counterpart of Gustav Vasa,
not in temperament and personality necessarily but in terms of his historical function; and with the scope of the drama enlarged to encompass
Europe, the central off-stage event would be the battle of Stalingrad.

Although Marxist critics relegate Strindberg to that group of nineteenth-century writers who fled from realism and politics into symbolism and religion—"Strindberg plunged into neo-Romanticism and wild
superstition," said one of them[14]—Strindberg is in fact one of the most
Marxist of playwrights. He succeeded better than any other dramatist in
putting on stage the dialectical process of history. When the German socialist Ferdinand Lassalle wrote a play about the Reformation, Marx reproved him for falling into the error of "placing the Lutheran-knightly
opposition above the plebeian Münzer opposition."[15] Engels pointed out
that Lassalle's hero, Franz von Sickingen, failed to liberate the people
from monarchic tyranny because he did not form an alliance with the
peasants, and consequently, his plan of action was "necessarily trivial,"
as far as progress was concerned. Strindberg, whose political inclina-
tions were much more radical than Lassalle's and who had the advantage
of writing after the Paris Commune rather than before it, instinctively
avoided these errors in the Vasa trilogy and was so much in tune with
Marx's thinking that he put a Münzerite, Gert Bookprinter, above both
Lutherans and lords in the order of merit.

Strindberg is even more successful than Bertolt Brecht in dramatizing the dialectics of history. Brecht wanted to make the spectator think
about the past by keeping him at arm's length from the events. Strindberg's method was to unsettle the spectator's complacency by bringing to
the surface the contradictions of history. Either way, the viewer was

made to see history as something other than a series of great events directly ensuing from the decisions reached by men in high position. But there is a vital difference between the two methods, the same difference that George Lukács found between Chekhov and Brecht. He criticized Brecht's alienation effect as being superimposed on the play and as not being a function of the theme itself. In contrast, Chekhov creates a tension between the charming and sympathetic people in his plays and the immoral and parasitical social system that they represent.[16] In Brecht, the message is sent out in songs and on banners; in Chekhov we discover it for ourselves. Chekhov's method is Strindberg's. Brecht, of course, could well reply that the indirect approach fails because the average spectator is incapable of learning the lessons of history unless they are hammered home.

Still, there is one cardinal point on which Strindberg differs from Marx, from Brecht, and from Chekhov and which puts him in the company of Bernard Shaw. Though Shaw and Strindberg may seem to be polar opposites, they share a world between them, for both men believed in a vital force that impelled all living things to a higher form of existence. Marx, Chekhov, and Brecht were materialists, for whom spirit was an epiphenomenon, froth and spume churned up by the restless sea of matter. Strindberg and Shaw were vitalists, who put their faith in a life force that had either coexisted with matter since the beginning of time or had been the one original source from which matter itself had been distilled. Both impugned, with wit and sarcasm, often with irrefutable logic, and just as often with relentless asseveration, the neo-Darwinist doctrine that life in all its forms evolved and improved itself simply through natural selection, the survival of the fittest, and chance mutations and that matter required nothing outside itself in order to develop and rise to higher levels. Both believed that the vital spirit, however erratic its actions might appear, represented, in contrast to Schopenhauer's indifferent and directionless world will, a beneficent will striving to perfect itself by overcoming matter. Shaw believed in a life force because he saw how much had already been accomplished by life in its struggle with matter, while Strindberg believed in a spiritual force because he looked at the world around him and saw how much needed to be done and saw no way of its being done without some help from the higher powers. For Shaw, the ultimate aim of life was to overcome matter, and when he looked into the future as far as though can reach, he saw the seed of life mastering "matter to its uttermost confines." On this point Strindberg's vitalist credo differed from Shaw's. For Strindberg the final goal of life was moral, not acquisitive, and where Shaw envisioned bigger brains and a more intense mental life that would eventually succeed in turning all matter into "a whirlpool in pure intelligence,"[17] Strindberg saw the spiritualization of matter as the means by which a moral universe is created and maintained.

As far as the history of man was concerned, both Shaw and Strindberg knew that the prince of this world was not the devil. If the ultimate purpose of the social movements of history was beyond Tolstoy's comprehension, Strindberg and Shaw understood that these social movements had led to the increased power and improved welfare of the people. Where Thomas Hardy saw only an unconscious, undirected will behind the events of history, a will that achieved its effects by chance and coincidence, Strindberg saw the unfolding of a great design worked out by a will or intelligence of a higher order, an intelligence that employed opposing forces for its purposes as if it were planning the strategies for both sides in a chess game, simultaneously urging on, for example, the prophet Mohammed and Gregory the Great. For him, history consisted in the "unconscious striving of mankind, ignorant of its goal but in the service of a conscious will." This is very close to Shaw's philosophy (as expounded in *Man and Superman*, which was published in 1903, the same year in which Strindberg published an essay on the mystical in history) in which a life force proceeds by trial and error and develops a brain in order to minimize the errors, with the significant difference that in Strindberg mind is present from the beginning, a point that also distinguishes Strindberg's post-Inferno view from his earlier Hartmannian outlook in which reason was secondary to an unconscious will.

Fundamental to Strindberg's conception is a governing agent whom he calls "the Creator, the Undoer, and the Preserver." This Trimurti regulates the majestic rhythms of history, making and unmaking civilizations and cultures but always with a higher end in view. Goethe thought of the historical process in terms of attraction and repulsion, of positive and negative forces, of diastole and systole. Strindberg thought of it in terms of concentration and diffusion and likened the process to chemical analysis in which a substance is thrown down or precipitated from a solution and in turn dissolved in another solution in order that yet another precipitate may be formed. The Vasa trilogy is his demonstration of this process. It begins with the nation in disorder and the church divided against itself. Gustav is the reagent producing the precipitate that is the Swedish state, while Erik and Göran are the reagents that cause the dissolution of the state. When the trilogy ends, the nation is plunged in chaos. This political disorder, in which the commentators see an image of a madman's world, a world without meaning, this social chaos that would have unsettled Olympian Goethe and untuned all of Shakespeare's strings, was for Strindberg a necessary step in the advancement of the common man.

"The progress of the people is brought about in two ways," he said,

through dissolution and through condensation. The task of the dissolver is surely the more difficult and the more thankless task, but it is also the more effective. The chemist knows well enough how difficult it is to get a clear solution while precipitation often seems to take place without any help at all.[18]

Strindberg admired what Gustav accomplished, and the trilogy attains its climax when Gustav is cheered by the Dalecarlians. But, fundamentally, Strindberg's sympathies lay with the common people. Although he fluctuated throughout his life between respect for the political strong man who acted while others theorized and love for the common man in whom he saw the generative power of history, his strongest bond was with the populace. In his own mind he was always "the son of a servant." That is why the last scene of *Gustav Vasa*, which is eminently satisfying theatrically and which effectively rounds off the story begun in *Master Olof*, could not be allowed to stand as a final statement. In *Master Olof*, the people were depicted as an unwieldy mass who let themselves be brought into line for their own good. In *Gustav Vasa*, they were shown as both main stream and undercurrent which together determine the direction of events. In *Erik XIV*, the current spills over its banks, swirls about, and seeks a new channel. The overarching design of the trilogy reflects the great rhythm of history as Strindberg sees it, and what Erik and Göran unknowingly bring about is more admirable than what Gustav deliberately achieves. The ending of *Erik XIV*, like that of Chekhov's *Cherry Orchard*, draws the curtains on one epoch in man's political history and sets the stage for the next.

When Ibsen and Strindberg are compared with each other, as they continually are, the older of the two
usually comes off the better, at least
in England and America. Ibsen, the
advocate in everyone's eyes except
his own of women's rights, appears as
the wise old man; Strindberg, the misogynist with a mother fixation, as an
obstreperous child. Ibsen's reasoning
powers are set off against Strindberg's
emotionalism; his finely honed verse
against Strindberg's ragged doggerel;

MAKING
MUSIC

his steady and laborious perfection of technique from play to play against
Strindberg's erratic experimentation with form; the consistently high
standard of his works against the uneven quality of Strindberg's; the coherence and comprehensiveness of his philosophy against the lightning-
swift changes and astounding reversals in Strindberg's thinking. Still,
there comes a point in this list of contrasts when the wise old man begins
to seem too nearly perfect and a little inhuman. An acquaintance described Ibsen as being utterly indifferent to the charms of music, flowers,
and children.[1] Strindberg seized on the remark to assail Ibsen and all that
he stood for (SS, 46:133). Strindberg adored music, flowers, and children, and they figure prominently in his stories and plays. Although
Ibsen had a painter's eye, he had no ear for music and no interest in it
until he was in his sixties and had fallen in love with a young pianist.
Strindberg, in contrast, had music in the roots of his being, and it was
partly through his love of music that he was able to advance the frontiers
of dramatic art beyond those explored by Ibsen.

To appreciate what Strindberg accomplished as an innovator in this
respect and to recognize his true place in the history of the drama, it is
helpful to remember that drama was not a product of spontaneous generation. It was the offspring of two parents, music and fable. It was born out
of man's desire to sing and dance and out of his curiosity as to how
things happen. In the drama of the Greek tragedians, music and story
formed a perfect union—but only for a while, as Nietzsche tells us. Then
music quarrelled with fable over who should be master of the house;
they went their separate ways; and there was no conscious effort to bring
them together again in their original relationship until the Renaissance.
Striving to recreate the Greek tragedy, the Italian composers produced

what we know as opera, a form in which music dominates the story. After that, the imbalance between the musical and narrative elements became more and more pronounced in spite of the efforts of Gluck and others to restore the original partnership.

In the meantime, the narrative drama, having never entirely forgotten its birth, made use of music to enhance the atmosphere of the story, to stress the pathos of a scene, or simply to preoccupy the minds of the audience while the stage was being reset. Shakespeare's employment of song is familiar enough not to require comment; it is less well known that the spectator at a straight play in eighteenth-century London spent about one-third of his evening in the theatre listening to music. In the nineteenth century, music became an even more vital ingredient in the narrative drama through the development of melodrama—tragedy for those who cannot read, as one of its practitioners defined it. Even if the theatregoer did not know the language the actors spoke, even if he were blind, he could pretty much follow the story by listening to the music that accompanied the entrances of the characters (rumble on the bass viol for the villain, a trumpet for the hero, trills on the flute for the heroine, a bassoon for the comic), the ominous chords struck as the villain pronounced his ultimate threat, "hurry music" for action scenes, crashing music for battle scenes, soft music for sentimental scenes—all of it appropriated by the moving pictures and later by radio and television drama.

It was also in the nineteenth century that both Richard Wagner and Henrik Ibsen reacted against the way in which music was being made to pander to the story. Wagner, emulating the Greeks, composed what he called music dramas. Ibsen, perfecting the narrative drama and bringing it to a degree of complexity it had never attained before, sought to make it completely independent of music. When *Ghosts* was performed in Norway, it was his wish, in violation of all custom, that there be no music at all before the curtain rose and none during the intermissions. While Wagner endeavored to fashion a modern form of Greek tragedy by fusing music and drama together, Ibsen created it by ruthlessly separating the two.

In the 1890s, Wagner and Ibsen were the dominant figures in the advanced theatre—not as rivals, however, for in Paris both had the admiration of the Symbolists, who wanted to restore to the cultural and intellectual life of Europe the spirit that had been banished by the materialists and the naturalists. It may seem odd that the author of *Ghosts*, the most notorious naturalist drama, should be highly regarded by the Symbolists;

but Ibsen in the 1890s had entered a new phase of his career and was writing plays like *The Master Builder*, that hypnotic drama which explored man's soul and made the outer world subservient to the inner world of will and spirit.

At this point Strindberg enters the story. Nearly twenty years younger than Ibsen, he was destined, it seemed, always to remain obscured by the huge bulk of the Norwegian master. But in the 1890s the rival ventured into fields that the master skirted. The course of Strindberg's life and the course of European drama had both reached a kind of terminus, and further development in each could only come about through radical change. Ibsen had exhausted the possibilities of the complex plot in which characters had cores as solid as atoms and events were linked together in cause-and-effect relationships, while Strindberg questioned the validity of those relationships and knew that the ego and the atom were both divisible. The plays he wrote after 1897 reflect this new view. Read as naturalistic works, they are impossible to understand, and if they have exerted a considerable influence on the drama of this century, it is mainly because they have been understood as freeing the drama from the restraints of the purely narrative element that informed naturalistic plays. The new world required a different kind of playwriting, and in developing it, Strindberg's musical interests became a source of inspiration.

2

Strindberg liked to describe his childhood as one of fear and hunger, of physical poverty and spiritual deprivation. He had come into the world, he insists on telling us, unwanted and unloved. He may have felt unloved, especially after his mother died and his father remarried; throughout his life, nothing was so abhorrent and painful to him as the infliction of stepparents on a child. Apart from the stepmother, the circumstances were quite different from those Strindberg describes. He was born into a middle-class family, quite legitimately—he was not the illegitimate child he represents himself as being in his autobiographical novels—and though his father's business had its ups and downs, the children were as well cared for as those in other middle-class families.

As was customary at the time, they were expected to acquire some musical culture and to play an instrument. The father liked music and encouraged his children to take lessons. Strindberg's older sister and older brother both received a formal education in music, attending the academy of music in Stockholm when they grew up. August Strindberg started to take piano lessons but, characteristically, grew impatient and tried to teach himself, without success. Consequently, he felt left out when family and friends gathered for musical evenings, playing Haydn and Mozart symphonies as transcribed for four hands, Anna and Oscar playing violin; Axel, cello; and Eleanor, piano; and he tried to enter the inner circle by memorizing the names and opus numbers of all the scores he could lay his hands on. When Strindberg attended the university at Uppsala, he sang in quartets and learned to play the flute and the guitar. At least up to the time of his Inferno crisis, his guitar accompanied him wherever he went, and when he was in a festive mood, with the schnapps flowing freely, he would break out into song, accompanying himself on the instrument, which he always kept a little out of tune (figure 7).

"Perfectly tuned instruments quickly become boring," he told his wife Frida, "like perfect beauties." Frida was flattered.[2]

He seems not to have taken music very seriously. It afforded amusement in his private life, and in his plays, he employed music in a conventional manner. In *Miss Julie*, the folk songs and dances on Midsummer Eve help to establish an erotic and threatening atmosphere, but they do no more than that.

In the 1890s, however, when Strindberg, divorced from his wife, separated from his children, shunned by his publishers, and reprobated by the guardians of Swedish morals, left Sweden to begin what he hoped would be a new literary career in either Germany or France, his attitude toward music began to change. In the Berlin bohemia, he learned to like Chopin's music, hearing it played passionately by Stanislaw Przybyszewski,[3] Chopin's compatriot who was obsessed with sex, black magic, and Nietzsche. In Paris, Strindberg developed a friendship with Sophie Kjellberg,[4] a pianist in the Scandinavian colony, who taught him to appreciate Bach and Sinding. He would sit for hours, listening to her play. He was responding to new impressions, new ideas. At the end of the first part of *To Damascus*, the Woman urges the Stranger to listen to new tunes. Although she has in mind more than music, it was music that helped open Strindberg's mind to a new outlook on life and to new forms of art.

As a young man, he had no consuming passion for classical music— far from it. He thought the Beethoven quartets banal—"four instruments prattling"[5] was his capsule description of them in 1872. He was only twenty-three, and the remark smacks of youthful bumptiousness. Still, even in the mid-1890s, he could mention with approval a pianist who

brought new life to the Beethoven "Pathétique" Sonata by playing it on a
piano that had been tuned at random.[6] After the Inferno crisis, he would
have regarded that jangling music a sacrilege. Beethoven became his
idol, the creator of some of man's sublimest works. Picturing his lone-
someness during the late hours of the night, hours that the aging Strindberg dreaded, he wrote on one occasion,

I wanted to cry out, to break free. I wanted release, I wanted to hear music, music
of the greatest kind, music by that greatest of souls who suffered all his life—I
wanted Beethoven, especially Beethoven, and I began to rouse to life in my inner
ear the last movement of the "Moonlight Sonata," which has become for me the
most sublime expression of mankind's yearning for liberation, of a sublimity beyond the reach of words. [SS, 38:189]

To the end of his life Strindberg found inspiration and solace in Beethoven. Once he found him, he never let him go. Beethoven was a kindred soul, not liked by "the so-called good people . . . , an unblessed and
unsettling spirit who cannot be called divine, but who is certainly un-
earthly."[7] Beginning in 1898, Strindberg and his brother Axel met nearly
once a week to study the sonatas,[8] giving especial attention to the sonata
no. 31. In December 1900, he acquired his own piano and learned to play
it in his "own special way, in slow tempo, as if squeezing the notes out of
the piano."[9] During the last twelve years of his life, his chief social entertainment was provided by what he called Beethoven evenings. A small
group of professional musicians, including his brother Axel, who now
held the position of musical director at the Royal Theatre in Stockholm,
would meet regularly in Strindberg's flat to play classical music, chiefly,
although not exclusively, Beethoven. They would gather punctually at
8:00 P.M. and play for an hour or so; then Strindberg would serve supper,
after which there would be more music. These Beethoven soirees, which
revived memories of the musical evenings of his childhood, continued
right up to the end of his life, the last meeting of "the Beethoven boys"
taking place on February 14, 1912, three months before Strindberg's death
from cancer.

Strindberg was drawn to serious music after the Inferno crisis because music could give direct expression to both the spiritual or ideal
side of existence and the subconscious or irrational life of the mind. He
would have agreed with Goethe, who in discussing "das Dämonische"
with Eckermann (March 8, 1831), said that "music occupies a realm so
lofty that reason cannot come up to it; from music emanates an influence
that dominates everything, an influence that no man can explain."[10] The
young Strindberg would have been familiar with Schopenhauer's praise

of music as the highest form of artistic expression, highest because it represented pure energy unadulterated by the phenomena of matter. All the same, when Strindberg in the 1890s came to recognize the power of music, he did not adopt Schopenhauer's point of view. For the pessimistic philosopher, music captured a bit of the meaningless energy of the universe and molded it into a object of contemplation. For the visionary playwright, music imbued the leaden world with poetry and meaning. It was the bond between man and a higher form of existence and was not to be trifled with. Great music was sacred, divine, and exalting; poor music was impious, satanic, and demeaning.

As a young man, he had laughed at the satire in Offenbach's operettas.[11] After the Inferno crisis, he reprehended Offenbach for caricaturing and debasing the nobleness and grandeur of ancient Greece. And, quite consistently, he disapproved of operetta and musical comedy in general for demeaning humanity instead of elevating it. This sort of music was like a pernicious infection. "You can't listen to an operetta without suffering some harm," he warned,

because it is as hypnotically suggestive as evil itself. Like a medium you sway to the tune of the unseen composer; your body dances as he pulls the strings. You are quite literally infected. . . . Better the cinema or the innocent circus with beautiful horses and crazy clowns, if you're looking for a little harmless entertainment. [SS, 50:155]

Even Beethoven failed to measure up to Strindberg's standards when the composer deliberately descended from the sublime.[12] He did not care for the scherzos in the Beethoven sonatas, called them "Mozartian doodling," and on the Beethoven evenings, the scherzos were usually omitted at his request. He also thought the "Ode an die Freude" of the Ninth Symphony "banal," an opinion that Stravinsky was to share.

Virtually all of Mozart seemed trifling to Strindberg, except the G Minor Symphony and parts of the *Requiem* (SS, 28:303–04).[13] In *Don Giovanni*, all he liked were Leporello's big aria and the music accompanying Giovanni's damnation, music from the abyss, Strindberg called it, professing to hear in it the outcry of Mozart's guilty conscience for having seduced a woman whose husband subsequently committed suicide. Among composers of string quartets, Haydn won his unqualified praise.[14] And Chopin's Nocturne in G, opus 37 no. 2, transported him by means of its fascinating modulations to a world of absolute purity and beauty (SS, 40:118–19). Other Chopin pieces he was particularly fond of were the Polonaise opus 40 no. 2, the *Fantaisie Impromptu* opus 66, and the Etude opus 25 no. 7. Of Schumann's works he liked "Aufschwung" and the Third Symphony, which he heard in a piano transcription. Bach's soaring spirit naturally won his admiration, and of the pieces Strindberg was able to hear he preferred the French and English Suites, the Toccata in D minor (BWV 913), and the great Chaconne from Partita 2 in D minor.

For lighter fare he turned to Brahms's *Hungarian Dances*, Mendelssohn's *Capriccio*, *Hebrides* Overture, and incidental music for *A Midsummer Night's Dream*, Weber's overtures to *Oberon* and *Der Freischütz*, Nicolai's overture to *The Merry Wives of Windsor*, Gounod's *Faust*, Mascagni's introduction to *Cavalleria Rusticana*, and even Rossini's overture to *William Tell* (SS, 54:474).[15]

Nothing tells us more about Strindberg's attitude toward music than his views on Richard Wagner. At first, when Wagner was a cult figure among the Symbolists in the 1890s, Strindberg saw him as a prophet raging against the prevailing philistinism and commercialism. Recovering from his Inferno crisis, he thought he recognized in the composer of *The Ring of the Nibelung* a comrade in arms. "Reading Wagner's *Rhinegold*," he wrote in 1897, "I discovered a great poet, and now I understand why I haven't understood before what is great about this composer, whose music is really only an accompaniment to his text" (SS, 28:313).[16] The curse on gold in *The Rhinegold* went straight to Strindberg's heart. To learn the magic that can forge the ring of gold one must forswear the ecstasies and powers of love, and Strindberg himself had turned his back on wife and child—second wife, fifth child—when he tried to transmute base elements into gold.

Yet within a year he was calling Wagner a satanist[17] because Wagner made use of the tritone, the unnatural interval, *diabolus in musica*. From then on, Strindberg went out of his way to assail the composer (SS, 41:177–78). Not only were Wagner's harmonic innovations offensive and "against nature," his orchestration was too heavy and drowned out the singers. The fact that he had made the recitative the essential part of his music dramas showed that he was fundamentally unmusical—and it was only the unmusical people who appreciated him. The whole Wagnerian cult was political at bottom and not musical. Wagner was loved by the Germans because he exalted the German nation, and he had become a cult figure in France because of the Franco-Prussian War. The 30,000 Germans in Paris promoted Wagner and won over the younger generation of Frenchmen who were in rebellion against the old-fashioned ideas of their parents.

This is Strindberg writing polemically and using the cult of Wagner to condemn cultism in general. Actually, his own ideas on musical com-

position (SS, 54:453–60) and harmony were very advanced, even radical. He said that if he were a composer, he would throw out the whole
theory of formal harmony and be guided only by his inner feelings. He
imagined that composers have always relied on instinct, except when
writing learned, academic, dull music. He questioned the need for a
dominant key, argued that the ear prefers transitions and that it is wrong
to speak of "permissible" intervals and chords, directly contradicting
what he had said about Wagner's unnatural harmonies. For his play The
Dutchman (written 1902 but left uncompleted), he wanted unseen in-
strumentalists[18] to play music consisting of new harmonies without melody. One critic avers that Strindberg had atonal music in mind.[19] In line
with this, Strindberg proposed a new system of notation in which key
signatures would have no function. He also desired to remove the bars in
musical notation and complimented Wagner for having virtually done
so. In one of his last dismissive comments on Wagner, he said that under
the German master music had reached such a pitch of complexity that
what was called for now was simplification.

What was there about Wagner that had disillusioned Strindberg?
And what was there about Wagner's music that aroused Strindberg's animosity? It was simply that Wagner's words belied Wagner's music. The
narrative said one thing, the music another. In the Ring cycle, the text
praised love and decried power and greed, while in the music itself,
there was the clamor of ambition and conquest, the noise of drums and
trumpets. It was, said Strindberg, music for the cavalry, "military music
for the drill field" (SS, 41:177), a comment that in the light of the events
of the twentieth century was prognostic. Far from being the prophet of
the new religious movement, as was assumed by the Parsifal addicts,
Wagner was the prophet of paganism. Strindberg found the story of Tristan and Isolde beautiful and moving because it showed how fleeting and
unfulfilling, how opposed to the enduring spirit of man and his divine
origins, were the deceptive joys of physical love. But the beauty lay only
in the narrative; the music was another matter. Strindberg knew that in
Wagner's drama the soul lay in the words, the body in the music, and he
understood perfectly well the meaning behind the orgasmic music.

I have praised the text of Tristan for its pure beauty, which reminds one of Maeterlinck. But the music—!
    Consider that andante with the words, "O sink' hernieder, Nacht der Liebe!"
    It is not only ugly but evil. That is why it is adored, worshipped; and those
who won't offer incense to the idol are persecuted with a kind of antireligious
fanaticism. [SS, 47:665–66][20]

(When Strindberg drew up a list of plays that he wanted to see staged at his Intimate Theatre, he included *Tristan and Isolde*, along with such items as Euripides's *Hippolytus*, Racine's *Phaedra*, and Grabbe's *Don Juan and Faust*—all of which would have made an extraordinary cycle on love. But he wanted *Tristan* done without the music!)

The young Strindberg would probably have been among the worshippers, if he had known Wagner's works. In connection with *A Dream Play*, I mentioned one of Strindberg's stories from the 1880s in which a daydreaming girl imagines herself in a vast cathedral with the organ thundering out the *Dies Irae* (SS, 15:20–22). The words become flesh, the pipes of the organ become the pipes of Pan, and the sound of the organ is drowned in a storm of nature. The whole story is a Rousseauistic indictment of high culture as a neurosis, of civilization as an unhealthy rupture in man's being. Even here, the music expresses a spiritual force in conflict with nature. But the music is defeated. That never happens in the works written after the Inferno crisis. There lies the whole difference.

In 1901, Strindberg responded to the eroticism of Wagner's *Tristan* by writing *Swanwhite*, a Maeterlinckian fairy play for adults. The parallels are obvious, even though Strindberg drew his material from Swedish folk tales. In Wagner's music drama, Tristan is sent to bring Isolde home as the bride of King Mark. In Strindberg's play, a handsome prince, nameless, is sent overseas to bring Swanwhite back as the bride of a young king. In *Tristan*, a potion causes Tristan and Isolde to fall in love with each other. In *Swanwhite*, the unutterable name of the prince fulfills the same function. In Wagner, Tristan and Isolde are caught making love. In Strindberg, the prince and Swanwhite are caught in bed together by Swanwhite's evil stepmother. Although the prince has carefully placed his sword between himself and Swanwhite, the stepmother accuses Swanwhite of betraying the young king.

Now for the differences. In Wagner, Tristan dies, and Isolde is united with him in a scene in which sexual energy is equated with the energy of the universe. In Strindberg, the prince dies but is restored to life and to Swanwhite in a scene in which charity and forgiveness are seen as the expressions of the highest love. "Eros is here only a symbol of great all-embracing Caritas."[21]

At first, Strindberg wanted the accompanying music to be played only on a harp and French horn and to consist entirely of newly composed pieces, not arrangements of familiar tunes [SS, 36:350]. Evidently, he could not find what he wanted, and subsequently, when the play was considered for production at his own Intimate Theatre, he suggested that some of Chopin's music, the *Impromptu Fantaisie* opus 66, and one of the Etudes opus 25, be transcribed, the first piece for harp and the second for oboe or French horn. When he needed advice on musical matters, he usually turned to his brother Axel, and on this occasion, Strindberg jotted down some thoughts in a note that survives.

Apropos our harp experiments this evening—
The Chopin *Impromptu Fantaisie*, Opus 66, could be transcribed thus: the bass plays as is, but the string of pearly notes in the treble is changed into chords, which, especially on page 2, are indescribably beautiful (followed by the bass).
Now my question is: since arpeggios come out best on the harp and should be in the treble, couldn't the one be exchanged for the other, putting the present bass into the treble and converting the pearly string into bass chords?[22]

Earlier, in the spring of 1906, Harriet Bosse—now divorced from Strindberg—had approached Sibelius[23] in Finland to ask him to compose incidental music for a production of the play to be given at the Svenska Teatern in Stockholm in which she would be featured as Swanwhite. This was the one occasion in Strindberg's life when a composer of the first rank wrote music especially for one of his plays. Unfortunately, he never got to hear Sibelius's entrancing score. The impresario Albert Ranft, owner of Svenska Teatern, delayed putting the play into production for several reasons, one of which was that Sibelius was asking royalties of 600 marks plus 2 percent of the gross box-office receipts.[24] In April 1908, *Swanwhite* had its premiere in Helsinki, without Harriet Bosse but with Sibelius's music. Half a year later, when Ranft's announced production gave no signs of getting into rehearsal, *Swanwhite* was staged at Strindberg's own Intimate Theatre, without Bosse and without Sibelius. Scored for flute, clarinet, two French horns, percussion, and strings, Sibelius's ethereal music demanded more in physical resources than the Intimate Theatre could supply.

3

As a playwright, Strindberg was constantly experimenting after the Inferno period with ways in which the narrative element in drama might become as evocative and suggestive as music, expressing more than mere words could. Some of his plays are lyric dramas in which music supports the narrative throughout. *The Bridal Crown* (written in 1901), for instance, makes use of folk tunes for this purpose (SS, 36:346–47; 53:525).[25] When Strindberg did not find exactly what he needed in the collection of folk songs that he consulted, he used a tune of his own com-

position. The song of the water sprite (*forskarlen*) is Strindberg's variation of a melody he dimly remembered from his own study of Swedish
folk songs and customs.

For his play on Charles XII of Sweden, the most poetic of his history
plays, Strindberg weaves the music of Bach through the narrative. Although the music helps to establish the atmosphere of the eighteenth
century, its larger purpose is to transcend the historical facts and evoke
not only Charles's state of mind but the forces at work on the man and in
the age. Strindberg makes the warrior king a music lover whose favorite
composer is Bach, and the sarabande played by the king's servant, a dwarf
named Luxembourg, becomes a death motif.

The play begins where plays about kings usually end. Charles XII,
who for years made all of Europe tremble, is shown in his last days, returning to a destitute Sweden whose resources he has exhausted on the
battlefields of Denmark, Poland, the Ukraine, and Bessarabia. Subsequently enshrined by hero worshippers who liked to summon to mind
the days when Sweden was a first-rate power while conveniently blotting out the fact that the net result of Charles's military exploits was to
reduce Sweden to a second-rate power, he appears in Strindberg's play as
a broken and defeated man who still goes through the motions of fighting
enemies while waiting fatalistically for the final blow to fall on him. In
Strindberg's rendering, Charles stands as the image of political absolut-
ism, and the sarabande, which is heard in each of the five acts, augurs
both the death of the king and the end of autocracy in Europe. In the
fourth act, in a scene reminiscent of the banquet at the end of *Erik XIV*
but more pointed and now visionary, grotesque, almost surreal, the rag-
tag are seen invading the king's garden, perching themselves on the wall,
while Charles and his minister of finance talk of the bankruptcy of Sweden, oblivious to what is going on behind them.

Although Strindberg had little use for hero cults and none at all for
the cult of Charles, whom he scorned as "Sweden's destroyer, . . . a bully,
the idol of hooligans" (SS, 50:251), it was impossible for him not to draw
some lines of sympathy on his picture of a brave but beaten soldier who
endures defeat without whimpering and embraces death with dignity.
Before the great leveler, Charles is as helpless and as pitiful as any other
man. Conversely, since all men must face death, Charles takes on the dimensions of Everyman. By treating his subject as a musician might,
Strindberg counteracts the political tendentiousness inherent in the portrait and suffuses it with the fellow feeling that music is capable of
providing.

The dramatic plot is so thin it virtually disappears, and in its place, Strindberg sketches a sequence of scenes that follow each other like the pieces in an orchestral suite or partita. He was undoubtedly led to utilize it here because the suite was the musical form most characteristic of the Baroque age. Bach provided the background music, and the suite established the form. As if to indicate his departure from orthodox dramaturgy, Strindberg divided his play into five tableaux rather than into acts: a tableau in general usage meant a subdivision of an act involving a change of set. Each act or tableau in *Charles XII* has its own rhythm and mood, and in structure, the play is less like Ibsen's *A Doll House* or Racine's *Phaedra* than Bach's Partita II in D Minor. The five acts are not linked together by a chain of events; they are loosely joined evocations of a man, a nation, and an era. The first act, which pictures a land wasted and desolate, is a somber allemand. The second act, revealing the intrigues at court, is a sprightly corrente. The third act, signaling the demise of absolute monarchy in Europe, is a wistful sarabande. The fourth act, a descant on love and war, is a lively gigue. And the last act, in which Charles is killed by a bullet that could have come either from the enemy or from one of his own soldiers, is in mood, if in no other way, the equivalent of Bach's haunting chaconne. Just as the popular dance forms were completely refined and exalted when composers like Bach made them parts of a suite, so the conventional acts of standard drama, comprising exposition, rising action, height of action or turning point, falling action, and close of action or catastrophe, are here transmuted into music and visual poetry.

To establish and maintain the appropriate atmosphere, Strindberg wanted selections from Bach played at the rise of the curtain and between the acts. The final chorus from the *Saint Matthew Passion* was to serve as prelude, while the Gavotte in G Minor from the third English Suite, the D Minor Sarabande from the first French Suite, and the G Minor Sarabande from the third English Suite, with the following *agréments*, were to be played during the four entr'actes.[26]

Music in the *Damascus* cycle has an even more important function than it does in *Charles XII*. In the history play, the music evokes a mood and tells the audience what attitude to adopt toward the subject. In *To Damascus*, it becomes as indispensable as the words or the physical action in letting us know what is occurring. Since the hero of the play is only subconsciously aware of what is happening to him, and the tale is told from his point of view, the music, along with other symbolic elements, allows the alert listener to follow the inner, psychological, and spiritual story. The funeral march indicates the death of the materialist outlook in the hero; judgment on him is pronounced to the accompaniment of the *Dies Irae*, which is followed by the singing of *Salve Regina*, suggesting the possibility of redemption.

For the premiere of this play in 1900, Strindberg suggested that the theatre orchestra play the following pieces as entr'acte music:[27] Beethoven's Sonata in D Major opus 10 no. 3, the "Largo e mesto" (as prelude), the *Allegretto gracioso* from Mendelssohn's Lieder ("Frühlingslied"), the "Lacrimosa" from Mozart's *Requiem*, the Allegro movement from Beethoven's Sonata in D Minor opus 31 no. 2, and the interlude from Schumann's *Manfred* Overture. Because of technical problems caused by the numerous changes of scene, the act division in this production was different from that in the printed script. The Mendelssohn "Spring Song" would have been heard immediately before the Stranger and the Woman show up at the house of her husband, the Doctor; the *Requiem* just before the Stranger is discovered in the asylum; the Beethoven D Minor Sonata before the ravine scene; and the excerpt from *Manfred* before the last meeting with the Doctor. No one but Strindberg would have thought of playing the sugary "Spring Song" between the melodramatic end of the first scene, with the sound of the *Ave Maris Stella* and the ominous shriek of voices from the church still ringing in the ears of the audience, and the resigned, world-weary dialogue that opens the second scene. This sudden shift of tone provided by the music is typical of the play as a whole and underscores the ironic mood established in the first scene. On the other hand, the *Manfred* music has a more symbolic function, hinting quite plainly at the return of the spirit of defiance, of Byronic rebelliousness, in the Stranger.[28]

This is music meant as a signpost, and Strindberg uses music that way throughout *Easter*, a fragile and lyrical drama that he wrote at about the same time as *The Dance of Death*, infusing the former with mawkishness, sentimentality, and Christian charity, and the latter with hatred, vengefulness, and misanthropy. In *Easter*, Strindberg has the theatre orchestra play selections from Haydn's *The Seven Last Words of Our Saviour on the Cross* to indicate that his narrative about domestic problems, the foreclosure of a mortgage, and a student's failing his examinations forms a parallel to the Passion of Christ, the action taking place on Thursday, Friday, and Saturday of an Easter week around 1900. (The narrative technique of making everyday contemporary incidents correspond explicitly with the deeds of legend and myth, a technique made familiar by

Joyce and other writers and now rather shopworn, is Strindberg's invention, as he rightly claimed [SS, 53:468].)

In *The Dance of Death*, less music is played than in *Easter*, but it is arguably a more musical drama. Strindberg would have had his captain, Edgar, dance to the tune of Saint-Saëns's "Danse Macabre" had not Ibsen forestalled him by using it in *John Gabriel Borkman*. He had to settle for Halvorsen's "Entrance of the Boyars," actually, as it turned out, a better choice for this play.

The essential music in *The Dance of Death*, however, lies in the structure of the play. Its scenes can easily be broken down into Stanislavskian "beats," each of which has its own rhythms, each ending with a pause or a sudden modulation to another key, and it is the rhythm of these beats, rather than complications of plot as in conventional drama, that provides the driving force of the play. Themes are repeated and echoed from scene to scene. Curt's admonition of the need for forbearance, in the third scene, unexpectedly becomes Edgar's in the last scene. Edgar's grotesque dance to Halvorsen's music in the first scene, the dance that causes his heart attack, is followed by Alice's triumphant version of it in the third scene. Edgar's first-act lines about human life as destined for the manure pile becomes a leading motif that inspires Alice's vitriolic tirade in the second scene of the act. Another leading motif is provided by Edgar's philosophy of "wipe out and move on," with which the play ends. As counterpoint to it is the theme that everything in life is repeated, that everything comes back, and that nothing can be wiped out, a theme that finds perfect expression in the very structure of the play.

4

Strindberg's experiments in combining musical and dramatic form were part of a general reaction against the neoclassic play and its offspring, the well-made play. Initiated by the naturalists, the movement was abetted by the antinaturalists, the Symbolists, and has continued up to the present time. The naturalists wanted to replace the contrived plot machinery with intimate photographs of life. Maeterlinck threw out plot and replaced it with verbal music and an aura of otherwordliness. Chekhov, who disdained the dead conventions of the well-made play as much as Zola did, diminished the element of intrigue and made up for it by giving plot a kind of musical treatment. No one can analyze *The Three*

Sisters without being struck by its symphonic structure, and the "Oh, to go to Moscow" theme is repeated as often and in as many ways as the "People are to be pitied" motif is in *A Dream Play*. Also, at about the same time, Shaw put all the plot of *Man and Superman* into one part of the play in order to make himself free in the middle section, the Don Juan in hell scene, to compose a pure play of ideas for tenor, baritone, countertenor, and soprano. Strindberg went even further. In his pursuit of the intangible "higher powers," he left behind nearly all the principles and rules of standard commercial theatrical fare and, in effect, asked his audiences to forget what they knew about the handling of plot and the drawing of character and to remember all that they might have known about variation of theme, use of counterpoint, resolution of discords, and the psychologically, rather than logically, satisfying fusion of seemingly unrelated elements that is characteristic of great music. The nineteenth-century play was all cogs and wheels, and what Strindberg wanted was a play in which the logic of events had to yield to the logic of emotions, of "the demonic."

After the Inferno crisis, the search for new dramatic forms led Strindberg to restudy Shakepeare. He came to understand that the unique artistry of Shakespeare, whom he now esteemed above all other dramatists, lay less in his insight into character and in the breadth of his canvas than in the unlabored manipulation of all the elements that build a play and in the creation of a poetic world in which meaning is not spelled out but felt. To describe Shakespeare's technique, Strindberg had to resort to musical terms. Of *Hamlet* he said,

It forms a symphony constructed throughout along polyphonic lines with separate motifs beautifully plaited together. . . . The andante of the first act acquaints us with all the secrets we need to know; the second movement or act develops the theme, which is varied in the third. The *largo mesto* of the fourth act (Ophelia's madness) undergoes a quiet transition in order to burst out into the presto of the finale. [SS, 50:69]

Strindberg also saw how Laertes's part contributed to the musical form. "Laertes has acquired Hamlet's *pathos*: to avenge a father's death. Shakespeare treats this like a fugue or canon with Laertes picking up and carrying Hamlet's voice but now in the bass. (Hamlet was a tenor.)" Even the fact that nothing comes of Laertes's rebellion against the king was explained by Strindberg in musical terms as an unresolved discord (SS, 50:65, 171).

To Damascus, the first play that Strindberg wrote under the new dispensation, was "composed," he said, "in strict contrapuntal form" (SS,

50:287. Cf. SS, 49:138), by which he meant that the scenes and subjects of the second half of the play repeated those in the first half. ("Canonic form" would seem to be a better term for this.)

Even more musical in structure is *A Dream Play*, in which story and plot are about as prominent as they are in a Strauss tone poem. As he explained in a note, Strindberg let himself be guided solely by thematic considerations and entirely ignored the demands and conventions of the well-made play.

> As far as the loose, disconnected shape of the play is concerned, even that is only apparent. On closer examination, the composition is seen to be quite firm and solid—a symphony, polyphonic, now and then like a fugue with a constantly recurring main theme, which is repeated in all registers and varied by the more than thirty voices. There are no solos with accompaniments, that is, no big roles, no characters, or rather, no caricatures; no intrigue, no act curtains where applause is expected.—The voice parts are subjected to strict musical treatment; and in the sacrificial scene of the finale, all that has happened passes in review, with the themes once again repeated, just as a man's life with all its incidents is said to do at the moment of death.[29]

Construed as a musical composition, *A Dream Play* is a marvel of Bachian dexterity and ingenuity. The phrase "People are to be pitied" is repeated often enough to seem to be the main statement or subject. Actually, it is the answer. The principal statement in its original form is heard when the Mother complains, "If you help one person, you hurt another" (SS, 36:229). Living means hurting others. Indra's Daughter descends to earth to experience life as a human being, and she learns how difficult it is. "And the most painful thing," said Strindberg, "is hurting others, which one is forced to, if one wants to live." [30] The fugal answer "People are to be pitied" follows from that and is spoken by the Daughter immediately after the Mother's remark. (Brecht borrowed the principal subject[31] and made it the basis of *The Good Woman of Setzuan*, which also employs the familiar device of having the gods descend from heaven to find out why people are not all good.) As the fugue progresses, the principal statement (helping one person hurts another) is augmented, reversed, and inverted. Joy quickly turns sour; sweet love decays into disillusionment or bitterness; hope is born of despair and despair, of hope; duty makes war against pleasure; nothing on earth endures; reality is a mirage; life is a dream; and death, an awakening. All these contradictions, these antinomies of existence, attain their fullest expression in the final moments of the play, in the immolation scene, in the image of the flame-lit chrysanthemum, and in the Daughter's revelation that the world, and everything in it, is the product of an irresolvable conflict on both the physical and metaphysical levels of being.

The three acts of the drama may correspond to the three movements of a symphony, as Strindberg seems to suggest in his note. Taking the hint, an American scholar has found that the first movement (act) is in sonata allegro form; the second movement is a theme and variations; and the third takes the form of adagio, rondo, and coda.[32]

When Strindberg considered producing the play at his Intimate Theatre, he hoped that selections from Bach, Beethoven, and Mendelssohn might substitute for an original score, which he would have preferred.[33] For the kyrie eleison played on the organ near the end of act 1, Strindberg proposed the first thirteen bars of duet no. 12 in Beethoven's *Fidelio*, act 2. For the music of the wind and the waves in Fingal's Cave, Mendelssohn's *Hebrides* Overture was an obvious choice, but Strindberg wanted only the first few bars with the main theme to be played. In act 2, a Boston waltz is called for in the script, and it clashes with the Bach Toccato in D-sharp. For the complaint of the winds in the third act Strindberg suggested the accompaniment (and only the accompaniment) to the first stanza of Beethoven's Lied no. 32 ("An die Hoffnung") and for the song of the waves, the accompaniment to Beethoven's "Adelaide," bars 39–70; for the Daughter's elegy "Why are you born in pain?" the accompaniment to Beethoven's Lied no. 5 ("Vom Tode"); and for the Daughter's last poem, "Farewell, child of earth," the passage from *Fidelio*, act 2, *grave*, as long as necessary.[34]

5

The fugue is inherently not the most dramatic of musical forms. If Strindberg wanted to give drama a musical shape, why did he not resort to sonata form, which is much more dramatic in feeling by virtue of the conflict and growth of themes in the development section? As a matter of fact, he did. Between the writing of *To Damascus*, Part One and the creation of *A Dream Play*, he composed a play in strict sonata form,[35] using as his model the last movement of Beethoven's D Minor Sonata opus 31 no. 2. He heard the sonata played in the house of a friend in Lund in 1897. The occasion was made memorable and worth noting in his diary on June 1 because he saw a moth dancing to the rhythm of the music. Strindberg was as entranced as the moth, particularly by one passage in the last movement, twelve bars that sounded like the drill of conscience boring into the mind.

Two years later, when he decided to follow up *To Damascus* with another dramatic and psychological study of guilt, he took that twelve-bar passage as his leitmotif and built the rest of the play around it. This time the plot he had in mind was complicated and suspenseful, and perhaps that is why, of all musical forms, only the sonata form could serve his purpose.

The narrative element of the play derives from Strindberg's Berlin period and from the melodramatic events in the life of that high-strung Polish writer Stanislaw Przybyszewski. He had a mistress, Martha Foerder. She was the child of middle-class parents; Stanislaw had been her tutor; she gave herself to him; and her parents threw them both out of the house.[36] A rather plain woman, she devoted herself completely to Stanislaw, lived in desperate poverty with him, and bore him three children. Strindberg had a mistress too: Dagny Juel, a Norwegian who had been introduced by the painter Edvard Munch to the bohemian group that gathered at Strindberg's favorite tavern. Dagny passed from Munch's bed to Strindberg's and thence to Przybyszewski's. Stanislaw married Dagny, and Martha, seeing that she had no hope of winning back her lover and the father of her three children, committed suicide. By this time Strindberg had married Frida Uhl, an advanced and independent woman, by profession a journalist, just the sort of wife who could be relied on to provide Strindberg with the conflicts his dramatic soul thrived on. They had moved on to Paris, where he had enjoyed two fleeting moments of fame as the author of *Miss Julie* and *The Father*. In June and July 1896 rumors reached Strindberg[37] that Przybyszewski had been arrested in Berlin for having killed Martha and the children. According to one story, Przybyszewski had attempted to carry out an abortion on Martha, with fatal results.

Strindberg saw similarities between his own case and Przybyszewski's and, in carrying out the experiment in madness, identified with him. A flake of soot fell into Strindberg's absinthe on the day the first news of Przybyszewski's arrest reached him, a clear indication to Strindberg that there were thoughts in his mind connecting him with the Pole. Strindberg had enjoyed Dagny's favors, and Przybyszewski was as jealous a man as Strindberg. More to the point, Strindberg was hardly more faithful to Frida than Przybyszewski was to Martha: in Paris, he had dallied with an English sculptress while Frida was in Austria. There was yet another connection, obscure but troubling, just the sort of mental link that fascinated Strindberg. The first rumors of the Berlin affair that reached him had said that the three childen had been killed, and Strindberg had once wished that the child of his second marriage might fall ill so that he would be called home and be reunited with his wife. The gods punished him as is their wont by answering half his prayer: they struck with illness a child of his first marriage. This gave Strindberg the idea for a drama about the havoc caused by our wishes and imaginings, which, as he said, "possess a kind of reality" (SS, 28:280),[38] and which, as a matter of fact, often overwhelm the other reality.

The point that Strindberg wanted to make was that certain imagined crimes can produce more anguish and remorse in the tender conscience than real crimes. In Vienna at this time, Freud was discovering that his patients often confessed to, and punished themselves for, misdeeds and offenses they had never actually committed but had only thought of committing, and the wish had become the father not to the deed but to the punishment for the deed. In attempting to explain how the mind works in cases of this sort, Strindberg postulated an inner tribunal that has jurisdiction over this kind of crime and its punishment. He came to understand why he had so often felt he had been unjustly accused and punished for crimes he had not committed. "I admit now," he said, "that I committed them in my thoughts. But how did people know this? Certainly there is an immanent justice that punishes sins of thought; and when people judge each other on the basis of suspicions, ugly looks, or simply 'by feel,' they do right" (SS, 46:84).

In August 1898, Strindberg had a couple of vivid dreams about Przybyszewski, and possibly at this time he read or recalled Przybyszewski's play Das grosse Glück (1894), in which the author tells of his infatuation with Dagny Juel, his abandonment of Martha Foerder, and the suicide of Martha—two years before the tragedy occurred.[39] By putting his own case beside Przybyszewski's, Strindberg saw that he had the material for a play dealing with success, arrogance, and the power of secret desires. In January 1899, he set to work, condensing characters and conflating incidents. The hero of his play is Maurice, a dramatist and a composite of himself and Przybyszewski. Henriette, the temptress in the play, is a recognizable portrait of Dagny Juel, with a few added traits drawn from the English sculptress. The painter Adolf, who impresses others as a pure soul and a paragon of all the virtues, including meekness, which the others noticeably lack, is a combination of Munch, whom Strindberg had known in his Berlin and Paris years, and Per Ekström, a painter whom Strindberg had known in Stockholm when they were both young. (He goes under the name Sellén in Strindberg's novel The Red Room.) Ekström had had to wait until he was fifty before success came to him and his pictures began to sell. In 1898, when Strindberg caught up on Ekström's career, he said deploringly, "What an awful life. He could never afford to have any vices." [40] With only a little touching up, Przybyszewski and Ekström emerged as a contrasting pair in Strindberg's sketchbook. The Polish writer had achieved considerable fame in the German avant-garde by 1898 when he was only thirty and had destroyed a woman and her children in the process; the Swedish painter had struggled and starved until he was fifty but had hurt no one except himself.

Strindberg could weave these two careers around his own. He had been famous at thirty and a failure at forty; he was the father of three children for whom he was unable to care properly and the ex-husband of a woman who had fallen on hard times; he had elbowed his way to notoriety in the 1880s and wandered in obscurity in the 1890s while others took his place on the Swedish literary scene. Using the two strands provided by Przybyszewski and Ekström and interweaving material from his own life, Strindberg transformed the sordid Berlin story into a sophisticated Parisian drama. Intoxicated by sudden success in the theatre, Maurice abandons his faithful mistress and his young daughter for another woman, fascinating, glamorous, and utterly lacking those moral scruples that have kept him from enjoying life to the fullest. Now, only his child prevents him from entering the carefree world that beckons to him, and for a moment, he wishes the child did not exist. No sooner said than done. The little girl dies under mysterious circumstances, and Maurice feels that his wish was somehow the cause of her death. [41] He and his femme fatale are picked up by the police for questioning; instead of spending evenings under starry Mediterranean skies, he spends a night in jail. Remorse and self-punishment make up the rest of the drama, which ends happily, and the tone of the play is, in spite of the subject, rather light and ironic. "All the characters are angels," said Strindberg, "and commit the most detestable deeds—just as in life."[42]

6

Although he unequivocatingly called his play a comedy, Strindberg had trouble finding a title for it. A Danish production bore the title *Guilty or Not Guilty?* In Germany it was known as *Rausch* (intoxication) and given the Lubitsch touch when filmed. Generally, however, it has been known as *Crimes and Crimes*, an elliptical form of "There are crimes, and there are crimes." One of the working titles was "In a Higher Court," and that title, as does *Guilty or Not Guilty?*, alludes to Kierkegaard. The subject of the play is Kierkegaardian; its denouement is Kierkegaardian; even its tone is Kierkegaardian. The subject is the guilt felt by the hero for imagined crimes. In Kierkegaard's essay "'Guilty?'—'Not Guilty?',", one of his "psychological experiments," a young man has a crime on his conscience although he has not actually committed one. The anguish he suffers is the result of an inborn melancholy and an active imagination. These qualms of conscience, which a lesser soul would not feel, are signs of divine election. The trial of probation he must undergo brings him into a direct relation with his true self and thus with God. The trial is not a legal trial since no crime that the lawbooks recognize has been committed. The young man is on trial in "a higher court" precisely because he is not on trial in the courtroom. The trial is temporary, like Job's, and the knowledge of being on trial does not come immediately. As with Job, after the trial of probation is over everything is doubly restored to the young man, except his child. Although he has lost the woman he loved, he has found himself in a way that is doubly significant, and that is true repetition (*Gjentagelse*). He is born to himself as a poet, belonging to a higher sphere.

I have combined here thoughts from both "'Guilty?'—'Not Guilty?'" and *Repetition*, for that is what Strindberg did in *Crimes and Crimes*. Strindberg sets the legal crime of which his hero is suspected against the crime of conscience of which the hero accuses himself. In his two days of anguish, his trial of probation, his sins come home to him. "Everything is dug up, everything repeats (*allt går igen*)" (SS, 30:215), he says, in what Strindberg intended as a transcription of Kierkegaard's Gjentagelse. The ending of the play, which has troubled viewers and commentators, is lifted from Kierkegaard. Instead of ending the story where it began, in the cemetery, as he originally intended and as would seem to befit the serious theme, Strindberg allows his playwright hero to regain everything doubly. At the moment the hero places himself in the hands of the church to do penance, the telephone, like the bolt out of the blue that brought everything back to Job, brings the news that the hero's play is back on the boards again and that money will come pouring in. Kierkegaard's young man gets everything back doubly, except his girl, and becomes a poet. Strindberg's young man gets everything back again, except his girl, and succeeds as a playwright. "Everything comes back (*Allt kommer igen*)," says one of Maurice's friends. "Except Henriette" (*SS*, 30:219).

Though most readers feel that Strindberg provided his drama with a false and happy end by letting Maurice off too easily, Kierkegaard would have understood that Maurice is being denied the highest merit and is left in the limbo of the unexceptional. Lacking a strenuously serious nature, he cannot make the leap to the religious level of existence. His sufferings are all too brief. If Strindberg had brought Maurice back to the cemetery into the realm of the four last things, he would have implied that Maurice is somehow being levitated to the religious stage. But, as was the case with Kierkegaard's young man, Maurice was not made to be exalted. He was only picked out to be instructed. Since there is nothing profound about him, neither his vastation nor his regeneration, he can quickly slip back into his normal mode of being, a little wiser and only a little the worse for wear. "Tonight I go to church," he says, "to settle accounts with myself. But tomorrow I shall go to the theatre" (*SS*, 30:220).

With crime and punishment so neatly balanced, Strindberg defended the denouement as strictly moral and went on to explain that Maurice and Henriette are made to suffer sufficiently in the last act, which, he said, was "Swedenborgian, with hell already on earth."[43] Taking that hint, a viewer familiar with Swedenborg's concept of the life of the soul would understand that the people who surround Maurice, whatever their roles as realistic characters, participate in his inner drama as spirits. Henriette is a contradictory spirit, one of those who teach the good by showing its opposite. Jeanne and Adolph are presumably chastising spirits who silently reprove Maurice and serve as his conscience. Jeanne's brother Emile, who in the second scene of the play blocks Maurice's attempted flight from Henriette and thus inaugurates the criminal drama, incarnates one of Swedenborg's instructing spirits, while Madame Catherine and the Abbé function as angelic spirits, guardians and overseers who moderate Maurice's punishment and see to it that the contention of good and evil does not get out of hand.[44] The business ledger kept by Madame Catherine is the Book of Life, the Ledger of the Almighty, in which all the pluses and minuses of one's life are recorded. To Swedenborg the Book of Life was the "interior memory," that is, the subconscious or unconscious, in which "all and every particular, which man has thought, spoken, and done" are inscribed.[45]

The title Crimes and Crimes alludes to two basic kinds of injustice. Some crimes go unpunished, and sometimes people are punished for crimes that were never committed. In the first instance there is a crime weighing in the scales but no culprit; in the second instance there is a culprit but no crime, at least not a crime of the sort that can be weighed and pondered in a court of law. These cases are brought before a higher court, the court of conscience and the "higher powers."

7

Now this is where music comes into play. Strindberg makes the allegretto movement of Beethoven's sonata the central symbol of crimes of the mind. It is actually heard in the third scene of the play, act 2, scene 1, when Maurice decides to spend the night with Henriette. Strindberg motivates the playing of the sonata by having a pianist in the neighboring room practice the finale, repeating it over and over again, especially bars 96–107, those notes that Strindberg said acted like a center-bit drilling into his conscience. In this scene Beethoven functions no differently than Mendelssohn did in To Damascus. But in the drama as a whole, Beethoven plays a much larger part. For Strindberg, the Kierkegaardian subject matter demanded a Beethovenesque treatment,[46] and he confided to a friend that the whole of Crimes and Crimes was built on the Beethoven sonata.[47] This is literally true: the finale of the sonata provides the matrix for the play.

Beethoven's allegretto finale follows standard sonata form, with two subjects being presented in related keys in the exposition. These subjects are fully worked out in the next section, the development. Then comes a recapitulation in which the themes are repeated in their original keys. A coda, which in this case includes a rondolike repetition of the main theme, brings the sonata to an end.

Strindberg's first subject concerns the higher powers, the spiritual forces at work within man; this is set forth in the richly symbolic first scene of the play, the Montparnasse cemetery, dotted with crosses and with the ivy-clad ruins of a mill in the background. The second subject is arrogance and the workings of the human will, as demonstrated by Maurice and Henriette in the second scene. Strindberg's alternate titles might be applied to these two subjects. *Crimes and Crimes* refers primarily to the first subject, which concerns crime and conscience. *Intoxication* refers primarily to the second: drunk with success, Maurice wants neither loyal friend, faithful mistress, nor loving child to stand in the way of what he thinks is happiness with Henriette. The rest of the play elaborates these two subjects pretty much in accordance with Beethoven's finale.

Crimes and Crimes	Sonata Form	Sonata no. 17, Allegretto
I, i Cemetery I, ii Crémerie	Exposition	Bars 1–95
II, i Auberge des Adrets II, ii Bois de Boulogne	Development	Bars 96–214
III, i Crémerie III, ii Auberge des Adrets	Recapitulation	Bars 215–318
IV, i Luxembourg Gardens IV, ii Crémerie	Coda	Bars 319–99

When bars 96–107 are heard as specified in the script, it is as if, for a few moments, the pattern broke through the tracing.

Because standard sonata form is similar to standard dramatic form, the musical structure of this play generally passes unnoticed. The thematic development, however, is almost purely musical, and what in an ordinary play would be described as a parallel situation is here more fittingly described as a thematic repetition. In the third act, the recapitulation, scenes and characters from the first two acts reappear. Maurice's mistress and the abbé, who were prominent figures in the first scene of the play, show up in the crémerie scene of the third act to restate the principal religious theme. In the second act, in the tavern l'Auberge des Adrets,* Maurice and Henriette, flushed with success, wait for the hum-

* Auberge des Adrets: Strindberg had his tongue in his cheek when he let Henriette and Maurice have their rendezvous in a tavern called l'Auberge des Adrets. This auberge was the locale of a melodrama of the same name. In 1823 the actor Frédérick Lemaître achieved instant fame by playing this unbearably banal criminal drama for laughs. His performance as the thief and murderer Robert Macaire made *L'Auberge des Adrets* one of the most notorious and subversive plays of the century and subsequently inspired some of Honoré Daumier's most incisive social caricatures. By setting two scenes of *Crimes and Crimes* in the Auberge des Adrets, Strindberg is hinting that his play, too, is a play of mixed modes, a melodrama with deeper implications and a comedy about crime.

ble and pathetic Adolph. In the auberge scene of the recapitulation, Adolph is the prospering artist, waiting with Henriette for the contrite Maurice. "Everything comes back, everything repeats itself," says Henriette, expressing one of Strindberg's favorite notions, and a notion that is eminently suitable to musical treatment.

The musical techniques of varying the principal themes and of transferring them from one voice to another are carried further by Strindberg in this play than in any of his other works. The musical development is intended to provide an esthetic delight for the viewer, who, no matter how deaf, cannot help noticing how the success-and-hybris theme, for instance, is transferred from Maurice to Adolph in the recapitulation. Where Maurice had blared in triumph like a Roman emperor, Adolph in his hour of success speaks like an undeserving and lowly penitent. Again, in the tavern scene of act 2, Maurice, seeking to ease his conscience by blaming others for his own deeds, refers to Adolph as a pimp who deliberately arranged for him and Henriette to meet. In the tavern scene of the recapitulation, act 3, the theme is heard again but in a different key when Maurice and Henriette find themselves being treated as pimp and prostitute by the police.

These are obvious examples. It is in enlarging on his main theme, crime and conscience, that Strindberg becomes more subtle and displays his virtuosity by using three voices, since nothing less than that will serve to exhaust the richness of the theme. One form of the theme concerns father and child. It is as if the playwright-composer made father and child the notes in his theme, and then tossed it back and forth from one voice to another. First voice: Maurice. His crime was to wish that his child had not been born. Second voice, same theme: Henriette. In her family the father was hated so much that he lost all will to live. Third voice, same theme: Adolph. As a young man he had on a certain occasion silently hoped that his father would die. Maurice's daughter died; Henriette's father died; and Adolph's father died. Yet in none of these instances was an actual crime committed, and the three ill-wishers have had to be tried and judged in the court of conscience. Publicly disgraced and pilloried as a murderer, Maurice suffers two days of agony, which he accepts as punishment for his selfish ambitions. Adolph has abased himself for years and cannot enjoy success and prosperity when he finds it. Henriette's case is more special. To complete the variations on the crime-and-conscience theme, there must be a real crime in addition to the imagined crimes, a crime whose perpetrator has not been caught. This is supplied by Henriette, who hints at her misdeed in the development section, act 2, and reveals it in the coda, act 4. Called upon to help a girl friend in distress, she had assisted in an abortion that had fatal results. Having committed a crime, Henriette feels set apart from other human beings. Her life has become half unreal; she exists as a creature of the night; and her pursuit of pleasure, her amoral existence, is only her way of running from a troubled conscience and from the police and from the girl's boy friend who she fears will eventually catch up with her. Treating Henriette's real crime and Maurice's imagined crime as motifs, Strindberg, like a good composer, sees to it that the one is only a variation of the other: Maurice wished that his child had not been born, and Henriette prevented a child from being born.

8

Tracing Strindberg's thematic developments may seem to be purely an armchair exercise. After all, can a theatre audience be expected to enjoy Strindberg's ingenuity any more than an untutored listener can hear what Bach accomplished in his great mirror fugues? In the theatre, however, the placement of the actors, the lighting of the sets, and the use of visual motifs can make the spectator aware of some of the elements that contribute to the musical structure. When Vsevolod Meyerhold[48] staged Crimes and Crimes in 1912, colors in the sets and costumes were associated with the leitmotifs of the play. Although he did not know about the sonata structure, his production suggests how the musical form might at least be hinted at.

Whether the underlying form should be heavily outlined for the benefit of the spectator, presented in cloisonné, so to speak, is another question. As is true of many plays written at the very end of the nineteenth century and well into the twentieth, the realistic story of Crimes and Crimes does not exist for itself, and the director must decide how much of the symbolic underpinning should be revealed. What Strindberg wanted can be inferred from some of his remarks. To his Swedish editor he confided that "the hero of the play, the plot-maker, is the Unseen One."[49] This was not an idea that would appeal to the producers of commercial theatre fare. Trying to sell the play in Germany, he took a different tack. He told his German translator that he wanted the surface of the play to be realistic, a picture of everyday life without the exaggerations of melodrama and tragedy, and the tone to be light and skeptical. A few years later, when the play was to be produced at his own Intimate Theatre, he said he wanted the sets to be simple and suggestive rather than solid and realistic down to the last detail. There was a practical reason for this: his theatre was too small and ill-equipped to provide five realistic sets and manage seven scene changes. But the overriding reason was that he wanted to "allegorize the stage," and he thought he might achieve this by letting drapes form an abstract background while a few tastefully selected props would set the scene without making it real.[50]

These remarks reveal the contradictions inherent in the play from its conception. Strindberg recognized that the religious aura would be dissipated by the realistic action and the flippant, often coarse, dialogue and that the moralizing element, the speeches by the abbé, would run counter to the indulgent philosophy of the play. To find a way of blending the two, he turned to music. He decided to write his play in two keys with the moralizing element in the tonic, and to provide the necessary modulation, he wanted the part of the abbé played rather roguishly, "in good humor and with humor."[51] More often than not, Strindberg used music to tap the wellsprings of the soul, but here music is used to solve a problem of style.

When Strindberg wrote *Crimes and Crimes*, audiences were not ready for plays in which the pleasures of pure form could override the logic of plot. He had to throw the sop of suspense and intrigue to audiences barking for conventional theatre fare. But his main concern was esthetic, and when forced to choose between the artificial tensions of crime drama and the well-made play on the one hand, and the psychological tensions of great art and music on the other hand, Strindberg always chose the other hand. There is a glaring example of this in act 3 when the police inspector summarizes all the evidence against Maurice in one long speech. In conventional drama, that evidence would be artfully revealed bit by bit in three or four scenes in order to build suspense. For that kind of suspense, Strindberg wanted to substitute the suspense of unresolved chords, inverted themes, incomplete variations, and deceptive cadences.

In avoiding standard playwriting conventions, Strindberg has made himself widely misunderstood as an artist. He endeavored to restore music to intellectual drama, and to do so, he dug at the roots of his art, studying Greek tragedy, of which music was an essential part, rereading Shakespeare, whose love of music shaped everything he wrote, listening to and playing Bach and Beethoven, those masters of the art to which

all the arts aspire, and preferring, even when writing a play like *Crimes
and Crimes* with which he hoped to have a popular success, to treat
drama as an art rather than as a trade. Now when the well-made play has
been unmade and when audiences have become familiar with nonrealis-
tic drama and accustomed to the fluid form and visual imagery of film,
his plays should be staged in a manner that allows one to hear clearly the
music that flows through them.

What New Yorkers think of as the off-Broadway theater had its beginnings in Paris in 1887 when André Antoine, a clerk for a gas company by day, a theatrical amateur by night, put down a whole month's salary to rent a theatre in Montmartre. He called his enterprise the Théâtre-Libre, and the first play he produced was *Jacques Damour*, which was based on a story by Zola about the Commune of 1871, still an inflammatory subject in Paris. Antoine's intention was to establish a home for plays orphaned by the national theatre, the Comédie-Française, and by the boulevard theatres. He wanted a liberated theatre whose doors would be open to plays that were not begotten especially for the *vedettes* of the French stage, plays about distasteful subjects, plays with indecorous language, plays too short to fill an evening, and plays written by foreign authors. The Théâtre-Libre attracted international attention in February 1888 when Antoine staged Tolstoy's *The Power of Darkness*. That a group of relatively untrained amateurs could present the world premiere of a powerful and controversial work by one of the world's most famous authors made serious playwrights and producers all over Europe sit up and take notice. It dawned on them that the Théâtre-Libre offered a feasible alternative to both the boulevard theatre that made art a business and the subventioned theatre that turned art into an institution.

Within a decade or so, other free or independent theatres sprang up all over Europe: the Théâtre d'Art (1891) and the Théâtre de l'Oeuvre (1893) in Paris, the Freie Bühne (1889) and the Freie Volksbühne (1890) in Berlin, the Independent Theatre (1891) and the New Century Theatre (1897) in London, the Independent Theatre in Barcelona (1896), the Art Theatre in Moscow (1898), and the Irish Literary Theatre in Dublin (1899). Since the purpose of these theatres was to promote the avant-garde drama, the author took the center of the stage, and the play was thought of as a vehicle for ideas and not for the leading actor. The plays had short runs or were put on in repertory with other plays; the theatres were generally small; and the audiences very select.

For a recondite poet like William Butler Yeats even the audiences at the Irish Literary Theatre were not select enough. As a dramatist, he sought to create "with an unpreoccupied mind," picturing life "as the

CHAMBER PLAYS

musician pictures it in sound and the sculptor in form."[1] To free himself
from the considerations that must constantly preoccupy the mind of the
commercial playwright—the need to provide big parts for the leading actors, obvious and strongly colored characterizations, acting "points" that
will garner applause in the middle of a scene, and effective act endings
that will bring down the house, all the claptrap of popular theatre—Yeats
finally turned his back on the common folk and wrote plays for "an un-
popular theatre and an audience like a secret society where admission is
by favour and never to many,"[2] in fact, only about forty or fifty who
would forgather in a drawing room.

In Sweden at this time, August Strindberg was also faced with the
problem of accommodating the demands he placed on himself as an artist and thinker to the expectations of an audience in the theatre. By instinct an actor, he craved an audience; but as a dramatist trying to express a very subtle and complex philosophy, he needed an intellectual
and sophisticated audience.

Several times in his career Strindberg had dreamed of establishing
his own theatre. This dream had been first realized in 1889 when Strindberg and his wife had established in Copenhagen the Experimental Theatre, a Scandinavian counterpart to Antoine's Théâtre-Libre. Although
two of Strindberg's finest works, Miss Julie and Creditors, were staged at
the Copenhagen theatre, the amateurish acting, highlighted by Strindberg's wife playing Miss Julie in a subdued fashion in order not to arouse
her jealous husband peeping at her from the wings, had turned the venture into a fiasco. Within a week it had been laughed out of existence.

Eighteen years later the results were somewhat better. In 1906, August Falck, a young and enterprising actor, toured the Swedish provinces
with his production of Miss Julie and finally brought it to Stockholm.
This was the first time that the notorious play had been seen in the capital, and its warm reception revived Strindberg's flagging interest in the
drama. He met with Falck, and together they rented, in the summer of
1907, a store which was renovated as a theatre seating 161 persons and
named the Intimate Theatre.[3]

Even before they found a location, Strindberg had written four plays
especially for this new theatre. Although he had a desk full of his own
unproduced scripts (a result of his having glutted the Swedish market
with the twenty-odd plays he wrote between 1898 and 1903), his genius
was fired by the very thought of having his own theatre in which he
would be free to experiment. When he set to work on the first of these
plays, he already had a pretty clear idea of what he wanted: a play

intimate in form; a simple theme treated with thoroughness; few characters; vast perspectives; freely imaginative, but built on observations and experiences, carefully studied; simple, but not too simple; no huge apparatus; no superfluous minor parts; none of those "old machines" or five-acters built according to the rules; none of those drawn-out plays lasting all night.

Miss Julie (without an intermission) has gone through its ordeal by fire and shown itself to be the kind of drama demanded by the impatient man of today: thorough but brief.[4]

At first glance, these remarks indicate that Strindberg had not advanced beyond the views expressed nineteen years earlier in his manifesto of naturalism, the preface to Miss Julie. Nor is there much in the first of the Chamber Plays, Storm Weather (Oväder), to suggest that Strindberg is about to enter virgin dramatic territory. The play seems to mark an end rather than a beginning. It evokes the atmosphere of a late summer evening, which becomes a symbol for the last years of life. The elderly hero of the play has settled down in a quiet and fashionable residential district in Stockholm to sit out the evening of his life on park benches and at the chess table. But his former wife, much younger than he and now remarried to a man her own age, bursts unexpectedly and unintentionally into the quiet of his home and reopens old wounds in his heart. The storm clouds of passion that he thought had drifted past him once and for all now lower again on the horizon. These, too, go scudding by, and the play ends with the long twilit evenings of summer coming to an end and the street lamps being lit to signal the beginning of autumn. "The first street lamp; . . . now it's autumn, old boys," says the retired gentleman. "It begins to get dark, but understanding comes and shines with its dark lantern, so we don't get lost. . . . Close the windows . . . so the memories can go to sleep in peace. The peace of old age" (SS, 45:74).

The play represents an attempt on Strindberg's part to wipe out the painful memories of his marriage to Harriet Bosse, his third wife, who was twenty-nine years younger than he. He wanted to even the score with this young woman who had divorced him after only three years of marriage and was now involved with an actor closer to her in age and in professional aims. Strindberg's intense jealousy reveals itself when his alter ego in the play gloats over the failure of his former wife's marriage to a card-playing drifter and gigolo. Harriet Bosse was naturally furious when she saw the play at the Intimate Theatre. Strindberg wrote her, "I warned you not to see it. It is a painful work with which I tried to write you and [our child] out of my heart: I wanted to draw in advance on the anguish I knew I would soon feel."[5]

This mood piece with its evocative dialogue answers very well to Strindberg's first description of what a Chamber Play should be. The next plays are of a different order and indicate that he had altered his conception of the form. In January 1907, when he was about to start writing *Storm Weather*, he had *Miss Julie* in mind as the prototype of a Chamber Play. In April, when he was concerned to justify the later Chamber Plays, he broke completely with the rules of standard drama and gave the playwright absolute freedom to follow the dictates of his imagination. No particular form was to bind the author; theme alone would determine the form; and the playwright could handle the theme in any way he chose as long as he did not violate the "unity and style of the original idea" (SS, 50:12). In short, a chamber play was to be written like a piece of music and to require from an audience attention to theme and development rather than to plot and character.

Strindberg's inclination to make use of musical form is apparent even in his realistic works, especially in *Miss Julie*. Beginning in 1898 with his first dream play, *To Damascus*, Part One, he very consciously set out to appropriate to the drama some of the techniques of music. His aim was to make the drama as suggestive as music and, at times, to render his audience as unthinking and defenseless as an audience caught in the relentless thematic development, the mysterious tremolos, the tonal surges, and the emotional storms of a Beethoven sonata.

In 1902, Shaw in his preface to *Mrs. Warren's Profession* had announced that

the drama of pure feeling is no longer in the hands of the playwright: it has been conquered by the musician, after whose enchantments all the verbal arts seem cold and tame. . . . There is, flatly, no future now for any drama without music except the drama of thought.[6]

In a way he was right. But it was still possible to create a drama of pure feeling if the dramatist did not rely entirely on the verbal arts but also made use of every possible physical resource of the modern theatre and recast the shape of the drama so that feelings could be aroused instantly, as they are in music, without the necessity of spending a great deal of time motivating a situation or etching in all the details in a character portrait to make it as lifelike as possible. In the well-made play, motivation simply meant giving every effect its cause. After his Inferno crisis, however, Strindberg could no longer view the world in terms of purely causal relationships. Instead of causes he saw correspondences. Since this view could not be expressed within the form of the well-made play, he was forced to modify it substantially and to create virtually a new kind of drama by reverting, paradoxically, to some old dramaturgical techniques. Writing in 1908, Strindberg contrasts the contemporary way of writing a play with Shakespeare's way:

What we call a "scene" according to the French idea (Sardou) is the result of skillful tactics and a carefully planned strategy. We have to prepare each scene, make use of hints and suggestions, the betrayal of secrets, upsets, peripeties, plots and counterplots, and parallelisms (which are my forte). But Shakespeare is a slap-dash writer who spills everything in the first act. . . .

Take *Richard III.* In the first act the corpse of the murdered Henry VI is brought in, the widow [sic] walking alongside. "Stay!" says Richard. He woos her, and after eight pages the murderer has almost got a yes from her. It is so skillfully done that no one can raise any objections. I have studied this scene in particular to achieve a similar end. A modern French playwright would have used all five acts to get the widow of the murdered man to say yes to his murderer. To Shakespeare, it is merely a detail, and he moves on past it. No harm is done. They are simply two different ways, both of them equally good. [SS, 50:52–53]

What Strindberg created was a dramatic form in which less attention is paid to preparing for the big scenes and to building up suspense, and more attention is given to drawing parallels between scenes and characters and to sustaining a mood at almost the same level of intensity throughout. Instead of working backward from the climactic scene as Sardou did, Strindberg conceives a symbolic situation and then explores all its possibilities. The advantage of the first method is that audience interest is likely to mount as the play goes on, since the playwright has saved his biggest surprises for the end;* and the danger inherent in the second method is that the playwright's inspiration is likely to flag before the play is over. Shakespeare generally begins stronger than he finishes.

2

In order to achieve a modern drama of pure feeling, the form of the nineteenth-century drama not only had to be altered radically, but the verbal arts also had to be supplemented by the other arts so as to create

---

* Strindberg learned how to combine Shakespeare's method with Sardou's only to encounter another difficulty: that of being understood. With regard to one of his more abstruse dramas, *Advent,* written in 1898, Strindberg explained: "The play isn't clear immediately because of a stratagem in the writing of it. I used to spill everything right away; now I hoard some secrets and sustain interest all the way through, and even provide a surprise in the fifth act. Perhaps you remember how they used to praise my first acts. That's where I was wrong. I was too fired up, too impatient. I piled it on too much in the beginning, and all my ammunition was shot off by the third act." Strindberg to af Geijerstam, 7 January 1899, *Brev,* 13:63.

what the German critic Diebold described as the *Theaterpoesie* of Strindberg. Strindberg could have had—and has had posthumously—a second career as a painter.[7] No other major dramatist offers such a rich feast for the eye of the spectator. To see his plays is to walk through a gallery of memorable pictures. The kitchen scene and the Rose Room of *To Damascus*, Part One, exist as images apart from the dialogue, and the sets for the play form a series of pictures in which even the colors have special significance.[8] *A Dream Play* is so thoroughly visual that half its meaning is conveyed directly to the eye. It has often been remarked that this play resembles a motion picture because the scenes fade in and out; actually, the dissolves are purely theatrical and would be less striking on the screen than on the stage. More cinematic is the banquet scene in Part Two of *To Damascus*, which seems to call for close and medium shots, dolly and pan shots, expertly edited. Similarly, the opening of *Charles XII* is like the first moments of a motion picture with all the significant shots appearing simultaneously in the script to be edited by the eye of the viewer as it roves over the stage picture: the cottage in shambles, the sand drifts obscuring part of it; the empty door frame; the broken windows; the missing roof tiles; the lone, leafless tree with one apple hanging from it blown by the wind; the ruins of a burned church and houses behind and to the right of the cottage; and still farther away, the dark sea with the first pale gray rays of dawn on the horizon; and in the midst of this scene of desolation, a man in rags searching among the ruins.

Aural effects are equally prominent in Strindberg's plays, notably in the dream cycle but no less so in the history plays. This theatrical poetry constitutes one of the charms of the Chamber Plays, and some of the strongest effects in them are visual and aural: the flash of lighting at the end of the first scene of *Storm Weather*; the revelation of the orchard in full bloom in *The Burned House*; the apparitions of the Milkmaid and the dead consul in *The Ghost Sonata*; the crunching of tea biscuits at the "ghost supper" in the same play; and in *The Pelican*, the creaking of the rocking chair. In production, the verbal, visual, and aural elements must be blended and balanced as delicately as the voices in a string quartet. The reader has only the score, and unless he remembers that, he may rush over some passages of great music. When the warm hand of the young, vigorous Student in *The Ghost Sonata* clasps the ice-cold hand of the eighty-year-old Hummel, and the Student is then unable to free himself from that deathlike grip, our blood should run a little colder as we watch the Student's strength being drained from him as surely as if a vampire were sinking its fangs into his neck. In that brief, concentrated incident the principal theme of the whole play is sounded clearly: everything else is an elaboration on it.

With so much happening between the lines, these plays are actually longer than they seem when read. Each is meant to take about ninety minutes in performance, apparently the optimum length for spellbinding an audience, since *Miss Julie* and *Creditors* are also that long. But it is quite possible for a tone-deaf director to rush the actors through one of these Chamber Plays in sixty minutes by eliminating the pauses and closing up the action. The result would be something like listening to a long-playing record at 78 r.p.m. No time would really be saved because all of one's time in the theatre would be wasted. When the history of the "pause" and the "long silence" in the drama comes to be written, Strindberg, along with his contemporary Chekhov, will be hailed as the great innovator. These numerous pauses place a heavy burden on the director and actor, for a pause does not mean that the action stops or that the rhythm of the play is interrupted. Indeed, the action usually becomes more intense, with stage business supplying what words have only hinted at or may even have hidden.

Strindberg was not one of those playwrights who regard their scripts as sacrosanct and inviolable. He encouraged actors to make minor changes; to add lines to cover an exit, to drop lines if the pace was sagging, to change the phrasing if they found lines difficult to speak. He wrote to his German translator:

You may certainly insert a few lines if you want to, but it would be better to have the actor smooth out his entrances and exits by repeating a line or by delivering his last words ritardando or by adding a few words of his own. . . . Perhaps even short improvisations or pantomimes, like the cadenzas in music.[9]

In return, Strindberg wanted the spirit of his play to remain inviolate. He allowed only those changes that intensified the overall effect and that made it as musical as possible. What holds a chamber play together is not plot but theme and mood. *Storm Weather* is lyrical and sentimental like the Waldteufel waltz heard in the background; *The Burned House* is mordantly comic and disdainful; while *The Ghost Sonata* and *The Pelican* fuse together a monumental scorn for the world and a genuine sympathy for the deluded and put-upon creatures who inhabit it. In each case, the mood must be imposed on the audience with such force that they will no more think of questioning what is happening than they would think of questioning what happens in their dreams.

In the preface to *Miss Julie*, Strindberg described the playwright as a hypnotist who transmits suggestions to the audience. Unlike Brecht, he did not want the audience to reflect on the events of the play until the curtain had come down. While the curtain was up, the audience was to be as entranced as the author had been when in the grip of inspiration. Strindberg is a perfect example of the poet as Plato saw him, a man who creates in a divine rapture. Ordinarily, dramatists must rely a great deal on conscious skill and art in putting together their theatrical machines. But Strindberg wrote best when he was dipping his pen in the inkwell of his unconscious. Asked to describe his writing habits, he replied:

You tell me, if you can. Something begins to ferment within me, a not unpleasant kind of fever, which is transformed into an ecstasy or intoxication. Sometimes it's like a seed that suddenly sprouts, sends down roots, draws to it all my experiences—but all the while selecting and rejecting. Sometimes I think of myself as a medium: everything comes so easily, half unconsciously, with just a little bit of planning and calculation. At best this lasts for only three hours (nine to twelve in the morning usually). And when it's over, things are dull and boring again until the next time it happens. But it doesn't come when ordered, and it doesn't come when it pleases me. It comes when it wants to come. Most often and most definitely after some major disaster. [SS, 54:472]

For him, the unconscious was the voice of God, and he would not fight it. Especially in the latter half of his career, after 1894, he could seldom bring himself to change what he had written, even if certain apparent inconsistencies or unrealized thoughts were called to his attention. His German translator asked him why the bishop's funeral is mentioned several times in the first part of *The Burned House* without being referred to again. Replying that he probably needed it to fill in the background and to underscore the death motive, Strindberg refused to drop it or to expand it. With regard to another of his plays, Strindberg explained more fully what function these "unrealized intentions or abortive thoughts" have in works that are not constructed like well-made plays.

An example from my own experience opened my eyes to this kind of "ellipsis" in the conception of a work. The German translator of my play *Easter* asked me whether a certain line of dialogue was a blunder or was supposed to have some significance. Eleanora asks Benjamin, who has flunked his Latin exam, what his teacher's name is. The boy replies, "Mr. Algren"; and Eleanora says, "I shan't forget that!" Later she actually does remember, and I believe it was the author's intention to have the teacher appear toward the end as the agent of providence. I say "I believe" because the creative process is just as much a mystery to me now as it was forty years ago, whether it takes place with clear deliberation and complete consciousness or not. At any rate, I told the translator that it was probably an oversight. But when he suggested striking it out and I was on the verge of doing so, I fould I could not. I had the distinct impression that it was to remain.

And then I asked myself why it should remain and what it might signify. I found that if I took it out, something seemed to be lacking; and that it gave a realistic touch to the scene when it was there, because it reminded one of how people in a desperate situation throw out a thousand ideas, only one of which is carried out. I insisted that it remain, calling it an unrealized intention. Possibly Laertes' revolution, which is never carried out in *Hamlet*, is another dissonant chord that is never resolved—quite against the rules but effective. [SS, 50:171]

It turns out that all the apparent oversights in the Chamber Plays have their hidden purpose and contribute to the *ambiance* of these works. One of the more interesting examples of what seems like a blunder, and which is always "corrected" by translators, is Hummel's remarking at the beginning of *The Ghost Sonata* on the Student's strange way of pronouncing the word "window." In fact, the Student has not pronounced the word at all. If this were a realistic play, there would be no explanation, just as there would be no explanation for the appearance of the Milkmaid as an apparition visible at first only to the Student. On the other hand, if the apparition can be accounted for as a symbol, so can the window. For Hummel is described later as a thief who enters through windows to steal human souls, and here we see him as he first steals into the Student's life by means of a "window." The point is lost if we insist on regarding these plays realistically rather than as a species of music drama.

If the director, the actors, and the scene designer have conspired successfully, all the seemingly disparate and irreconcilable elements in these plays will join to recreate the fantasy that first fired the poet's imagination. The unrealized intentions will have the proper dissonant effect; the pauses will be as filled with tension as in a Beethoven sonata; and the principal themes will sound as clearly as fate knocking at the door.

3

Strindberg referred to these plays as his "last sonatas."[10] All four of them are concerned with death, or, more accurately, they are written from the point of view of a man who is getting ready to die. Death is looked upon as an escape from a corrupt and disgusting world and the portal to the life beyond. The author of the Chamber Plays is a mystic seeking a Swedenborgian resolution to the struggles of earthly life in the life after death. Strindberg associated himself with no church and no creed. All he was certain of was that religion meant a connection with the world beyond. The philosophical excursions of the late Strindberg, in the *Blue Books* for example, become easier to follow if one recalls that religious mystics have generally interpreted the unconscious as the link with God, a fact of which Strindberg was conspicuously aware. That is why he placed so much faith in the workings of his own unconscious. The "higher powers," which Strindberg thought of as controlling our destinies, apparently use our minds as their field of operation, and when Strindberg tries to put down on paper what they are up to, his attempts read like excerpts from Freud and Jung.

From childhood on, Strindberg tended to view the inner life as more real than the outer life. After his Inferno crisis, reality, as far as he was concerned, existed only in the life after death or in one's mind, while the world as most of us know it was only an illusion or a bad reflection of reality, with everything turned backward, as the Daughter discovers in *A Dream Play*. After the dissolution of his third marriage in 1904, Strindberg suffered another "major upheaval," his second Inferno, which lasted until after he had finished the Chamber Plays. "What has kept my soul from plunging into darkness during my work [on *The Ghost Sonata*]," he wrote,

is my religion (= *Anschluß mit Jenseits*); the hope of something better, and the firm conviction that we live in a world of illusion and folly from which we must struggle to free ourselves.

On the contrary, things seem brighter than before, and I have been writing with the feeling that these are my "last Sonatas". . . .

Now I am very likely about to enter a new phase. I long for the light, always have, but have never found it.

Is this the end? I don't know, but I suspect it is. Life is forcing me out, in a way—or pestering me to get out, and for a long time now I have placed my hopes on "the other side", with which I am in close touch (like Swedenborg).

And the feeling has come over me that I've done my tour of duty and have no more to say. My whole life often strikes me as if it were put on stage for me, both to cause me pain and to make me write. Consequently, my deeds might, from one point of view, be considered with indifference (morally speaking); but that hasn't prevented my suffering from the dirt I've been dragged through, a suffering in the form of *conscientia scrupulosa* (pangs of conscience). And the strange thing is that the deeds (?) I have reproached myself with have been conditioned by or have been necessary for my development, often appearing to be simply reflex actions when I have been provoked by somebody or something. I have struck back when others have struck me, but it has hurt me more to strike than to be struck.[11]

The last part of this quotation touches on another point which is crucial for an understanding of the Chamber Plays. Not only did death offer the possibility of escape from the anguish and darkness of life; it was also a final settling of accounts. One set of books is all each human being is allowed, and when his accounts balance, the books are closed. "It does indeed seem true," says Strindberg in his *Blue Books*, "that one doesn't get out of this life until everything has been settled, the small along with the big" (SS, 46:125). In *Storm Weather*, the house, with its brides and corpses passing through, is a symbol of life and all its emotional conflicts. Having settled accounts with his wife, the gentleman is through living; in moving away from the house, he is preparing himself for the last journey.

The thought that life is a carefully kept ledger is behind all the Chamber Plays. The second opus among the Chamber Plays, *The Burned House* (*Brända tomten*), shows how the ledger of life is kept. This is a more heavily symbolic work than *Storm Weather* and, in respect to the handling of the theme, is more musical in its structure. The symbol of life in this play is a little suburb known as the Swamp, halfway to the cemetery. Everybody in this community is involved in the life of everyone else—"they stick together like clay"—and one of the difficulties in reading the play is keeping in mind the various strands of the web of guilt in which everyone is ensnarled. The key thematic speech is the Stranger's describing the loom of destiny as it weaves human lives into a pattern of meaning, a pattern that is revealed only when the shuttle has moved for the last time.

When you're young, you see the loom being set up. Parents, relations, friends, acquaintances, servants—they make up the warp. Later in life you see the woof. And from then on the shuttle of fate weaves the thread back and forth. Sometimes it breaks, only to be tied together and go on its way. The heddle rises and falls, the threads are shoved together to make little meaningless curlicues, and then the fabric is complete. When you get old and your eye can really see, you discover that all those little curlicues make a design—a monogram, an ornament, a hieroglyphic, which now for the first time you can interpret. That's your life! And the World Weaver has woven it. [SS, 45:96–97]

Strindberg's early title for the play was "The World Weaver," and he clearly had in mind the cosmic web that is central to the philosophy of Tantric Buddhism. For the Buddhist, the outer and inner worlds are two sides of the same fabric, and all deeds and thoughts are woven into a web in which each strand is affected by every other strand. Strindberg probably read about the cosmic web in 1896 in Madame Blavatsky's theosophical writings.[12] Explaining Karma, she writes that

there are *external and internal conditions* which affect the determination of our will upon our actions, and it is in our power to follow either of the two. Those who believe in *Karma* have to believe in *destiny*, which, from birth to death, every man is weaving thread by thread around himself, as a spider does his cobweb; and this destiny is guided either by the heavenly voice of the invisible *prototype* outside of us, or by our more intimate *astral*, or inner man, who is but too often the evil genius of the embodied entity called man. Both these lead on the outward man, but one of them must prevail: and from the very beginning of the invisible affray the stern and implacable *law of compensation* steps in and takes its course, faithfully following the fluctuations. When the last strand is woven, and man is seemingly enwrapped in the net-work of his own doing, then he finds himself completely under the empire of this *self-made* destiny. It then either fixes him like the inert shell against the immovable rock, or carries him away like a feather in a whirlwind raised by his own actions, and this is—KARMA.[13]

To represent dramatically the weaving of the cosmic web is no easy thing. In order to show how the external and internal worlds form an inseparable whole, how all the aspects of one's life and the lives of others are interrelated, and how the final design is a demonstration of the law of compensation, of measure for measure, the plot must be made so complicated that it will be hard to follow. The spectator must see with the eye of the young man in the midst of things the little curlicues, the trivial incidents and simultaneously with the eye of the old man the emergent grand design. Strindberg first tried his hand at this in a long short story, *The Roofing Feast* (*Taklagsöl*), which is about a dying man, dosed with morphine, who reviews his life as it flits by in his mind in bits and pieces. The story, a masterpiece of the narrative art, is in form an interior monologue in which memories of tunes played on a phonograph strike sparks in the fevered mind of the dying man. It was written in 1906 and is a prelude to the Chamber Plays. As a matter of fact, Strindberg first conceived it as a drama,[14] and at one point, he had in mind a play in which the phonograph would provide the fragmentary record of a life, leaving the old man free to comment on his own past, a device that Beckett would employ fifty years later in *Krapp's Last Tape*.

In *The Burned House*, Strindberg uses a version of that method. The play is in two acts. The first presents all the contradictory information[15] about the persons whose lives have some connection with the burned house. The second, largely a monologue by the Stranger, who after years of wandering has returned to his childhood home, sorts out the information, establishes the hidden connections between incidents remote in time from each other, and reveals the pattern of justice, the balancing of the books.

The play begins with the police looking for the arsonist who set fire to the house owned by a man whose trade is dyeing cloth. Their chief suspect is a student who has been having an affair with the Dyer's wife. The play ends with the disclosure that the Dyer sought revenge against the Student by falsifying evidence against him. The Dyer's plot to incriminate the Student is exposed by a mason who had been sent to jail by the Dyer for commiting forgery, a forgery which was quite justified in the long view since the Dyer, as a child, had stolen a book from his brother by means of forgery. Thus the loom of fate weaves its patterns and settles accounts.

The Stranger, the Dyer's brother, is the ostensible protagonist of the play. The dramatic effectiveness of the play seems to be spoiled by the superior, know-it-all attitude of the Stranger, who goes around exposing the crimes and deceptions of others without being exposed himself. But the audience should not be led to assume that he is one of those who will be unmasked. He is not part of the Swamp and has not been from the moment he tried to kill himself as a boy of twelve. He has had a glimpse of life "on the other side," symbolized by his travels throughout the world, and sees through all the sham of life on earth. His disillusion began when he ate of the fruit of the tree of knowledge by reading Casanova's memoirs. After that, one thing led to another until he was truly cast out of paradise and saw the world in all its nakedness. A momentary recovery of innocence and a vision of the world as it was in the beginning occurs when the ruins of the burned house are cleared away and reveal an orchard prematurely in full bloom from the heat of the fire that exposed all the sham and deceit on which the house was built. Another Adam and Eve appear toward the end of the play, two youngsters about to get married, but they have not been onstage more than two minutes before the loom begins to weave another pattern of deceit.

4

The Burned House, opus 2 of the Chamber Plays, was written simultaneously with opus 3, The Ghost Sonata, which was completed on March 8, 1907, only a few days after Strindberg had finished opus 2. Yet the two plays are strongly contrasted in tone and style, and the views of justice and of a moral universe that they offer are diametrically opposed. The Burned House,with its touches of local color, its use of dialect, and its humorous characters, is a kind of wry comedy in which the law of compensation is allowed to work and justice prevails at the end. To go from it to The Ghost Sonata is to traverse the distance Shakespeare traveled in 1604 when he finished Measure for Measure and began King Lear.

The Ghost Sonata seethes with indignation as Strindberg's scorn and contempt for the world find expression in some of the most grotesque and theatrically stunning scenes in modern drama. To say what he felt Strindberg had to invent a new dramatic language that we now call surrealistic, a language in which metaphors assume life. To say "time hangs heavy" is one thing; to picture, as Dali has done, a watch hanging heavily is another. To say that the sweet young thing you once knew now looks like an old mummy is one thing; to have this woman imagine herself a mummy and comport herself like one, as Strindberg has her do, is another.

The artistic originality of *The Ghost Sonata* and the visionary intensity of its best scenes have made this by far the most well-known of the Chamber Plays. But critics seem reluctant to declare that the play possesses any great coherence. The stumbling block to most interpretations is the last scene, which can easily appear redundant. The plot peters out after the "ghost supper" of the second scene, and the third scene comes as an anticlimax. After the unmasker Hummel has been unmasked, what more is there to hold our attention?

Strindberg wrapped his play in mystery when he sent it off to his German translator and rebuffed all questions.

As far as *The Ghost Sonata* is concerned, don't ask me what it is about. *Discrétion, s'il vous plaît!* One enters a world of intimations where one expresses oneself in halftones and uses the soft pedal, since one is ashamed to be a human being.[16]

Indiscretion being the better part of a critic's valor, let us enter this world of intimations and see where they lead. The Student's first dialogue with the Milkmaid suggests that he is a Christ-like figure, an impression deepened by his being a Sunday child and gifted with second sight, and that she is the woman of Samaria who gave Jesus water to drink at the well. Later in the first scene, several references to Wagner's *Ring of the Nibelung* prompt the thought that the Student is Siegfried, and the Brünnhilde he is to set free is the Hyacinth Girl, who is costumed in riding habit and boots when we first see her. In the same scene, the Student, entranced by the beauty of the Hyacinth Girl, quotes a line from the "Witch's Kitchen" scene of Goethe's *Faust* and immediately afterwards refers to his agreement with old man Hummel as a pact, a devil's bargain. Thus the Student reminds us fleetingly of Jesus, Siegfried, and Faust.

In a way, Strindberg is using the *Damascus* method here, but with a difference. These muted allusions are short motifs that are combined with others to form statements, just as Wagner in his music dramas combined leitmotifs to convey the underlying sense of the action. Strindberg's method here is exactly analogous to Wagner's. When Brünnhilde tells Siegmund that he must die, the orchestra mingles the fate motif with the death motif and the Walhalla motif. When Strindberg wants to enlarge the symbolic import of the Student's role, he proceeds in the same way. The Christian will notice the aura of the Savior that emanates from the young man as he stands at the fountain being given water to drink, but the Buddhist will note that the young man is a student and that he has just saved a child from a decayed and collapsing house. Buddha became a student when he left his family, and he too was a savior. He endeavored to save people from the "old decayed burning house" that stands for the world of sensual craving, spiritual ignorance, and longing for individual existence ("The Parable of the Burning House"). In the last scene, in which a statue of the Buddha is clearly visible, the Student renounces the young girl who has aroused his passion. She is surrounded by flowers just as the wife of Buddha was at the moment of his great renunciation.

Jacob Hummel, the old man, is the gathering point for an extraordinarily complicated set of allusions or leitmotifs. Making a pact with the Student, he is Mephistopheles. As a cripple, he is *le diable boiteux*, the limping devil, Asmodeus,[17] who in Lesage's novel helps a student marry a beautiful woman and enables him to peer into the lives of other people. Riding in his wheelchair, he is Thor. "All day long he rides around in his chariot like the great god Thor," says his manservant (SS, 45:169). As a former resident of Hamburg with a shady past, Hummel is an avatar of Heinrich Heine's Hirsch, collector, operator, appraiser, cupboard lover, and a caricature of a Jew. Hirsch was the name of a Jewish business man in Stockholm whom Strindberg disliked;[18] Heine's Hirsch (who appears in *Reisebilder*: "Die Bäder von Lucca") assumed the name Hyacinth; and Strindberg's Hummel is the real father of the Hyacinth Girl.[19]

The ramifications do not end there. A true Swedenborgian will track down more allusions. When Hummel is described as breaking into houses, sneaking in through windows, the Swedenborgian adept will recall the mystic's gloss[20] on Joel 2:9: "They shall climb up upon the houses; they shall enter in at the windows like a thief." Climbing into houses signifies the destroying of the good things appertaining to love and wisdom; entering through windows denotes the use of the truths of the intellect to destroy the truths of faith. Indeed Hummel enters the Colonel's home to steal the souls of its inhabitants, and in the supper scene, he unmasks and destroys the Colonel by revealing the true facts about him. Furthermore, the Student's way of pronouncing the word "window" is the means by which he is inveigled into Hummel's plot. The Student's name is Arkenholz, and the window of the ark (Gen. 6:16) signifies the intellectual part of man.[21] Arkenholz is drawn into Hummel's sphere of influence because of a desire for material things, or, as Swedenborg would say, cupidity takes the place of spiritual love, and intellectual understanding of true wisdom. Arkenholz relished the thought of having an apartment like the Colonel's when he saw the sun glittering on its windows. (See figure 24.)

5

But is this the way to write a play—even a play for the cognoscenti? All these allusions and references, the obvious as well as the obscure, threaten to swamp the play and drown the viewer. For that matter, is it any way to write a poem or a novel? Sometimes it is. *Ulysses* and *The Waste Land*, both written within a decade and a half after *The Ghost Sonata* and both compact of allusions and literary echoes, use a method similar to Strindberg's. But there is a difference, too. Eliot appended explanatory notes to aid, or tease, his readers, and Joyce helped to provide a book-length key to his book. Strindberg the dramatist did not even furnish a program note. How could he justify, even to himself, the procedure he followed in this play?

The answer lies in what he was trying to say. "No predetermined form is binding on the author because the subject matter determines the form" (SS, 50:12): that was the principle behind the Chamber Plays. He wanted the theatregoer to respond to this new kind of theatre music in the same way that a listener responds to chamber music in the recital hall. The ordinary listener cannot do what the music student does when he pores over the score and sees how the parts are related to each other and how the themes are intertwined. But the listener will be able to follow the music all the same, just as the sensitive theatregoer will be able to catch the drift of Strindberg's play without understanding what is going on at every moment. In fact, absolute clarity would dispel meaning because a major concern of the play is our inability to know exactly what is going on in life. As in life, so in science. The modern physicist has found that the more precisely he determines the position of a subatomic particle, the less he knows about its momentum, and the more he knows about its momentum, the less he knows about its position. This vexing situation, which led Heisenberg in 1923 to formulate his indeterminacy principle, has its counterpart in the macrocosm. The more narrowly we focus our attention on a particular human crisis, the less we know about the general tendency of our lives; and the more clearly we delineate the general tendency, the less able we are to isolate the specific cause of an event. Nothing is easier to prove or disprove than why a person acted as he did. Yet just as the physicist, though ignorant of the behavior of a specific particle, can predict statistically what the aggregate of particles will do, so Strindberg believed that human activity in its entirety was governed by some law.

Long before Heisenberg discovered the indeterminacy principle, Strindberg made use of something like it in this drama. Hummel's explanation to the Student of the relationship of the people of the house to one another is hopelessly complicated. In an ordinary play, this explanation, which explains nothing and confuses everybody, would be exposition of the worst sort. Here it establishes the confusing entanglements that constitute the subject. Strindberg's aim was to create a network of allusions, of interrelated images, that would be the theatrical counterpart of the infinitely complicated cosmic web woven by inner and outer forces. In the naturalistic view of man, causes and effects can be isolated; in the Buddhist view, the strands that go into the making of our lives are so numerous and so entangled with strands from other lives in the making that all one can perceive, at best, is a general pattern. Just how the little curlicues that are continuously being woven into the fabric of our lives come to form this particular pattern can be observed only occasionally. It is this sense of complexity, this growing awareness that things are somehow related without our knowing exactly how, that Strindberg wanted to convey.

The problem was one of organizing the myriad allusions and references into a schema that would guide the half-conscious thoughts of the viewer. In dramatic terms, it was a question of finding a through-line. Eliot and Joyce faced the same problem when they had to sacrifice narrative development for inner revelation in order to express a view of life that had less to do with time and space and progress than with stillness and spirit and regeneration. While picturing the fragmentation of life in modern times, Eliot brought order into his poem by making the various sections of it represent the search for the Holy Grail. He found his through-line in Jessie L. Weston's Frazer-inspired examination of medieval legend. Strindberg found his in Swedenborg and Blavatsky.

The World Weaver is as diligent in *The Ghost Sonata* as she was in *The Burned House*. The two plays are intimately connected and were written almost simultaneously. Speaking of the family entanglements in *The Ghost Sonata*, Strindberg used words that are perfectly applicable to *The Burned House*. "This is how the World Weaver weaves the destinies of people, and just as many secrets can be found in every home."[22] The difference between the two plays reflects Strindberg's inability to convince himself that there can be a final settling of accounts, a completion of the pattern, an exact doling out of measure for measure in earthly life. In *The Burned House*, he arranges all the details so that the pattern is fully revealed and completed. The credits and debits balance each other, and the books are closed. In a Swedenborgian vision of what goes on in the realm of the dead, Strindberg said that there "the whole strange web of life is untangled, and [the dead] could see the threads of their destinies, could see why they had to do the deeds they hated to do, and why others had been allowed to be unjustly cruel to them" (SS, 48:1035; 46:124–26, 152–55).

This was only his conviction of the moment, however. At other times he doubted that justice of this sort prevailed even in the grand view. "If on the other side of the grave," he said,

we were to meet Rhadamanthus, the judge, and he were to set about untangling the affairs of men, there would be no end to it. Because life is such a web of lies, errors, misunderstandings, of debts due and owing, that a balancing of the books is impossible. [SS, 46:173]

For that reason, Strindberg, who could not bear the thought that injustice might be eternally triumphant, although he saw the evidence for it all around him, made the leap of faith and flew from the pagan underworld to the Christian other world. "What Rhadamanthus could not untangle the man on the cross could, and that with but a single word to the repentant malefactor: 'Today shalt thou be with me in paradise'" (SS, 46:174). Madame Blavatsky's theosophy and its law of compensation, with its implicit advocacy of revenge, now seemed too strict and petty to Strindberg, whereas the teachings of Christ advocated forgiveness without revenge and "without a bookkeeping of all the mistakes and idiocies one has committed."[23]

In *The Ghost Sonata*, the unknotting of the skein of guilt proves to be impossible. Hummel, who assumes the role of judge, is himself judged by the Mummy, who stops the clock and wipes out the past with suffering and remorse. "We have erred, we have transgressed, we, like all the rest," she says,

We are not what we seem to be. At bottom we are better than ourselves, since we abhor and detest our misdeeds. But when you, Jacob Hummel, with your false name, come here to sit in judgment over us, that proves that you are more contemptible than we are! And you are not the one you seem to be! You are a slave trader, a stealer of souls! [SS, 48:192]

6

The view in this play is not from a point near the end of life, as in *The Burned House*, but from a point on the other side of the grave. In this, his most extravagant work, Strindberg takes us on a journey into death, lets us leave the body and enter the world of spirits. The steamship bells at the beginning signal the start of the journey, which will end at the Isle of the Dead. Like the people in the play, we hardly know that we have left the natural world because the life of the body is continued into the other world. "The first state of man after death," says Swedenborg,

resembles his state in the world, for he is then likewise in externals, having a like face, like speech, and a like disposition, thus a like moral and civil life; and in consequence he is made aware that he is not still in the world only by giving attention to what he encounters.[24]

What we encounter is a spectral milkmaid, a dead consul who appears in his winding sheet to count his mourners, and a young student who tells a strange story about saving a child from a collapsing building only to have the child disappear from his arms. By this time, it should dawn on us that the child disappeared because she was saved and remained in the natural world.

Before us is the facade of an elegant apartment house. This set represents exteriors, the first state of man after death, the state that corresponds to the world of social accommodation and legal inhibition. The second scene takes us into the house, into the Round Room, where the Mummy appears (figures 25 and 26). This represents the state of interiors, where the spirits become, to quote Swedenborg, "visibly just what they had been in themselves while in the world, what they then did and said secretly being now made manifest."[25] Here Swedenborg provided the inspiration for the graphic and theatrical disrobing scene in which Hummel strips the Colonel of his decorations and exposes him as a social sham, only to be unmasked himself by the Mummy as a criminal and a stealer of souls. The Round Room is what Strindberg elsewhere calls "the undressing room into which the deceased are led immediately after death. There they remove the vesture they were compelled to put on in society and with friends and family; and the angels soon see them for what they are" (SS, 46:49–50).[26]

The hymn to the sun, intoned by the Student, provides a fitting conclusion to the scene both because of what it says about kindness and guilelessness and because of its source. Strindberg freely adapted it from some stanzas of the Icelandic *Sólarljóð*, a visionary poem, Catholic in inspiration, containing a description of the moment of death—"I saw the sun"—and of hell and heaven by a man who from the other side of the grave is able to communicate with his living son.

The third and last scene, the Hyacinth Room, represents in the Swedenborgian plan the third state of man after death, a place of instruction and preparation for those who may merit a place in heaven. The essentially good spirit, like the Hyacinth Girl, must be vastated and purged of evils and falsities acquired on earth. The Student functions here as a vastating spirit, confronting her with the ugly truths of life and removing evils and falsities from her in order that she may receive the influx of goods and truths from heaven. As he speaks to her, she pines and withers away.

The three sets of the play also correspond approximately to what the theosophists, following the cabalists, call the three dwellings of the soul: "Earth for the physical man, or the animal Soul; Kâma-Loka (Hades, the Limbo) for the disembodied man, or his *Shell*; Devachan for the higher Triad."[27] The shell is the astral form of the soul; it is the body that is left behind when the highest aspect of the soul, the mind, departs for Devachan or nirvana, that condition of the soul in which passion, hatred, and delusion are no more.

The Buddhist and Christian hints dropped at the beginning of the play continue to ripple through it and to intermingle, especially in the latter half. The room in which the unmasking of the Colonel and the old man takes place is both Kâma-Loka and hell. In the last scene, the Student speaks of Christ's sufferings on earth, while a small statue of Buddha expresses purity of will and the patience to endure. The shallot in its lap symbolizes the relation of matter to spirit (Swedenborg's correspondences) and man's striving to raise earth to heaven.[28] In the final moments, what is seen and what is heard fuse together into a sublime poetic image of radiant theatricality: the harp bursting into sound, the Student's solemn hymn to the sun, the white refulgent light burning away the reality that is only an illusion, and the emergence in the distance of the Isle of the Dead. The light that floods the room and causes it to disappear is the light of death, of nirvana, and of divine wisdom and love. In the Só-larljóð, the dying man sees the sun and knows the truth about life as he passes over the threshold. In Swedenborg, the sun is the symbol of God's love, and when the angels draw the film from the eyes of a dying person, he sees a bright white light that represents eternal life.[29] In Mahayana Buddhism, the Buddha is the pure light that banishes the darkness of ghosts, of the animal world, of hell; it is the light of the great mind and power that lights the way to the land of happiness; it is the light of truth, purity, and mercy.

7

On the cover of the manuscript of the play, Strindberg drew a picture of Buddha's shallot. He gave the play the subtitle "Kâma-Loka"; he thought of calling it "The Ghost Supper"; but he finally settled on *The Ghost Sonata*,[30] which suggests both the extraterrestrial setting of the play and its musical structure. The *Sonata* title is certainly the most fitting, for unless one treats the play as a kind of musical composition, it is impossible to appreciate its artistic wholeness and the way in which all the pieces fit together. Although it is often faulted for lacking coherence, especially in the last scene, the play is, in fact, a miracle of artistic organization, a work of Wagnerian intricacy and contrivance composed with Mozartian ease in which everything seems casual and improvised and yet nothing in it is adventitious. In an ideal production, the perfect Strindbergite would quickly forget about character analysis and conventional plot development, and would respond to symbols and elusive harmonies and thematic development. He would quickly understand that the plot is not designed to reveal what Hummel once in his dark past did to the Milkmaid. He would sense immediately that Hummel and the Milkmaid are thematic opposites and nod at the recognition of Hummel and the Cook as thematic companions. When Hummel is described as a man who tears down houses, sneaks in through windows, and ravages human lives, the Strindbergite would remember that the Student saves the life of a baby caught in a collapsing house and that the Milkmaid offers aid to the Student. He would hear character answering character, but he would sense theme answering theme. He would know that it is both musically and morally right that after Hummel exposes the Colonel as a valet who used to flirt with the maids in order to scrounge in the kitchen, Hummel himself should be exposed as being exactly what he accused the Colonel of being. And he would experience esthetic delight in seeing the evil Cook in the last scene suddenly emerge from the kitchen in which Hummel and the Colonel had their beginnings. But instead of perfect Strindbergites, we have critics who shake their heads grumpily at the Cook and reproach Strindberg for putting his petty domestic problems into a play.

Being distinct from one another in setting, tempo, and mood, the three scenes must be regarded as corresponding to the three movements of a sonata,[31] even though the themes set forth at the beginning are developed through the whole work. The first and longest scene, unsurpassed in modern drama for sheer dramaturgical virtuosity, is a brisk allegro, its mood sustained by the youthful buoyancy of the Student and by the grasping eagerness of the Old Man as they lay their plans for entering the house of elegance. In sharp contrast is the second scene or movement, the largo. To its slow tempo and its long silences the ghost supper is eaten, the masks removed, the interiors revealed. The final scene is a quiet andante, which stresses the principal theme of the whole sonata and brings it to a close with a brilliant coda that restates all the themes.

In physical terms, the play takes us from the street in front of the imposing apartment house into a salon of the house, from the salon into a symbolic bedroom, and from there to the Isle of the Dead. The effect of this arrangement is not only to make us feel that we are going on a journey but that we are also penetrating the heart of some mystery and losing some of our illusions as we do so, for in each scene some masks are dropped. In Kâma-Loka "the scales fall from one's eyes and one sees *Das Ding an sich*,"[32] which means that everything here is the reverse of what it was among the living, whose eyes are veiled by Maya. Each time we move, we also lose a few characters until, at the end, only the Student is left. There is a death or a funeral in each scene, the play beginning with the Consul's funeral, reaching its climax in the hanging of old Hummel, and culminating in the death of the Young Lady. Death, however, is not the principal theme of the work; it merely provides the occasion for the work.

The subordinate themes in this play—to save the main theme for the last—are ones that were primary in *The Burned House*: the world is a sham compounded of lies, deceits, and illusions; to live is to be guilty; and death represents a settling of accounts. In the first scene, the residents of the house are shown to be bound together in a web of mutual guilt and deception. In the second scene, Hummel swells up like a blood-sucking insect as he exposes all this guilt and deception and reminds the residents that they are all in his power. But his turn comes when the Mummy exposes him as a criminal who was responsible for the drowning of a milkmaid. That finishes the Old Man and would seem to finish the play were it not for the fact that we have been ignoring the main subject of this sonata.

That subject is vampirism. It is presented to us visually at the very outset when the Milkmaid, the Student, and the Old Man are on stage, and it is announced with stark clarity when old Hummel grasps the hand of the Student and sucks strength from him. Hummel is a vampire who feeds on human souls, and opposed to him is the supplier of milk, who recognizes the Student as an ally. The opposition of Hummel and the Student is made clear when we learn that Hummel enters into houses to tear them down, while the Student saves those who are caught in collapsing houses. At the end of the first scene, in a brilliant recapitulation, the Old Man sees the Milkmaid for the first time and recoils in fear. Thus, at the end of the first scene, the battle lines are clearly drawn: the vampires against the savers of souls, the bloodsuckers versus the nourishers.

The second scene removes any doubts we may have had about Hummel as a bloodsucker. In the first scene, he can and should win some of our sympathy, just as he wins the sympathy of the Student. But in the second scene, all our doubts about Hummel as a vampire are removed along with his mask as the pretended benefactor of the Student. This scene is devoted to the old people, who have suffered and done penance for their sins.

But what of the young who are not yet guilty? And what of love as a force to overcome the vampires? In Kâma-Loka, where we see *Das Ding an sich*, everything is the opposite of what it appeared to be. The benefactor is a vampire; the good provider is a kitchen sponger; and instead of giving food, the Cook sucks the nourishment out of it. Quite consistently, the Old Man's greed and craving for power has its reverse here too. To redeem himself, Hummel, like Wotan, has arranged for the two young people to fall in love and start a life free from corruption. Love is to undo the curse of the Ring of Gold. Hummel-Wotan introduces his substitute son, the Student, into the house of the Colonel to meet the Hyacinth Girl, Hummel's real daughter. Like Siegfried, the Student is to awaken his Brünnhilde and marry her. After the decaying atmosphere of the ghost supper with its mummies and skeletons and stagnant waters, the Hyacinth Room is vibrant with youth, passion, and sensuousness. But opposed to this riot of the senses is the stillness of Buddha. The mood of this scene is like that evoked by Strindberg in a letter to Harriet Bosse.

I find my only consolation now in Buddha, who tells me clearly that life is a phantasm, an illusion that we shall see turned right way round in another life. My hope and future lie on the other side; that's why life is so difficult for me. Everything here disappoints and mocks one, and should only be seen at a distance. This morning I saw my favorite landscape from my desk. You know, in sunlight, and so supernally beautiful I fell into an ecstasy. I wanted to go down to the field and take a closer look. But then it vanished behind the knolls, and when I got closer, it didn't look the same. What you go after runs away from you.[33]

The colors and fragrances of the hyacinths—and the flowers are everywhere in the room—overpower the Student. In them lies all the beauty and allurement that binds one to the physical world. For that reason they are dangerous, poisonous. They stir the senses and trouble the spirit without satisfying either. To Swedenborg, the hyacinth signified knowledge deriving from the "affection of an infernal love."[34] To Strindberg, the hyacinth resembled those people whose beauty is skin-deep, enormously attractive to look at but empty within, creatures who move through life like sleepwalkers, breathing, breeding, and dying without any deep perception or understanding of the world around them.

The hyacinth is beautiful to look at, perfectly beautiful; its perfume delights our sense of smell; and perhaps it is even capable of perceiving something like pain and pleasure. But without self-consciousness, reason, and free will there is no possibility for a soul to develop, and to be without a soul is virtually to be dead— at least to those of us who are alive. [SS, 48:847]

The Hyacinth Girl in the Sonata is too weak to have an independent soul and too ethereal to endure the attrition of daily life: planning meals, leveling the wobbling desk, sorting the week's wash. Her strength has been taken from her by the Cook, the ogre who haunts the house and who belongs to the Hummel family of vampires. In a way, it is the girl's weakness that draws the Student to her. In the first scene, he is on the verge of forgetting about her when her bracelet falls off her arm—an arm too thin to hold a bracelet—and the Student hastens to pick it up. But without strength and without soul, she is a leech on the Student. The girl turns out to be akin to the Cook and Hummel. In the economics of the psyche, they are parasites who consume without producing. It is this that makes her beauty poisonous. When the Student repels this poison, he must render it back in the form of truth, which to the Young Lady is the strongest poison in the world. She is in a trance, her eyes are closed, and she glides through life like a sleepwalker. To tell her the truth will wake her and cause her to fall from the rooftop, but the Student has no choice. He is fully awake, his eyes are open, and he sees the world for what it is. He cannot lie, nor can he remain silent, for silence is a form of lying. He tells her the ugly facts of life, and the truth kills her.

In Wagner's *Ring*, the love of Brünnhilde and Siegfried for each other augurs the death of the gods, the end of Walhalla, of the world of power and of the kingdom of gold. In Strindberg, love also brings death but does not bring an end to the curse. The Ring of Gold becomes the girl's bracelet, and love becomes its own curse. The quiet horror of the last scene lies in this: after seeing how greed and deception have ruined the lives of the old ones, we see how truth and love destroy the young ones.

The *Sonata* ends with a Beethoven-like coda in which all the themes are sounded again. When the Student describes his father's disastrous dinner party at which all the guests were told off and their true natures were revealed, we are reminded not only of the ghost supper of the second scene but also of what is happening at this moment as the Student speaks to the girl and destroys her. The Student's strength is now being sucked from him and only the death of the Hyacinth Girl* saves him. Freed at last from the Three Poisons that Buddha speaks of—the poison of desiring individual existence, the poison of ignorance, and the poison of sensual longing—the Student faces nirvana, the state of perfect calm, the extinction of aversion, confusion, and passion, as the Isle of the Dead looms in the distance.

Strindberg thought of having a sign appear over the Isle of the Dead with these words from Revelation written on it in flaming letters: "And

---

* Hyacinth girls are rare in both life and art, and there is the odd circumstance that the only hyacinth girls in literature appear in Strindberg's *The Ghost Sonata* (1907) and Eliot's *The Waste Land* (1922). Moreover, in both drama and poem she plays the same ambiguous role, provoking desire yet suggesting death. Eliot's narrator seems to be calling to mind the last moment in Strindberg's play when, seeing the girl's arms filled with hyacinths, he says, "I was neither / Living nor dead, and I knew nothing, / Looking into the heart of light, the silence." The fact that Eliot follows Strindberg in using fragmentary allusions and quotations can be explained as due to indirect influence; so can the juxtaposition of Christian and Buddhist elements. ("A Buddhist is as immanent as a Christian in *The Waste Land*," says Craig Raine, "Met him pikehoses: *The Waste Land* as a Buddhist Poem," *Times Literary Supplement*, 4 May 1973.) But the appearance of the Hyacinth Girl seems to be a deliberate echoing of the last scene in Strindberg's play. Eliot was in Germany in 1914 and 1915 when the cult of Strindberg was at its peak. To the younger generation, Strindberg was more than a classic; he was the prophet of an age of turmoil and doubt, an incarnation of the modern conscience—just the sort of writer who would appeal to the spiritually troubled Eliot. Replying to an *enquête* conducted by a Swedish newspaper on the occasion of the Strindberg centenary, Eliot stated that he had learned to know some of Strindberg's plays during the most impressionable period of his life and before he had given any thought to writing for the stage. *Svenska Dagbladet*, 20 January 1949.

God shall wipe away all tears from their eyes; and there shall be no more death, neither sorrow, nor crying, neither shall there be any more pain: for the former things are passed away." [35]

8

Strindberg also wanted these words to be sung by an invisible chorus at the beginning of a play, *Toten-Insel*, which was meant to continue the mystical journey into the realm of the dead. A recently deceased teacher arrives at the Isle of the Dead in the boat pictured in Böcklin's famous painting, and he wakes up among the dead just as he had often woke up among the living, trying to catch a few more minutes of sleep before rushing off to his early morning class, his mind troubled by unpaid bills and uncorrected student papers. After a while, when he has become acclimated to Hades, he has the privilege of hearing what his wife, two daughters, and a colleague thought of him. Their views are so divergent and inconsistent that they seem to be talking about four different people. After this Pirandellian beginning, Strindberg intended to show what the teacher's life was really like, but he abandoned the project, torn between his desire to write about happier matters and his compulsive need to be honest. He told himself that though he wanted to put joy and happiness into his writings, he was irresistibly driven to speak the ugly truth (SS, 46:406–07).

Here he was being a bit evasive. He should have said that he could create drama at that time only by seeing the contrast between the Platonic ideal and sordid reality. He had to put aside *Toten-Insel* because the Isle of the Dead was no place for drama. When he described that island as he liked to imagine it, his description was purely lyrical.

Here the dead could rest after the horrors of life. . . .
The whole strange web of life was unraveled, and they saw the threads that made up their destinies. Saw why they had to do certain deeds they hated to do; why others had been allowed to cause them pain unjustly. What they gained in enlightenment they lost in bitterness. The spirit of reconciliation spread its soft light over the horrible past. In their hearts they forgave their enemies, and sometimes even blessed them. All that had happened, even the most awful things, appeared to be propitiated, and in that way, only in that way, were they able to erase the terrible memories they had thought they could never be rid of. They cried with joy and fell into raptures. They could never have imagined this: that a reconciliation with the past was possible. . . .
This was the resting place, the summer holiday after the first death. [SS, 48: 1035–36]

In this wistful rhapsody of life on the Isle of the Dead, this dream of the afterlife, Strindberg could pacify the ghosts that haunted him. One of these ghosts was that of his brother-in-law, Hugo von Philp, the principal of a private school in Stockholm, whom he had portrayed as the ego-centric captain in *The Dance of Death*. Philp had died in January 1906 after enduring much pain and suffering. In his last moments, as Strind-berg recorded them, Philp had suddenly said, "It is summer outside. I want to sleep." Then he had lain down on his bed and gone "to sleep," becoming like a child in appearance.[36]

It was to make amends for his cruel portrait of Philp that Strindberg drew him again as the teacher in *Toten-Insel*. "It is as if the 'departed' demanded satisfaction from me," said Strindberg, "or required that I pic-ture him *also* from his good side, where he was innocent and had his merits."[37] It soon became obvious, however, that the play began where it should end, with summer outside and the ship waiting to take the happy vacationers to the island of rest. Although *Toten-Insel* continued the story of *The Ghost Sonata*, it lacked drama and added nothing that was not already implicit in the *Sonata*. The coherence of the Chamber Plays had to be maintained, and what unites them is not a developing narrative or a similarity of technique but the inquisitive and searching mind of the artist as it deals with the matter at hand in every possible way. After the *Sonata*, the dramatist had to conceive a plot that would extend the lines of thought laid down in the previous Chamber Plays. Exorcizing the ghost that haunted his moral conscience was secondary to satisfying his artistic conscience. Or, to put it more accurately, the two were one and the same because his vision as an artist was ultimately a moral vision.

As he worked on these plays, his view of human life darkened. He saw corruption and injustice everywhere. He saw people preying on one another, the vampires feeding on the weak, the parasites consuming the strong. And he saw that most people moved through life like automa-tons, ignorant of anything but their bodily needs, utterly deluded about themselves and others. Only a small part of this vision is presented in *Storm Weather*, which is merely a prologue to the other Chamber Plays. An exceptionally good play for the philistines,[38] Strindberg called it; the story is simple, the treatment is realistic, and justice is allowed to pre-vail. In the second opus, *The Burned House*, the vision expands. Human destinies form a skein of deceptions and falsehoods, of accusations and recriminations. Still, when the yarn is unraveled, it is all woven into a pattern in which there are no loose threads. The weaver is a meticulous worker. Again, the philistine is satisfied—or would be if the pattern were simple enough for him to comprehend it. He recognizes these people, their way of talking, their small jokes and petty motives, and understands that fundamentally all is right with the world. But the artist is not satisfied. He knows that this realistic picture of the world only seems real, for it is not true. When the visionary in him looks intensely and steadily at the world, when the scales fall from his eyes and he sees through Maya, sees the Ding an sich, the human forms that inhabit the streets and rooms appear to him as vampires and sleepwalkers, parasites and hyacinth people. Now the moralist is upset, suspecting that the neat pattern of justice woven by the World Weaver is an illusion like everything else. He sees no completed pattern, only loose threads, and when he gathers them together and attempts to weave them back into the pattern, he only makes things worse. He tries to be ruthlessly honest, but ruthlessness tears the fragile web. Compassion should repair the harm done, but pity and understanding are only the spider's snares.

In The Pelican, opus 4 of the Chamber Plays, the vampires and sleepwalkers appear again. The Book of Life is opened and audited, not to balance accounts, which is seen to be impossible, but to find the error, the mistake that began the embezzlements and defalcations, the thefts and peculations, the deceptions and lies on which the vampires have lived and of which the sleepwalkers are ignorant. Mother, Daughter, and Son in The Pelican are sleepwalkers, stumbling blindly through life, their eyes closed to the truth. The spirit of the recently deceased father wakes them, and the settling of his estate represents the settling of accounts with which all these plays are concerned. When they have been awakened, they die.

There is nothing complicated or subtle in the story Strindberg has to tell. After the atmospheric impressionism and pastel work of Storm Weather, after the homey realism and intricate drawing of The Burned House, after the sourdine, otherworldly poetry and finespun allusiveness of The Ghost Sonata, Strindberg, like Beethoven in his last string quartet, retreats to the more familiar and well-trodden paths of his art and offers a straightforward plot and gaudy theatricality, as if to say that the brutal and simple truth must be told with brutal and searing simplicity. The conventional spine-chilling effects of popular drama appear here but are transformed into symbols and leitmotifs. The spirit of the dead father gathers in the chair that rocks by itself and in the wind that rattles the window panes and howls in the stove (figure 27). This wind is, as one critic calls it, the awakener of the sleepwalkers and their tormentor.[39] It is the undying voice of the past, while the fire that the mother tries to put out, the fire that she has denied her children, the fire that the wind feeds, the fire that finally consumes the house, is the fire that burns away iniquities and purifies by destroying.

The plot, too, is simple, uncluttered, and primal; it could serve and has served for Hollywood melodrama, French comédie rosse, and Greek tragedy. Brother and sister learn that their mother has destroyed their father, and they avenge his death. It is the basic situation in the Oresteia,[40] with Strindberg adding a twist to the plot by making the mother's paramour the daughter's husband.

The Daughter, sexually undeveloped and sterile, is another version of the Hyacinth Girl. Her brother is an alcoholic and, like his sister, is too weak to face the tribulations and struggles of daily life. To whom do they owe their weakness? After The Ghost Sonata it is not difficult to guess. The Milkmaid and the Cook, appearing respectively in the first and last scenes of that play, represent two sides of the same symbol. And in the coda to the Sonata, the Student, by way of summing-up, says that children are nipped in the bud either in the kitchen or in the bedroom. Who is this nipper in the bud, this cook who gives water instead of milk, if not Mother? In The Pelican the ominous, ogrelike Cook of the Sonata becomes the mother of these two helplessly doomed children who are thin from lack of food, cold from lack of affection, and blind from lack of soul. The whole play is a scathing attack on the Mother as a great fraud. She too is a sleepwalker, of Hummel's sort, blind from selfishness. When the settling of accounts comes, the Son and Daughter turn upon their mother, wake her from her sleep, and make her cringe and crawl and eat the insubstantial food she has fed them. But taking vengeance upon her cannot undo what has been done. The only way out is to put an end to all their suffering. The drunken Son sets fire to the house, and in a magnificent scene, a domestic Götterdämmerung that announces the bankruptcy of the family as an institution and the end of bourgeois drama, the Mother leaps to her death, while brother and sister ecstatically and incestuously embrace each other (figure 28), as brother becomes Papa and sister, Mama; and as the flames leap up to consume them, they sink back to the innocence of childhood, back to the warmth of the spring of life, calling for their dear mother.

Gerda, hurry up, come on, will you, the boat bells are ringing, and Mama's sitting in the salon. No, she's not, oh, poor Mama, she's not with us, did we leave her on shore? Where is she? I don't see her anywhere, it's no fun without Mama. Here she is, she's coming!—Now it's summer again!

With that scene, the chamber music comes to an end. These Chamber Plays occupy roughly the same place in Strindberg's oeuvre as do the last quartets in Beethoven's. Both men were in their late fifties when they produced these works that represent their last great creative efforts. Greeted at first with incomprehension, Beethoven's quartets are now recognized as among his supreme achievements. But Strindberg's Chamber Plays are still all too frequently relegated to the drama's museum of freaks. It is time that they came into their own, for they represent not the blather of madness but the mysteriously controlled utterance of genius working at the top of its bent.

It is a fact worth noting that Strindberg composed *The Ghost Sonata* and liberated drama from its long enslavement to character and motivation in the same year that Picasso painted *Les Demoiselles d'Avignon* and shattered the old concepts of the relationship of art to nature. The unresolved contradictions and unnerving dislocations in these works signalized a new epoch in the arts and possibly in Western culture. A revolutionary year in many ways, 1907 was also a year of strange coincidences. While Picasso painted *Les Demoiselles*, Schönberg set to work on his Second String Quartet, which was to lead him to upset the traditional concepts of musical harmony and rhythm. And at about the same time Einstein had what he later called "the happiest thought of my life":[1] the flash of insight that led him to develop the general theory of relativity and to overturn the accepted notions of gravity, space, and time. What Picasso did for painting, Schönberg, for music, and Einstein, for science, Strindberg did for the drama.

Occupying a lonely outpost in the arts, Strindberg was often ignored and misunderstood and never more so than in *The Ghost Sonata*, which employs techniques that were accepted as legitimate means of expression only after his death. The last scene of the play, for instance, clearly anticipates the techniques of collage and montage as used by Braque and Picasso in art, by Eliot and Joyce in literature, and by Griffith and Eisenstein in the film. On stage are bouquets of hyacinths, a statue of Buddha, a hospital screen, and a harp, which I take to be the "prophet's harp" described by Rydberg in his poem "Dream Life." To them will be added at the very end a radiant light and Böcklin's painting *The Isle of the Dead*. This visual montage is supplemented by an aural one in which fragmentary quotations from, or references to, Christ, Buddha, Swedenborg, and a medieval poet are juxtaposed. These elements pull the mind in different directions, but out of the conflict emerges a higher concept that unites all the fragments in a single object of contemplation. The apparent difference between Strindberg's method and that of the later experimenters is in fact only the difference between theatre and the other arts.

Undoubtedly, there is an elaborate network of subtle influences that

CHAPTER FIFTEEN

THE LAST OUTRAGE

connects artistic and scientific discoveries and transmits ideas from one field to another.* There must also be a kind of pattern underlying the events and giving form to the network, a pattern that escapes the notice of the ordinary man and is only dimly discerned by men of genius. One of the most remarkable aspects of Strindberg's genius was the way in which it not only traced the pattern but collaborated with the maker of the pattern. When Strindberg seemed to be most subjective and most personal, utterly lost in himself, he was actually most in touch with world affairs and most deeply enmeshed in the network. His way of anticipating the developing and emergent pattern was to weave himself into it. When the feminist controversy raged most furiously, Strindberg's marriage broke up. When the new psychology of Freud was being born, Strindberg hurled himself into a psychological inferno. And when the old conventions of art were being decisively abrogated, Strindberg entered a second inferno. The conjunction of these crises in his personal life with the larger events of cultural history has little to do with chance. He brought these crises on himself. He knew what he was doing and understood the nature of his kind of insight. He was fully aware that his most original and innovative work was done after the "major disasters" in his life; it was then that he saw most deeply into the heart of things. Just before he embarked on his 1896 experiment he wrote, "In the great crises . . . when one's very existence is threatened, the soul acquires transcendental qualities" (SS, 28:274–75).[2]

His best plays were written when he had been galvanized into writing them by some tremendous emotional storm. In the case of the Chamber Plays, it was not so much the fortuitous entrance of the actor August Falck into his life that brought him back to writing for the theatre as it was the death of his brother-in-law and the irrevocable loss of Harriet Bosse to another man. Those events provided the necessary emotional

*As an example of this transmission of ideas one might take Strindberg's indirect contribution to the development of modern music. At the time that Schönberg was formulating his new theories of tonality, he read many of Strindberg's works, including the Blue Books, and he studied Swedenborg. His monodrama Erwartung and his drama with music, Die glückliche Hand, both composed between 1908 and 1913, derive from the Damascus cycle and A Dream Play. Also at about this time, Schönberg, inspired by Strindberg's Jacob Wrestles, planned to write an oratorio presenting modern man wrestling with the forces of materialism and socialism, and finding God. According to Professor Stuckenschmidt, one of the impulses behind Schönberg's Drei Stücke für Orchester and thus of atonality was his reading of Jacob Wrestles. (On this point see Lars Gustafsson, "Strindberg as a Forerunner of Scandinavian Modernism," The Hero in Scandinavian Literature, ed. John M. Weinstock and Robert T. Rovinsky [Austin and London, 1975], p. 136.)

crisis. The crisis by itself, however, could not be translated into art any more than an actor can convert his genuine passion into a great performance without a script. The actor in Strindberg knew that the traumatic experience had to be preceded by a period in which the material to be used was collected and worked over. The peculiar nature of his genius lay in his ability and willingness to plan the catastrophe. The still prevalent and naive view that Strindberg was a semi-psychotic, demi-demented artist who wrote because he suffered from certain profound psychological disturbances that could be ameliorated by writing about them puts the cart before the horse. One need only set in order the pieces of his life and his works to see that he was an artist to the depth of his being and that he created the disturbances in order to write. His madness was the madness of the true artist who, in the words of Shaw's John Tanner, "will let his wife starve, his children go barefoot, his mother drudge for his living at seventy, sooner than work at anything but his art," the artist who is "half vivisector, half vampire," and who "steals the mother's milk and blackens it to make printer's ink to scoff at her and glorify ideal women with."[3]

In this creative process the major upheaval was not the crucial element; any crisis would serve to precipitate the creative outburst as long as it came after a certain period of preparation. The Chamber Plays were in a sense conceived when Strindberg wrote the novels *Gothic Rooms* and *Black Flags*, which were experiments with form as well as panoramic surveys of the intellectual concerns of the times. The dream plays began their gestation when Strindberg resolved to investigate the psyche by bringing matter and mind together in a series of experiments that started in 1894. The seeds of the sex tetralogy of his naturalistic period were planted in 1884 when Strindberg assailed the feminists in *Married*. The imaginative work culminating in the great plays in each phase of his career did not commence with an unpredictable earthquake upsetting his life, but with a decisive act deliberately committed. Devoting his life to art, he could not afford to let chance rule, even though he liked to give the impression that it did. To be steadily creative, he could not rely on the springs of Helicon or the hoofs of Pegasus. He had to dig his own well and produce his own inspiration.

One of his most revealing confessions is in the form of a short story he wrote in 1905, "The Saga of Stig Storverk's Son," the first in a collection of tales dealing with Scandinavian heroes from the Middle Ages to 1700 (SS, 43:7–53). Just as the best art conceals art, so the most revealing confessions conceal confession. Although Strindberg in this tale is remarkably successful in entering into the life of ancient Sweden, in summoning up its spirit and enduing its primitive inhabitants with the rude glamour of a lost age, in bringing them to life yet keeping them at the distance an effective saga requires, the story he has to tell is actually about himself. Like Strindberg, the hero is a man of mixed parentage. His father, who belongs to the people of the dark, once caught a glimpse of Balder and the people of the sun. He fell instantly in love with one of the beautiful sun maidens and by means of trollish powers was able to mate with her. The offspring of this union, Stig, is slated for greatness. Like the archetypal hero of legend, he is exposed and abandoned as a baby, found and raised by a stranger, and becomes in his youth a warrior. His best friend is Vikar, and when Vikar becomes ruler of the land, he invites Stig to share the throne with him. Stig declines the offer. Later, when Vikar's ships are becalmed and when precious stones thrown into the sea and burnt offerings do not appease the gods and raise the winds, a human offering is called for; and the leaders of the tribe draw lots to determine who will be immolated. Vikar is chosen, and Stig is designated as executioner. Tormented by the thought of having to slay his warrior comrade, Stig has a vision in which he sees his father Storverk on trial before a Viking tribunal. Sitting in judgment on him are Odin and Thor, and they let Storverk, whose name means "great deeds," know what life has in store for Stig, the son of Great Deeds. The two gods say they will intervene in Stig's life but in opposing ways. What Odin will do for Stig, Thor will undo. Odin bestows victory in war; Thor, the wounds of war. Odin promises wealth; Thor reduces the amount. Odin offers the gift of poetry, while Thor will see to it that the poet will be forgotten. Odin will bring a number of women to Stig; Thor will take them all away. Odin gives Stig three lives; Thor condemns him to commit a dastardly deed in each. Stig himself is to be kept in ignorance of all this, for "woe betide the man who knows his destiny." Only in this vision does he apprehend what his fate is to be.

At this point, "The Saga of Stig Storverk's Son" becomes patently autobiographical. What Odin bestows on Stig is what Strindberg received in life, and the visionary setting of the trial (in Saxo's original tale, the trial is a real event and not a vision) is meant to suggest that in the deepest recesses of his mind Strindberg knew what plots the gods had laid for him and had known ever since his publisher, Bonnier, had suffered for Strindberg's blasphemy in 1884.

The vision fades and gives way to reality. Stig must now assist in the execution of Vikar, stabbing him with a marsh reed that magically turns into a spear. He becomes a social outcast, although the warriors in the tribe esteem him as a poet. His next deed is to attack the fortress of women, one of whom he captures and marries, only to become virtually her captive and slave. One day he espies his wife in the company of a strong warrior. Aroused by jealousy, he stabs the man in the back, drinks his blood, and thus regains his manhood. Behind this episode lurks the story of *A Madman's Defense* in which Strindberg disclosed intimate details about his first wife Siri and her first husband, Baron Wrangel. The Swedish establishment never forgave him for his ungentlemanly conduct, his violation of the aristocrat's code.

In the next episode, Stig and Alf, one of his admirers, set off to do battle against an unspecified enemy. Alf discreetly removes himself from the scene of carnage, which is so violent that all nature is in turmoil. Stig returns, severely wounded, nearly dead, and learns that in the confusion of the fighting he has accidentally slain his wife. Subsequently, a spirit informs him that he had only wounded her. This mysterious war recapitulates Strindberg's literary campaigns. He fought at first as a naturalist but emerged from the smoke of battle as a symbolist or, rather, as a supranaturalist. During the naturalist campaign Strindberg was assisted by Gustaf af Geijerstam (Alf). Later, however, when the battle between the writers of the 1890s raged most furiously, Geijerstam gave Strindberg no support. The slain wife is Siri, whom Strindberg divorced in 1891.

The third era in Stig's life begins when he is urged to kill the king of Uppsala. Stig is easily persuaded because the king had once publicly ridiculed him. After having slain the king, Stig, old and tired, looks forward to his own death. He sings his own exequy, and the people recognize him as the true skald of their country. He plunges a spear into his heart and dies on a funeral pyre, rejoining in death his mother and the "white" people of the sun. As the fire dies down, Alf pipes up: "The son of Great Deeds you were indeed; the father of Great Deeds you were not." Whereupon, one of the warriors unceremoniously kicks Alf into the fire.

In this saga à clef, the king of Uppsala is Viktor Rydberg, the most highly respected scholar-poet of his generation in Sweden. He had once satirized Strindberg[4] in a poem, caricaturing him as a dog-hating, woman-disdaining social upstart and setting him up as representative of the modern spirit, ambitious, ruthless, simple, and crude. Strindberg avenged himself tit for tat in the novel *Gothic Rooms* by making Rydberg an antichrist, the prophet of the paganism and irreligion that was corroding the soul of modern man. As if this calumniation of a distinguished man who was no longer in a position to defend himself, since he had died in 1895, were not enough to infuriate the Swedish literati, Strindberg in the same novel subjected Geijerstam to such a pitiless and malicious pillorying that it was believed to have hastened his death.

Strindberg used this *Heldenleben* of Stig Storverk's son to disclose the direct connection between the most scandalous events of his life and the beginnings of the most creative phases of his writing career. In the first phase, the scandal came as a gift from the gods, or as a curse, when Strindberg committed blasphemy and had to stand trial with his publisher. Strindberg had certainly not foreseen that eventuality. In the other phases, however, the outrageous acts were deliberately committed by a man who knew what the artist in him required. When his creative fires threatened to die out, he rekindled them by placing a wife or a friend on the coals, and when the fire was blazing, he threw himself into it.

Strindberg used a different metaphor in describing his professional methods. "What an occupation!" he lamented. "To sit at your desk flaying your fellow man, and then to offer him the skin and expect him to buy it. Like a starving hunter who cuts off the tail of his dog, eats the flesh on it, and feeds the dog the bone—the dog's own bone."[5]

2

Although the cruel caricature of Geijerstam and the screed against Rydberg evened old scores, Strindberg's purpose in lampooning them was to entice the main force of the opposition out into the open where they would show their true colors. It was his way of challenging the establishment. He knew he was at his best when he was in the midst of battle, and although he would tremble before a bill collector, he showed absolutely no fear in attacking literary moguls, political bosses, business magnates, scientific authorities, religious gurus, and even God himself. "I don't write in order to be known as a poet," he said at the beginning of his career; "Writing is my way of fighting."[6] And at the end of it he said, "I fight; therefore I live" (SS, 51:92). He saw himself sometimes as Laocoön raging against Apollo and as Jacob wrestling with God but mostly as Loki, the eternal rebel, the irrepressible troublemaker, constantly subverting the pantheon and always refusing to become part of it. "You have the power; I have the word. I have the word in my power" (SS, 13:28).

With these words, he flung down the gauntlet to the establishment in 1883 in a poem of insurrectionary exultation, "Loki's Calumnies" ("Lokes smädelser").

The motive behind this belligerence was not the masochist's desire to be knocked down and humiliated, although that is what happened to Strindberg. It was the moralist's anger at the Boetian indifference of human beings to the injustice in the world. It was also the dramatist's instinctive desire to create a scene. Clearly, he could hardly admit this last motive without alienating his moralistic supporters. As always, an esoteric reason existed alongside the exoteric. He had to color his deepest motives by reproaching himself for what he called his reflex actions when others provoked him. But in the same breath he admitted that these "reflex actions" were indispensable for his development as an artist.[7] In the story about Stig Storverk's son he could more forthrightly suggest the close relationship between his art and his outrageous acts. Great art and a bad conscience have often kept shop together, but with Strindberg, the partnership was synergetic in the sense that the need to create created the outrage. For him, there could be no art without intensity of feeling, and like Henry James, he could argue that there was a strict dependence of the moral sense of a work of art on the amount of felt life that went into its making.

Strindberg could not have written the Chamber Plays in 1907 if he had not calumniated Rydberg and Geijerstam in 1904. The second great creative outburst of his life had come to an end, diminuendo, with the lyrical autobiographical novel *Alone*, a slim volume of Andersen-like fairy tales, and an unfinished cycle of plays on world history—all written in 1903. In the same year, new ideas began to float about in his mind, ideas touching on all aspects of modern culture, amorphous ideas without a center. He recorded them in the form of conversational sketches that he called "preludes and fugues." (Later these sketches took the form of an omnium-gatherum, the *Blue Books*.) He saw the new cultural front as the advancing tide of mercantilism and irreligion and felt that he had been shunted into the past and put among the naturalistic writers of the 1880s who had nothing to say to the present generation. Fuming, he girded his loins and ventured into the battlefield by writing *Gothic Rooms* and *Black Flags*, the latter so unsparing in its abuse and so flagitious in its personal animosity that it took Strindberg nearly three years to find a publisher for it. With these works, calculatingly planned to be as offensive as possible to the literary and political pantheon, he set out on the third stage of his journey as an artist.

But they carried him only a short way toward his goal as an artist. Although they glow with moral zeal and bristle with indignation at a world gone wrong, they are intellectually flabby and esthetically untidy, with some of the "preludes and fugues" being roughly pressed into service. Strindberg could not tone up his new thoughts to the ultimate degree of artistic refinement and definition until the inner emotional pressure was made equal to the outer cultural pressure. He tried to accomplish this by compressing his thoughts about earthly justice into a couple of novelettes, *The Roofing Festival* (*Taklagsöl*) and *The Scapegoat* (*Syndabocken*). These are superb examples of narrative art, but they lack the range and vision of the two novels. What had been gained in intensity and form had been lost in breadth. Next, he considered rewriting *The Roofing Festival* as a monodrama,[8] which would not have required much work since the story is itself interior monologue, the transcription of the thoughts and memories of a dying man dosed with morphine. Still nothing came of it. At about the same time he made an effort to adapt "The Saga of Stig Storverk's Son" for the stage. Again the drama failed to materialize. Greater inner pressure was needed, and that was supplied by Harriet Bosse.

Legally divorced from her in 1904, Strindberg continued to live with her constantly in his thoughts, to have sexual intercourse with her occasionally, and to enjoy whenever possible the company of the child she had borne him. Near the end of 1906 and in the first weeks of 1907, his feelings toward her cooled, perhaps because he could sense from her demeanor what others already knew: that she had found another man, closer to her in age than Strindberg and, since he was an actor, closer to her professionally. Now the Strindbergian volcano erupted and poured hot ashes on Harriet's head. He immediately set to work on his first Chamber Play, *Storm Weather*, in which Harriet's infatuation with her actor is reflected in the degrading affair of the divorced wife with a gambler and ne'er-do-well. Having found its vent, Strindberg's long-gathering resentment against the world and its injustices spread its lava in the succeeding four or five months over the whole of bourgeois society. (See figure 8.)

3

In the cooling-off period that followed, Strindberg wrote several more plays, none of which belong in the front rank of his works. The dramatic impulse had exhausted itself, and another chapter in his life was drawing to a close. When Harriet married the actor, Strindberg moved from the apartment he had shared with her to another one less elegantly situated. He pawned his library of three thousand volumes for 400 kronor to keep the Intimate Theatre afloat.[9] In the spring of 1908 he concluded the third volume of his *Blue Books* with a description of the Isle of the Dead. In July 1908, he made the final entries in his *Occult Diary*, closing the books on his psychological speculations. And at the end of the year he wrote a lyrical drama, *The Black Glove* (*Svarta handsken*), in which he reaffirmed his belief in the primacy of spirit over matter and in the inevitability of justice in the affairs of men, however deviously it must make its way.

He labeled it Opus 5 among his Chamber Plays, and on dramaturgical grounds, it belongs with the others,[10] though it has little in common with them thematically. It is of the same length and represents yet another mode of drama: a fairy play for adults. The time is Christmas; the setting is an apartment house. This house is a modern tower of Babel in which there is a confusion of values, not tongues, and two of its occupants are taught a lesson in ethics by the Spirit of Christmas, who appears in the shape of a woman in white with stars in her hair. Present also—omnipresent, in fact—is the Christmas elf, who creates disorder as a means of setting everything right. Before the play is over, a selfish lady who treats her maid harshly will be punished for her haughtiness and disregard of others, and a taxidermist who has spent sixty of his eighty years looking for the answer to the riddle of the universe, working on the assumption that there is a unity of all matter, will learn that he has failed in his pursuits because he has ignored the spirit that informs matter. "Where you thought you perceived the law of nature," the elf tells the stuffer of dead bodies, "you now shall meet the maker of the law. . . . Where once you saw rude nature and the monsters of chance, you now will apprehend beings no different from you" (SS, 45:313–14). The stories of the lady and the taxidermist are plaited together by means of the black glove, which is lost by the lady, found by the old man, and employed by the elf to teach them that the universe is dualistic and that happiness lies in helping others.

By adding *The Black Glove* to the other Chamber Plays, Strindberg recanted the pessimism he had voiced in *The Ghost Sonata* and *The Pelican* and reverted to an earlier position. The plot recapitulates the great conversion of the Inferno period, and the moral harks back to *A Dream Play*. The taxidermist is the glazier all over again.

The next play he wrote, the last that he was ever to write, suggests even more strongly that Strindberg was closing up his shop. *The Great Highway (Stora landsvägen)*, which bears the descriptive subtitle "seven stations in the life of a wanderer," takes its hero from the Alps to the Last Gate and finally to the Dark Wood, where to the tune of Chopin's Nocturne 13 opus 48 no. 1, he dictates to his maker the inscription for his tombstone.

Here rests Ishmael, son of Hagar,
Once called Israel because he
Prevailed on God to fight with him,
And who did not give up until laid low,
Conquered by His almighty goodness.
Nor, Eternal One, shall I let go your hand,
Your hard hand, until you bless me.

Bless me, your human creature,
Who suffers from the life you gave;
Me first, who suffered most,
Suffered most the pain of not being
The human being I wanted to be. [SS, 51:100]

If one did not know the order in which these two last plays were written, *The Black Glove* would seem to make a more fitting epitaph and final confession than *The Great Highway*, which is certainly not the drama of a man trying to make his peace with the world. The sentimental treacle of *The Black Glove* has turned into bitter gall, and the hard hand that is felt throughout the play is not the Lord's but Strindberg's own striking his enemies. The seven stations of this un-Christian via dolorosa are stations in which the sufferer avenges himself on those who have wronged him. On the road to Damascus, Strindberg was pursued by the Wild Huntsman; in *The Great Highway*, Strindberg calls himself the Hunter.

There is in this play little of the conciliatory spirit usually found in last testaments, at least in literary ones, because it was not meant to be the last word of an exhausted author. This pilgrim's progress is a transitional work between two stages of the artist's progress. The Dark Wood represents worldliness, as in Dante, and implies the beginning of another journey into the Inferno. The Hunter's epitaph intimates death but presages rebirth. Through the agency of the gods, Strindberg had given himself three lives, with an outrageous act marking the beginning of each. That arrangement had been made in 1905. By the end of 1908, the three lives had been used up, and Strindberg was still alive and kicking. To take a new lease on life, he would have to commit another outrage. In *The Great Highway*, the Hunter is beating the bush, trying to rouse the game.

4

What fields were left that he had not hunted in? He had scandalized good society by publicizing the intimate details of his married life as no gentleman would do; he had dumbfounded the scientific community by disowning Darwin and by embracing Swedenborg as no educated man in his right mind would do; and he had offended the arbiters of culture, upholders of tradition, and national patriots by lampooning them as self-seeking hypocrites, corrupters of justice, and moral idiots, as Alceste might have done but as no enlightened man of the world with some sense of the ridiculous would ever do. After having offended in marriage, madness, and misanthropy, how else could he offend?

The political events of 1909 came as a godsend to him. When the conservatives won at the polling booths, the workers responded by going out on strike—a general strike that disrupted the economic life of Sweden. Strindberg took his stand with the workers. This was not surprising since he had always been opposed to the conservatives and had consistently attacked the vested interests. He had lived his whole life as an outsider. The members of the social and political establishment abhorred him and had ostracized him for encouraging sexual immorality among the young, for debunking Sweden's national heroes, and for degrading human beings in general. Their position was that an artist was obliged to picture the ideal and to uphold the eternal spiritual values. Strindberg was, of course, more highly idealistic than any of them and knew that what the establishment meant by the ideal was what was ideal for them: the preservation of their way of life. He put the matter succinctly in a jingle he wrote in 1883:

What's heavenly and divine
They said I had no respect for.
True! For isn't it divine
To be rich and still expect more? [SS, 13:12]

Since Strindberg refused to support the established order, the established order refused to recognize him as a creative artist and looked upon his fame as mere notoriety. A cartoon that appeared in 1898 in Sweden's leading humorous magazine shows how far Strindberg was beyond the pale of literary respectability. The cartoonist, Albert Engström, who certainly harbored no ill feelings toward Strindberg, placed the most highly esteemed literary figures on ascending plateaus of Mount Parnassus.[11] At the top sit Verner von Heidenstam and Oscar Levertin, the Castor and Pollux of the antinaturalistic movement, which they coyly insisted was not a movement but a plea for individualism. In fact, it was the Swedish equivalent of the English aesthetic movement and, like it, emphasized the cultivation of talent and beauty. Somewhat lower down the slopes of Mount Parnassus are Gustaf af Geijerstam, who had made his reputation with naturalistic novels, and Axel Lundegård, who had once collaborated with Strindberg in rewriting *Comrades*. There are a dozen other literary lights in the drawing, but nowhere, not even on the lowest slopes, is Strindberg to be found.

Flying above Parnassus is a winged creature, Apollo Musagetes, the leader of the Muses, in the likeness of C.D. af Wirsén, the doyen of Swedish literary critics since 1880 and the head of the Swedish Academy. The eighteen members of the academy distributed certain government funds to worthy writers and, after 1900, named each year's winner of the Nobel Prize for literature. It had pointedly never given an award or grant of any sort to Strindberg, even in the 1890s when he had to be sustained financially with money collected by friends and admirers through a public appeal. The reason for the academy's indifference, explained Wirsén, was that "Strindberg has still not repented,"[12] meaning that Strindberg had not abased himself before the academy for having written and published *A Madman's Defense*. A number of years later when William Butler Yeats came to Sweden to receive the Nobel Prize, the attitude of the academy was unchanged. Yeats was told that, although Strindberg was the Shakespeare of Sweden, the academy "could not endure his quarrels with his friends nor the book about his first wife."[13]

The scandal that attaches to Strindberg's name for his sometimes scurrilous treatment of well-known and possibly better deserving people is insignificant compared to the stigma that has fastened on the academy for the contempt and scorn with which it treated him year after year. Although the academy presumably awarded artistic merit, its decisions were heavily influenced by what it considered moral considerations. It could have said so and at least been honest; instead, it played politics and was both hypocritical and obtuse.

When Strindberg skirmished with the establishment in 1904 and 1905, impartial observers thought he was being no less hypocritical.

Even though his ostensible concern was with the materialism and Darwinism that were making themselves felt in every aspect of life, his jeremiads seemed to be directed at easily identifiable personalities rather than at the larger issues, and though he had Swedenborg and the angels of heaven as his witnesses, his motives smacked of envy and jealousy. Which was perfectly understandable in a middle-aged writer who did not rate a place even in the shadow of Mount Parnassus.

The circumstances were different in 1909. In the first place, he was now able to support himself by his writing, for the first time since the early 1880s; he did not need to rely on the kindness of friends, and he was in a position to thumb his nose at government grants. Money in itself had never meant much to him; he was proud of the purity of his motives. "I know how I should have written to make writing profitable," he said, "but I congratulate myself for not having written that way" (SS, 54:238). Obsessed by his art, he was in debt nearly all his life, and when money did come his way, most of it went immediately to pay old obligations. Even when he was able finally to cancel all his debts and have some money left over, he plowed it back into his art. In 1907, when his income for the year suddenly soared to 32,000 crowns, he unhesitatingly invested 19,500 in the Intimate Theatre[14] and promptly lost them. Still, having money to lose was better than having no money at all. By 1909, his financial position was secure.

Moreover, the growth of his income from royalties was evidence that he had a broadening base of support in the common people, especially in the younger generation, while the good will shown toward him on his birthday in January 1909 convinced him that the support was as deep as it was broad. Although he had totally alienated himself from the official taste-makers, he now felt more than ever that the path he had chosen had been the right one. He had taken enormous artistic risks in his career and made great sacrifices, human as well as economic, while others had found the climb up Parnassus eased for them with money and favors. There was a growing awareness on the part of the workingman that the cultural arbiters were the isolated ones, removed from the life of the people, and that Strindberg, in spite of his mysticism and exotic beliefs, had always been deeply immersed in the life around him. The fundamental sympathies of the man who called himself the son of a servant when he could just as legitimately have called himself the son of a merchant had always, except for a brief flirtation with Nietzsche, been with the common people. In the novel The Red Room (1879), he had exposed the moral rot in the pillars of society; in his history of the Swedish people

(1882), he had written a history of the oppression of the lower classes; in his long poem *Sleepwalking in Broad Daylight* (*Sömngångarnätter på vakna dagar*, 1883), he had charged the governing classes with the neglect of moral concerns in favor of esthetic concerns; and in his history plays written after the Inferno crisis, he had again affirmed his belief that the only meaningful progress was the result of the labors of the common man. Consequently, no one should have been surprised when Strindberg aligned himself with the workers in the political turmoil that followed in the wake of the general strike of 1909. What astonished everyone was his ability to make himself the center of controversy and to arouse a whole nation (see figure 5).

He managed this feat by committing the fourth great outrage of his life. In April 1910, acting on an invitation that had been extended four years earlier, Strindberg submitted to the liberal Stockholm newspaper *Aftontidningen* an article on the cultist adulation of Charles XII, Sweden's warrior king of the eighteenth century. He entitled it "Pharaoh Worship" and in place of payment asked that it be printed without any editorial interference. This was the first of about eighty articles that he published in two Stockholm newspapers in 1910 and 1911, articles that provoked the most violent literary controversy in Sweden's history and that could not have fomented such intense passions and shaken so much of the country if it had been merely a literary quarrel. "Pharaoh Worship," which struck everybody at first as ineffective sniping at an indestructible monument by a man whose aim was no longer good, had in fact been conceived with admirable tactical skill. Like a well-placed piece, it simultaneously raked two of the enemy's files with fire.

Heidenstam, who sat at the top of the Swedish Parnassus, had written in 1897 and 1898 a lyrical prose work, *The Charles Men* (*Carolinerna*), which some enthusiasts had extolled as the greatest piece of creative writing in the Swedish language. It depicted Charles XII as a tragic figure pursuing a mysterious destiny in which Sweden was called upon to make immense sacrifices. Three years later, in 1901, Strindberg had had his say on the subject in his drama on Charles XII. Although the two royal portraits may appear to be very similar when viewed by foreigners, there is a radical difference between them when seen with Swedish eyes. The king that Heidenstam portrays is a glamorous figure, fascinating in his power to compel a nation to commit heroic deeds even against its will and estimable for his military skill and personal fortitude. Strindberg's king is a bully who ravages Europe and impoverishes Sweden; his play is a Hitler-in-his-bunker sort of play. Heidenstam's portrait of the

king was naturally the one that appealed to the establishment. They bought it and gave Heidenstam a token of their appreciation. On the two volumes of *The Charles Men* he climbed a bit higher up Parnassus, and while Heidenstam was awarded an honorary degree by the University of Uppsala, Strindberg found himself in the Dark Wood at the end of *The Great Highway*.

By attacking the cult of Charles XII, Strindberg not only fired at Heidenstam, who occupied the center of the literary citadel; he also got in a few shots at the government troops. Charles XII, who had caused all Europe to tremble, was the idol of Swedish chauvinists, and in "Pharaoh Worship," Strindberg underscored the connection between the worship of Charles and modern militarism.

In the articles that followed, Strindberg besieged the establishment from every side, usually by taking aim at particular individuals. After having fired his squib at Heidenstam, he ambushed Sven Hedin, the world-famous explorer, by producing an eighteenth-century map of Tibet that recorded certain places that Hedin claimed to have discovered in the 1890s.

The response to Strindberg's onslaught was entirely predictable. He was accused of envying the success enjoyed by the cultured and aristocratic Heidenstam and by the adventurous and recently ennobled Hedin.

One critic proposed that the Swedish nation should give Strindberg a fitting monument by erecting a statue to him in which he would personify *Invidia*.[15] Another critic made the same point somewhat less elegantly by calling Strindberg "a base, envious, clumsy mudslinger, and nothing more."[16] Hedin defended himself against Strindberg's denunciations and then gave vent to his personal feelings.

When Strindberg writes criticism, he personifies the crude rabble. What he produces will not outlive the moment, and during its brief existence its place is in the gutter and the toilet.

What a pity! Because Strindberg does have a phenomenal talent. But he also has a rotten character, an amazing mixture of Titan, sphinx, vampire, and parasite. Like the jackal, he prefers corpses [a reference to his attack on the dead Rydberg], but will also have a go at the living, as long as they cannot bite.[17]

By letting it be inferred that he himself was one of those toothless and harmless creatures whom Strindberg found it safe to attack, Hedin let his emotions get the better of his reason. Silence would have destroyed Strindberg; when the establishment defended itself by calling him names, he knew that his strategy was working. Never one to spare feelings, mince words, or chop logic, Strindberg was a formidable pamphleteer and polemicist, a master of invective, reckless in his accusations but with an unerring instinct for the jugular. What at first had seemed like a quixotic skirmish with imaginary enemies turned out to be a well-planned campaign against the entrenched interests, and within two months of the time he had marched out alone to do battle, he had transformed the sedate Swedish cultural scene into a beerhouse brawl. He no longer stood alone. He had become a rallying point for the discontented laboring classes, and a host of writers and commentators had joined forces with him. The first collection of his newspaper articles, published with the title *Addresses to the Swedish Nation* (*Tal till svenska nationen*), echoing the title of Fichte's *Reden an die deutsche Nation*, went through several printings in two months.

His greatest victory came when the controversy had been raging for a year. Although Heidenstam had figured in the article that had started the whole affair, he had sensibly remained aloof from the battle, preferring to let his young disciples defend his position and reputation. Finally, however, he too came into the field with two articles that attracted extraordinary attention and brought the controversy to its climax. After upbraiding Strindberg for resorting to the use of insults and ad hominem arguments, Heidenstam went on to describe him as the full-blooded barbarian in our culture. . . . The civilizing forces are hateful to him, heart and soul. . . . Driven by hate, he is totally lacking in that humble love of the truth that is above the personal. That is to be found only in the man of culture. But Strindberg, his ice-gray eyes peering mistrustfully upwards, is a runaway slave.[18]

Nothing could have pleased this runaway slave more than to see the aristocratic Heidenstam stooping to sling mud with the other brawlers. In descending from his perch on Parnassus, Heidenstam made a tactical error, becoming vulnerable on all sides. His adherents had accused Strindberg of envying Heidenstam's literary accomplishments; now it was Heidenstam who was accused of envying Strindberg's popularity. Although Heidenstam thought he had written the epos of the Swedish people, the people were gathering around Strindberg. "It must be difficult for Heidenstam," wrote one of the participants in the debate, "to learn that Strindberg in spite of being the son of a servant, perhaps just because of that, captures the attention of a whole nation, and that his collected articles, ridiculed by all intelligent persons, are reprinted ten times in only a couple of months."[19]

Moreover, Heidenstam's remarks disclosed the fundamental nature of the conflict between him and Strindberg. It was, as Strindberg had known since 1885,[20] a class conflict. By implying that Strindberg's achievements as playwright and novelist were somehow vitiated and nullified by his being a barbarian and a slave—a fugitive slave, no less—Heidenstam exposed the nexus between politics and literature, between social class and esthetic ideals.

The more the establishment critics endeavored to undermine Strindberg's reputation and character, the more irresistibly did the facts implant themselves in the public consciousness. First, Strindberg was unquestionably Sweden's most fertile literary genius. Second, he had never received any official recognition for his creative work. Third, Heidenstam and a host of nonentities had received such recognition in various ways. The inevitable question prompted by these incontestable facts was, Why had not Strindberg been honored?

The mentality that found it inappropriate to recognize Strindberg's genius because he was a runaway slave and behaved to his betters like a guttersnipe was the mentality that dominated the heart and soul of the literary establishment, the Swedish Academy. When the academy had the opportunity of awarding the Nobel Prize to Ibsen, Zola, or Tolstoy, they gave it to Sully-Prudhomme, a member of the French Academy; to Bjørnson, who professed his belief in the good, the true, and the beautiful; and to Sienkiewicz for having written *Quo Vadis*. But not to Ibsen, who had professed anarchist sympathies in the 1890s; not to Zola, who had arraigned the French military establishment for its bigoted treatment of Dreyfus; nor to Count Tolstoy, who had betrayed his class, given away his property, and was preaching pacifism.

Nobel's purpose in establishing the prizes in literature and in other fields was to further the cause of peace and to promote the brotherhood of man, and when the academy failed to confer the first Nobel Prize on Tolstoy, a group of Swedish writers and artists, including Strindberg, protested to the academy and apologized to the great Russian on behalf of the Swedish people. In a newspaper article in 1903, Strindberg scoffed at the academy—"an illiterate society" of "archeologists, philologists, theologists, and histologists" (SS, 54:410–11)—and later, during the great debate of 1910 and 1911, he praised Tolstoy for exposing modern war as an invention of the upper classes. "When the revolutionary pressure from below becomes too intense, threatening the upper classes, then war relieves the pressure" (SS, 53:484).

5

The great debate that Strindberg had opened made the literary wrangle a skirmish in the class conflict, precisely as he had expected. In July 1910, the third month of the feud, a workingman named Adolph Lundgrehn, making note of the fact that Strindberg had no chance of being elected to the academy or of being awarded the Nobel Prize, proposed in an open letter that the Swedish people should give a special prize to Strindberg for his contributions to the cultural life of his country.

"From the time of his trial for *Married* [in 1884] to the present," wrote Lundgrehn,

even glimmers of recognition for his Herculean labors are practically non-existent. That the Swedish Academy [of eighteen immortals] is closed to him is perhaps no cause for sorrow in him or in others now that it has become a disgrace to belong to it. Strindberg is immortal anyway. But that he was passed by when the Nobel Prize was awarded is an insult not only to him but to Swedish literature and to wide sections of the public both in and outside our country who have come to feel a growing respect for the master in work after work, and a growing love for the characters he has created.[21]

It was this suggestion of a special prize for Strindberg that unleashed the wrath of the establishment, and from the moment it was made, the controversy became overtly political. In April 1911, Heidenstam published *The Decline and Fall of Proletarian Philosophy* (*Proletärfiloso-fiens upplösning och fall*) in which he reprinted his animadversions on Strindberg. At the same time there appeared in the leading daily papers an appeal, signed by 217 writers, artists, musicians, actors, scientists, and members of parliament, for contributions to a special Strindberg fund to be presented to the author on his next birthday, January 22. In part it read:

With Strindberg begins a new era in Sweden's cultural history, and his works mirror our land and our people more variously and graphically than that of any other writer. His robust spirit has given our literature works that shall continue to be a force in times to come through their steadfast idealism, their manly courage, and their penetrating knowledge of life. He has ranged from the depths of the human soul to its heights. He has descended into the fiery abysses of life at its most painful and risen to the sunlit realms of love and redemption. His inquisitive mind, ever seeking the truth, has never been satisfied with ready-made answers. Through his life and works runs a strain of moral self-examination and an intense feeling for human justice and human suffering. August Strindberg is the true creator of our national drama, and in his plays are to be found the richest possible variety of characters from different times and different social classes. He is the great renewer of Swedish prose, and his books speak a Swedish that is forceful, precise, and of incomparable freshness. No one is more intimate with the genius and temper of the Swedish language than he. His works already form an inseparable part of our heritage and, because of their inner truth and artistic power, are making their way beyond our borders. Future generations, far and wide, shall find in them a witness to the life and struggles of our times.[22]

Forty thousand people[23] responded to this appeal and subscribed 45,000 crowns, most of it in small amounts sent in by workingmen. For a man who had never shown much respect for money, and who now needed it less than ever before, 45,000 crowns was not the most fitting form of recognition. But since it was intended as an anti-Nobel Prize, the gesture would have been less pointed if it had not taken the same form as the Nobel Prize.

The gift was presented to Strindberg on his sixty-third birthday by a three-man delegation, which included Hjalmar Branting, the leader of the Social Democratic Party. Strindberg's first words to them were, "Don't look so damn solemn." All day long, bouquets of roses were delivered to him. In the evening, the members of the Stockholm Workers Union marched in a torchlit procession through Stockholm and gathered in the street below Strindberg's apartment. He made a brief appearance on his balcony, holding the hand of his nine-year-old daughter. When the crowd below began to shout hurrah, she strewed roses over them. The gesture was so appropriate that Strindberg followed suit, answering the shouts of the people with roses.[24] The symbolism of the moment was felicitous and the occasion unique in Swedish history. Other writers had received medals from the monarch, stipends from the administration, honorary degrees from the universities; only Strindberg received his award of merit directly from the people.

On the following day, he sent his thanks to the Social Democratic Party. "Now that I have finally found my true self once again and my true position, which, because of my occupation as a writer, could not be a firm one, you know where I stand, and consequently all your doubts must vanish."[25]

6

It was now nearly two years since Strindberg had inaugurated the fourth phase of his evolution by writing "Pharaoh Worship," and, predictably, his thoughts began to turn to the drama. The newspaper articles he had written performed the same function as the short stories and novels of the previous phases. In these articles, he was free to range widely over all areas of modern life, recognizing its complexity without having to compress it into a bold and encompassing symbol.

"I am old," he told his newspaper editor in May 1910. "Have no time to lose. Find it hard to wait since I feel I still have left unsaid so much that might clarify my unclear position both in literary and other matters."[26]

He looked upon the world as continually changing.

Having grown old (and venerable), I should, according to tradition, become conservative, but I don't seem able to. I don't even understand how older people can become conservative. How can one believe in maintaining the established order when nothing is established. Everything is in flux, everything changes. How many philosophies and systems haven't I seen collapse and give way to others in my time? Laws, even holy writ itself, have been annulled by parliaments and governments; customs and ideas about what is fitting and right have all changed; attitudes and ways of thinking about those above and those below, parents and children, man and wife, master and servant, have all been disturbed. How then can anyone set much store on an order that is not really established now and was only temporarily so, fifty years ago? [SS, 53:509–10]

When the laboring class bestowed the anti-Nobel Prize on him, Strindberg began to outline a play about Robespierre and the French Revolution to be called "The Bloody Bread" ("Det blodiga brödet"). On his rebellious nature the French Revolution had exerted a life-long attraction. In his 1903 essay on historical cycles, he had said that that cataclysmic chapter in European history had comprised events "both beautiful and ugly, but on the whole beautiful, and in the final view utterly sublime" (SS, 54:380). Undoubtedly his drama would have combined political and religious themes. He was highly censorious of socialist reform programs as vulgarizations of the Christian ideal, rooted as they were in a materialist philosophy, and he hailed Cromwell and Robespierre as great revolutionaries because they were religious men (SS, 53:19).[27]

The play was never written. In April, Strindberg learned that he had inoperable cancer of the stomach, and he died a month later, on Tuesday afternoon, May 14, 1912. The funeral ceremonies were delayed until Sunday to allow ordinary workingmen to take part in them. Thousands of the laboring class marched, along with hundreds of university students and a large number of members of parliament. Eight workingmen of imposing stature served as pallbearers. The king of Sweden sent a laurel wreath. As for the Swedish Academy, it took no notice whatsoever of the death and burial of Sweden's greatest writer. (See figures 9 and 10.)

7

In his native country, Strindberg has always been looked upon as a political figure, a publicist and controversialist as much as dramatist and storyteller. In this respect, his position in Sweden is comparable to Shaw's in England. When he was a young man in the 1880s, Strindberg made the terms upper class and lower class resound through the nation, and he died in the midst of a political confrontation between the left and the right, a confrontation inflamed and exacerbated in no small way by his writings. Even his sexual battles were politically colored because he insisted on underscoring the connection between class structure and social morality. The feminist movement in his view was "an aristocratic movement, a political upper-class movement, in which women were employed as agitators," and he cautioned his feminine readers that beneath the rosy promise of their emancipation lay the expectation of another kind of submission and a new thralldom (SS, 17:87). For him there could be no meaningful change in women's social position without a political upheaval. In his last altercation with capitalism and the upper class, the sexual element was replaced by religious concerns without any loss in the vehemence with which he carried on his war against the "established" social order.

In Germany, on the other hand, Strindberg was accepted as a religious writer, exposing the vices of a materialistic age. In the dark years before the First World War, his reputation mushroomed. By the time of his death, two hundred editions of various Strindberg works had been printed in Germany,[28] and the number of performances of his plays skyrocketed after Reinhardt's impressive production of *The Dance of Death* in 1912. For a decade or so, he was the most frequently staged dramatist in Germany. But his plays disappeared from the German stage as suddenly as they had arrived. His popularity coincided with the rage for expressionism, and his visionary plays were interpreted exclusively as dramas of man's soul—metaphysical dramas, not Freudian ones. He was reproached by some commentators for having diverted attention from the essential social questions to transcendental ones, as at the end of *A Dream Play*. For them, as for Brecht, Strindberg was the poet of the middle class.[29]

Yet another Strindberg emerged in France in the 1920s. It was the deranged Strindberg, the poet of the Inferno, who appealed to Cocteau, Artaud, and the surrealists.[30] Outside that circle, he won little recognition in France, partly because the Germans had so thoroughly made him over in their own image.

In England and America, he had even worse luck. He came on the scene just at the time when Ibsen was being installed as a literary classic and enshrined as the saint of the feminists and liberals. Compared to the stolid and rational Norwegian, Strindberg seemed like a cranky upstart. How could one take seriously a misogynist who married three times, as if he could not get enough of a bad thing?

Everywhere, in Europe as well as America, in his homeland and abroad, there was bound to be a misunderstanding of Strindberg as long as a part of the man was taken for the whole. But there was another reason for the general failure to understand his thought and to appreciate his artistry, especially in the drama. Whereas it was easy to relate the form of Ibsen's plays to the standard drama of the past, Strindberg's seemed to lack form, and this was taken to mean that, though there were flashes of insight in them, they contained no coherent philosophy. He was misunderstood because what he saw and experienced and intuited required new forms of expression. He fashioned the most experimental group of plays in the history of drama not because he hoped to revolutionize the theatre but because the world as he comprehended it was not the world that other dramatists had dealt with. In traditional Western philosophy, it was thought possible to encompass the universe in a definite conceptual scheme governed by certain basic laws connecting observable phenomena in a cause-and-effect relationship. All the evidence amassed by modern scientists, especially those working in the outer reaches of physics, has all but annihilated that possibility, at least for the time being. The failure of scientists to develop any comprehensive theory explaining the behavior of subatomic particles releasing high energies and traveling extremely short distances has produced a crisis in the study of matter that can only be resolved by casting out the deterministic laws of classical mechanics and constructing another domain, a substratum of the world the nineteenth century thought was absolutely fundamental.

Strindberg endeavored to chart that elusive substratum by surveying both the physical and psychological realms.

Body and soul are not two different things, but only two different ways of perceiving the same thing. Similarly, physics and psychology are only different attempts to link our experiences together by way of systematic thought.[31]

These are the words of Albert Einstein, jotted down in 1937, but they might have been written by Strindberg, who was the first writer to see the disintegration of the atom and the dissolution of the ego as parallel events auguring a new concept of the cosmos, and perhaps because he was present at the birth of it, he succeeded better than anyone else has so far done in giving dramatic form to this new concept. The twentieth-century thinker knows that the relationship of events to one another has become so complicated that ordinary equations cannot express them. Robert Musil in his epic novel *The Man without Qualities* abandoned the old narrative techniques because they could not represent the modern world any more than Euclidean geometry could picture Einstein's universe. For Musil, life appeared to be "an endless system of relationships" in which

there were no longer any such things as independent meanings, such as in ordinary life, at a crude first approach, are ascribed to actions and qualities. In this system the seemingly solid became a porous pretext for many other meanings; what was happening became the symbol of something that was perhaps not happening but was felt through the medium of the first.[32]

In order to see the world in all its complexity, Strindberg kept changing his point of view, circling around his subject until he had seen it from all sides. The contradictions in his thought reflect the contradictions of a relativistic world and an evolving life. Where his critics saw inconsistency Strindberg saw progress. "All my writing," he said when still young, "is the record of a constant changing of beliefs, from the worse to the better; a disavowal of my former, homespun self; a struggle against the old ideals (prejudices); and that is why I am so much at odds with myself, so full of contradictions" (SS, 17:18).

When he could not resolve the contradictions in a single work, he let them stand unresolved in two separate works. Both A Dream Play and Queen Christina were planned and written right after Harriet Bosse had walked out on him. In the first play, she appears as a heavenly being who tries to raise men to her level through the power of love. In the second, she becomes the flirtatious, self-centered woman who makes a game of love and who enjoys seeing men on their knees before her. Easter and The Dance of Death were both written in October 1900, but into the first went compassion and forgiveness; into the latter, malice and vengefulness.

Nor is the comic side lacking in this many-sided man, though one often hears it said that he had no sense of humor. This is because most of his humor went into his stories and poems, and by the time he had succeeded in forging the material into drama, much of the laughter had been hammered out of it. The successive versions of Comrades, for instance, become progressively less funny; and he moved on from Comrades to The Father. But the young, rebellious Strindberg was essentially a comic writer, totally without respect for great men and revered social institutions. As a social satirist and political agitator, admiring Dickens and Mark Twain, he made his humor serve a moral cause, and his wit was not that of a free spirit. His Ariel remained enslaved to Prospero. A jest was a weapon to him, and, like Shaw, he believed that a joke was an earnest in the womb of time. Unlike Shaw, however, he did not wish to have a reputation as a comic writer and carefully guarded his image as a solemn thinker, knowing that the public hates to be confused. "Once you are branded as a jester," he said, "the public will laugh at your tragedies."[33]

Naturally, the feminists in the 1880s found as little to laugh at in Strindberg's jokes as did the capitalists, militarists, and academicians in 1910. Humor is not an absolute; it has its seasons and its history. Strindberg's sense of the comic acquired a different philosophical basis during his Inferno crisis. Before that, his jokes were made at society's expense. The Inferno experience, which some would say reduced him to a humorless madman, actually caused him to see life as a divine comedy. After

1896, there were moments when he saw that his whole life was a vast joke played on him by a god who was a prankster and a confidence man (SS, 28:191).[34] "How can one help not believing that the gods are playing a joke on us mortals?" he asked. "That is why some of us, snickering because we are in on the joke, can laugh in the midst of our worst torments. How can anyone be expected to take seriously what is so manifestly a gigantic joke?"

When the Germans took him most seriously, he was most humorous. His sense of the comic was, admittedly, not one that most people could share. It was part and parcel of the new reality that he had encountered. It was humor energized by anxiety and torment. At a certain point, his gravity became so enormous that it collapsed under its own weight and disappeared into something like those black holes of outer space to emerge instantly in another reality as antianxiety and antitorment. It is the kind of comedy that flashes out unexpectedly in *To Damascus* and makes the ending of *The Dance of Death*, Part One, an existential jest. Passing through his Inferno, Strindberg moved beyond tragedy and comedy into a no-man's-land where contending forces meet and opposites are joined. This kind of humor is not unlike Chekhov's in some respects but is perhaps closer to Jewish humor. Laughter is miraculously heard just when there is nothing to laugh about. The humor of the Inferno is romantic humor to a large extent, what Jean Paul called "the sublime inverted." But Strindberg passed beyond this. The romantic, melancholy humorist learned to amuse himself with the thing that caused his sadness; Strindberg obliterated it.

He said of himself that when he showed his teeth, it was hard to tell whether he was about to smile or bite (SS, 51:19). Beneath this characteristic ambiguity, this unnerving humor, lay the absolute indifference of the inexhaustible poet and creator. He insisted that his life was a succession of lives, a series of experiments, an examination of different attitudes and philosophical postures. "I don't hold any opinions," he said;

my views are impromptu. Life would be pretty monotonous if one thought and said the same things all the time. We've got to keep it new and fresh. One's whole life, after all, is only a poem, and it is much more pleasant to float over the swamp than to stick one's feet in it to feel for solid ground where there isn't any.[35]

Like a god who finds he does not like the world he has made, Strindberg more than once discarded what he had created and made a new world for himself. When he had stripped sex and marriage of their richest ores, he quarried the unconscious. When finally, after more than twenty years of labor, he grew tired of building a paradise around an Eve who was both madonna and mistress, he threw her into the fire at the end of *The Pelican*, burned down the house in which she had ruled and exercised her powers, and ran into the streets to join the workers on the barricades and to help them build a new social order.

Only his creative powers constituted reality for him. The physical world was a stage set, illusory and changeable, and life, a scenario that could be rewritten. Nothing in the theatre of life was permanent, not even the deepest anguish. Strindberg is "proof against anything," said an acquaintance, "because he is more sound than he thinks he is, and there is no core within him to destroy." [36] He said of himself that he could not be utterly depressed by a sorrow because he felt that "life was not entirely real." [37] Sooner or later, he would find himself laughing at his own wretchedness, and this divine insouciance was the source of his resilience.

Although he was thin-skinned and extremely sensitive, the wounds he suffered and the tragedies he endured were like those of the actor who knows that the dagger is wooden and that he who dies must rise for the curtain call. He lived most intensely and was most happy when he was writing. Then the difficulties and pains of living were converted into the joys of creating. When the horrors became unbearable, he made them unreal. The world became a poem and a dream, and since it made more sense in that form, the poem in turn became the reality.

But there could be no art without life, and Strindberg practised his craft by constantly transforming the water of everyday experience into poet's wine. In his *Occult Diary* he kept a record of these little miracles, which to the ordinary mind seem like ordinary events, even when Strindberg embroidered them for the benefit of less poetic minds, as he did in the incident of the pressed trousers. One day when the rain was pouring down, he had to call on his publisher. Strindberg possessed only two pairs of trousers, one new and clean, the other old and barely presentable. Which should he wear? He decided on the better pair, went out into the rain, saw his publisher, returned home, took off his wet and muddy trousers, and hung them up to dry. Back at his desk, he thought more about those trousers than about his writing. What a fool he had been to put on the good pair! And then when he glanced round to look at them, there they were pressed and cleaned, as good as new. A miracle!

Strindberg told this anecdote to his friend Albert Engström, the humorist, who was a little vexed that Strindberg should try to impose on his intelligence with such an inane story. It was obvious that Strindberg's maid had come in, had seen the dirty trousers, and had cleaned and pressed them. Strindberg replied to Engström, "You're impossible! You're a simple realist, and that's why nothing ever happens to you." [38]

Confusing mechanics with meaning, Engström missed the point of the incident. Strindberg knew how the trousers had been restored to their original state; what delighted him was to see an unspoken wish become solid reality. "I trembled as one does before a miracle," he wrote in the *Diary*, "but smiled at the ridiculousness of it at the same time. Still, I took it as a friendly gestre from the 'unseen,' a sign of approval." [39]

When there was no sign of approval, no little miracle to make poetry out of an unhappy fact, he performed the greater miracle of transforming reality into its opposite.

Do you know what makes life bearable to me? It is that every now and then I convince myself that life is only half real, a bad dream inflicted on us as a punishment, and that at the moment of death we awaken to the true reality, becoming aware that the other was only a dream—all the bad things one had done, only a dream. In that way the remorse vanishes with the act itself, which had never really been committed. That is redemption, salvation. [SS, 28:316] [40]

In his last play, in the role of the Hunter lost in the Dark Wood, he said, "*I have no existence; only what I have created does*" [SS, 51:92]. On his deathbed, before slipping off into his last sleep, he echoed these words. "Don't bother about me," he told the nurse who attended him; "I no longer exist." [41] It was a good exit line for the actor who had played many parts and who now, having made his life into a poem and reality into a dream, was himself about to become pure spirit.

ABBREVIATIONS AND SHORT TITLES

SS. August Strindberg, *Samlade skrifter*, ed. John Landquist, 55 vols. (Stockholm, 1912–20).

Brev. August *Strindbergs brev*, ed. Torsten Eklund, 15 vols. (Stockholm, 1948–).

Inferno, 1966. Strindberg, *Inferno*, ed. C. G. Bjurström (Paris, 1966).

Légendes, 1967. Strindberg, *Légendes*, ed. C. G. Bjurström and Georges Perros (Paris, 1967).

Vivisektioner, 1894. Strindberg,. *Vivisektioner*, ed. Torsten Eklund (Stockholm, 1958). Written in 1894.

Occult Diary. Strindberg, *Ockulta Dagboken* (Stockholm, 1977). Published in facsimile.

NOTES

PREFACE

1. Torsten Eklund, "Från Riddarholmen till Blå tornet," *Meddelanden från Strind-bergssällskapet*, no. 21 (April 1957), pp. 1–21.
2. Strindberg to Meijer, 11 December 1890, in Uno Willers, *Strindberg om sig själv* (Stockholm, 1968), pp. 35–36.

CHAPTER 1

1. Victoria Benedictsson [Ernst Ahlgren], *Dagboksblad och brev*, ed. Axel Lundegård, 2 vols. (Stockholm, 1928), 2:184.
2. See Evert Sprinchorn, "Brandes and Strindberg," *The Activist Critic: A Symposium on the Political Ideas, Literary Methods and International Reception of Georg Brandes* (special issue of *Orbis Litterarum*), eds. Hans Hertel and Sven Møller Kristensen (Copenhagen, 1980), pp. 109–26.
3. Strindberg to Bonnier, 4 January 1885, *Brev*, 5:7.
4. See Anna von Philp and Nora Hartzell, *Strindbergs systrar berätta om barndom-shemmet och om bror August* (Stockholm, 1926).
5. Thomas Rymer, "A Short View of Tragedy," *Dramatic Essays of the Neoclassic Age*, ed. Henry Hitch Adams and Baxter Hathaway (New York, 1950), p. 146.
6. Edmond and Jules de Goncourt, *Préfaces et manifestes littéraires* (Paris, 1888), p. 54.
7. Axel Lundegård, *Några Strindbergsminnen knutna till en handfull brev* (Stockholm, 1920), pp. 114–15.
8. Karin Smirnoff, *Så var det i verkligheten* (Stockholm, 1956), p. 100.
9. Carl Ludwig Schleich, *Hågkomster om Strindberg*, trans. Gust. Lindelof (Stockholm, 1917), p. 47.
10. Strindberg to Schering, 2 April 1907, *Brev*, 15:356. To his daughter Kerstin he wrote in 1909, "But I'm a writer, and for me life is only material for dramas—generally tragedies." Strindberg, *Brev till min dotter Kerstin* (Stockholm, 1961), p. 164.
11. Strindberg to Schering, his German translator, 6 May 1907. Strindberg, *Från Fjärdingen till Blå tornet*, ed. Torsten Eklund (Stockholm, 1946), p. 382.
12. A. Jolivet, *Le Théâtre de Strindberg* (Paris, 1931), pp. 349–50.

13. Strindberg to Bonnier, 21 June 1886, *Brev*, 5:356–57.

14. Strindberg to Bonnier, 9 August 1886, *Brev*, 6:18.

15. Strindberg to Bonnier, 22 December 1887, *Brev*, 6:335.

16. Karl Otto Bonnier, *Bonniers. En bokhandlarefamilj*, 5 vols. (Stockholm, 1930–56), 4:161.

17. Strindberg to Pehr Staaff, 5 August 1887, *Brev*, 6:241.

18. Strindberg to Axel Strindberg, 13 June 1887, *Brev*, 6:223.

19. Strindberg to Lundegård, 17 October 1887, *Brev*, 6:282.

20. Strindberg to Lundegård, 12 November 1887, *Brev*, 6:298.

21. For a discussion of the various narrative techniques that Strindberg employs, see Sven Rinman, "En dåres försvarstal," *Svensk litteraturtidskrift* (1965), pp. 63–75.

22. Strindberg to Hansson, 20 February 1891, *Brev*, 8:188.

23. Smirnoff, *Så var det i verkligheten*, p. 203.

24. Strindberg to von Heidenstam, 22 November 1885, *Brev*, 5:211.

25. Strindberg to Axel Strindberg, 13 June 1887, *Brev*, 6:223.

26. Strindberg to Dörum, September 1871, *Brev*, 1:80.

CHAPTER 2

1. Strindberg to Zola, 29 August 1887, *Brev*, 6:262.

2. See Strindberg to Zola, 29 August 1887; *ibid.*, and the discussion in Børge Gedsø Madsen, *Strindberg's Naturalist Theatre* (Seattle, 1962).

3. Knut Hamsun in his contribution to *En bok om Strindberg* (Karlstad, 1894) pointed out that the asymmetrical set derived from impressionistic painting and from German stage experiments (pp. 25–26).

4. On the influence of the French pantomime, see Carl-Olof Gierow, *Documentation—Evocation. Le Climat littéraire et théâtral en France des années 1880 et "Mademoiselle Julie" de Strindberg* (Stockholm, 1967), pp. 65–90, 129–32. More relevant to *Miss Julie* than anything Gierow mentions is the use the duke of Saxe-Meiningen made of pantomime in his production of Molière's *The Imaginary Invalid*. He substituted for Molière's intermezzo between acts 1 and 2 a scene in pantomime in which the maid makes the bed and puts the room in order. Thus he avoided an act curtain in the same way Strindberg did in *Miss Julie*. The duke first staged Molière's play in 1874, but it was kept in the repertory when the Meiningen company toured Europe.

5. See André-Paul Antoine, "Le Naturalisme d'Antoine: Une Légende," *Réalisme et poésie au théâtre*, ed. Jean Jacquot (Paris, 1960), pp. 233–40.

6. Strindberg to von Heidenstam, 5 October 1886, *Brev*, 6:78.

7. In his 1909 pamphlet *Öppna brev till Intima teatern* Strindberg says that in Sweden the wing-and-drop set was in use up till 1880. Since the box set was in use much earlier in Scandinavia, as early as the 1830s in Copenhagen, he evidently means that by 1880 the closed-in set had completely replaced the wing-and-drop for interior scenes at the principal theatres.

8. Wilhelm von Humboldt, "Uber Goethes Hermann und Dorothea," *Wilhelm von Humboldts Gesammelte Schriften*, ed. Albert Leitzmann, 15 vols. (Berlin, 1903–18), 2:133.

9. Emile Zola, "Proudhon et Courbet," *Mes Haines. Causeries littéraires et artistiques* (Paris, 1880), p. 25.

10. Strindberg to Josephson, 8 October 1884, *Brev*, 4:341. The locomotive had appeared on the Scandinavian stage in the 1870s for the climax of *Arbetaren*, Lorentz Dietrichson's play about George Stephenson, the inventor of the steam locomotive. The commode would shortly be seen in August Lindberg's production of *The Wild Duck*.

11. Letter written about 6 March 1889, *Brev*, 7:263.

12. Yeats said that he met Strindberg in Paris and that it was in his company that he "heard for the first time of stage scenery that might decorate a stage, and suggest a scene while attempting nothing that an easel painting can do better." ("The Bounty of Sweden," *The Autobiography of William Butler Yeats* [New York, 1953], pp. 327–28.) Early in January 1897, shortly after this meeting, Yeats wrote to Fiona Macleod, "My own theory of poetical or legendary drama is that it should have no realistic, or elaborate, but only a symbolic or decorative setting. A forest, for instance, should be represented by a forest pattern and not by a forest painting. One should design a scene which would be an accompaniment, not a reflection, of the text." (*The Letters of W. B. Yeats*, ed. Allan Wade (London 1954), p. 280.) Two or three years later, Yeats saw these ideas given reality in the settings designed by Gordon Craig for Purcell's operas.

13. Strindberg to Lundegård, 17 October 1887, *Brev*, 6:282–83.

14. Strindberg to August Falck, 23 December 1887, *Brev*, 6:337.

15. See Strindberg to Schering, 14 June 1905, *Brev*, 15:135; and Strindberg, *Öppna brev till Intima teatern* (1909), *SS*, 50:290. Craig in his account, "A Visit to August Strindberg," *The Listener*, 10 January 1957, pp. 53–54, misdates the visit and has it taking place in 1907.

16. Strindberg to August Falck, 1 April 1908, *Strindberg och teater. Bref till medlemmar af gamla Intima teatern* (Stockholm, 1918), p. 38.

17. Strindberg to Alexandersson, 23 April 1908, *Strindberg och teater*, p. 44.

18. Strindberg to Falck, 18 August 1908, *Strindberg och teater*, pp. 70–71.

19. Arno Holz, "Die Kunst—Ihr Wesen und ihre Gesetze," *Arno Holz Werke*, ed. Wilhelm Emrich and Anita Holz, 7 vols. (Berlin-Spandau, 1962–64), 5:14.

CHAPTER 3

1. See the preface to *Miss Julie* and Strindberg to Edvard Brandes, 4 October 1888, *Brev*, 7:130; and Strindberg to Georg Brandes, 4 December 1888, *Brev*, 7:192.

2. See Lennart Josephson, *Strindbergs drama Fröken Julie* (Stockholm, 1965), pp. 232–35.

3. Strindberg to af Geijerstam, 7 January 1899, *Brev*, 13:63. The relevant passage is quoted below in the footnote to page 250.

4. "Introduction to *Fröken Julie*," *August Strindbergs dramer*, ed. Carl Reinhold Smedmark, 4 vols. (Stockholm, 1962–70), 3:290.

5. Strindberg to Georg Brandes, 29 November 1888, *Brev*, 7:184.

6. Strindberg to von Heidenstam, 21 September 1885, *Brev*, 5:170.

7. *Vivisektioner*, 1894, pp. 36–37.

8. Paul Lafargue, "Le Matriarcat, Etude sur les origines de la famille," *La Nouvelle Revue* 39 (15 March 1886): 301–36. Before proceeding to an analysis of the *Oresteia*, Lafargue gives credit to Bachofen (*Das Mutterrecht*, 1861), L. H. Morgan (*Ancient Society*, 1877), and Engels (*Der Ursprung der Familie*, 1884) as the formulators of the new theory of man's prehistory, and to Vico as a precursor who recognized a sexually promiscuous stage in the development of primitive society.

9. Strindberg would also have read Georg Brandes's foreword to the second edition (1885) of the Danish translation of John Stuart Mill's *The Subjection of Women*, in which Brandes summarized the argument of Engels's *The Origin of the Family*. Completely in tune with Strindberg's thought was Brandes's remark that monogamy does not arise from a reconciliation of man and woman but, on the contrary, out of a conflict of the sexes hitherto unknown in history. (Brandes, *Samlede Skrifter*, 18 vols. (Copenhagen, 1899–1910), 12:54–59.)

10. See also Strindberg to Hansson, 10 March 1889, *Brev*, 7:274, in which he writes, "Misogyny . . . can never be treated poetically, but must always remain philosophy. *The*

Father still comes under the poetic because it contains the worship of woman (that is, the overvaluation of woman's qualities), the cult of mother."

11. Martin Lamm, *Strindbergs dramer*, 2 vols. (Stockholm, 1924–26), 1:281.

12. Bertha was to be the central figure in the trilogy. She appears as the child in the first part, *The Father*. In the second play, *Marauders* (a version of *Comrades*), she is a married woman. The third part, which was never written, was to be a comedy ending with the reconciliation of the warring spouses. See Strindberg to Cederborg, 29 August 1887, *Meddelanden från Strindbergssällskapet*, nos. 59–60 (May 1978), p. 25; and *Brev*, 6:165.

13. Strindberg to Lundegård, 17 October 1887, *Brev*, 6:282.

CHAPTER 4

1. Strindberg to Bonnier, 21 August 1888, *Brev*, 7:105.

2. The major studies of this period in Strindberg's life are Gunnar Brandell, *Strindbergs Infernokris* (Stockholm, 1950) (English translation: *Strindberg in Inferno*, trans. Barry Jacobs (Cambridge, Mass., 1974)); and Göran Stockenström, *Ismael i öknen: Strindberg som mystiker* (Uppsala, 1972). For an informal account of Strindberg's activities, social, scientific, and artistic, during the crucial years, see my introduction, "Strindberg from 1892 to 1897," *Inferno, Alone, and Other Writings* (New York, 1968).

3. Strindberg to Hansson, 23 October 1891, *Brev*, 8:361.

4. Strindberg to Littmansson, 22 July 1894, *Brev*, 10:152.

5. Samuel Butler, *Luck, or Cunning, As the Main Means of Organic Modification?* rev. ed. (London, n.d.), p. 8. Cf. Bernard Shaw, preface to *Back to Methuselah*, *The Bodley Head Bernard Shaw Collected Plays with Their Prefaces*, 7 vols. (London, Sydney, Toronto, 1970–74), 5:300, 318.

6. Strindberg to Frida Uhl, 16 January 1895, *Brev*, 10:361.

7. Strindberg to Frida Uhl, February 1895, *Brev*, 10:386.

8. Strindberg to Hedlund, 23 August 1896, *Brev*, 11:307.

9. Strindberg to Hedlund, (?) October 1895, *Brev*, 11:89.

10. Ernst Haeckel, *The History of Creation*, 5th English ed. 2 vols. (New York, 1911), 2:497–98.

11. Strindberg to Mörner, 31 May 1894, *Brev*, 10:68.

12. *The Riddle of the Universe at the Close of the Nineteenth Century*, trans. Joseph McCabe (New York and London, 1900), p. 90.

13. Ibid., p. 4.

14. Ibid., ix.

15. Strindberg to Frida Uhl, 22 May 1895, *Brev*, 11:16.

16. Holger Drachmann et al., *En bok om Strindberg* (Karlstad, 1894), p. 33.

17. Strindberg to Bergh, 26 November 1894, *Brev*, 10:314.

18. *Vivisektioner*, 1894, p. 106 ff.

19. See also "Etudes funèbres," *Inferno*, 1966, pp. 85–86.

20. See also *Inferno*, 1966, p. 57.

21. Strindberg to Hedlund, 21 June 1896, *Brev*, 11:219.

22. Strindberg to Hedlund, ca. 10 April 1896, *Brev*, 11:157.

23. Strindberg said, "Thoughts are the deeds of the emotions" (*SS*, 46:193). Was he echoing and modifying Nietzsche? "Thoughts are but the shadows of our feelings—always obscurer, emptier, and simpler." Friedrich Nietzsche, *Die fröhliche Wissenschaft* (sec. 179), *Werke in drei Bänden*, ed. Karl Schlecter, 2d ed., 4 vols. with index (Munich, 1960–65), 2:145.

24. See also *Inferno*, 1966, p. 55.

25. See also *Légendes*, 1967, p. 25.

26. Strindberg to Prager, 12 June 1896, *Brev*, 11:210.

27. Strindberg to Hedlund, 11 July 1896, *Brev*, 11:261.

28. See also *Inferno III, Légendes*, 1967, p. 180.

29. Strindberg to Thaulow, ca. 23 July 1896, *Brev*, 11:285.

30. Quoted in *The Autobiography of William Butler Yeats* (New York, 1953), p. 189.

31. Maeterlinck, "The Tragical in Daily Life," *The Treasure of the Humble*, trans. Alfred Sutro (London, 1907), p. 119. Maeterlinck's essay first appeared in *Le Figaro* with the title, "A propos de Solness de Constructeur." Revised and lengthened, it was reprinted as "Le Tragique quotidien" in Maeterlinck's collection of essays, *Le Trésor des humbles*, in 1896. The 1894 version appeared in Norwegian translation in *Verdens Gang*, 7 April 1894.

32. Strindberg to Mörner, 7 October 1894, *Brev*, 10:276.

33. Leo Berg, *Der Ubermensch in der modernen Litteratur* (Paris, Leipzig, and Munich, 1897), p. 124.

34. Edgar Steiger, *Das Werden des neuen Dramas*, 2 vols. (Berlin, 1898), vol. 1: *Henrik Ibsen und die dramatische Gesellschaftskritik*, p. 82.

CHAPTER 5

1. Stellan Ahlström, *Strindbergs erövring av Paris* (Stockholm, 1956), p. 272.

2. Strindberg to Schering, 14 October 1902, *Brev*, 14:219. The essay was printed in *Zukunft*, 11 October 1902.

3. See also *Inferno*, 1966, p. 130.

4. Later these notes were more securely stored in a chest, but "The Green Sack" remained the generic name for Strindberg's scientific notes. See *Brev*, 9:206–07, 287; *Brev*, 13:184; *Brev*, 14:181–82, 229; *SS*, 46:222, 341, 343; and Strindberg, *Klostret*, ed. C. G. Bjurström (Stockholm, 1966), p. 74.

5. Strindberg to Hedlund, 23 March 1896, *Brev*, 11:143.

6. Strindberg to Hedlund, 29 April 1896, *Brev*, 11:177–78.

7. Strindberg to Hedlund, ca. 22 February 1896, *Brev*, 11:133.

8. Nietzsche, *Die fröhliche Wissenschaft* (sec. 319), *Werke*, 2:186.

9. Rimbaud, *Oeuvres complètes*, ed. Antoine Adam (Paris: Bibliothèque de la Pléiade, 1972), pp. 249–51.

10. Strindberg wanted "Sensations détraquées" to serve as the introduction to *Inferno* and *Legends*. See Strindberg to Bröchner, 5 May 1899, *Brev*, 13:105.

11. Carl Du Prel, *Det dolda själslifvet, eller, Mystikens filosofi*, 2 vols. (Stockholm, 1890), 1:111–24, 132.

12. Strindberg to Hedlund, 19 July 1896, *Brev*, 11:275.

13. See also *Inferno*, 1966, pp. 119–21. Strindberg in his diary noted with interest a newspaper article describing the effect that tobacco and absinthe consumption had on Musset. Musset would go into a kind of trance, and in that condition, while still at his table in the restaurant, he would write poetry, and, having written, he would be helped off to bed by an obliging waiter. See *The Occult Diary*, February 1901.

14. For the effect that absinthe may have had on Strindberg's behavior and on his writings, see Bo Bäfverstedt and Erik Carlsson, "Strindberg, alkohol och absint," *Recip Reflex*, nos. 2–4 (1975) (with a bibliography of earlier items on the subject), and Sven Stolpe, *August Strindberg* (Stockholm, 1978), pp. 135–44.

15. See also *Légendes*, 1967, pp. 78–79. Originally in the essay "L'Irradiation et l'extension de l'âme," printed in the July 1896 issue of *L'Initiation*. The passage from *Jardin des plantes* (*SS*, 27:208) is quoted below on p. 86.

16. See, for example, Strindberg to Hedlund, 28 August 1896, *Brev*, 11:308.

17. See Orvar Nilsson, "Dr. Anders Eliasson, Strindbergs vän," *Från Ystadsspråk till Strindbergsdrama*, eds. Sven Carlquist and Nils Olsson, Ystads Fornminnesförenings Skrift, no. XI (Ystad, 1966), p. 118.

18. See "Sulfonal," *La Grande Encyclopédie. Inventaire raisonné des sciences, des lettres et des arts*, 32 vols. (Paris, 1886–1902), 30:694. Strindberg to Hedlund, 1 December 1896, *Brev*, 12:5.

19. See editor's notes in *Brev*, 11:136, 138. In all Strindberg received 1,200 kronor, some of which went to pay off debts he had accumulated in Paris. The 1,200 kronor was about as much as he would have made from the publication of a book, and more than he would have made as an ordinary workingman.

20. See also *Légendes*, 1967, p. 78. Originally printed in the essay "L'Irradiation et l'extension de l'âme" (1896).

21. Strindberg to Hedlund, 17 May 1896, *Brev*, 11:195.

22. See also *Vivisektioner*, 1894, pp. 36–55 and *Inferno*, 1966, pp. 133–35.

23. *Occult Diary*, June 18, 1896, *Brev*, 11:215–17, 223, 227, 232, 234, 237. *Inferno*, 1966, pp. 125–29. *SS*, 28:76–79.

24. Strindberg to Eliasson, 26 June 1896, *Brev*, 11:227.

25. Strindberg to Torsten Hedlund, 18 June 1896, *Brev*, 11:212.

26. Strindberg's version of the Philps's visit can be pieced out from his letters. See *Brev*, 11:209, 212, 215, 227, 260, 286. His sister's account is in *Strindbergs systrar berätta om barndomshemmet och om bror August* (Stockholm, 1926), pp. 76–80.

27. The original version, called "Ave Spes Unica," was rejected by the editors of the periodical *Gil Blas* in the autumn of 1895. The paragraphs in question are to be found in *Inferno*, 1966, pp. 77–78; and in *SS*, 27:667–68. When the essay was later translated into Swedish, Strindberg excised these paragraphs.

28. Sverker Hällen, "Vem förföljde Strindberg? Kryptogram blev utmaning," *Ystads Allehanda*, 19 September 1970. Translated into French, "Qui donc poursuivait Strindberg? (Un cryptogramme menaçant)," *Obliques* (Revue trimestrielle), no. 1 (1972), pp. 62–68.

29. This and the other quotations in this paragraph are from Strindberg to Hedlund, 6 July to 20 August 1896, *Brev*, 11:236, 261, 282, 293, 301, 304.

30. Strindberg to Littmansson, 4 October 1902, *Brev*, 14:217.

31. Strindberg, preface to *Samlade romaner och berättelser* (Stockholm, 1899), n.p.; and Strindberg to af Geijerstam, 5 August 1899, *Brev*, 13:176.

CHAPTER 6

1. Ronald Hingley, *Chekhov* (London and New York, 1950), p. 233.

2. "The Tragical in Daily Life," *The Treasure of the Humble*, trans. Alfred Sutro (London, 1907), pp. 99, 105–06.

3. Ibid., p. 105.

4. "Mystic Morality," *The Treasure of the Humble*, pp. 71–72. This essay appeared first in *La Nouvelle Revue*, June 1895.

5. *Vivisektioner*, 1894, p. 71.

6. *Samlade otryckta skrifter*, 2 vols. (Stockholm, 1918–19), 2:127–45.

7. Strindberg to Bergh, 30 January 1901, *Brev*, 14:16–17.

8. See also "Nemesis divina," *Vivisektioner*, 1894, p. 51.

9. Goethe, *Aus meinem Leben, Sämmtliche Werke*, ed. Karl Goedeke 15 vols. (Stuttgart, 1881), 9:613.

10. See also *Inferno III, Légendes*, 1967, p. 180.

11. See also *Occult Diary*, 4 June 1898.

12. See also *Occult Diary*, 23 February 1898.

13. Strindberg to Hedlund, 23 July 1896, *Brev*, 11:289.

14. Henry Maudsley, *The Physiology and Pathology of the Mind* (New York, 1871), p. 193.

15. Strindberg, *Klostret*, ed. C. G. Bjurström (Stockholm, 1966), p. 58.

16. *Introduction à l'étude de la médecine expérimentale*, ed. R. P. Sertillanges, 8th ed. (Paris, 1917), p. 75.

17. Jerome Bruner, "Psychology and the Image of Man," *Times Literary Supplement*, 17 December 1976, p. 1590.

18. Strindberg to Eliasson, 28 October 1896, *Brev*, 11:369.

19. Freud, *The Origins of Psycho-Analysis: Letters to Wilhelm Fliess, Drafts and Notes: 1887–1902*, ed. Marie Bonaparte, Anna Freud, and Ernst Kris, trans. Eric Mosbacher and James Strachey (London, 1954), p. 236.

20. Bruner, "Psychology and the Image of Man," p. 1591.

21. See Stockenstrom, *Ismael i öknen*, p. 284.

22. *Inferno III, Légendes*, 1967, p. 173.

23. Strindberg's summary of the story of Zanoni is in his letter to Marie Uhl, 23 February 1897, *Brev*, 12:80.

24. H. Taine, *De l'intelligence*, 2 vols. (Paris, 1914), 1:278. Originally printed in 1869, *De l'intelligence* was revised several times by Taine. The passage I have quoted seems to have been added in one of the editions published after 1875.

25. Du Prel, *Det dolda själslifvet*, vol. 1, chap. 3.

26. Strindberg to af Geijerstam, 17 March 1898, *Brev*, 12:279.

27. *To Damascus* is a late, and perhaps culminating, version of the circular plot that romantic writers used to represent the spiritual journey of man. In early romantic literature the return of the traveler to his starting point symbolized the reunion of the individual soul with universal nature. M. H. Abrams in his study *Natural Supernaturalism* (New York, 1971) gives numerous examples of this sort of journey.

28. Meister Eckhart, *Selected Treatises and Sermons*, trans. James M. Clark and John V. Skinner (London, 1958), p. 170 (trans. slightly revised).

29. See also *Inferno*, 1966, p. 132.

30. See also *Inferno*, 1966, p. 132.

31. Freud, "Zur Psychotherapie der Hysterie," *Gesammelte Werke* 18 vols. (vols. 1–17, London, 1940–52; vol. 18, Frankfurt am Main, 1968), 1:272.

32. R. D. Laing, *The Politics of Experience* (New York, 1967), p. 101.

33. Rev. 5:9: "And they sung a new song, saying, Thou art worthy to take the book and to open the seals thereof: for thou wast slain." Also, on the last page of *To Damascus*, the Woman says, "The mountains hide," evidently in allusion to Rev. 6:16.

34. *Klostret*, p. 116.

35. In an interview with the Danish journalist Georg Bröchner in 1899; first printed in *Svenska Dagbladet*, 20 May 1912. Quoted here from Thérèse Dubois Janni, *August Strindberg, En biografi* (Milan, 1970), p. 229.

36. Strindberg to af Geijerstam, 2 November 1897, *Brev*, 12:191.

37. Emil Kléen, *August Strindberg: Mannaår och ålderdom*, ed. Stellan Ahlström and Torsten Eklund (Stockholm, 1961), p. 140. Originally in *Malmö-Tidningen*, 7 April 1898.

38. See also *Inferno*, 1966, p. 218.

39. Strindberg to Harriet Bosse, 19 November 1900, *Brev*, 13:337.

CHAPTER 7

1. See also "Etudes funèbres," *Inferno*, 1966, p. 87. Originally printed in *Revue des revues*, 15 July 1896. Strindberg may have been quoting secondhand from Du Prel, *Det dolda själslifvet*, 2:177.

2. See also *Inferno*, 1966, p. 235.

3. See also *Inferno*, 1966, p. 167.

4. Goethe, *Sprüche in Prosa, Sämmtliche Werke*, ed. Karl Goedeke (Stuttgart, 1881), 2:530.

5. Strindberg mentions Swedenborg in February 1896 only as a mineralogist who also delved into the spirit world. Not until the following May does he acquire a larger understanding of Swedenborg, by reading Balzac's Swedenborgian novel *Séraphita*. In August, he read excerpts from Swedenborg's writings, and in September, he was ready to praise Swedenborg as a great visionary. See Strindberg to Hedlund, ca. 15 February, 15 May, and 17 September 1896, *Brev*, 11:132, 192, 327.

6. Strindberg to af Geijerstam, 17 March 1898, *Brev*, 12:279.

7. *Heaven and Its Wonders and Hell*, trans. J. C. Ager (New York, 1949), n. 551 (hereafter cited as *Heaven and Hell*).

8. Ibid., nn. 343, 507, 512.

9. Ibid., nn. 89, 90, 510, and *Arcana coelestia (The Heavenly Arcana)*, ed. John Faulkner Potts, 12 vols. (New York, 1949–70), n. 687.

10. See Stockenström, *Ismael i öknen*, pp. 83, 400, 413, 505–06.

11. See also *Légendes*, 1967, p. 88.

12. Sartre to *Dagens Nyheter*, Stockholm, 28 January 1949, on the occasion of the Strindberg centenary.

13. On the influence of *The Dance of Death* on *No Exit*, see Anthony Swerling, *Strindberg's Impact in France 1920–1960* (Cambridge, 1971), pp. 90–100.

14. Heinz Herald, *Max Reinhardt* (Berlin, 1915), pp. 182–83.

15. *Heaven and Hell*, n. 553.

16. August Falck, *Fem år med Strindberg* (Stockholm, 1935), p. 282.

17. *Heaven and Hell*, n. 506.

18. *Arcana coelestia*, n. 2441; cf. *Arcana coelestia*, n. 8487, and *Heaven and Hell*, n. 561.

19. On the faces of those in hell, see Swedenborg, *Heaven and Hell*, n. 457.

20. Kela Kvam, "'Dødsdansens' danske førsteopførelse," *Teatervidenskabelige studier*, ed. Svend Christiansen (Copenhagen, 1969), 1:102.

21. *Heaven and Hell*, n. 296.

22. On what the sea signifies: *The Apocalypse Revealed*, trans. John Whitehead, 2 vols. (New York, 1949), n. 238. On casting into hell: *Heaven and Hell*, n. 510.

23. Adolf Winds, *Der Schauspieler in seiner Entwicklung vom Mysterien–zum Kammerspiel* (Berlin, 1919), p. 270.

24. Gunnar Ollén, *Strindbergs dramatik*, rev. ed. (Stockholm, 1966), p. 180.

25. Strindberg to Schering, 31 January 1902, *Brev*, 14:169.

CHAPTER 8

1. Gunnar Ollén, *Strindbergs dramatik*, rev. ed. (Stockholm, 1966), p. 124.

2. On the chemists congress, see Strindberg to Prager, 19 June 1896, *Brev*, 11:215; and Strindberg to Jolivet-Castelot, August 1896, *Brev*, 11:296. On the night cafés, see Gunnar Brandell, "Chineur och timmerman," *Meddelanden från Strindbergssällskapet*, nos. 40–41 (May 1968), pp. 9–12; and A. Jolivet, *Le Théâtre de Strindberg* (Paris, 1931), p. 250.

3. Strindberg to Kléen, 9 July 1898, *Brev*, 12:335.

4. Jung, *Aion: Researches into the Phenomenology of the Self*, 2d ed., *The Collected Works of C. G. Jung*, ed. Gerhard Adler, Michael Fordham, and Herbert Read, trans. R. F. C. Hull, 20 vols. (New York and Princeton, 1953–79), vol. 9, pt. 2, p. 8.

5. Ibid., p. 9.

6. Ibid., p. 13.

7. The material in this paragraph draws on Jolande Jacobi, *The Psychology of C. G. Jung*, 8th ed. (New Haven, 1973), pp. 107–08, 114–26.

8. Material from Frieda Fordham, *An Introduction to Jung's Psychology* (Harmondsworth, England, 1953), pp. 61–63.

9. See Stockenström, *Ismael i öknen*, p. 380.

10. Strindberg to von Bülow, 1 April 1898, *Brev*, 12:285.

11. "Commentary on *The Secret of the Golden Flower*," *Collected Works*, vol. 13, *Alchemical Studies* (Princeton, 1967), 35.

12. In *Inferno*, Hedlund is called "a messenger employed by Providence, a paraclete." *Inferno*, 1966, p. 131. See also *SS*, 28:82.

13. See note 22, chap. 5.

14. See also *Légendes*, 1967, p. 77.

15. Eliphas Levi, *Transcendental Magic: Its Doctrine and Ritual*, trans. A. E. Waite (London, 1896), p. 51.

16. Jungian interpretations of Strindberg's writings are to be found in Guy Vogelweith, *Le Psychothéâtre de Strindberg* (Paris, 1972); and in Eric O. Johannesson, *The Novels of August Strindberg* (Berkeley and Los Angeles, 1968).

17. Strindberg to Kléen, 9 July 1898, *Brev*, 12:335.

18. Ibid.

19. *Arcana coelestia*, n. 1108.

20. *Arcana coelestia*, nn. 1883, 1884. See also *SS*, 28:289–90.

21. If he is to be believed, Strindberg's own experiences of being transported in spirit to another place rivaled Swedenborg's. See the essay "L'Irradiation et l'extension de l'âme," *Légendes*, 1967, pp. 73–79; *SS*, 28:273–82.

22. Nietzsche, *Die fröhliche Wissenschaft* (sec. 333), *Werke*, 2:193.

23. *Divine Wisdom*, n. 252.

24. *Heaven and Hell*, n. 440.

25. See also *Inferno*, 1966, p. 186.

26. *Heaven and Hell*, n. 182.

27. *Divine Wisdom*, n. 276.

28. See also *Légendes*, 1967, pp. 40–41; cf. Stockenström, *Ismael i öknen*, p. 228; and editor's note in *Brev*, 12:274.

29. *Arcana coelestia*, n. 968.

30. *Inferno*, 1966, p. 241; *SS*, 28:199.

31. Unpublished essay, written November 1897; quoted in Martin Lamm, *Strindberg och makterna* (Stockholm, 1936), p. 94.

32. *Arcana coelestia*, n. 1977.

33. *Divine Wisdom*, n. 186.

34. Ibid., n. 189.

35. On the letters as a dramatic device, see Stockenström, *Ismael i öknen*, pp. 357–59.

36. Swedenborg, *The Earths in the Universe, Miscellaneous Theological Works*, trans. John Whitehead (New York, 1970), n. 137. The Stranger himself refers to "that green witch's dress that bewitched me one day between the café and the church on a Sunday afternoon," *To Damascus*, Part Two, scene 9(*SS*, 29:230). Cf. *Légendes*, 1967, p. 103; *SS*, 28:312.

37. See also *Légendes*, 1967, pp. 87–88.

38. "Réponse à une enquête," *L'Hyperchimie*, December, 1897. Quoted here from A. Mercier, "Auguste Strindberg et les alchimistes français," *Revue de littérature comparée*, 43 (1969): 39.

39. Swedenborg, *The Earths in the Universe*, n. 79.

40. *Arcana coelestia*, n. 5893.

41. *Arcana coelestia*, n. 696.

42. See also *Légendes*, 1967, p. 78.

CHAPTER 9

1. See Stockenström, *Ismael i öknen*, pp. 358–59 and p. 534, n. 73.

2. *Occult Diary*, 11 February 1901.

3. See Gunnar Ollén, *Strindbergs dramatik*, pp. 196–98.

4. *Divine Providence*, n. 307.

5. See Howard James Jensen, "Swedenborgian and Other Religious Influences upon Strindberg's Dramatic Expressionism" (Ph.D. diss., Wayne State University, 1972), p. 89.

6. This scene superficially resembles the sections in Swedenborg's *Conjugial Love* (*The Delights of Wisdom Pertaining to Conjugial Love after Which Follow the Pleasures of Insanity Pertaining to Scortatory Love*, trans. Samuel M. Warren, rev. Louis H. Tafel [New York, 1971]) in which the angels in a mountain setting discourse on chaste and scortatory love (nn. 74–82). The mercury and sulphur used in treating the luetic patients have both medical and symbolic significance, as Strindberg further explains in *En blå bok I* (SS, 46:375–78).

7. In *Conjugial Love*, Swedenborg writes, "Two married partners most commonly meet after death, recognize each other, consociate again, and for some time live together; which takes place in the first state, that is, while they are in externals as in the world. . . . But successively, as they put off things external and come into their internals, they perceive the quality of the love and inclination which they mutually had for each other, and then perceive whether they can live together or not." (nn. 45, 48).

8. Jung, "The Phenomenology of the Spirit in Fairytales," *Collected Works*, vol. 9, pt. 1, *The Archetypes and the Collective Unconscious* (New York, 1959), 219 n. 14.

9. On Klemming's psychological significance for Strindberg, see Johan Mortensen, *Strindberg som jag minnes honom* (Stockholm, 1931), pp. 46–47; my edition of Strindberg, *Inferno, Alone, and Other Writings* (New York, 1968), p. 166 and n., p. 268 and n.; and Gunnar Brandell, *Strindberg in Inferno*, trans. Barry Jacobs (Cambridge, Mass., 1974), pp. 5–6 (*Strindbergs Infernokris* pp. 10–11).

10. See also *Légendes*, 1967, p. 109.

11. Gunnar Ollén, *Strindbergs dramatik*, pp. 212–13.

CHAPTER 10

1. Strindberg to Schering, 13 May 1902, *Brev*, 14:187.

2. Diebold, *Anarchie im Drama* (Frankfurt am Main, 1921), pp. 205–10.

3. See Martin Lamm, *August Strindberg*, 2d ed. rev. (Stockholm, 1948), pp. 293, 301, and Helmut Müssener, *August Strindberg "Ein Traumspiel"*, Meisenheim am Glan, 1965 (Deutsche Studien #4), pp. 29–30, 53–54.

4. *Strindbergs dramer*, 2:318.

5. *Occult Diary*, 6 September 1901. Strindberg later noted that Hegel had also remarked on the conjunction of the organs of love and excrement.

6. Strindberg to Aulin, 20 January 1908, *Från Fjärdingen till Blå tornet. Ett brevurval 1870–1912*, ed. Torsten Eklund (Stockholm, 1946), p. 389.

7. See Vagn Børge, *Strindbergs mystiske Teater* (Copenhagen, 1942), p. 194 fn.

8. The idea of a lawyer as the embodiment of humanity's miseries may have come to Strindberg from Balzac, his favorite writer at this time. In *Colonel Chabert* there is a passage that runs in part, "There are three persons in our society, the priest, the doctor, and the man of law, who cannot have any respect for humanity. They probably wear black robes

because they are in mourning for all the virtues, all the illusions. The most unhappy of the three is the lawyer. . . . We lawyers, we see the same evil feelings manifest themselves again and again; nothing rectifies them; our offices are sewers that can never be cleansed." *La Comédie humaine*, ed. Marcel Bouteron and Henri Longnon, (Paris, 1947), p. 79.

9. See my article, "Strindberg and Samuel Butler," *Meddelanden från Strindbergssällskapet*, nos. 57–58 (May 1977), pp. 27–30.

10. See the frontispiece to J. P. MacLean, *An Historical, Archaeological and Geological Examination of Fingal's Cave in the Island of Staffa*, (Cincinnati, 1890). As an avid gleaner of scientific facts and fancies, Strindberg might have read MacLean's book, which in its original form was a report made to the Smithsonian Institution. When Strindberg in his *Blå bok* (SS, 46:310) discusses what he calls the man-made architecture of Fingal's Cave, he directly challenges some of the arguments that appear in MacLean.

11. See *Strindbergs måleri*, ed. Torsten Måtte Schmidt (Malmö, 1972), plate 40, pp. 183–85, 347. The grotto motif recurs in several of Strindberg's paintings: two versions of the "saga grotto" dating from 1894, a *Fingal's Cave* from 1902, and *The Grotto* from the same year.

12. Source critics point out that Strindberg had in mind an actual building in Stockholm that he could see from his apartment and that he mentions several times in his writings. The fact that a troop of cavalry were quartered there may have begun a chain of associations in Strindberg's mind. As for other uses to which he put the building, there is his poem "My Troll Castle," written at about the same time as *A Dream Play*, in which a magic castle is built by two lovers on a spring day out of the air and mist and the sun of their senses.

13. In the last instance the statement is made in connection with *A Dream Play*. See also *Légendes*, 1967, p. 107.

14. Swedenborg, *Heaven and Hell*, n. 575. Freud, *The Origins of Psycho-Analysis*, p. 159 (in a letter to Dr. Fliess, 1 March 1896); Strindberg, "Etudes funèbres," *Inferno*, 1966, p. 85; SS, 27:603. See also SS, 47:530, 693, 767.

15. Vagn Børge, *Strindbergs mystiske Teater*, p. 237, and Müssener, *Strindberg "Ein Traumspiel"*, pp. 48–49.

16. Freud, *The Origins of Psycho-Analysis*, pp. 198–200.

17. Børge, *Strindbergs mystiske Teater*, p. 240, and Müssener, *Strindberg "Ein Traumspiel"*, pp. 48–49.

18. Strindberg to Hedlund, 10 November 1895, *Brev*, 11:100.

19. *Occult Diary*, 28 September 1901. The second quotation, "dark underworld," was added by Strindberg some time after 1901.

20. *The New Jerusalem*, n. 36. This passage is quoted by Du Prel in *Det dolda själslifvet*, 2:151.

21. Strindberg to Schering, 17 April 1907, *Brev*, 15:361.

22. Most of Strindberg's remarks and suggestions on staging *A Dream Play* have been collected in *Strindberg Uber Drama und Theater*, ed. Marianne Kesting and Verner Arpe (Cologne, 1966), pp. 138–48.

23. Iwan Bloch, *The Sexual Life of Our Time in Its Relation to Modern Civilization*, trans. M. Eden Paul (New York, 1928), p. 510. (First published in 1908.)

24. *Occult Diary*, 18 November 1901.

25. Freud, *Complete Psychological Works*, 4:63 n.

26. Freud, *The Interpretation of Dreams, Complete Psychological Works*, 4:280 n. Du Prel, *Det dolda själslifvet*, 1:94.

27. *Det dolda själslifvet*, 2:105.

28. Ibid., 1:76–86.

29. Ibid., p. 80.

30. Ibid., p. 65.

CHAPTER 11

1. "'Det uendeligt Smaa' og 'det uendeligt Store' i Poesien," first printed in 1689, and reprinted in 1870 in Brandes's *Kritiker og Portraiter*. Its influence on Strindberg has been discussed in English by Joan Bulman, *Strindberg and Shakespeare* (London, 1933), pp. 44–49 passim.

2. "On the Tragic Art," *Essays Aesthetical and Philosophical* (London, 1882), p. 348. Schiller, *Werke*, ed. Ludwig Bellermann, 8 vols. (Leipzig and Vienna, n.d.), 8:40–41.

3. *Coleridge's Shakespearean Criticism*, ed. Thomas Middleton Raysor, 2 vols. (Cambridge, Mass., 1930), 1:138.

4. Schiller, *Werke*, 4:340.

5. See Benno von Wiese, *Die deutsche Tragödie von Lessing bis Hebbel*, 3d ed. (Hamburg, 1955), p. 242.

6. For the impact of the Paris Commune on the writing of *Master Olof*, see Allan Hagsten, *Den unge Strindberg*, 2 vols. (Stockholm, 1951), 1:404–17; Sven-Gustaf Edqvist, *Samhällets fiende. En studie i Strindbergs anarkism till och med Tjänstekvinnans son* (Stockholm, 1961), pp. 52–87; Gunnar Brandell, *Revolt i dikt* (Stockholm, 1977), pp. 1–30; and Brandell, "'Ils voulaient brûler Paris:' Strindberg et la Commune," *La Revue d'Histoire du Théâtre*, no. 3 (1978), pp. 213–23. Strindberg's own comments are in *I Röda rummet*, *SS*, 19:30.

7. On Gert's radicalism as a reflection of Strindberg's, see Hagsten, *Den unge Strindberg*, 1:388 ff. Also on this point and on the parallels between Olof and Jesus, see the introduction to *Mäster Olof* in *August Strindbergs dramer*, ed. Carl Reinhold Smedmark (Stockholm, 1962), 2:14–16.

8. Preface to *Back to Methuselah*, *Bodley Head Bernard Shaw Collected Plays*, 5:314. Cf. Shaw to A. J. Marriott, 28 October 1894, *Collected Letters*, *1874–1897*, ed. Dan H. Laurence (New York, 1965), p. 456.

9. On the conservative victory at the polls, see Strindberg to Fahlstedt, 30 September 1872, *Brev*, 1:126.

10. Henry Thomas Buckle, *History of Civilization in England*, 3 vols. (London, 1882), 2:554.

11. See also Erik Lindstrom, *Strindbergs "Mäster Olof"-dramer* (Lund, 1921), pp. 7–11, 22–23, and Carl Albert Helmecke, *Buckle's Influence on Strindberg* (Ph.D. thesis, University of Pennsylvania, 1924), pp. 23–26.

12. Smedmark, introduction to *Mäster Olof*, *Strindbergs dramer*, 2:251.

CHAPTER 12

1. A comparison of this outline with Strindberg's first sketches (reproduced in Walter Johnson's study *Strindberg and the Historical Drama* [Seattle, 1963], pp. 95–96) reveals how radically he altered his first thoughts and how the symmetry and balance of the play in its final form was achieved only after the leading motif had been changed.

2. Strindberg to af Geijerstam, 5 August 1899, *Brev*, 13:176.

3. Ibid., p. 177.

4. Strindberg compares Erik with Hamlet point for point in his 1908 essay on Shakespeare's play.

5. Martin Lamm, *Strindbergs dramer*, 2 vols. (Stockholm, 1924–26), 2:155, 152. See also Martin Lamm, *Strindberg och makterna* (Stockholm, 1936), p. 139.

6. Strindberg's perceptive comments on *Henry VIII* have been neglected by Shakespeare scholars. He was among the first to assert that the structure of the play was solid and coherent. In his interpretation, the design of the play deliberately emphasizes the ambigu-

ity in human actions and in the judgments passed on those actions. Opposing explanations are carefully juxtaposed by Shakespeare in order to contrast the hasty and biased inferences men are compelled to draw in their daily affairs with the larger view that a historical or religious perspective offers. *Shaksperes Macbeth, Othello* . . . .

7. *The Messingkauf Dialogues*, trans. John Willet (London, 1965), p. 103.

8. Tolstoy, *War and Peace*, trans. Louise and Aylmer Maude (New York, 1942), pp. 1359, 1361.

9. See Allan Hagsten, *Den unge Strindberg*, 2 vols. (Stockholm, 1951), 1:362–63.

10. See Strindberg to Schering, 1 December 1902, *Brev*, 14:231–32. The fragments of the cycle are printed in Strindberg, *Samlade otryckta skrifter*, 2 vols. (1918–19), 1:5–197. The cycle is discussed by Harry V. E. Palmblad, *Strindberg's Conception of History* (New York, 1927), passim; and by Johnson, *Strindberg and the Historical Drama*, pp. 237–46.

11. Leon Trotsky, *The History of the Russian Revolution*, trans. Max Eastman, 3 vols. (New York, 1932), 1:435.

12. See Michael W. Kaufman, "Strindberg's Historical Imagination—*Erik XIV*," *Comparative Drama*, Winter 1975–76, p. 327.

13. The quoted phrases are from Hegel, *Lectures on the Philosophy of History*, trans. J. Sibree (London, n.d.), p. 26.

14. Ernst Fischer, *The Necessity of Art: A Marxist Approach*, trans. Anna Bostock (Harmondsworth, England, 1963), p. 78.

15. Marx to Lassalle, 19 April 1859, Marx and Engels, *On Literature and Art* (Moscow, 1976), p. 100.

16. Lukács on Brecht and Chekhov: see Henri Arvon, *Marxist Esthetics*, trans. Helen R. Lane (Ithaca and London, 1973), pp. 105–12.

17. Shaw, *Back to Methuselah, Bodley Head Bernard Shaw Collected Plays*, 5:631, 630.

18. Apart from what is found in his history plays, Strindberg's most important speculations on progress are contained in a long and desultory essay "Världshistoriens mystik" (*SS*, 54:337–401), printed in installments in a Swedish newspaper in 1903. Harry V. E. Palmblad in his *Strindberg's Conception of History* (New York, 1927) offers the most thorough discussion of these ideas. According to him, most of Strindberg's thoughts as expressed in the essay date back to 1893 and some, to the 1880s. But the idea of a conscious will in history almost certainly dates from the Inferno period. The passages I have quoted or paraphrased are to be found on pages 351, 396, 398, and 363 of Strindberg's essay. The analogy of historical development to a chemical process is also made elsewhere: for example, in *Religiös renässans* (1910), *SS*, 53:248; and in "Bevittna vi en upplösning eller en utveckling av den religiösa känslan?" (1907), *SS*, 54:464.

CHAPTER 13

1. John Paulsen, *Mine Erindringer* (Copenhagen, 1900), p. 19.

2. Frida Strindberg, *Strindberg och hans andra hustru*, trans. Karin Boye, 2 vols. (Stockholm, 1933–34), 1:115.

3. F. Servaes, "Vom jungen Przybyszewski," *Pologne Littéraire*, 11 (15 January 1936).

4. Gerda Kjellberg, *Hänt och sant* (Stockholm, 1951), p. 49.

5. Strindberg to Fahlstedt, September 1872, *Brev*, 1:127.

6. Strindberg, "Des arts nouveaux! ou le Hasard dans la production artistique," *Vivisektioner*, 1894, p. 60. By 1884 Strindberg had succumbed to the power of Beethoven's piano sonatas. See Hélène Welinder's description of Strindberg in Chexbres, Switzerland, in *August Strindberg, ungdom och mannaår*, ed. Stellan Ahlström (Stockholm, 1959), p. 148. (Originally in *Ord och Bild*, 1912.)

7. Strindberg to Gerber, 8 December 1903, *Brev*, 14:325.

8. Strindberg to Littmansson, 25 September 1902, *Brev*, 14:215.

9. Albert Engström, *August Strindberg och jag* (Stockholm, 1923), p. 29. Cf. Anna von Philp and Nora Hartzell, *Strindbergs systrar berätta om barndomshemmet och om bror August* (Stockholm, 1926), p. 100.

10. Goethe, *Gespräche mit Eckermann* (Leipzig, 1923), p. 604.

11. See the description of *La belle Hélène* in chap. 8 of *The Son of a Servant, SS*, 18:179–82.

12. Strindberg to Littmansson, 4 July 1903, *Brev*, 14:276. Strindberg to Littmansson, 21 June 1903, *Brev*, 14:271. Cf. *Taklagsöl, SS*, 44:23.

13. See also Strindberg to Littmansson, 4 July 1903, *Brev*, 14:276, and *Légendes*, 1967, p. 96.

14. Strindberg to Littmansson, 4 July 1903, *Brev*, 14:276.

15. See also Victor Hellström, *Strindberg och musiken* (Stockholm, 1917), pp. 26–30.

16. See also *Légendes*, 1967, p. 104.

17. *Occult Diary*, 4 June 1898.

18. *Samlade otryckta skrifter*, 1:242.

19. Karl Sam Åsberg, "Strindberg och musiken," *Svenska Dagbladet*, 14 May 1937, quoted by Vagn Børge, *Strindbergs mystiske Teater*, pp. 269–70.

20. For Strindberg on Wagner, see *SS*, 46:214; *SS*, 41:176–8; and Strindberg to Tor Aulin, January 1908, *Från Fjärdingen till Blå tornet*, p. 391.

21. Strindberg to Anna Flygare, 24 October 1908, August Falck, *Strindberg och teater* (Stockholm, 1918), p. 78. Cf. Strindberg to Flygare, 5 May 1908, ibid., p. 52; and Strindberg to Grandinson, 6 July 1901, *Brev*, 14:99–100.

22. Letter of 25 April 1907; *Brev*, 15, pp. 365–66.

23. Erik Tawaststjerna, "Sibelius svenska Kontakter," *Svenska Dagbladet*, 8 December 1965. Strindberg to Anne-Marie Strindberg, 21 July 1907, *Breven till Harriet Bosse*, ed. Torsten Eklund (Stockholm, 1965), p. 172.

24. Falck, *Fem år med Strindberg*, p. 232.

25. See also Hellström, *Strindberg och musiken*, pp. 2–3, 20–21, 46, and Ollén, *Strindbergs dramatik*, pp. 183–84.

26. Hellström, *Strindberg och musiken*, p. 43. According to this source, Strindberg substituted the Bach Gavotte in G Minor for the sarabande called for in the script.

27. Hellström, *Strindberg och musiken*, p. 35. Ingrid Hollinger, "Urpremiären på Till Damaskus I," *Dramaten 175 år. Studier i svensk scenkonst*, ed. Gösta M. Bergman and Niklas Brunius (Stockholm, 1963), pp. 313–14, 343–45.

28. On the Titanism in *To Damascus*, Part One, see Gunnar Brandell, *Strindberg in Inferno*, pp. 274–76.

29. This commentary on the musical structure of *A Dream Play* was originally part of Strindberg's prefatory note. He deleted it, leaving only the well-known section on the dream quality of the play. For the rest of the note, see Helmut Müssener, "Ett drömspel. Tillkomst och textproblem," *Meddelanden från Strindbergssällskapet*, no. 36 (December 1964), p. 26; or Müssener, *Strindberg "Ein Traumspiel,"* pp. 26–27; or *Strindberg Über Drama und Theater*, pp. 140–41.

30. Strindberg to Schering, 13 May 1902, *Brev*, 14:187.

31. Marianne Kesting, introduction to *Strindberg Über Drama und Theater*, p. 20.

32. Raymond Jarvi, "*Ett drömspel*: A Symphony for the Stage," *Scandinavian Studies* 44 (Winter 1972):28–42.

33. Strindberg tried to persuade the violinist and composer Tor Aulin to write music

for a condensed "chamber" version of *A Dream Play*. See chapter 10, note 6, and Walter A. Berendsohn, *Strindbergs sista levnadsår* (Stockholm, 1948), pp. 72–74.

34. Falck, *Fem år med Strindberg*, p. 274.

35. Strindberg also experimented with sonata form in poetry. See Strindberg to Schering, 2 December 1902, *Brev*, 14:233; his comment in "Omkring 1890," *SS*, 53:97; and the discussion in Gunnar Ollén, *Strindbergs 1900-talslyrik* (Stockholm, 1941), pp. 94–95, 165–68, 202–03.

36. F. Servaes, "Vom jungen Przybyszewski," *Pologne Littéraire*, 11 (15 January 1936).

37. *Occult Diary*, 18 June, 1 July, 4 July, and 5 July 1897. *Brev*, 11:215–17, 227–28, 232.

38. See also *Légendes*, 1967, p. 78.

39. See Andrzej Uggla, "Przybyszewski och Strindberg," *Meddelanden från Strindbergssällskapet*, nos. 53–54, (May 1974), pp. 12–20.

40. Johan Mortensen, *Strindberg som jag minnes honom* (Stockholm, 1931), pp. 36–37.

41. Maurice's child died from the flowers she was playing with in the Montparnasse cemetery in the opening scene of the play. Symbolically (that is, esoterically), this places the responsibility for all that happens of the Higher Powers, that which lies beyond the cause-and-effect logic of the mechanical universe. Realistically (that is, exoterically), her death was caused by the arsenic that had accumulated in dangerous amounts in the ground in certain Paris cemeteries. The eminent toxicologist Mathieu J. B. Orfila had warned of such dangers. Through his chemical studies, Strindberg knew Orfila's work quite well, and he owned a copy of Orfila's *Traité de toxicologie*.

42. Strindberg to Kerstin Strindberg, 1 February 1899, *Brev*, 13:82.

43. Strindberg to af Geijerstam, 22 March 1899, *Brev*, 13:117. The Swedenborgian elements in the play are discussed by Stockenström, *Ismael i öknen*, pp. 426–49 (summarized in English, pp. 479–80).

44. Swedenborg, *The Earths in the Universe*, nn. 71–78. Cf. Strindberg, *Inferno*, 1966, pp. 228–31; *SS*, 28:185–89; and *Légendes*, 1967, pp. 98–99; *SS*, 28:306–07.

45. Swedenborg, *The New Jerusalem*, n. 52. Cf. Strindberg, *En blå bok I*, *SS*, 46:33.

46. Strindberg wrote to the composer Tor Aulin on February 4, 1912, "You brought Beethoven with you—Beethoven and Kierkegaard! who are one and the same." (Quoted in Berendsohn, *Strindbergs sista levnadsår*, p. 174.)

47. Strindberg to Littmansson, 21 March 1899, *Brev*, 13:115. See also Strindberg to Herrlin, 23 January 1900, *Brev*, 13:248; and *The Occult Diary*, 1 June 1897, with a marginal note of a later date.

48. Vsevold Meyerhold, *Ecrits sur le théâtre*, trans. Béatrice Picon-Vallin, 2 vols. (Lausanne, 1973–75), 1:214–15. See also Konstantin Rudnitsky, *Meyerhold the Director*, trans. George Petrov, ed. Sydney Schultze (Ann Arbor, 1981), pp. 171–73.

49. Strindberg to af Geijerstam, 12 March 1899, *Brev*, 13:117.

50. Strindberg to Schering, 10 September 1902, *Brev*, 14:210. Memo to Intimate Theatre, *Samlade otryckta skrifter*, 2:236.

51. Strindberg to Schering, 10 September 1902, *Brev*, 14:210.

CHAPTER 14

1. Yeats, "First Principles," *Explorations* (London, 1962), p. 154.

2. Yeats, "A People's Theatre," *Explorations*, p. 254.

3. The best account in English of Strindberg's theatrical experiments at the Intimate

Theatre is Gösta M. Bergman, "Strindberg and the Intima Teatern," *Theatre Research/ Recherches Théâtrales*, 9 (1967):14–47.

4. Strindberg to Adolf Paul, 6 January 1907, *Brev*, 15:334.

5. Strindberg to H. Bosse, 4 May 1908, *Breven till Harriet Bosse*, ed. Torsten Edlund (Stockholm, 1965), p. 189.

6. *Bodley Head Bernard Shaw Collected Plays*, 1:249.

7. The standard works on Strindberg as painter are: Gunnel Sylvan, "August Strindberg som målare," *Dikt och konst, Tidskrift för konstvetenskap* (Stockholm, 1948), 27 (1948):63–125; Göran Söderström, *Strindberg och bildkonsten* (Uddevalla, 1972); and *Strindbergs måleri*, ed. Torsten Måtte Schmidt (Malmö, 1972). On Strindberg as art critic: Gösta Lilja, *Strindberg som konstkritiker* (Malmö, 1957).

8. See Egil Törnqvist, "Strindberg and the Drama of Half-Reality. An Analysis of *To Damascus I*," *Strindberg and the Modern Theatre* (Stockholm: The Strindberg Society, 1975), pp. 119–50.

9. Strindberg to Schering, 4 July 1907, Falck, *Fem år med Strindberg*, p. 77.

10. Strindberg to Schering, 27 March 1907, *Brev*, 15:354.

11. Strindberg to Schering, 27 March and 2 April 1907, *Brev*, 15:354, 356.

12. Strindberg received copies of Blavatsky's *Isis Unveiled* and *The Secret Doctrine* in September 1896 and read enough to make derogatory comments on them. See Strindberg to Hedlund, 12 September 1896, ca. 26 September, 30 October, 31 October, and 7 November; and Strindberg to Eliasson, 8 November 1896, *Brev*, 11:323, 346–47, 374, 375–76, 384–85, 386. Also, Strindberg, *Inferno*, 1966, p. 203; *SS*, 28:159–60; and *Légendes*, 1967, pp. 108–09; *SS*, 28:319. Cf. Martin Lamm, *Strindberg och makterna*, pp. 132–34.

13. H. P. Blavatsky, *The Secret Doctrine*, 2 vols. (Point Loma, California, 1925), 1:639.

14. Strindberg to Schering, 17 April 1907, *Brev*, 15:361–62.

15. The contradictory information in the play is the subject of Göran Lindström's article, "Strindberg's Chamber Play, Opus 2, *After the Fire*," *Essays on Strindberg* (Stockholm: The Strindberg Society, 1966), pp. 49–64.

16. Strindberg to Schering, 7 April 1907, *Brev*, 15:367.

17. Göran Lindström, "Asmodeus i Madrid och Lund," *Sydsvenska Dagbladet Snällposten*, 27 June 1971; and Lindström's commentary in Strindberg, *Spöksonaten* (Skrifter utgivna av Modersmålslärarnas förening, no. 96) (Lund, 1963), pp. 99–100.

18. Isaac Hirsch was an almsgiving businessman whom Strindberg saw frequently on the streets of Stockholm. (Falck, *Fem år med Strindberg*, p. 85.) When he gave him the name Hummel, Strindberg probably had in mind either the composer Johann Nepomuk Hummel or the notorious New York lawyer Abraham Hummel. Richard Wagner despised Johann Nepomuk Hummel as a philistine. Asked what he thought of while composing a rondo, Hummel answered: the eighty ducats of his publisher. (Wagner, "On Poetry and Composition," *Prose Works*, trans. William Ashton Ellis, 8 vols. [London, 1895–99], 6:144.) The other Hummel was the most famous criminal lawyer in New York from 1890 to 1905, the associate of gangsters and socialites, theatrical personalities and politicians. He often won his cases by blatant chicanery, and the subornation of witness was one of his standard methods. In September 1905, he was finally indicted for criminal conspiracy, brought to trial in December, and found guilty on 20 December 1905. He resorted to every legal stratagem to avoid going to jail. His conviction was confirmed by the New York State Supreme Court in the spring of 1907 and he was incarcerated 21 May 1907. (*Dictionary of American Biography*, vol. 5; and Richard Rovere, *Howe & Hummel* [New York, 1947].)

19. Evert Sprinchorn, "Heine, Hummel, and the Hyacinth Girl," *Meddelanden från Strindbergssällskapet*, no. 56 (May 1976), pp. 16–17.

20. *Arcana coelestia*, n. 3391.

21. *Arcana coelestia*, nn. 651–55. The name Arkenholz comes from Johan Arcken-

holtz, a Swedish mystic coeval with Swedenborg (Lindström, commentary on *Spöksonaten* [Lund, 1963], p. 81).

22. Strindberg to Schering, 27 March 1907, *Brev*, 15:354.

23. Strindberg to Harriet Bosse, 6 October 1905, *Brev*, 15:183.

24. *Heaven and Hell*, n. 493.

25. Ibid., n. 507.

26. Cf. Swedenborg, *Arcana coelestia*, n. 6495: "In the real world an evil man is kept in bonds by his loves themselves, whose loss he fears, thus by the loss of honor, gain, reputation, and life. . . . Hence he appears moral and civil in act, sometimes like an angel, and does no harm to society and his neighbor; and if he does harm, there are civil laws to punish him. But in the other life this plane is non-existent; there man is in the spiritual world, consequently in the sphere of his interiors; thus such as he had been inwardly, such he is there, and not such as he had appeared in externals; for externals are taken away from him, and when they are taken away, his quality in the world, whether that of a devil or that of an angel, is manifest."

And what if the man is without qualities and his whole character is nothing but pretense? Strindberg describes one of his former acquaintances (af Geijerstam) as being like that. "I sometimes think of him in Swedenborg's disrobing room on the other side of the grave. A shave comes first, then off comes one piece of clothing after another; then they remove the skin, the muscles, the bones—since every part of him is false, until there is absolutely nothing left of the man" (*SS*, 47:787).

27. Blavatsky, *The Secret Doctrine*, 1:244. Cf. Strindberg, *SS*, 46:248: "The theosophists speak of the seven planes in Kâma-Loka, the state after death."

28. Strindberg to Schering, 30 April 1907, *Brev*, 15:368.

29. *Arcana coelestia*, nn. 183–86.

30. Strindberg told his German translator that the Swedish title *Spöksonaten* should be rendered as "Gespenster Sonaten," not as "Spuk Sonaten," and pointed to Beethoven's "Gespenster" Sonata and "Geister" Trio. "Spook" suggested hobgoblin, "ghost" suggested spirit, and it was the latter connotation that he wanted. Strindberg to Schering, 1 April 1907, *Brev*, 15:355. Beethoven's Sonata 17 opus 31 no. 2, generally known as the "Tempest" Sonata, had, for unfathomable reasons, acquired among Strindberg's musical friends the appellation "Ghost" Sonata. Strindberg did not learn this until after he had used the sonata in *Crimes and Crimes*. Strindberg to Herrlin, 23 January 1900, *Brev*, 13:248.

31. For a different view, see Raymond Jarvi, "Strindberg's *The Ghost Sonata* and Sonata Form," *Mosaic*, no. 4 (1972), pp. 69–84.

32. Strindberg to Schering, 27 March 1907, *Brev*, 15:354.

33. Strindberg to Harriet Bosse, 4 October 1905, *Brev*, 15:181.

34. *Apocalypse Revealed*, n. 450.

35. Strindberg to Schering, 7 March 1907, *Brev*, 15:360.

36. *Occult Diary*, 18 January 1906.

37. Strindberg to Axel Strindberg, 29 November 1907, Martin Lamm, *Strindbergs dramer*, 2:405–06.

38. Strindberg to Schering, 27 March 1907, *Brev*, 15:354.

39. Bernhard Diebold, *Anarchie im Drama* (Frankfurt am Main, 1921), p. 220.

40. There is also a striking similarity to the plot of Przybyszewski's novel *The Mother* (1902), in which the son discovers the reasons for his father's death, decides he cannot live in this house of lies and crime, and sets fire to it.

CHAPTER 15

1. Walter Sullivan, "The Einstein Papers: Growth of Theories About Relativity Lead to a Flash of Insight," *New York Times*, 28 March 1972, pp. 1, 32.

2. See also "L'Irradiation de l'âme," in Légendes, 1967, p. 74.

3. Man and Superman, Bodley Head Bernard Shaw Collected Plays, 2:557–58.

4. See Olle Holmberg, "Viktor Rydberg och August Strindberg," Samlaren, 1935, pp. 41–43. Cf. Hanna Bellander, "Ett gräl om Viktor Rydberg," August Strindberg. Mannaår och ålderdom, ed. Stellan Ahlström and Torsten Eklund (Stockholm, 1961), pp. 42–46.

5. Klostret, pp. 130–31.

6. Strindberg to Ossian Ekbohrn, 26 July 1879, Brev, 2:72.

7. See Strindberg to Schering, 27 March and 2 April 1907, Brev, 15:354, 356.

8. On Strindberg's plans for other monodramas, see Fritz Paul, "Strindberg og monodramaet," Edda, 1976, pp. 283–95; Fritz Paul, "'Indras Dotter': Zur Genese von Strindbergs Dramenentwurf aus dem Jahre 1905," Scandinavica, 15 (1976):19–28; and Strindberg's own remarks in his letters to Schering, 17 April 1907, Brev, 15:361–62; and 6 May 1907: Från Fjärdingen till Blå tornet, ed. Torsten Eklund (Stockholm, 1946), pp. 382–83.

9. Walter A. Berendsohn, Strindbergsproblem (Stockholm, 1946), p. 196.

10. Raymond Jarví has carefully analyzed the musical structure of The Black Glove in "'Svarta Handsken': A Lyrical Fantasy for the Stage," Scandinavica, 12 (1973):17–25.

11. The cartoon appeared in Strix. It is reproduced in Ny illustrerad svensk litteraturhistoria, ed. E. N. Tigerstedt, 2d ed. rev. (Stockholm, 1967), 4:224.

12. Johan Mortensen, Strindberg som jag minnes honom (Stockholm, 1931), p. 70.

13. Yeats, "The Bounty of Sweden," The Autobiography of William Butler Yeats (New York, 1953), p. 327.

14. Gustaf Uddgren, Andra boken om Strindberg (Gothenburg, 1912), p. 128.

15. See Erik Hedén, Strindberg. En ledtråd vid studiet av hans verk (Stockholm, 1921), p. 426.

16. Strindbergsfejden, ed. Harry Järv (n.p., 1968), p. 464.

17. Ibid., p. 228.

18. Ibid., p. 878.

19. Ibid., p. 881.

20. See Strindberg to von Heidenstam, 21 September 1885, Brev, 5:170–71.

21. Strindbergsfejden, p. 97.

22. Ibid., p. 1018.

23. Berendsohn, Strindbergs sista levnadsår, p. 168.

24. Hedén, Strindberg, pp. 441–42.

25. Strindberg to Branting and Magnusson, 23 January 1912, Från Fjärdingen till Blå tornet, p. 436.

26. Strindberg to Spångberg, 25 May 1910, Från Fjärdingen till Blå tornet, p. 422.

27. Cf. SS, 47:617–19.

28. Hedén, Strindberg, pp. 461–62. See also Berendsohn, Strindbergs sista levnadsår, pp. 128–31.

29. See for instance Otto Kaus, Strindberg (Munich, 1918), p. 111; and Bernhard Diebold, Anarchie im Drama, pp. 233–36.

30. See Anthony Swerling, Strindberg's Impact in France 1920–1960 (Cambridge, 1971).

31. Albert Einstein, The Human Side: New Glimpses from His Archives, ed. Helen Dukas and Banesh Hoffmann (Princeton, 1979), p. 38.

32. Musil, A Man without Qualities, trans. Eithne Wilkins and Ernst Kaiser, 3 vols. (London, 1954–60), 1:297–98.

33. Strindberg to Schering, 23 March 1902, Brev, 14:176.

34. See also Inferno, 1966, p. 233.

35. *Klostret*, p. 58.
36. Per Hallström to af Geijerstam, 1902, *Strindberg, Mannaår och ålderdom*, p. 174.
37. See the complete quotation above, page 100.
38. Albert Engström, *August Strindberg och jag* (Stockholm, 1923), pp. 44–46.
39. *Occult Diary*, 23 January 1902.
40. See also *Légendes*, 1967, p. 107.
41. From the record of Strindberg's last hours by nurse Hedvig Kistner, in *Strindberg. Mannaår och ålderdom*, pp. 293–95.

INDEX

Acting, 25, 252; in Chamber Plays, 252; comic style of, 31; in *Father, The,* 31–32; naturalistic, 25, 30–33; tragic style of, 30–33
Addresses to the Swedish Nation, 291
Advent, 250n
Aeschylus: *Agamemnon,* 46, 47, 48; and Strindberg, 46–48
Albee, Edward: *Who's Afraid of Virginia Woolf?,* 113, 120
Alchemy, 64, 71, 79, 82, 124, 134, 224; Jung on, 133; in *To Damascus,* 123–25, 136
Alcohol, 66, 81; Strindberg's experimentation with, 67–68
Alone, 282
Anarchism, 70, 73
Anima: Jung on, 127–29, 134. *See also* Psychological themes
Antibarbarus, 55
Anti-Nobel Prize, 294–95
Antoine, André, 24, 246, 247; naturalism of, 24, 25, 32; Strindberg influenced by, 25. *See also* French theatre
Aristotle, 57, 65, 109, 184, 205
Art: as science, 83–84
Association of ideas, 81–83, 85, 87–89, 102; Freud on, 158
Atheism, 1, 78–79, 115
Author, The, 11, 26
Autobiographical writings, 6–7, 279–81; letters as, 8, 10–11, 19; novels, 8, 9–14, 51, 282. *See also* names of works
Avant-garde theatres, late nineteenth-century, 246–47

Bach, Johann Sebastian, 224, 228–29, 233, 234

Bachofen, J. J., 47
"Battle of Brains, The," 26
Baudelaire, Charles Pierre, 65, 66, 67
Beckett, Samuel, 257; *Waiting for Godot,* 120, 153
Beethoven, Ludwig van, 221–22, 223, 230, 234, 275; and *Crimes and Crimes,* 240–41
Benedictsson, Victoria, 6
Bergman, Ingmar, 88
Bernard, Claude, 83
Bernheim, Hippolyte, 24, 26, 78, 157, 158
Berthelot, Pierre, 64
Black Flags, 278, 282
Black Glove, The, 284, 285
Blasphemy trial (1884), 13, 279, 281, 293; financial difficulties due to, 12
Blavatsky, Helena, 69, 256–57, 263
Blue Books, 255, 256, 276n, 282, 284
Böcklin, Arnold: *Isle of the Dead, The,* 271, 277
Bosse, Harriet (third wife), 146–48, 151, 157, 227, 255, 268, 277, 284; divorced from Strindberg, 283; as subject matter, 166–67, 176, 248, 283, 299
Brandes, Georg, 1, 15, 179
Brecht, Bertolt, 205, 214–15, 233, 253
Bridal Crown, The, 227
Büchner, Georg, 179
Buckle, Henry Thomas, 188–89, 194, 206
Buddhism, 256–57, 260, 265–66, 268–69, 270 and n. *See also* Religious themes
Burned House, The, 251, 252, 257–58, 263, 272; death theme in, 253, 256, 263, 264; religious themes in, 264–66
Butler, Samuel, 53, 161–62
By the Open Sea, 54, 58

Self-experimentation. *See* Experimentation
Set design: asymmetrical, 25, 28; for
  Charles XII, 30, 251; for *Crimes and
  Crimes,* 243, 244; for *Dream Play, A,* 153,
  154, 155–56, 160, 167, 251; for *Father,
  The,* 32; for *Miss Julie,* 28, 29; naturalism
  in, 25, 28–30, 32; solid vs. painted scenery, 24–25; symbolic, 29–30; synthetic
  method of, 30; for *To Damascus,* 30,
  251
Sex tetralogy, 48, 61, 63, 278. *See also Comrades; Creditors; Father, The; Miss Julie*
Sexual themes: in *Comrades,* 48; in *Dream
  Play, A,* 160–68, 171–75; in *Father, The,*
  47–48; jealousy as, 12, 14, 16–21, 70–71,
  248, 280; in *Miss Julie,* 38–44, 48; and
  music, 225, 226; sado-masochism as,
  41–43; and social conflict, 37–44, 47–49,
  296; in *To Damascus,* 128, 148, 149. *See
  also* Feminism; Love themes; Marriage
  theme; Maternal theme; Misogynistic
  theme; Paternal theme; Psychological
  themes; Women
Shadow: Jung on, 127–29, 134; in *To Damascus,* 127, 129, 130, 139, 150. *See also*
  Psychological themes
Shakespeare, William, 2, 5, 8, 27, 184, 201,
  210, 219, 258; *Hamlet,* 232; *Henry IV,*
  179–80, 197; *Henry V,* 182, 199; *Henry
  VIII,* 182, 204; *Julius Caesar,* 182; *Macbeth,* 104–05, 109–10; *Othello,* 17;
  Strindberg on, 232, 250 and n
Shaw, George Bernard, 1, 8, 53, 189, 191; use
  of music by, 232, 249; and Strindberg,
  215–16, 278, 296, 299
"Sighing of the Stones, The," 63
Sir Bengt's Wife, 36
Sleepwalking in Broad Daylight, 289
Socialism, 51
Social themes, 215–17, 296–301; class conflict as, 3–5, 35, 37–44, 48, 185, 198, 211,
  289, 292–96; in *Creditors,* 48; Darwinist,
  46, 47, 48; in *Erik XIV,* 198–99, 203,
  204–12; in *Gustav Vasa,* 194–95, 210,
  211, 217; in late anti-establishment works,
  286–96; Marxist, 46, 47, 214; in *Master
  Olof,* 185, 187–89, 202, 211; in *Miss Julie,*
  35, 37–44, 48; and sexual conflict,
  37–44, 47–49, 296. *See also* Feminism;
  Maternal theme; Paternal theme; Psychological themes; Sexual themes
Somnambulism, 67, 70, 78, 80, 169, 273
Sonata form, 234–35; in Chamber Plays,
  254, 267; in *Crimes and Crimes,* 240–43.
  See also Musical themes
Son of a Servant, The, 12, 51
"Soul Murder," 17

Spencer, Herbert, 26, 57
Staaff, Per, 13
Stanislavsky, Konstantin, 25; emotion-mem-
  ory technique of, 19–20; and *Lower
  Depths, The,* 6
Station drama: *To Damascus* as, 76–77
Steiger, Edgar, 62
Stockholm, 3, 176–77; description of, in
  Red Room, 22
Storm Weather, 248, 249, 251, 252, 272,
  283; death theme in, 256
Stravinsky, Igor Fëdorovich, 223
Strindberg, August: anti-Nobel Prize given
  to, 294–95; artistic conventions broken
  by, 9–10, 277–78, 297–301; childhood of,
  4–5, 220–21; death of, 222, 276, 296; deliberate insanity of, 16–18, 60, 67–74,
  277–78; fame of 15, 63, 235; health of, 74,
  124, 296; influence of, on twentieth-century artists, 276 and n, 277; influences on
  (*see names of authors, philosophers, and
  psychologists*); irrationality, use of, by,
  1–5, 49, 277–82, 298–99; late anti-establishment works of, 286–96; marriages of
  (*see* Bosse, Harriet; Essen, Siri von; Uhl,
  Frida); misunderstanding of, 1, 2, 23,
  244–45, 286–88, 297; moods of, 20, 100,
  103; musical interests of, 218, 220–27
  (*see also* Musical themes); nondramatic
  work, use of, by, 8, 36; productivity of, 1,
  20; role-playing of, 5–9, 14–21, 51–52,
  82, 277; as scientist, 52–64, 71, 79, 84,
  90, 124; on truth, 4–5; works of (*see
  names of essays, novels, plays, poems,
  and stories*)
Stronger, The, 30, 51
Suffering: and conscience, 103–05, 111–12,
  126, 142–44; in *Dream Play, A,* 155–57,
  161, 162, 175, 233. *See also* Guilt theme
Suicide, 86; in Ibsen, 40–41, 44–45; in
  Miss Julie, 34–35, 40–45. *See also* Death
  theme
Supranaturalism, 62, 67, 117, 280. *See also*
  Naturalism
Swanwhite, 226–27
Sweden: *1909* general strike in, 286, 289;
  social class system, *1880s,* 3–4 (*see also*
  Social themes). *See also* History plays;
  Stockholm
Swedenborg, Emanuel, 65, 104, 263; mysti-
  cism of, 106–07, 109–10, 113–19,
  136–46, 151, 167, 239–40, 264–66
Swedish Academy, 287, 292–94, 296
*Swedish People on Holiday and at Work, in
  War and Peace, at Home and Abroad, or,
  A Thousand Years of Swedish Culture
  and Customs, The,* 177–78